A GENERATION AT WAR

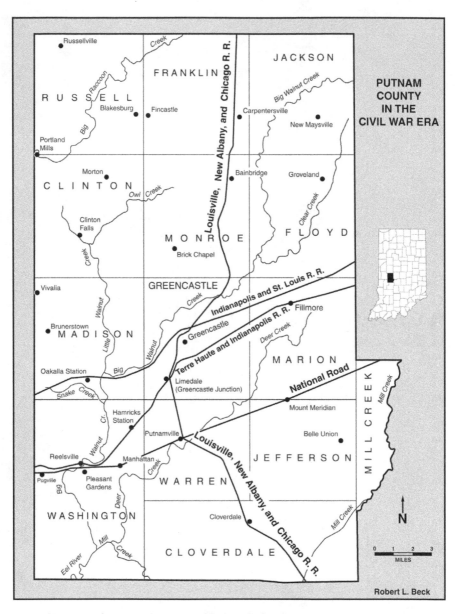

Map of Putnam County. (Courtesy of Robert L. Beck)

Nicole Etcheson

A Generation at War

THE CIVIL WAR ERA IN A
NORTHERN COMMUNITY

University Press of Kansas

First paperback edition published in 2023.

Published by the University Press of Kansas (Lawrence, Kansas 66045),
which was organized by the Kansas Board of Regents and is operated
and funded by Emporia State University, Fort Hays State University,
Kansas State University, Pittsburg State University, the University of
Kansas, and Wichita State University

Library of Congress Cataloging-in-Publication Data
Etcheson, Nicole.
  A generation at war : the Civil War era in a northern community /
Nicole Etcheson.
    p.   cm.
  Includes bibliographical references and index.
  ISBN 978-0-7006-1797-5 (cloth : alk. paper)
  ISBN 978-0-7006-3515-3 (paperback : alk. paper)
  ISBN 978-0-7006-3516-0 (ebook)
1. Putnam County (Ind.)—His ry—19th century. 2. Indiana—History—
Civil War, 1861–1865—Social aspects. 3. United States—History—Civil War,
1861–1865—Social aspects. 4. Putnam County (Ind.)—Race relations.
5. Indiana—Race relations. I. Title.
  F532.P9E73 2011
  977.2'49—dc23   2011022638

British Library Cataloguing-in-Publication Data is available.

Printed in the United States of America

10 9 8 7 6 5 4 3 2 1

PARA LOS DOS ROBERTOS

Contents

Acknowledgments

Two men are responsible for this project. The first is Daniel Voorhees, who, as a newly elected congressman in the Civil War era, vowed, in Greencastle, Indiana, that he would not send one man or raise one dollar to fight against the South. Voorhees spoke during the secession crisis, and a few months later, after the firing on Fort Sumter, Putnam County quickly filled its quota of volunteers. I did not cover the Civil War years in my previous book, *The Emerging Midwest,* but these two tidbits, uncovered during research for that book, indicated that there was strong prowar and antiwar sentiment in the county. I decided to investigate what happened in Putnam County, using it as a microcosm of the Civil War in the North.

I was further curious because the second man, my father, Gerald Ray Etcheson, had grown up in the county. He always wanted one of his daughters to go to DePauw University. None of us complied, although, as he pointed out, two of us went to small midwestern liberal arts colleges much like DePauw. I have no regrets about my degree from Grinnell College; my only regret is that my father did not live to see me go there. This is not a family history, but Putnam County is the ancestral homeland of the Etchesons.

Many people and institutions have helped me with this book. First and foremost, I have benefited from the generosity of Alexander M. Bracken, whose bequest to Ball State University has made possible the position that I hold and the time and resources it has allowed for work on this book. I also thank the Department of History at Ball State University for awarding me the Alexander M. Bracken Professorship and Frank A. Bracken for his interest in Civil War history. A National Endowment for the Humanities summer stipend in 2004 made it possible to begin the research for this book.

At DePauw University, Barbara Steinson and John Schlotterbeck of the History Department and Wesley Wilson at the archives have been invaluable. Wes Wilson's staff, including Linda Sebree and Linda Butler, helped with research and illustrations. Barbara and John have provided some much-needed companionship during research trips to Greencastle. In 2009, DePauw invited me to be one of the Walker Horizon lecturers. I thank John Schlotterbeck and David Gellman for hosting me and my fellow Walker lecturer, John Elliff, for providing materials from his research at the Library of Congress. John Baughman, DePauw professor emeritus, graciously provided many tips on sources and illustrations. At the Putnam County Museum, I have been welcomed by Judge Diana LaVioletta, Ellie Ypma, and Sally Gray.

Steve Towne generously gave of his extensive knowledge of Indiana's Civil War materials and commented on drafts of two chapters. He also copied material from letters between Alice and Lucius Chapin in the Indiana State Archives for me. He truly is the indispensable guide to the Civil War in Indiana. At the Indiana State Library, Randy Bixby answered many queries and helped guide the beginning of my research. Monique Howell helped with questions about newspapers, and Mark Vopelak provided photos.

The staffs of the Indiana Historical Society, Indiana State Library, and Archives and Special Collections at DePauw University have been unfailingly helpful and cheerful. The staff at the Clerk's Office in the Putnam County Courthouse gave me access to the old records. Ernie Phillips, superintendent of Forest Hill Cemetery, was extremely kind in locating several graves. Susan Harmon, local history librarian at the Putnam County Library, cheerfully pulled numerous records for me on a Friday afternoon and has continued answering queries by e-mail.

For over a year, I tried to get Ransom E. Hawley's pension file from the Department of Veterans Affairs. Another year passed, and I mysteriously received a call from Connie Smith at the VA's Baltimore office. She said the file was in the mail. I laughed derisively—I had heard that before. But it was. My deepest thanks go to the staff at the Baltimore Regional Office of the Department of Veterans Affairs, including Smith, Bonnie J. Miranda, and Director George Wolohojian.

Those who provided helpful information and contacts include Thomas E. Rodgers, whose work on west-central Indiana has been invaluable. Tim Phipps, an indefatigable researcher, generously gave me research materials that related to Putnam and provided the photo of John G. Davis. John Gastineau kindly gave free legal advice about historical cases. Don Elder and Eloise Duff provided the photograph of Mary Vermilion. Robert L. Beck did the map, patiently incorporating many changes. Michael A. Ross directed me to his article—with Stacy Lorraine Braukman—on privy examinations. Greg Witkowski, my colleague at Ball State, spent some time looking through a book in German and translating portions about African American migrants to Robertsport, Liberia. Thanks to Wilma L. Moore of the Indiana Historical Society and Jeannie Regan-Dinius of the Indiana Department of Natural Resources for their help in answering questions about African American graves. Wilma Moore, along with Richard Blackett, has fielded many questions about African American history. Racquel Henry shared citations and information from her dissertation on Indiana African Americans who settled in Liberia. A. J. Aiseirithe provided references to the *Liberator.*

An early version of the chapter on women in the Civil War was presented at the Ohio State University's Department of History seminar in early American history. I appreciate the input from John Brooke, Randy Roth, Drew Cayton, Les Benedict, Carla Pestana, and others.

At the University of Texas at El Paso, where I began work on this book, Interlibrary Loan librarians Gracie Castañeda and Maria Reyes cheerfully put up with and filled my unending requests. The Interlibrary Loan Department at Ball State has proven equally speedy and efficient, particularly in getting microfilm from Indianapolis. Jason D. Stratman of the Missouri Historical Society provided me with information about Josiah Williams's life in that state.

At Ball State University, my fellow nineteenth-century historian Scott Stephan read a first draft and provided his usual insightful and penetrating comments. I have also benefited from the assistance of some fine graduate students: Brian Burns, Jeff Wing, Matthew Stephenson, Jeremy Bohonos, and Jessica Oswalt. Marsha Andrews scanned photos—over and over again to get them right.

Fred Woodward and all his staff at the University Press of Kansas, including Susan Schott, Mike Briggs, and Ranjit Arab, are always a delight to work with and to chat with at conferences. Sara Henderson White and Kelly Chrisman Jacques patiently guided me through working with photographic scans. Jennifer A. Dropkin expertly oversaw production, and Joan W. Sherman thoroughly edited the manuscript. Matthew Gallman read an overly long draft and provided extensive helpful comments for revision. I am deeply in his debt.

Jim Madison is the greatest historian of Indiana and deserves to be a Sagamore of the Wabash. He is also the best friend and mentor an Indiana University Ph.D. could ever have. As always, Jim provided useful contacts and generous encouragement.

I want to thank my aunt, Thursa Evens, and my uncles, Warren and Kenneth Etcheson. I have not met anyone in Putnam County who does not know

Aunt Thursa—a pillar of the Bainbridge community, former bursar at De-Pauw University, and award-winning dessert chef. I have had many a free dinner while doing research for this book. Uncle Tinker's and Uncle Kenny's reminiscences not only provided context for this work but also cheered me on the path to its completion.

As always, my husband, Robert J. Williams, aided with many nonhistorical but nonetheless essential tasks: helping me learn to use the new laptop and notebook computers (I went through two before finishing this book) and the new research and note-taking programs. He edited the manuscript and helped with illustrations. To borrow a phrase from a famous marriage, he is my dearest friend. I may have failed to make a historian of our son, Rob, who prefers photography and Japanese, but his middle school teacher told him he was the only History Day student she had ever had who used footnotes. "My mom made me," was his reply. He also endured a hot afternoon in the Bainbridge Cemetery. I remain hopeful that someday he will see the value of footnotes and history if not the fun of looking at old tombstones.

Introduction

The Murder of Martha Mullinix

In the spring of 1857, Greenbury O. Mullinix brutally murdered his teen-age wife, Martha Ann. A bride of less than a month, Martha was the seventeen-year-old daughter of David Sublett, a local farmer. Wielding an axe, her assailant, who was probably standing in front of her, smashed her skull. After she fell against the brick hearth, the murderer continued to strike the side and back of her head, gouging wounds an inch deep. Bleeding profusely, the poor girl was still alive when her husband's brother-in-law and cousin reached her. By the time the local physician, Daniel W. Layman, arrived an hour later, she was dead.[1]

Greenbury's family had strong local ties, having been among the earliest settlers of Putnam County, Indiana, where Greenbury was born in 1832. His grandfather had moved to the county in the 1820s from North Carolina, a migration pattern from the upland South common in the county's settlement. Greenbury's father died when the future murderer was only two years old. Although Greenbury had several aunts and uncles on his father's side, Jonathan Mullinix became closest to his orphaned nephew. Indeed, Jonathan strove so hard to help Greenbury that a newcomer to Putnam County mistook him for the murderer's father. The large Mullinix family prospered in the county. Jonathan owned real estate worth $3,640, well above the county average, and several relatives served in local office in the pre–Civil War period. Even Greenbury himself was not doing badly. In 1850, the teen-age Greenbury lived in Greencastle, the county seat, where he worked as a baker. The census listed him as owning $1,300 in real estate, placing him near the middle of local property owners. The trial record described him as a laborer, but he had been elected constable of Washington Township a year earlier. His term ended the month he killed his wife.[2]

The Sublett family lived about 4 miles away from the Mullinixes. David Sublett had been born in Kentucky. He, his wife, Mary, and their five oldest children had migrated to Indiana within a couple of years of Martha's birth in 1840. The Subletts were thus a generation later than the Mullinix family in settling in Putnam County. Perhaps this late arrival explains why they were noticeably less prosperous than the Mullinixes. In 1850, David owned only $400 in real estate, putting him in the bottom third of property owners. Martha's alliance with Greenbury may have seemed a chance to marry into a more prosperous, better-established local family. The Subletts lost their farm a few years after their daughter's death.[3]

Twenty-five-year-old Greenbury was not a large man. At 5 feet 9 inches and weighing only 125 pounds, he was described as "slender" with light brown hair and light-colored eyes, either gray or blue. He was sloppy in his personal appearance, wearing pants without suspenders and a cap set back on his head. The new husband initially claimed that an unknown intruder had attacked Martha while he was feeding the hogs. Later, he changed his story, recalling that it was his horse he had been feeding, perhaps because a neighbor contradicted his hog-tending story. Greenbury pleaded not guilty "in emphatic terms" at his October trial, for which at least fifty potential jurors had been summoned. The jury required only an hour and a half to dispense with the defense's argument of insanity, sentencing Greenbury to death for first-degree murder. Defense lawyers John A. Matson and Delana Williamson moved for a new trial, but Judge James M. Hanna refused to grant it. On October 16, Hanna sentenced Greenbury Mullinix to be "hanged by the neck until dead."[4] Mullinix was stoic. Upon sentencing, he said, "It's a hard *dose,* and I might as well take it *now.*" Sarcastically, he told the judge, "I thank you for the *execution.*"[5]

Greenbury's uncle made a desperate, but unavailing, attempt to save his nephew's life. Jonathan Mullinix petitioned the governor, urging him to commute the sentence to life on the grounds that Greenbury was insane. Between 200 and 300 men signed the petition, testifying to a general consensus that Greenbury was not normal—or perhaps to the connections of the Mullinix family or even to conscientious objections to the death penalty. On November 19, which should have been Greenbury's last full day on earth, Governor Ashbel P. Willard granted a month's stay, allowing the defense time to make an appeal to the state supreme court.[6]

The stay of execution procured by Jonathan Mullinix provoked "intense excitement" in the county. The last execution for murder had been sixteen years earlier. (Coincidentally, Jonathan had been a juror in that case.) Novelty as well as the brutality of the slaying doubtless prompted the attention it received. Tom Walpole, the Indianapolis lawyer hired by Jonathan, together with the governor's private secretary and two other men went to Greencastle to get the trial transcript. They left town immediately, as a "feeling of mob violence" prevailed in reaction to the governor's meddling. After Sheriff William Farrow read the governor's stay of execution, Rev. E. W. Fisk and Capt. W. H. Thornburgh, a respected local merchant, spoke, "calling on the people to submit quietly, and avoid mob violence." Although the majority agreed, "some few cried 'hang him,' and then there was a rush. The jail was soon surrounded by a large multitude." The sheriff ordered a small party of men, armed with fixed bayonets, to protect the jail. The mob was unorganized, and the show of force stopped them.[7] A professor at Indiana Asbury University, Miles Fletcher, knew how close to violence the mob had come. He wrote his father, "Our citizens of all parties are very indignant." Fletcher believed that the greatest deterrent to a lynching was the expectation that the legal authorities would carry out the execution. He was "certain that if the Sheriff does not hang the man on the day appointed, the people [will]."[8]

Putnam's citizens got their wish. Jonathan Mullinix's efforts gained Greenbury only a respite. The state supreme court never received the evidence, perhaps because the locals had prevented Walpole and his cohort from getting the transcript. Moreover, Mullinix's attorneys had failed to file a bill of exception with the judge specifying errors made during his trial. In the absence of the evidence—and especially without the bill of exception—the Indiana Supreme Court affirmed the lower court's judgment. On the morning of December 18, a dark and cloudy day on which a light rain fell, Greenbury Mullinix was hanged.[9]

The last execution in the county had been in 1841 and had been public. By the late 1850s, however, Northern sensibilities increasingly rejected the deterrence value of public executions and deplored their brutality. But crowds still gathered hoping to satisfy their curiosity. Miles Fletcher even invited his younger sister, Lucy, to "visit me, & see the 'hanging.'" Although the execution was to be private, Miles thought they could get a view from an overlooking building or that his friendship with Sheriff Farrow would gain them admittance and even allow Lucy to meet the murderer. Either Lucy was less eager than her brother to see a hanging or their father did not consider this outing suitable for a teen-age girl because she does not appear to have made the visit. Despite the fact that the sheriff had erected an enclosure to prevent the public from seeing the execution, people came by train, horseback, and carriage. The streets, especially near the jail, "were thronged with a moving mass of human beings, eager to gratify curiosity." The sheriff admitted only witnesses to the execution.[10]

Mullinix proved defiant to the end. On the scaffold, he protested his innocence. When the sheriff tied his hands, placed a hood over his head, and fastened the rope around his neck, he said to the sheriff, "Bill, that is rather tight," and he laughed a "big laugh." It was as well he maintained his equanimity because the first attempt to hang him failed when the rope broke. Mullinix landed on his feet and walked a few yards before being led back to the scaffold. The authorities let his body hang for over half an hour before declaring him dead and taking the corpse down.[11]

The hanging of Greenbury O. Mullinix was the last execution in Putnam County, although the murder of Martha Mullinix was certainly not the last violent death. The next spectacular murder, of a young husband and wife, occurred in Groveland on the night of January 6–7, 1861, and when the case went to trial in April, it had to compete for attention with the beginning of the Civil War. In that case, Tilghman H. and Lydia W. Hanna were murdered in their beds with an axe, with their infant child left alive between them. Suspicion soon focused on Robert G. H. "Harper" Evans. Sentenced to life, Evans escaped from the state prison at Jeffersonville before the end of the Civil War and disappeared. Rumors about sightings of him persisted in the county for many years. A robbery and arson spree that occurred in Groveland in 1865 was blamed on Harper Evans, supposedly returned to exact revenge on those who had testified against him.[12]

The Hanna murders shared characteristics with Martha Mullinix's slaying. Harper Evans and his victims were well-established county residents. Like Martha Mullinix, nineteen-year-old Lydia Williamson Hanna appeared to have married into a family of slightly higher status than her own.[13] Although the murderer, a youth of twenty, "neither look[ed] vicious, cruel, nor hardened," he shared the bad character of Greenbury Mullinix. He was described as profane, "a prodigal and reprobate youth, disobedient to parents, of bad habits and evil associations." Evans was depicted as indifferent to his mother's feelings just as Greenbury Mullinix had allegedly been four years earlier.[14]

The murder of Martha Mullinix would have been just another sordid crime that occasionally marred Putnam County's tranquility except that Miles Fletcher made it into a commentary on the county's politics and society. Writing for an Indianapolis Republican newspaper, Fletcher exploited Martha's death to indict the Democratic party and advance the temperance cause. Mental illness, alcohol, and economic strain often contributed to spousal violence.[15] All three factors probably played a part in the Mullinix murder, but locals did not use her death to campaign against domestic violence or address mental illness or the strains on marriage that certainly must have existed given the dismal economic times brought about by the Panic of 1857. Miles Fletcher, an up-and-coming young politician, turned the murder into a saga of Democratic iniquity, even as the capital's Democratic newspaper condemned "the infinitessimal littleness and meanness" of the Republican paper's treatment of Greenbury Mullinix, "this unfortunate man," and emphasized that he had "protested his innocence to the last."[16]

First, Fletcher attacked Democratic corruption. Although Jonathan Mullinix was initially rebuffed upon approaching Governor Willard, he gained entrée, Fletcher alleged, by engaging the services of lawyer Walpole, reputedly a drinking buddy of the governor's, for the considerable fee of $500. Fletcher faulted the Democratic governor not only for refusing "the heart broken father"—here, Fletcher misidentified Jonathan Mullinix—but also for granting the stay of execution "to a favorite who has been paid to get it." For that hefty fee, he said, Walpole persuaded the governor to grant the month's respite. Democrats, however, insisted that no bribes had been paid and that Governor Willard had acted correctly in allowing the defense lawyers time to make their case to the supreme court.[17] Though not without their own ethical lapses, members of the infant Republican party saw themselves as less corrupt than the Democrats. They pointed to President James Buchanan's administration as a particularly egregious example: the president or those close to him bribed or coerced politicians and overlooked electoral fraud in Kansas Territory. As Miles Fletcher was writing, Republicans were pressing the corruption issue at the national level.[18]

The Mullinixes were Democrats, and local Republicans believed that the Mullinix family represented all that was wrong with the Democratic party. Jonathan Mullinix not only voted Democratic but was also "a person without education, opposed to free schools, and destitute of any liberal ideas concerning society, religion or government. His associations, chiefly, during life have been such as a person of his cast of mind would naturally choose—those who would be to him 'kindred spirits.'"[19] The use of the word *spirits* may have been an intentional pun, for local Whigs and Republicans saw alcohol as a central component of the Democratic ethos, and Fletcher further reported that Jonathan Mullinix and even Greenbury's grandfather were "drunkards."[20]

Republicans emphasized the role of alcohol in the murder. A leading citizen of Putnam and neighbor of the Mullinix family, A. D. Hamrick, maintained that the murder showed the necessity of protecting "the young of our land from the demon of INTEMPERANCE."[21] Fights involving alcohol were a common occurrence and were regularly reported in the local newspaper and private correspondence. But though alcohol no doubt contributed to the mayhem, Greenbury lived in a violent culture. Even temperance men went armed, and "a quarrel about some trivial matter" could result in wounds from canes or bowie knives. Miles Fletcher himself once responded to an alcohol-fueled fight at a concert between town youth and college students by asking his brother to send him a revolver.[22] Greenbury Mullinix's use of an axe against his wife was indeed considered a heinous crime, but he lived in a community where stabbing and shooting "affrays" between men occurred frequently.

It is not known whether Greenbury had been drinking on the morning Martha died, but there is reason to believe that he trafficked in liquor. Elijah Edward Evans, who had been a student at Indiana Asbury almost a decade earlier, penciled a poem in response to the news of Martha Sublett Mullinix's death:

> The Salt Creek spring forever flows
> And its waters taste of rye
> And the Salt Creek boys who visit it
> Are always on a "high."
>
> And some who wish their fellow men
> This beverage to share
> Have bottled it up in barrels huge
> And sent it every where
>
> And though perchance the license law
> It is got them in a fix
> Still we may draw potations deep
> Ex parte Mullinix*————
>
> (*Greenberry Mulinix (now dead rest his soul) sold corn juice
> by the jigger—pint—or quart*)[23]

Greenbury Mullinix, his grandparents, and a cousin were defendants in suits concerning the illegal sale of alcohol from the 1830s through the 1870s.[24]

And in addition to being intemperate, the murderer smoked tobacco and used "profane language," even on the day before his execution. Although Jonathan Mullinix was a "hardshell Baptist," another marker of Democratic affiliation, his nephew seemed unconcerned with religion and uninterested in spiritual consolation from the Presbyterian and Methodist ministers who attended him during his imprisonment and at the gallows. Harper Evans also showed moral indifference, had a jocular attitude, and used profanity—formulaic sins attributed commonly to criminals.[25] In the Mullinix case, Fletcher made these peculiarly Democratic faults.

As much as Fletcher saw the Mullinix murder as a condemnation of immorality, especially drinking, he also viewed it as a commentary on gender roles. Greenbury felt more comfortable in the male realm of the doggery, or saloon, than in the female realm of domesticity. William T. Good, who was married to Greenbury's sister, testified to problems in the Mullinix marriage. On the night before the murder, Good had seen Greenbury and Martha at the home of other relatives. Greenbury told Good that he intended to emigrate because he disliked maintaining a household. When Good asked if he meant to take Martha, Greenbury replied, "'No, he'd be d—d if he would; he would leave her here.'" It was common to leave a wife behind while establishing oneself in a new country, but Greenbury's vehemence suggested that the couple's newlywed bliss had quickly eroded. One witness, Stephen Harvy, testified that he had overheard Greenbury "abusing his wife. He said 'you d—d bitch, I'll slap hell out of you.' She appeared to be crying." Looking into the house, Harvy saw Greenbury with "a stick in his hand, [he] struck it on the floor, and said 'you G—d d—d bitch, I'll knock your head off of you.'"[26] Greenbury even admitted to problems in his marriage in order to make a bizarre claim to self-defense. He said "that he acted only in self-defence in committing the deed;—that if he had not killed her when he did that she would have poisoned him, and thus ended his life,—and that God would punish no man for committing murder in self-defence."[27]

Martha, however, was described as a "retiring girl, of a modest, gentle disposition." She was uneducated, and her family "associations were not of the best character," perhaps indicating the struggling nature of David Sublett's position in the county. But Mullinix was depicted as "a *bad, corrupt* man," who kept company with unchaste women, possibly contracting a venereal disease and infecting Martha. He had maligned the virtue of his mother and sisters and was indifferent to the pain he caused his family.[28] Martha may not have been an exemplar of "true womanhood," but the qualities of modesty, reticence, and gentleness that were attributed to her were characteristics held to belong to women. It was her desire to establish a home that angered her husband, and it was at her own hearth that she died. If she was in fact ready to abandon the woman's sphere of the home, it was because of abuses no woman should bear. It was Greenbury who failed to accept proper gender roles. He associated with loose women, not true women. He had little regard for the feelings of any women, including his mother. And he rejected the man's role as provider and intended to go west and leave Martha behind. Although Greenbury obviously crossed the line by murdering his young wife, Stephen Harvy apparently did not think to intervene when he heard him swear at Martha and threaten her. It is likely that others in the Mullinix and Sublett families knew of Martha's treatment as well, but there is no evidence that anyone tried to help her before it was too late.

In the course of the murder trial, gender and generational roles assumed significance. Greenbury was shown to be indifferent not only to his mother's feelings but also to male authority. Judge Hanna, it seems, had irritated the defendant by a long speech from the bench in which he highlighted testimony that Greenbury was disobedient, presumably to his uncle Jonathan. Society frequently invoked a failure to obey parents—along with drinking, swearing, and keeping low company—to explain criminality.[29] And father-son relationships were important to Miles Fletcher, Greenbury's principal chronicler. His own father, Calvin Fletcher, was a wealthy, self-made man. Miles never forgot he was a Fletcher. As a relative newcomer, he might have made an honest mistake in identifying Jonathan Mullinix as Greenbury's father, but the mistake also obscured Greenbury's status as an orphan, which might have gained the murderer some sympathy. Or perhaps portraying Greenbury as a foul-mouthed, drunken, disobedient son satisfied Miles's need to prove his own worth to Calvin Fletcher.

Class also played a role in how the murderer was judged. Jonathan Mullinix belonged to the solid yeomanry. His family had long resided in the county, he had considerable property, and he had sufficient political connections to at least temporarily delay his nephew's execution. Fletcher, however, depicted Greenbury as lower class: drunken, profane, slovenly, and the keeper of low company both male and female. Fletcher was himself the scion of as upper-class a background as Indiana could produce in the 1850s. But certainly, the politically ambitious Miles Fletcher played up Greenbury as the product to be expected from a Democratic household, associating Democrats with the lower-class world of the doggery, the stabbing affray, and unchaste women. Similarly, the murder of Tilghman and Lydia Hanna fit a nineteenth-century model in which the spurned suitor loses control of his passions, resolving that if he cannot have the girl, no one else will. Such a lack of self-control was also deemed a marker of class. Middle-class men more than working-class men were expected to be able to restrain their natural aggression.[30]

In his zeal to depict Greenbury as exemplifying the flawed values of lower-class Democrats, Miles Fletcher may have missed the obvious. Jonathan based his appeal for his nephew's life on Greenbury's insanity. Governor Willard evaded the controversy by asserting that sanity was to be determined by the judge and jury.[31] Some of the testimony indicates that the jurors were perhaps too quick to dismiss the insanity defense. Local men who served as guards reported Greenbury's wild mood swings and odd statements. Miles Fletcher said Greenbury's eyes tended to wander, "rolling from side to side and resting somewhat confusedly on different objects when addressed by any one." Greenbury himself said that "he 'had been out of his mind' several times in his life but had never been crazy," an unconvincing assertion of sanity.[32] Even stranger was his behavior on the eve of execution. He seemed indifferent to the idea of his death, disbelieving that it would occur, which some attributed to the stay of execution. When told in December he would hang the next day, "he said he had been fooled once, and that he could not be deceived again."[33] When his brother asked for a picture of Greenbury on the morning of his execution, "Greenbury remarked that he would rather have the likenesses of his family than that the family should have his." When asked why, "he replied that he wished to keep the pictures to remember his family by."[34]

Yet despite having recounted Greenbury's peculiar behavior, observers were disinclined to call him insane. Antebellum juries also preferred to find the accused guilty—particularly if the crime was as ghastly as the one Greenbury committed—rather than insane. In the nineteenth century, a finding of insanity did not guarantee removal to an institution, and it might seem altogether too convenient a means of evading punishment.[35]

The Mullinix and Hanna murders offer a window on Putnam County in the years before the Civil War. The land that became Putnam County had been purchased from the Miami, Delaware, and Potawatomi in the Fort Wayne Treaty of 1809 and the St. Mary's Treaty of 1818. White settlement began about the time of the latter. Some of these tribes, as well as the Shawnee, had had hunting camps in the region that became Putnam County, but the Native American presence was gone by the time white settlers arrived. The county was organized in 1821 and named after a hero of the American Revolution, Israel Putnam. Successive legislatures altered its boundaries, with the final adjustment not being made until the outbreak of the Civil War. Putnam County was heavily timbered, drained by several creeks, and rolling in some parts but not too hilly for farming or pasture. Its blue grass reminded the many settlers from Kentucky of their home state, and occasional caves and sinkholes in the limestone strata provided excursions for young people. Weather could be extreme, with very cold periods in the winter, humid and hot summers, torrential rains that flooded the county's creeks and swept away property, and "hurricanes" (tornadoes) capable of "carrying trees through the air as though they were feathers on the breeze."[36]

The county seat, Greencastle, a town of between 1,500 and 2,000 residents in the 1850s, was also home to a Methodist university, Indiana Asbury. As befitted a town with a Methodist college, Greencastle had a reputation for piety. Schoolteacher Almira Harrah on a Sunday evening heard "singing and praying at the church a few rods from where I am." She noted, "The people in Greencastle are really the most religious people I ever was acquainted with." There were religious exercises throughout the Sabbath: class meetings in the morning, church service at eleven, Sabbath school in the afternoon, and then another service. According to Harrah, "there was prayer meeting or preachings every night but one last week."[37] In addition to regular church services, Putnam hosted a number of revivals throughout the Civil War era. All the denominations held them, and newspapers reported on the progress of the "good work." By the 1870s, however, reporters were at pains to stress the orderliness of the meetings and their lack of the "uproarious clamor" known in the "antique" days of the Second Great Awakening.[38] Methodists initially preached in the county in 1821, and the Presbyterians' first church in Putnam County was established in 1825 by Isaac Reed, a Connecticut missionary. The Baptists had organized by 1823, and in 1855, a Christian church was built in Greencastle after a debate between a Methodist and a Disciple of Christ at Cloverdale led to sixty-nine conversions to the Disciples.[39]

Greencastle's courthouse, in which Greenbury Mullinix was tried, was only a decade old at the time of his trial. A "classic structure, with massive columns at either end," it towered over buildings on Greencastle's square. It remained at the center of civic life until its replacement at the dawn of the twentieth

Putnam County Courthouse (1848–1901), where Greenbury Mullinix was tried and much of county civic life occurred. (From Jesse W. Weik, *History of Putnam County, Indiana* [Indianapolis, Ind.: Bowen, 1910])

century. The churches in the town were built of brick, but houses were "mostly old fashioned farm buildings" at the beginning of the 1850s. Like many a college town, Greencastle did not always reflect county sentiments: it remained a solidly Republican outpost in a heavily Democratic county. Although Greencastle became a railroad hub, the National Road ran south of the town, through Putnamville. It initially seemed a setback not to have the National Road, but railroads soon spurred improvements, and during the 1850s, Greencastle built sidewalks to connect the courthouse square with the depots. Locals joked about "*wading the sidewalks* in muddy weather," but by the end of the decade, the town was macadamizing roads as well as directing the building of sidewalks in residential neighborhoods. Within two decades, the frame buildings around the courthouse would give way to businesses built of stone, and more prosperous residents would construct elegant residences. Even the sidewalks ceased to be a joke.[40]

A generation of men and women shaped by the same forces of class, gender, and political division that influenced the Mullinixes and Hannas would soon face the increasing conflict between the North and South that culminated in civil war. Certainly, Greenbury Mullinix and Harper Evans were not typical county residents. But the Mullinix murder, as interpreted by Miles Fletcher, highlighted gender roles, the importance of alcohol, and political divisions within the county. Civil war and its aftermath would reshape some of these divisions but leave others intact.

A wealth of home-front studies address how the war affected the South, tackling such issues as Southern nationalism, the erosion of slavery and rise of black rights, the effects of Union occupation and military mobilization, and changes in gender and class relations brought by the war. Edward L. Ayers's work is unique in looking at two counties, one in Virginia and one in Pennsylvania, to emphasize the commonalities as well as the differences on both sides of the sectional border.[41] At a time when most Northerners lived in the country, studies of the Northern home front have concentrated on cities: New York, Boston, Chicago, or Philadelphia. They have explored the soldiers' experience, wartime economic development, and dissent. When they have examined social history, they have not, with a few exceptions, focused on Northerners' changing racial attitudes, concentrating more on the effect of the war on women and immigrants. Furthermore, these studies, both of the North and of the South, have been generally confined to the war years, with perhaps some discussion of the immediate pre- or postwar periods.[42] This study of Putnam County seeks to understand how the Civil War changed the North and the country by widening the chronological period. By looking at Putnam County from the Compromise of 1850 to the end of Reconstruction, we can gain a better sense of the changes the war brought for the generation of which Miles Fletcher was a part. In addition, the rural and small-town nature of the county offers a contrast to the urban focus of previous Northern home-front studies.[43]

Although the chronological period is wide, the focus on Putnam County may seem a narrow one. But as Jill Lepore has eloquently explained, microhistories allow us to tell stories that have larger meanings. Through microhistory, the historian can illuminate truths about the culture under study. Richard D. Brown emphasizes that microhistories allow one to test generalizations and to give ordinary people a voice. Excellent general histories of the war in the North, such as those by Matthew Gallman and Philip Paludan, cannot capture in as much depth the individual experiences of men and women whose lives, whether they were in combat or not, "were touched by fire." Eric Foner has asserted that the Civil War was the central experience for nineteenth-century

Americans; to a significant extent, microhistory allows us to feel that experience as they did—their passions, hatreds, anxieties, and joys.[44] Microhistory allows us to see how ordinary Americans understood the causes and meaning of the war and how they sought to shape the peace.

For microhistory to have validity, the community under study must have some claim to representativeness or significance. No single location, of course, can represent the larger society, but a rural midwestern community such as Putnam County, Indiana, may tell us much about a Northern society that was itself still primarily agrarian. In 1860, Putnam was one of the most populous of Indiana's counties. Nationally, only five states had more people than Indiana: New York, Ohio, Pennsylvania, Illinois, and Virginia. In agriculture, Putnam ranked in the top third of Indiana counties in 1870, and Indiana as a whole was fifth in the value of its products, outranked only by Illinois, New York, Ohio, and Pennsylvania. Settled not long after Indiana became a state, Putnam was one of the state's richest agricultural areas. In 1860, 12 acres of land per person was improved in the county, twice the amount for the rest of the state. In the Civil War era, Putnam was a leading producer of corn, beef cattle, sheep, and hogs in Indiana. According to a state auditor's report in 1853, only one Indiana county—neighboring Montgomery—had more sheep. In early 1854, some 24,000 hogs were slaughtered and packed, earning $400,000. Putnam produced half as much corn and hogs per capita as other states of both the North and the South but roughly twice as many sheep and beef cattle. Greenbury Mullinix's murder weapon, an axe, was a basic tool of a rural, agricultural society.[45]

Indiana was in the top third of states in the annual value of its manufactures, outranked by several New England and mid-Atlantic states and some other midwestern states, including Illinois, Michigan, and Ohio. Putnam lagged behind the rest of Indiana, however, in manufacturing. Marion County, with a population four times that of Putnam, led the state with a per capita value of products in manufacturing of $277 in 1880. Cass County, number ten in the state in the value of its manufacturing products and number of people working in industry, had a per capital value of $93 and 1,342 industrial workers. By comparison, Putnam had only $39 per capita value of production and less than half the number of manufacturing workers as Cass in 1880.[46] Putnam was thus a relatively wealthy farming region with more industry than much of the state but hardly at the forefront of nineteenth-century industrialization.

Some of the most important political trends of the 1800s were occurring in Putnam County. Indiana was a key swing state in the nineteenth century.

Throughout the period, it was closely divided between parties and generally ended up in the winner's column. Only twice between 1848 and 1880 did Indiana vote for the loser in the presidential race, in both cases a Democrat: in 1848, when the Whig Zachary Taylor was elected, and in 1876, when the Republican Rutherford B. Hayes won a controversial election. In no presidential election was the winner's share of the state's popular vote greater than 54 percent, the margin by which Abraham Lincoln was reelected in 1864. More often, the winning party received no more than 51 percent of the vote and often less. Putnam County reflected these trends. Linked to the larger state and national economies by the National Road and, later, the railroads, Putnam was generally Whig. But many of the county's residents were Democrats. Elections were hotly contested and close, often leading to shady electoral practices, fights at the polls, and fraud.[47] It was a community with such deep political divisions that the horrific details of a young bride's death were exploited to indict an entire political party.

Putnam County also reflected the nation in its demography. Throughout the Civil War era, the population of Putnam continued to increase. In 1850, there were 18,615 people in the county. Over the next decade, the population grew 11 percent. The rate of increase slowed to 4 to 5 percent in the decades after the Civil War. But just as migration continued into the county, some young men were leaving. In the late 1840s, the California goldfields beckoned, and throughout the 1850s, Putnam County men would look westward for opportunity—if not to California, then to Pike's Peak, which was the mining frontier of the later 1850s, or to Kansas, Missouri, or some other frontier. Whereas Ohio had begun to lose population by 1860, Indiana and the states to the west and southwest continued to have a net in-migration. Indiana's population growth was slowing in the 1850s, however, and the state would begin to experience significant out-migration in the next decades. Studies of persistence rates, which focus on heads of households, show the western regions to have been more mobile, with only about one-third of the population remaining from census to census, compared to almost two-thirds in New England. One study of Indiana Asbury's graduates shows that a third migrated west in the 1850s, mostly to Kansas and Iowa.[48]

Indiana's population was a mix of Southern and Northern settlers. Some 18 percent of the state's population had been born in the South according to the 1850 census, mostly in upper South states such as Kentucky, Virginia, and North Carolina. By that period, two-thirds of the state's residents had been born in the Old Northwest itself, the majority of whom were probably children of migrants from the upper South. About 10 percent of the state's population came from mid-Atlantic states and only 1 percent from New England. Putnam County reflected a similar mix of settlers. The Mullinixes were originally from North Carolina, and other Putnam settlers migrated from Kentucky or Virginia. According to the 1850 census, 19 percent of the county's residents had been born in Kentucky. If one includes those born in other upper South states, the proportion rises to nearly a third. Like the state, almost two-thirds of Putnam's residents had been born in the Old Northwest, over half in Indiana itself. The Fletchers had New England roots, but only .5 percent of the county's population had been born in New England in the 1850s.[49]

The building of railroads in the 1850s brought Irish laborers to Putnam County. During the 1850s, the number of immigrants doubled over that of the previous decade, totaling 228 people. But Indiana lagged behind other midwestern states in attracting immigrants. Many traveled farther west in search of better and more abundant land, and unlike other states, Indiana did not recruit immigrants. Still, their numbers more than doubled in the 1850s, approaching 5 to 6 percent of the state's population. Over half of the foreign born were Germans, the largest immigrant group in the state. Next were the Irish at about 23 percent of the immigrant population. However, in Putnam County, where immigrants made up only 1 percent of the population, it was the Irish who were dominant, composing 65 percent of the immigrant population, compared with the Germans at only 18 percent. Immigrants had a disproportionate role in the temperance debates. Augustus Werneke, a naturalized citizen from Prussia, was a liquor dealer. Charley Michael, another German immigrant, owned a beer shop on the courthouse square.[50]

Some native-born Hoosiers felt sympathy for the Irish, who performed backbreaking labor on the railroads. And almost everyone recognized that the foreign born were "the subjects of an ungenerous prejudice here."[51] During a Fourth of July oration, Rev. Thomas S. Webb attacked the Catholic Church, deriding it as a "drunken church" whose priests sought political domination. Local Catholics relied on priests from Terre Haute and Indianapolis to say mass in private homes until Fr. William Doyle arrived in Greencastle and established St. Benedict's in 1853. Local lore has it that Gustavus H. Lilly, the Protestant owner of the church site, refused initially to sell the lot to the Catholics and so was told it was to be used for a vinegar factory. That story is likely untrue, but Father Doyle certainly did face harassment, especially from the local Whig newspaper, the *Putnam Banner,* which accused him of trying to control the local Irish.

A walk through the Bainbridge Cemetery, in the northern part of the county, shows that immigrants, no matter how successful, remained segregated from their fellows. Buried in the northwest corner are Currans, Heaneys, Kelleys, Mungavans, and Sullivans. Their gravestones, unlike those of Protestants buried there, often bear engravings of crosses, a practice common among Irish Catholics. Placed along the last rows at the cemetery's edge, their graves form a separate community in death just as the individuals did in life.[52] This was true even though some were prominent in the community: Patrick Heaney, for instance, was a leading Democrat and officeholder.

In its demographic patterns, Indiana reflected the country in the mid-nineteenth century. With its mix of Southerners and Northerners and its influx of immigrants, Putnam was slightly more Southern in its population than other parts of the North. Allegiances to the South would be a prominent feature of the county's reactions to civil war.

Class shaped the county much as it did the nation. The life of the doggery and its stabbing affrays—one type of male, lower-class culture—conflicted with the increasingly idealized and middle-class life represented by women's domesticity and by the home life that Greenbury so disliked. These elements often overlapped. Miles Fletcher, an aspiring young Republican with New England roots, stigmatized the Democratic Mullinixes with their Southern birth as lower-class, drunken threats to the social order. Fletcher exaggerated these characteristics to make his political point, but temperance was indeed a political issue that divided the parties as well as the native-born and immigrant populations. More than that, in an era that saw the rise and fall of political issues connected to westward expansion, sectionalism, economic development, and race, conflict over alcohol was a constant. Although many Putnam residents joined national temperance movements, the fight over alcohol was carried out on the local scene, involving city ordinances and church crusades.

Putnam was also a community about to be torn apart by national political events. A generation of young men who, like Miles Fletcher, were just embarking on their adult lives confronted the most violent episode of U.S. history, the Civil War. The violence of war shaped the lives of those who fought and of those who opposed the war. It affected as well women who, trying to fulfill their domestic roles, were left temporarily or permanently without a male breadwinner. The Mullinix and Hanna cases had reflected some aspects of society's conception of gender roles. The war challenged Putnam's young men and women to maintain those gender roles under vastly changed circumstances. Yet one element that would become extremely important to residents in the county over the next two decades was missing in these murder cases: race played no role in the murder of Martha Mullinix or of the young Hannas. In the ensuing years, however, the Civil War would make race an inescapable element of the county's life.

How did the Civil War change the North? That the war ended slavery and established the federal government's supremacy over the states, all the while expanding that government, has long been acknowledged. "How decisively and thoroughly did it alter American life in general?" asks historian George M. Fredrickson. Similarly, Matthew Gallman has queried, "What was the war's enduring impact on the North?"[53] This microhistory provides some answers to those questions. In Putnam County, a generation of men forged their identities in the Civil War and, as veterans, demanded continued recognition of their sacrifice. Women hoped to preserve traditional roles but found war often made that difficult. They maintained their dependence on male providers, and when circumstances, such as the death of a soldier husband, forced their independence, they only partially embraced it. As this Civil War generation matured, much of their society changed. Immigrants became more readily accepted members of the community, and though controversy over temperance remained constant in the county's life, women's antialcohol work challenged traditional roles. Antiwar Democrats remained unyielding white supremacists and maintained their political popularity despite Republican accusations of treason.

The most significant and deepest change, however, occurred in regard to race, which assumed a prominence that it had lacked before the war. In the 1850s, racism was pervasive in Putnam County, where few African Americans lived. But the sectional crisis of the 1850s, the Civil War, and Reconstruction forced residents to directly confront slavery and racism. Many in the county remained unremittingly hostile to African Americans, but others began to accept a greater measure of black rights. At the end of Reconstruction, Putnam County even became a destination for migrating Exodusters, who were fleeing the return of white supremacy in the South. Despite a long history of hostility to black migrants to the state, Putnam Republicans encouraged and welcomed the Exodusters. In Putnam County, the Civil War era forced white Northerners to confront the country's racial fissures. Neither the county nor the country would be entirely the same again.

PART 1
BEFORE THE WAR

1

A NORTHERN PARTY

Ned McGaughey's death at the James Hotel in San Francisco marked a transition in Putnam County's political life. McGaughey had been congressman from the Seventh Congressional District, which included Putnam. A Whig, he had supported the Compromise of 1850, including the controversial Fugitive Slave Act. Defeated for reelection, he headed west for California but contracted "Panama fever" during the crossing. By the time a doctor was found, McGaughey was past saving. "Emaciated" from travel and illness, he died immediately after his arrival.[1] It was perhaps fitting not only that he perished in California—the place over which the crisis of 1850 had arisen—but also that Putnam's leading Whig died at a time when the Whig party itself was dying. John G. Davis, the Democrat who had supplanted McGaughey as congressman, would become one of the leading political figures of the 1850s. Davis broke with his own party and formed an alliance with the Whig's successors, the new Republican party. Again, it was a controversy over slavery's expansion, this time to Kansas Territory, that provoked Davis's unlikely—and brief—dalliance with the Republicans. His chief nemesis in the Putnam Democratic organization was

Judge Delana Eckels, who supported the extreme Southern rights wing of the party. A young politician named John Hanna left the Democrats for the Republicans and was among those who worked with Davis during his break with the Democratic party. Hanna went on to campaign for Abraham Lincoln in 1860, and Davis reverted to the Democratic party, supporting Stephen A. Douglas. All these politicians insisted they wanted to protect what Hanna called the interests of "the white laborer." But whereas Hanna argued that the Democratic party's subservience to its Southern wing worked against those interests, Judge Eckels decided that Southern, not Northern, whites were the aggrieved party.[2]

These shifting political alliances marked the 1850s as a period of political realignment. McGaughey's party, the Whigs, had coalesced in the 1830s around an economic program grounded in a belief in the federal government's power to stimulate the economy through a national bank, protective tariffs, and federal money for internal improvements. By the 1850s, the salience of the economic conflicts had diminished. New issues such as temperance and immigration competed for voters' allegiance. And, as Ned McGaughey found, race and slavery expansion assumed greater importance, with disastrous consequences for both Whigs and Democrats. Historians have examined how slavery destroyed the Union, particularly emphasizing Southern fears of assaults on that institution, but less attention has been paid to how Northerners themselves felt threatened.[3] As the Whigs died, as the Democrats fractured, and as the "black" Republicans were born, Putnam residents longed for a Northern party that would accord the South its rights, respect the rights of the North, and deny rights to African Americans.

As a member of the Indiana legislature in the 1830s, Delana Eckels voted against the so-called Mammoth internal improvements bill, a Whig program of canals, roads, and railroads. The Kentucky-born Eckels began practicing law in Putnam County in the 1830s, eventually becoming a judge.[4] Throughout his long career in county Democratic politics, Eckels earned an unenviable reputation as "a man void of principle . . . the most vindictive, unscrupulous and tyranical little scamp that the sun shines on."[5] But he did have core Democratic principles. Although the Mammoth bill promised to increase his constituents' access to distant markets, Eckels, as a good Democrat, simply could not support it. His vote cost him reelection, although he took pride in being defeated "by only *three* votes." And when the state went bankrupt after the Panic of 1837 and could not finish the improvements, Eckels claimed prescience.[6]

Internal improvements were an important economic issue because farmers needed access to markets. Before the Civil War, Putnam farmers drove hogs to packing plants at Madison, Indiana, and Cincinnati, Ohio, or carted wheat to Lawrenceburg, Indiana, on the Ohio River—100 miles or more overland. An Indiana Asbury student assessing Greencastle's economic potential in the late 1840s noted the lack of "any facilities for transportation."[7] An English traveler found the so-called National Road poorly kept up through Putnam County: rain had made deep channels in the roadbed, planks had been laid down to compensate, or a corduroy bed of bone-jolting logs lay where the gravel had worn away altogether.[8] On the national level, economic issues split Whigs from Democrats, but as a practical matter, many Putnam Democrats appreciated the need for economic development. Judge John Cowgill, for example, believed railroads were the answer to the county's transportation needs. He proposed that the county lend its credit for the purpose of buying railroad stock in the two lines that would traverse the county.[9] Opponents feared that such "an enormous debt" would lead to "exorbitant taxes," not an unreasonable point after the failure of the state's grand internal improvements plan. Greencastle's Democratic newspaper scolded the opponents of Cowgill's plan for their fear of "public improvement," arguing that the railroads would create a "home market," increase population, and stimulate "public spirit."[10] Voters were not persuaded, and the measure was defeated. The railroads were still built. The Englishman passed "many scores of labourers . . . at work on cuttings and embankments for the railroad from Indianapolis to St. Louis." East-west and north-south routes would bisect the county and make Greencastle a railroad hub by the 1870s.[11]

Just as the railroads served the county's transportation needs, so did access to capital increase. One of the county's leading merchants, William H. Thornburgh, known as "Captain" Thornburgh for his early career on a Mississippi River steamboat, acted as a kind of banker because he possessed "the first money safe in the county."[12] Perhaps because he considered his safe inadequate to the county's financial needs, he was also among those who moved to organize a bank in Greencastle. The Central National Bank was formed by February 1856 and had bipartisan support. The state bank, chartered a year earlier, had been opposed by Democrats out of both political ideology and revulsion at the "bribery and corruption" by which the charter had passed the legislature.[13] Republicans conceded that the state bank "was conceived in sin and brought forth in iniquity," but it was managed by the highly respected Calvin Fletcher, surviving the financial Panic of 1857.[14]

Education also had some bipartisan support. Democrats took a leading role in pushing for better education in the county. William Larrabee, an Indiana Asbury professor, became the state's first superintendent of education under the constitution of 1851. The female academy operated by his wife, Harriet, was one of the premier institutions for young women in the state. Delana Eckels, who served as a school trustee, sued the Greencastle town council to force it to provide better education for local youth. Some Democrats protested against what they felt was an unjust school taxation, but others pointed out that an educated citizenry was necessary to free government, a sentiment echoed by Whigs and Republicans. Yet twice in the late 1840s, county voters overwhelmingly rejected the funding of free public schools.[15]

Although Indiana's 1851 constitution required a "general and uniform system of public schools," local jurisdictions that tried to build schools soon ran afoul of the "uniform" provision. The Indiana Supreme Court ruled that local taxation to fund schools violated that clause in a case that arose when a Greencastle taxpayer sued to prevent the collection of taxes the town had levied to support the schools.[16] Eckels lamented that the court had "knocked free schools into the middle of the next century."[17] With state funding limited and with the local ability to raise funds hampered by the courts, many districts failed to provide much education at all. On average, Indiana schools were in session only two and a half months of the year.[18] Putnam earned its title as "the banner county for ignorance" by having the highest proportion of illiterate adults in the state. And since Indiana had the highest rate of illiteracy of any Northern state, Putnam's record as the most illiterate county in the most illiterate free state was particularly ignominious.[19]

As befitted a college town, Greencastle fared better educationally than most places in Indiana. In the early 1850s, the town adopted a graded system with four primary schools and a high school, the latter a rarity in the 1850s. Still, many parents enrolled their children in private "subscription schools" held in the teacher's house.[20] In one of his fits of pique, Miles Fletcher called Greencastle "a lifeless, low, dirty, ignorant Kentucky town" with a largely illiterate population.[21]

Although economic and education matters were less partisan than the rhetoric often suggested, other issues split very clearly between the parties. For example, immigrants to Putnam County were few in number, but their presence was controversial. Anti-immigrant Know-Nothings asserted that Catholicism was inherently inimical to free political institutions. And according to the editor of the *Putnam Republican Banner,* it was "impossible for a Catholic to be a republican."[22] That the immigrants voted largely for the Democrats only exacerbated hostility. Democrats such as Judge Eckels became the strongest defenders of immigrant rights.[23] Within the Democratic organization, native-born individuals and immigrants vied for plum patronage jobs. M. J. Lynch, hoping to get the Greencastle postmastership, complained, "The office I am aspiring to will be given to some Irishman I think."[24] Patrick Rigney felt he had "a claim . . . for a small situation" as a reward for Irish support of the party.[25] Meanwhile, another Irishman, Patrick Heaney, became the most successful immigrant politician in the county. During the Civil War, he was made first deputy district prosecuting attorney for the county and then prosecutor for the Ninth District, which included Putnam County. A modern marker placed on Heaney's grave describes him as "a descendant of the house of Plunkett," a reference to the notorious early twentieth-century Tammany Hall politician George Washington Plunkitt, who famously boasted of his ability to profit from public office.[26]

But it was not just the immigrants' Catholicism and their voting for the Democrats that many Putnam residents disliked. The immigrants were also proalcohol. (Whig temperance advocacy, local Democrats claimed, was "a shot at our adopted citizens.")[27] It did not go unnoticed that many of the liquor traffickers were foreign: of the half dozen doggeries in Greencastle, one was run by a German and the others by Irishmen.[28] And when Miles Fletcher passed three drunken men on the town's streets, he assumed that they were Irish.[29] The Whig newspaper publicized the temperance cause and the steady stream of speakers and lecturers who chronicled "the dreadful curse of intemperance."[30]

To the forces resisting temperance, the immigrants were merely new recruits. Indeed, Dr. A. C. Stevenson gave the county's first temperance lecture in 1828, long before there was a sizable immigrant population. The lecture was disrupted by "topers [who] came in with their bottles and drank bumpers to one another, and to the speaker."[31]

Temperance, in fact, was the most highly contested issue of the pre–Civil War period in the county. In 1853, the legislature passed a local option law by which township voters decided whether to permit the sale of liquor.[32] Temperance forces also lobbied for a prohibition, or Maine, law as the only effective way to stop "the dram shop" from "dispensing ruin, misery and death to the unguarded and inexperienced sons of men."[33] The existing township option law was ruled unconstitutional by the Indiana Supreme Court, which found it violated the state constitution's provision that all laws be "general and uniform."

This finding renewed demands for a prohibitory law, which the legislature passed, bringing short-lived joy to temperance advocates in Putnam County. "We had a real Jubilee here when we heard the news that Governor Wright had signed the prohibitory liquor law," Samuel Landes wrote, "the whole Town was Illuminated court house & college—they throwed fire balls that I thought they would fire the town & you might have heard the shouts of the people a considerable distance from Town."[34] But this law, too, was quickly overturned by the Indiana Supreme Court as an unconstitutional infringement of property rights.[35]

Denied a prohibitory law, temperance advocates tried economic pressure. Citizens of Bainbridge and Greencastle boycotted retailers of alcohol. "We are having some exciting temperance meetings," Miles Fletcher reported to his father. "We have a mass meeting tonight to adopt resolutions, that we will patronise no one who engages in the sale of ardent spirits."[36] After the prohibitory law's failure, Greencastle passed an ordinance requiring a license of $100. This closed the doggeries "in front," but liquor dealers were believed to be surreptitiously selling out their back doors. A "committee of visitation" was formed to call on liquor shop owners and inform them that they must stop their trade. The liquor sellers agreed to quit but then simply moved their businesses. Frustration led to vigilante action. In the summer of 1858, citizens of Greencastle "broke up one establishment." German immigrant Charley Michael also received such a visit. The temperance men got into an altercation with Charley's wife, Barbary, and were charged with assault and battery when they tried "to break up and destroy a lot of *rot-gut* whiskey" found in the Michaels's home. In early 1859, the Cincinnati press reported a "liquor riot" in which the residents of Greencastle had gone on a rampage, destroying all the saloons in town, although local Republicans insisted that "the contents of *one* liquor shop only was destroyed" by one person and not a mob.[37]

When Eckels lost the race for the Sixth Circuit judgeship, he blamed "whiskey and whigery combined." He was aware that some Democrats crossed party lines to vote against alcohol.[38] Eckels, in fact, considered himself a "a devoted Temperance man," but he avowed, "I love my old party and will vote it whiskey or no whiskey."[39] The county's Democratic newspaper ran temperance fiction, and Democrat William H. Durham noted that even though he thought the state's prohibitory law was "a lame affair," he hoped it might help an alcoholic friend who had "no control of his appetite."[40] Nonetheless, Democrats were clearly the party of whiskey. H. B. Pickett of Groveland saw the division as "the whigs for and de[m]ocrats against" restricting alcohol.[41] James M. Cooper concluded he was not a Democrat because he was a temperance man and no temperance man could be a Democrat. Moreover, he observed that *"Free Liquor* is the *key stone* of modern Democracy in Indiana."[42] A leading partisan issue, temperance encompassed the entire era before, during, and after the Civil War. Yet even as it remained a perennial issue, sectionalism and slavery increasingly dominated voters' attention.

EDWARD W. "NED" MCGAUGHEY was as deeply rooted in the county as any of its residents. His younger sister, Mary Jane, was the first white child born in Putnam County, where their parents, Arthur and Sarah, had settled in 1821. The McGaugheys were thus among the county's oldest white residents, and both parents were community leaders. Arthur was the longtime clerk of the court, Sarah an active member of the Baptist church. When Ned joined the bar in 1835, he was only eighteen. In the 1840s, he had a seemingly swift political rise, serving in the state senate and twice in the U.S. Congress. The war with Mexico was remembered as his downfall. According to county historian Jesse Weik, McGaughey opposed that war and spoke strongly against it in the House of Representatives. Because of lingering resentment toward his antiwar stance, he was defeated in his next reelection bid and even denied a patronage post as governor of Minnesota Territory. Politically dead in Indiana, McGaughey left for California and an early grave.[43]

But Weik appears to have mistaken the moral of the story. McGaughey's downfall was not his antiwar position but his stance on the Compromise of 1850. It is true that he opposed the war with Mexico, in part for good Whig fiscal reasons that the war had "prostrated the public credit, and destroyed the revenues of the country." McGaughey also followed traditional Whig preferences for a strong Congress when he objected to President James K. Polk's maneuvering the United States into war: "The war-making power in this country is vested in Congress," he asserted, "not the President." Among these other issues, McGaughey recognized that acquisition of territory from Mexico raised troubling questions about slavery, and he thought it "the part both of prudence and patriotism to avoid this question, by refusing to receive any more territory."[44] Racism also contributed to his antiwar position, for McGaughey believed the Mexicans to be "semi-barbarous" and incapable of sustaining republican government.[45] He knew that his position opened him to attack, even to "charges of treason."[46] But whatever backlash there was against him, it did not cause Whigs to lose the district. McGaughey did not run in 1847, but the Whig candidate who did seek election, Richard W. Thompson of Terre Haute, also opposed the war. And Thompson held the Seventh Congressional District for the Whigs by the same narrow margin by which McGaughey had prevailed two years earlier.[47]

Within heavily Democratic Indiana, Putnam was a relative stronghold for the Whigs. The state had actually voted for the Whig presidential candidate, William Henry Harrison, in 1836 and 1840, but Harrison was the former territorial governor of Indiana, making the vote less a partisan referendum than support for a fellow westerner. In all the other presidential elections of the 1840s and 1850s, Indiana supported Democrats. By 1850, Democrats controlled all the state offices, the legislature, and most of the congressional seats as well as both of the Senate seats. And when delegates convened to write a new state constitution, two-thirds were Democrats. Yet of the nineteen men Putnam County elected to the Indiana General Assembly between 1844 and 1851, fourteen were Whigs but only five were Democrats.[48] Still, the Seventh Congressional District of which Putnam was part was tightly contested. When McGaughey first won election to Congress in 1845, it was by a margin of only 1 percent. Despite the common wisdom that the Mexican War had rendered him unpopular, McGaughey easily won the election in 1849 against a relative unknown, Grafton F. Cookerly; in fact, he was the only Whig to win in Indiana. But in 1851, he lost the seat by a narrow margin to John G. Davis, the Democrat who would hold it for much of the next decade.[49] It was not the Mexican War that cost McGaughey his seat but the Compromise of 1850.

McGaughey voted for parts of the compromise—even the proslavery fugitive slave bill, making him one of only three Northern Whigs who voted for the "nigger catching law."[50] A public meeting in Putnam County after the passage of the 1850 Compromise brought together Whigs such as A. D. Hamrick and Democrats such as Delana Eckels to endorse the compromise. McGaughey spoke, and one of the meeting's resolutions praised his vote in favor of the fugitive slave bill. Nonetheless, this reputation as a "slave catcher" hurt him among some local Whigs who contested his renomination.[51] Having demonstrated his pro-Southern bona fides by voting for the Fugitive Slave Act, McGaughey now sought to prove his sensitivity to the Free Soil movement. He expressed support for imposing the Wilmot Proviso—the prohibition on expanding slavery into territory acquired from Mexico that was the bedrock Free-Soil position—in the territories formed by the 1850 Compromise: Utah and New Mexico. Mc-Gaughey was believed to have written that "no man who speaks lightly of the *Proviso,* can be elected in our district," but he did not seem to know which position—the Southern-leaning fugitive law or the Northern-leaning proviso—would most appeal to voters. His dilemma was that of the Indiana Whig party, which faced not only the loss of voters to Free-Soilers willing to oppose slavery expansion but also pressure from Whigs in southern Indiana who supported the compromise.[52]

Meanwhile, local Democrats perceived an opening for their candidate, John G. Davis. The Indianapolis Democratic newspaper predicted, "Hundreds of Whigs will vote for Davis, and hundreds will refuse to vote altogether."[53] Bainbridge merchant Abiathar Crane, whom McGaughey assumed was a supporter, backed Davis.[54] Certainly, other Whigs feared that their own "dissention" would hand the Democrats a "victory."[55] For their part, the Democrats resoundingly supported the compromise. Governor Joseph A. Wright, McGaughey's former law partner, famously told the state legislature, "Indiana takes her stand in the ranks, not of *Southern destiny,* nor yet of *Northern destiny.* She plants herself on the basis of the Constitution; and takes her stand in the ranks of American destiny."[56] Wright reiterated these sentiments in Putnam County, where he spoke at Asbury University in July 1850, asking his audience to "renounce all sectional parties—sternly rebuke any and every effort to form a northern party!"[57] The Putnam Democratic newspaper, the *Sentinel,* endorsed the Compromise of 1850, and correspondents insisted that the law—even the Fugitive Slave Act—had to be respected.[58]

McGaughey's strategy in the election was to make Davis look like an opponent of the compromise. During a joint debate at Putnamville in 1851, he accused Davis of having expressed "disapprobation to some of the details of the Fugitive Slave Law."[59] But Democrats, in fact, held this up as Davis's great virtue—that he was an even greater advocate of the Compromise of 1850 than McGaughey, who had not voted for the Texas boundary bill. Democrats claimed that Davis would have supported all parts of the compromise.[60] As a result, McGaughey was too proslavery for some Whig supporters but not procompromise enough to attract either Democrats or those Whigs who were willing to make concessions to the South.

"GLORIOUS TRIUMPH! JOHN G. DAVIS, DEMOCRAT, ELECTED!" the *Indiana State Sentinel* pronounced. Still, it was a close victory. Davis received 51 percent of the district's votes, losing in Putnam and Parke counties. The *Putnam County*

John G. Davis. (From Isaac
R. Strouse, *Parke County
Indiana Centennial Memorial
(1816–1916)* [Rockville,
Ind.: Rockville Chautauqua
Association, 1916], 51;
courtesy of Indiana State
Library)

Sentinel called the 1851 election "disastrous" for McGaughey.[61] And it was certainly disastrous for the Indiana Whig party, as only one congressional district went Whig.

At the time, McGaughey's defeat seemed only a temporary setback, for a year later, Whig candidates swept the local elections; even the Whig presidential candidate, Winfield Scott, won Putnam County in 1852, though he was defeated by a large margin in the state.[62] The year 1852, however, proved to be the Whigs' last presidential race. The party's obituary had not yet been written, but it was in its death throes. Like many other Whigs, McGaughey had lost focus when confronted with the issue of slavery's expansion. He had waffled between pro-Southern support of the Fugitive Slave Act and pro-Northern support for the Wilmot Proviso, being a convincing advocate for neither side. By contrast, Davis backed the compromise and won.[63]

Calvin Fletcher called John G. Davis "a fine looking fellow."[64] Davis was born in Kentucky, where his family had settled in Parke County in 1819. He himself had been clerk of the county court from 1833 until his election to Congress.[65] Like McGaughey's, Davis's political career would be challenged by the sectional issues of the 1850s. For the Whig congressman, it had been the Compromise of 1850; for the Democrat Davis, it would be the Kansas-Nebraska Act of 1854. This legislation repealed the 1820 Missouri Compromise in the northern part of the Louisiana Purchase, where it instead established popular sovereignty, giving settlers the right to choose whether to have slavery. Incorporated into the legislation in order to gain Southern votes to organize the territory, popular sovereignty quickly became Democratic party doctrine even as it drove many Northern Democrats out of the party. Davis voted for the act in Congress and later maintained "it had no truer or more devoted friend" than himself. Its principles, he said, were "just and right" and capable of resolving not only the slavery issue but any other matter that might arise.[66] Eckels also accepted the new principle and dismissed protests as inconsequential. "Politically we are in a calm," he advised Davis. "Abolitionism, what little we have about the college keeps shady. . . . I do not know of an open enemy here to [the Kansas-Nebraska Act's] passage. The Compromise of 1850 unfettered by the act of 1820 or none seems to be the maxim of all."[67]

By referring to opponents of Kansas-Nebraska as abolitionists, Eckels revealed that the measure had reopened the slavery expansion question. He exploded with racially tinged language against Democrats who opposed the legislation: "He that will appoint a Woolly head with a black heart to office for the sake of policy or power is no better than an open abolitionist." Eckels defended popular sovereignty as "the assertion of a great political truth . . . that man is capable of self government and of the political axiom that all power is inherent in the people."[68] He insisted that the Kansas-Nebraska bill was supported by "a good sound majority in Putnam."[69]

But Putnam County was not as quiet as Eckels claimed. At Bainbridge, citizens met in late February to protest the bill. Higgins Lane, a Whig politician and former state representative from Putnam, drafted resolutions deeming the Kansas-Nebraska bill "unsound in principle and calculated to subvert the common rights of humanity" and urging opposition to "a measure fraught with so much mischief to the advancement of Freedom and Republicanism."[70] At

Putnamville, forty people signed a petition against the Kansas-Nebraska bill and sent it to Congressman Davis to present in Congress.[71] Other petitions "praying Congress to respect and adhere to the Missouri Compromise" were circulating at Portland Mills.[72] Those who opposed the Kansas-Nebraska bill were not concerned with the morality of slavery—as the editor of the *Putnam Banner* wrote, "You cannot put a negro on a level with a white man"—but they *were* profoundly disturbed by the opening of the territories to slaveowners.[73]

Already under attack from temperance men and Know-Nothings, the Democrats did not need another issue making inroads on their party's faithful. In the tumultuous spring of 1854, however, the Kansas-Nebraska Act threatened to do just that. In the tumult, Eckels saw an opportunity to replace Davis as the Democratic candidate. Perhaps he realized, despite reassurances to the contrary, that Davis's vote for the Kansas-Nebraska Act had fatally weakened his hopes of reelection. At any rate, Eckels sought to avoid a party convention. Good Democrats were surprised to learn that there had been a local convention in Putnam County and that it had appointed delegates to the district congressional and state conventions. Eckels's plan to replace Davis with Andrew Humphreys of Greene County faltered, in part, because Davis's friends in the county rallied to protect his candidacy.[74]

Eckels was right to be worried. Only two Indiana congressional Democrats who voted for Kansas-Nebraska were reelected—and John G. Davis was not one of them. He was defeated by Harvey D. Scott, a graduate of Indiana Asbury, a Terre Haute lawyer, and a Know-Nothing. Putnam County gave Davis only 45 percent of its vote in the 1854 race. While in office, Scott advocated admitting Kansas as a free state.[75] Meanwhile, the turmoil in Kansas gave rise to a new party. In the wake of the Kansas-Nebraska Act, the People's party appeared in opposition to Democratic territorial policy. After holding a convention in Indianapolis that summer, the People's party swept the state elections that fall, with its entire ticket of state officers elected by wide margins and winning nine of Indiana's eleven congressional districts. This party, later taking the name Republican, was a "fusion party" composed of Whigs and Know-Nothings. Democrats sometimes called their opposition "Abolition fusionism" and sometimes "Know Nothing ruffians" and "their fusion cohorts," indicating they were unsure which issue posed the real threat: the anti-Nebraska movement or the anti-immigration campaign.[76]

Richard M. Hazelett, a justice of the peace for much of the 1850s, would later be recalled in a county history as an active Republican. But in his memoirs, composed in the 1890s, Hazelett remembered being a "radical Democrat" until the Kansas-Nebraska Act. But when he decided that Northern Democrats were helping the South to spread slavery, he abandoned the party for one that "acted on a principle and advocated a principle that was more consistant [with] democracy and coinsided more fully with his views of democracy and justice he became what was called a know nothing." By the 1890s, Hazelett would say nothing about the anti-immigrant agenda of the Know-Nothings, remembering them only as precursors—"the start of the Republican party." He voted for the first Republican presidential candidate, John C. Frémont, in 1856 and remained an "unswerving Republican" until post–Civil War developments checked his faith in that party as well. Although county Know-Nothings had long included temperance and opposition to slavery among their issues, their members were increasingly drawn into the fusion movement, which had made fear of the Slave Power its focus.[77]

In addition to former Know-Nothings, the Republicans clearly relied on the old Whigs. One Republican and former Whig blamed the demise of his prior party on its accommodation of slavery. First, he observed, "the whig party was required to shoulder the compromise of 1850," which meant accepting "the ever infamous fugitive slave bill." When Whigs found the Constitution was to become "merely a 'life preserver' for the slaveholders oligarchy . . . the whig party itself went down, for it outlived its good name." Some old Whigs, in searching for a new party home, "mistook the leer" on the Democratic party's countenance for a welcoming embrace. But the Democratic party had created Kansas-Nebraska—"a bill which broke down the Missouri Compromise to keep out the sons of white men and let the Southern oligarch pass in with his man-servants and his maid-servants, his concubines and his slaves."[78] Whigs therefore could not be comfortable among the Democrats. Now, old Whigs such as Higgins Lane of Bainbridge stumped for the Republicans.[79]

Although Republicans poured themselves into campaign activities, decorating wagons and organizing speeches, Democrats prevailed.[80] Both state and county went for James Buchanan in the 1856 election. Democrats fared better in Putnam County than in the state at large. Buchanan received almost 52 percent of the county's vote for president and Republican John C. Frémont only 37 percent, compared to 50 percent and 40 percent statewide. Millard Fillmore, the Know-Nothing candidate, garnered just over 11 percent of the vote, a point more than he received in the state.

The Democrats held on to Indiana in the election of 1856 and were stronger in Indiana than in any other state of the Old Northwest, though the new People's party showed surprising strength. Ashbel P. Willard, the Democrats' candidate for governor, defeated Oliver P. Morton by fewer than 6,000 votes.[81] All that was left to complete the Democratic triumph was to reclaim the Seventh District's congressional seat. Eckels had hoped for the nomination, but it went to John G. Davis. Republicans condemned Davis for "his crime in Congress of repealing the Missouri Compromise and sustaining the Kansas iniquities," but he nonetheless prevailed over his opponent, John P. Usher, garnering 53 percent of the vote in Putnam County.[82]

Davis's political path, however, became no smoother. In late 1857, a convention at Lecompton, Kansas, submitted a proslavery state constitution to Congress. Because the convention had rigged the ratification process so that Kansas voters could not exclude slavery from the proposed new state, many Northern Democrats, led by Stephen A. Douglas, author of the Kansas-Nebraska Act, rejected Lecompton as a travesty on popular sovereignty. Southerners, supported by President James Buchanan, insisted that the process had been fair and legal. Furthermore, they asserted that if Kansas wanted to join the Union as a slave state, it was an insult to the South to deny its admission.[83] Davis supported Douglas. In a major speech in the House of Representatives, he announced that he was "reluctantly compelled to dissent" from the president's recommendation to admit Kansas under Lecompton. He also stated that Lecompton was a "violation and perversion" of popular sovereignty and "tainted with fraud." Davis agreed with free staters that a fair ratification had been denied and calculated that four-fifths of Kansas voters opposed Lecompton. He insisted that he did not act out of opposition to the South or slavery: "I am a native of a slaveholding state. I have no prejudices against the South, nor against the institution of slavery where it exists. I make no war upon the rights of the people of the South. I have defended those rights more frequently than southern gentlemen themselves; because my position as a public man, and as a national Democrat of the North has required it at my hands."[84] Yet for all his denials, Davis was declaring his independence from the South. Congressman William Smith of Virginia responded to his speech, insisting that Lecompton was a party measure, strongly endorsed by the head of the Democratic party, President Buchanan. Davis countered that Smith had no right to expel him from the party, and he denied the president had the power to dictate his vote, which would be "political despotism." When Davis accused Buchanan of having changed position on Lecompton, Smith replied, "That is the language of

rebellion." But Davis retorted—followed by shouts of "Good!"—"It is the language of a freeman, and not the language of a slave."[85] His retort indicated that
many Northerners were beginning to equate support of a Southern measure
such as Lecompton as enslavement to the South, a sentiment echoed by Democrats in Putnam County.[86]

When it became apparent to congressional Democrats who stood with the
administration on this matter that Lecompton would not pass, Representatives
Alexander Stephens of Georgia and William English of Indiana put together a
compromise and gave it the Hoosier's name in order to better appeal to disaffected Northern Democrats. The architects of the English compromise professed to find an irregularity in the Lecompton constitution's land grant. This
irregularity became the pretext for returning the constitution to Kansas for
another ratification vote, one in which Kansans would be allowed to reject the
constitution in its entirety, which they promptly did. The English compromise
reconciled enough Northern Democrats to the administration to secure passage, but Stephen Douglas did not vote for it. Neither did John G. Davis.[87]

The English compromise further divided Putnam County's Democrats. Daniel Sigler called it "the most dambable and dishunurble proposition that could
have originated in an american Congress."[88] Other Democrats, however, supported the measure. A. Bowen thought local Democrats "are almost as unanimous now in favor of admitting Kansas under the Lecompton Constitution as
they were against it short time ago."[89] An anti-Lecompton meeting in Greencastle drew an uncomfortable mixture of Democrats prepared to denounce
the "Lecompton English swindle" and those more hesitant to make public pro-
nouncements. George W. Ames doubted the propriety of a Democrat speaking
at such a meeting.[90]

This discomfort extended to the nomination for Congress. Davis became
only one of eight potential candidates whose names the Indianapolis Democratic paper put forward. Not surprisingly, a split occurred at the county convention, where delegates to the congressional convention were chosen: on one
side were pro-Douglas, pro-Davis members; on the other were pro-Buchanan
men such as Eckels and Pat Heaney. The Buchanan men successfully pushed
through instructions directing the delegates to back Henry Secrest, thereby
outmaneuvering Davis's disgusted supporters. Secrest was a Kentucky-born lawyer, former member of the state legislature, reformed alcoholic, and Eckels
loyalist.[91] A month later, a contentious meeting of the Seventh Congressional
District Democrats at Terre Haute nominated Secrest as the candidate. Secrest

had been anti-Lecompton but now supported the English compromise, which the convention endorsed.[92] The Republican *State Journal* concluded that the anti-Lecompton Democrats may have wanted Davis, "whose nomination would have been a direct rebuke of Lecomptonism," but "they got nothing but Henry Secrest, who is an approver of the English bill."[93]

Administration Democrats may have turned to Secrest because Delana Eckels was not available. Eckels, a staunch administration supporter, had received a patronage appointment as chief justice of Utah Territory—despite Davis's opposition—before the Lecompton constitution became a national issue. In the summer of 1857, his friends saw him off with a farewell "levee" at the courthouse. Arriving in Utah during the Mormon War, Eckels preferred to take a hard line against Mormon resistance to federal authority.[94] Willing to accept the Democratic party doctrine of nonintervention in the territories when it applied to slavery, Eckels refused to apply that same doctrine to the Mormons' "domestic affairs" involving polygamy.[95]

Whether Eckels would have been a better advocate for administration Democrats in 1858 remains unknown. Secrest, however, would be tarred with having shifted positions from supporting Davis's stand against the Lecompton constitution to accepting the English compromise.[96] When Terre Haute voters wanted to know if he supported the compromise, Secrest was evasive: "I am not aware that any person supports or indorses that measure as an independent original proposition." Yet somehow, the English compromise had become law, and Secrest expected "all good citizens to submit to it."[97]

Meanwhile, the Democratic papers dismissed fears that Davis might "run in opposition to the regular nomination of his party. He loves his life-long Democracy too well to lay it at the feet of men who have loved, in days past, to denounce him in the vilest and most unmeasured terms."[98] But these were exactly the men Davis hoped to court. In an anti-Lecompton speech in March, he declared, "My life has been spent in the service of the Democratic cause. I have been true to its principles, rejoiced in its successes, and mourned its defeats." Nonetheless, he recognized that he now stood with the "Black" Republicans, although he insisted that this was because the Republicans were willing to endorse popular sovereignty, not because he or other anti-Lecompton Democrats had adopted Republican principles.[99]

Anti-Lecompton Democrats and Republicans urged Davis to run as an independent, but regular Democrats were aghast when he decided to bolt his own party. He had had his share of party office, the *Sullivan Democrat*—once his organ—complained, and he had no right to deny his friend and former political supporter Secrest a chance at office. "If he throws himself in the arms of the Republicans, and is run by them, every Democrat should repudiate him without hesitation," advised the Indianapolis party newspaper.[100] "Mortified" by Davis's independent candidacy, Putnam County Democrats rallied to Secrest, who belonged to what the local Democratic newspaper called the "regularly nominated Democratic Ticket."[101]

Republicans set aside their misgivings and adopted Davis. In the heat of the Lecompton controversy, many had embraced him. Miles Fletcher reported an "earnest feeling" as the county convention approached, noting that "we have drafted some resolutions, taking the Douglas view of Squatter Sovreignty."[102] Worthington B. Williams wrote Davis a cordial letter. Years earlier, Williams had requested documents from Davis, informing the congressman that he was a Whig so that the request could be refused "if you was a person who confined such small favor to democrats." Davis sent the documents, remarking, "If I was not a democrat you was sure I ought to become so." Williams never imagined he would vote for Davis, "yet that time did arrive."[103] Republicans chose to support Davis by not holding a district convention; consequently, there would be no Republican candidate to oppose him. The *Indiana State Journal* urged Republicans in the Seventh District to vote for him.[104]

Putnam Republicans exploited local Democrats' hope for a Republican candidate to draw votes away from Davis by playing a practical joke. D. A. Farley altered a letter to make it look as if former congressman H. D. Scott intended to speak in Greencastle. When Farley showed the forgery to Secrest supporters, "their countenances lit up with Joy." The fraud was so successful that Farley had to intervene to keep word of a Republican candidate from spreading.[105]

The election was a "Waterloo Defeat" for the Democrats. Davis drew 1,820 votes in Putnam County, compared to Secrest's 1,656, and won reelection to his seat. At the state level, Republicans increased their seats in Congress and narrowly gained control of the statehouse, although Democrats won the state offices. Local Democrats complained of fraudulent voting in Putnam County, where "a purgation of the polls of illegal votes would strip nearly all the successful republicans of their majorities," and they even accused temperance men of using alcohol to sway voters. Despite such embittered remarks, Democrats recognized that their election losses betokened "a general shifting of parties" toward the Republicans.[106]

Buchanan Democrats might have gained hope from pondering the stability of the alliance between anti-Lecompton Democrats and the new Republican party. Farley urged Davis to remember those Republicans who contributed to his victory. Davis might, for instance, support D. C. Donnohue, a candidate for canal trustee, as "he perhaps had more to do in keeping of[f] a Republican convention than any other man." But Farley did not consider repaying the Republicans obligatory.[107] Indeed, Republicans risked being co-opted by their new allies. Abraham Lincoln, who was running for the U.S. Senate in Illinois that year, pointed out that the alliance between Republicans and Douglas Democrats was potentially dangerous. Although Lincoln endorsed the fusion with Davis in Indiana, he warned that Republicans might be swallowed up by the powerful Douglas. And Putnam Republicans soon had cause to regret their support for Davis, as he reconciled with the Buchanan Democrats.[108] John Cowgill exhorted him, "Whatever distractions we [Democrats] may have in our ranks, they must be brought together" to defeat the Republicans. "Our motto from this until after the fight of 1860 is over," Cowgill insisted, "must be 'the union of Democrats for the sake of the union.'"[109] Within a year of his election with Republican support, Davis was welcomed back into the Democratic fold.[110]

All eyes were now turned to the coming presidential election. Perhaps the power of the old Whig element in Putnam's Republican party explains the initial enthusiasm for Missourian Edward Bates as the party's nominee in 1860. John Hanna supported him, as did the *Putnam Republican Banner,* the local party newspaper. At the county convention, Bates also received support from Miles Fletcher and Higgins Lane. The convention resolved to back Bates at the state convention. Bates was an old Whig, and his mild antislavery views appealed to moderates in the Republican party, such as former Whigs. In addition, he had some appeal for the Know-Nothings.[111] When Henry S. Lane, the Republican candidate for governor and Higgins Lane's brother, spoke in Greencastle in February 1860, his mention of the presidential race provoked cries of "Bates!" from the crowd. Lane equivocated by endorsing "that honest and eloquent, conservative and very pure statesman and peerless orator"—whereupon several people again called out "Bates"—"who shall be nominated at the Chicago Convention."[112] Of course, Bates's previous support of Know-Nothings would hurt him with German Americans. The national Republican convention nominated Abraham Lincoln of Illinois, who was also a former Whig but had offended neither immigrants nor nativists. Putnam County's Republican convention promptly passed resolutions that endorsed Lincoln's nomination.[113]

Republican strategists in 1860 knew that for Abraham Lincoln to win, he had to take not only the states Frémont had claimed in 1856 but also other crucial Northern states—such as Indiana. To appeal to the lower North, including Indiana, the Republicans needed a moderate candidate, hence the selection of Lincoln. In fact, Henry Lane insisted to delegates at the national convention in Chicago that New York's William Henry Seward was too radical to win Indiana. Lincoln's astute operatives made overtures to the Hoosiers, and Indiana supported Lincoln on the first ballot. Henry Lane, worn out with lobbying delegates, leaped on a table and joined the full-throated convention yell when Lincoln was nominated on the third ballot.[114]

Ironically, the candidate selected for his moderation seemed to many in the county—and to future historians—an extremist. Since the emergence of the slavery expansion issue, Democrats dismissed all opposition as undermining white supremacy. The Putnam Republican newspaper characterized Davis as "denounc[ing] every one who favored free territory as an abolitionist!"[115] Republicans, according to their opponents, stood for "*Negro Equality.*"[116] Many Democrats found it impossible to believe that anyone could go over "to the *nigerites* with all their heresies. *No never.*"[117]

Lincoln's inflexible adherence to the Republican position against slavery expansion—and his refusal to endorse slavery as a moral good—left him vulnerable to being labeled a "Black Republican." After events at Harpers Ferry, where the abolitionist John Brown led an abortive attack in 1859, many Southerners saw no difference between Lincoln's measured statements and Brown's violence. At best, Lincoln seemed hostile to Southern rights; at worst, he seemed to be another Brown ready to lead a bloody slave uprising.[118]

Putnam Republicans certainly did not view themselves as extremists. Always defensive about race, they took pains to deny any sympathy for the raid on Harpers Ferry. A Republican county convention condemned "inciting slaves to insurrection" and "all violators of law and order," specifically mentioning Harpers Ferry but also Southern attacks on individuals.[119] Henry Lane, taking care in 1860 to deny the charge of abolitionism in his Greencastle speech, dismissed John Brown as "a felon" who "properly met a felon's doom."[120] Beyond that, Republicans reiterated their doctrine of not interfering with slavery in the states but not extending it into the territories. "They desire to have the territories for free homes, for free men," wrote an editorialist, who left unstated the preference that those homes be for free white men.[121] Finally, Republicans categorically denied any interest in black rights. "The Republicans want nothing to do with the negro," the *Banner* declared after Harpers Ferry.[122] In fact, the pro-Southern Democratic party, whose members "array themselves under the sectional black banner of slavery and wage an unnatural and cruel war upon the rights of free labor," had the greater interest in race.[123] John Hanna, in a speech to a Republican county convention in early 1860, "contrasted the course of the Democrats with that of the Republicans, declaring that they (Republicans) are willing to respect *all* the rights of the South, so far as they are guaranteed them by the constitution; but in doing so could not believe that the North had no rights which should be respected."[124]

Republicans hoped that in Putnam County, even residents of Southern birth would understand grievances against the South. When he spoke in Greencastle, Henry Lane "appealed to the large number of Kentu[c]kians around him to know why they were here in the free State of Indiana. It was not because the soil was any better than Kentucky, but because they loved a free State better than a Slave State."[125] In order to appeal to Putnam residents, Republicans brought in Kentuckian Cassius M. Clay as one of their prominent campaign speakers. Clay was an abolitionist, but local Republicans expected him to draw a big crowd in the Kentucky-settled county.[126] To an assemblage estimated at 5,000, he made a "conservative" speech, calling for Lincoln's election but distinguishing between the Republican party and the abolitionists. "He showed the degrading influence the institution of slavery has upon the poor white laboring men of the South, the tyranny exercised over this class by slave holders and capitalists, as well as the manner in which he is made the willing and pliant tool to fight the battles of his landlord and to actually go against his own interest."[127] The association with Clay, however, reopened Republicans to charges of abolitionism. After Clay's appearance, Democratic congressional candidate Daniel W. Voorhees, who was seeking John G. Davis's old seat, told a Bainbridge audience that Clay "'sat in a nigger convention at Cincinnati with Fred. Douglas on one side and an other buck nigger on the other side.'" Republicans did not repudiate Voorhees's racism but merely his facts: "C. M. Clay has a character as high as any man in the United States, and would no sooner equalize himself with a negro, than he would with Dan. Voorhees; which money could not hire him to do."[128]

Even though the Republicans brought in prominent speakers such as Clay and gubernatorial candidate Henry Lane, John Hanna emerged as a key party leader during the 1860 campaign. A graduate of Indiana Asbury University, he became a lawyer and practiced in Greencastle. A fierce defender of popular sovereignty, he had condemned the emerging anti-Democratic movement of 1856 as abolitionist. He was mayor of Greencastle from 1851 to 1854—presumably as a Democrat, as he had studied law under Delana Eckels. Hanna became a partner in Eckels's law firm, and it was Eckels who presented him at the county courthouse for admission to the bar in November 1850. As mayor, Hanna presided over the organization of Greencastle's graded school system, which involved working closely with Eckels, the chairman of the school trustees. In the spring of 1858, Hanna migrated to Kansas, where he was elected to the territorial House of Representatives and served as speaker pro tem. But John Hanna had strayed from the Democratic organization even before he left for Kansas. Evidently uncomfortable with the party's antitemperance and proimmigrant policies, he sojourned in the Know-Nothing party before becoming a Republican. After he returned from Kansas, he supported the 1858 fusion movement between the anti-Lecompton Democrat Davis and the Republicans. In 1860, he stood for election as a Republican presidential elector from the Seventh District and led the county's Republican forces.[129]

John Hanna's campaign for Lincoln mixed free labor and opposition to slavery with a dose of racism. In a speech at Terre Haute, he warned that if Hoosiers failed "to redeem our beloved Indiana from the thraldom of corrupt Democratic leaders . . . our children in after days will rise up to reprove us for a want of fidelity to the Heaven blest cause of free labor." He argued that those who opposed Lincoln's election "subserve the interest of a power which is everything for the 'nigger' and nothing for the white man." Lincoln's "election will settle this damnable 'nigger' question now and forever." Lincoln would make clear to the South "that it is no part of the policy of the Republican party to interfere with slavery in the States, and that we will live up faithfully to the compromises of the Constitution on our part, and require the same of them."[130] Though Republicans would abide by constitutional obligations to slavery, they would stand up to the Slave Power, whose continual demands for concessions to slave labor came at the expense of free white laborers.[131]

Democrats hoped to protect Northern rights by nominating Stephen Douglas, but they feared opposition from party members whose fealty lay farther south. Douglas Democrats were convinced that only the Illinois senator could win. A Russellville Democrat, upon learning that the Republicans had nominated Lincoln, exclaimed that with Douglas at the head of their ticket, "we can beat the *world the flesh* & *the Devil*." And for a Greencastle man, Douglas was "the only *Democrat* that can beat Lincoln in Indiana."[132] John Cowgill agreed with these sentiments but feared that Indiana's leading Democrats, including Governor Willard and Senator Jesse D. Bright, opposed Douglas.[133] Others, too, worried that Douglas might not be the candidate. A. M. Puett feared Southerners would prove ungrateful to "the larger portion of Democrats who have stood by the south and defended them."[134] "So help me god," Puett thundered, "if the South is by fools enough to . . . refuse to support Douglass I & thousands more will stand off & let the Hell hounds in the shape [of] Osawattomie Brown pitch into them."[135]

Reporter Murat Halstead captured such sentiments by describing the mutual incomprehension of Mississippi and Indiana delegates to the national Democratic convention in Charleston. Although Hoosiers insisted they were "fighting the battles of the South in the North," they received neither gratitude nor understanding. The Mississippians dismissed Stephen Douglas as no better than a black Republican. The convention deadlocked when Southern delegates walked out rather than see Douglas nominated. At a subsequent meeting in Baltimore that many Southerners did not attend, the national Democrats nominated Douglas for president. Southern Democrats, however, nominated Vice President John C. Breckinridge. President Buchanan, still smarting from Douglas's failure to support Lecompton, endorsed Breckinridge rather than his old rival.[136]

Even before the national convention that June, the divisions that would emerge there were visible among Putnam Democrats. A Democratic party convention in Greencastle endorsed Douglas for president, although the resolution "met with serious opposition in committee." Patrick Heaney, an anti-Douglas man, tried to overrule the endorsement but failed. Douglas Democrats later punished Heaney by denying him a nomination for office.[137] Putnam Democrats held a massive public meeting to ratify Douglas's nomination. Huge posters, 10 feet square, appeared in Greencastle to announce the gathering. An estimated 10,000 people attended. As this was more than had attended the state Democratic convention in Indianapolis, the Republicans suspected that the eager crowds had been imported from elsewhere. Nonetheless, even the Republicans conceded that "the procession, was a grand affair, reaching from the South to the North Depot, and doubling three times round the Square! It was headed by a brilliant band of music consisting of the Bass and Kettle Drums and fife, and was brilliantly adorned with banners." After the parade, the crowd assembled in front of the courthouse to hear a speech by Judge Cowgill that emphasized Douglas's fight against "the Slave holders, hand to hand."[138] Douglas himself passed through Greencastle "in the rounds of his electioneering tour." His train made an early morning stop at the depot, where a sleepy and hoarse Douglas received a delegation but declined to make a speech.[139]

Douglas faced opposition not just from county Republicans but also from Breckinridge Democrats. Not having prevailed at the county Democratic convention, Patrick Heaney and Henry Secrest broke with the Douglas Democrats and supported Breckinridge, the nominee of the Southern Democrats. Eckels's experience in Utah had shaken but not broken his loyalty to the president. In the spring of 1860, Eckels resigned and returned home to Putnam County, where he threw his support to the Breckinridge movement organized by Douglas's enemies in Indiana, Senators Jesse Bright and Graham N. Fitch. A few days after the large Douglas meeting in Putnam County, Breckinridge supporters met. Judge Eckels spoke for two hours, condemning Douglas as false to the Democratic organization. Republicans found it an unusually harsh speech for Eckels, perhaps testifying to the bitterness in the national as well as the local Democratic party.[140] Throughout the campaign, Eckels delivered a speech for Breckinridge that had "been preached so often in the little towns around the Capital that the people have almost got it by heart."[141]

According to one description, Eckels overtly defended slavery in this speech. He "built his whole slavery argument upon what are called our 'treaty obligations'" in acquiring the Louisiana Purchase. Having purchased territory in which slavery was established, the United States by treaty "pledged itself to protect the property of the inhabitants of the territory; therefore, slavery could not be abolished or prohibited in any part of this vast domain except in violating of treaty obligations."[142] Breckinridge's Hoosier supporters adopted the Southern Democratic doctrine that slavery could not be prohibited in the territories, either by congressional exclusion as the Republicans advocated or by Douglas's popular sovereignty. Instead, all citizens were said to "have an equal right to settle in [the territories] with whatever property they may legally possess."

Just as the Southern delegates who nominated Breckinridge scrupulously avoided the word *slavery* in favor of *property*, the Hoosiers spoke of "the right of property in the service of negroes." Breckinridge's Hoosier supporters warned that Republicans intended "to destroy the domestic institutions of the South, and to place the four millions of negroes now in this country upon a legal and political equality with the whites, leading to a mixture of races and consequent social equality . . . and would thus, under pretense of freedom to the negro, render freedom to the white men impossible."[143] Historian Sean Wilentz has said that leaders of the national Breckinridge movement could not decide whether they had a real program or whether they only wanted to defeat Douglas.[144] The Indiana Breckinridge convention's passionate adherence to white supremacy and protection of slave property, however, indicates more than just a movement for intraparty revenge. These Democrats resisted the cry for Northern rights made by Republicans and Douglas Democrats; instead, they saw the South as the victim and its rights as the ones in jeopardy.

The local Breckinridge Democrats nominated Dr. Hiram R. Pitchlynn, an Asbury graduate and Choctaw Indian originally from Mississippi, and Patrick Heaney for the legislature, although Breckinridge supporters in the state did not nominate a ticket for state offices. The Breckinridge meeting was much smaller than its Douglas counterpart, but Republicans purported to sense great support in the townships for Breckinridge. Douglas Democrats complained that most of those attending the Breckinridge convention were Republicans who hoped to divide the Democratic party.[145]

The Breckinridge campaign in Putnam County climaxed in late September with a rally at the courthouse. Jesse Bright spoke, as did Breckinridge's vice presidential candidate, Joseph Lane. Bright attacked both popular sovereignty and the irregularity of Douglas's nomination, predicting that Douglas would not get a single electoral vote. According to rumor, Daniel Voorhees, a Douglas man, had met with Putnam County Breckinridge men at Carpentersville, where he attempted to heal the breach in the party. If that is true, his effort failed. Voorhees was an 1849 graduate of Indiana Asbury, had married a Greencastle girl, and practiced law in Terre Haute. In addition to the Republican candidate, Thomas H. Nelson of Terre Haute, the Breckinridge men chose J. A. Scott to run against Voorhees.[146]

The state elections were a disaster for Putnam County's Democrats. They had been "overpowered by *the combined forces of abolitionism and disunionism.* . . . The defeat of the Democratic party in Putnam county is to be ascribed, not to the superior numbers of its Republican opponents, but the unconcealed opposition of men *professing* to be its friends."[147] Those professed friends were the 5 percent of Putnam voters who cast ballots for Breckinridge candidates. Although totaling only a couple of hundred voters in any race, the margin between Republicans and Democrats was so thin that the Breckinridge men made the difference. In state races for governor and lieutenant governor, Republicans Henry S. Lane and Oliver P. Morton won the county with 51 percent of its vote.

For other offices, however, the Breckinridge Democrats clearly contributed to a Democratic defeat. Although Voorhees won the congressional seat, he had been hurt in the county by the Breckinridge men. Nelson got 48 percent of the Putnam's vote and Voorhees 47 percent. J. A. Scott, the Breckinridge candidate for Congress, got 205 votes—5 percent of the total, a margin that could have given Voorhees the county. A similar result emerged from the state senator's race for the district of Putnam and Clay. The Republican James McMurry got 49 percent of Putnam's vote, and the Douglas Democrat Arch Johnson got 46 percent, with 5 percent going to Breckinridge Democrat J. G. Martin. Fortunately for Johnson, he won enough votes in Clay to secure the state senatorship. Samuel Colliver and John Adams, the Democratic candidates for state representative, were not so lucky. The Breckinridge candidates, Patrick Heaney and H. R. Pitchlynn, got only 141 and 200 votes, respectively—enough to give the election to the Republicans Reuben S. Ragan and Higgins Lane.[148] When the party nominated Henry Lane for governor and Morton for lieutenant governor, it was understood that if the Republicans won the legislature, Lane would be elected to a U.S. Senate seat and Morton would become governor. That was, in fact, what happened, with Lane serving the shortest term as governor in Indiana history—two days.[149]

Grafton F. Cookerly, editor of the *Terre Haute Journal,* condemned Eckels's maneuverings and the results produced by the disorganization in the Putnam County Democratic Party: "The loss we sustained was in Putnam county, where the Breckinridge men, under the leadership of Buchanan's Mormon Judge, D. R. Eckels, voted, almost to a man, the Republican State ticket. . . . But for the willful desertion of the Breckinridge men from the Democratic party, and its nominees, our majority in the District would have been several hundred more than it is." Cookerly believed Eckels was acting on instructions from the Buchanan administration. "But notwithstanding all this," he concluded, "we achieved in this District a glorious triumph," referring to Voorhees who, even though he lost Putnam County, had still carried the Seventh District and been elected to Congress.[150]

The presidential election was still to be held. Despite the Republicans' general sweep of the county, Voorhees's election to the congressional seat caused John Hanna to redouble his efforts on Lincoln's behalf. The presidential election went quietly in Greencastle except for a "little *rumpus*" when two men tried to raise a Douglas flag over the *Banner*'s office. Lincoln won Indiana's electoral votes—the first time since 1840 that the Democrats had lost the state.

Once again, if the Democratic party had stayed united, they would have won the county.[151] But Lincoln's election spurred Southerners to make good on long-standing threats of disunion. South Carolina seceded in December, and by February, the lower South had formed the Confederate States of America. County Republicans had voted knowing that secession might be the result. A year before the election, the Portland Mills Union Republican Club informed John Davis, "If there are those in this Union that would resist the government passing into the hands of a Republican administration constitutionally elected . . . we believe our government is strong enough and patriotic enoug[h] to deal with all the Treason of the South."[152]

Threats to the Union had previously been resolved by compromise, and Putnam citizens still hoped that such might be the case during the secession crisis. In late December, a meeting "irrespective of party" assembled to consider the Crittenden compromise, which called for a series of unamendable constitutional amendments to protect slavery. Republicans in Congress, however, refused to support the Crittenden measure because its provisions violated the party's opposition to the expansion of slavery. But when the Putnam County meeting assembled in December, Republican opposition to the Crittenden compromise had not yet solidified. Among the meeting's prominent attendees were Breckinridge Democrat Eckels, Douglas Democrat Arch Johnson (the newly elected state senator), and even Republican Higgins Lane. The attendees endorsed the Crittenden compromise and were prepared to reassure the South by guaranteeing slavery.[153]

Some Republicans at the meeting, however, spoke against conciliating the South.[154] In an editorial, the *Banner* supported "a settlement a like honorable and satisfactory to both North and South" but warned that no compromise could endure that violated public opinion or overturned the election results: "The recent vote at the polls shows that public sentiment is overwhelmingly against establishing slavery in any public territory." Yet, in defiance of the election results, men sought to legally enact "the principle thus overwhelmingly condemned." Pointing to the South's unwillingness to be satisfied with previous compromises, the *Banner* also observed, "Thus the public history shows that these men who threaten to overturn the Government have broken faith with us at every turn, while we are now asked meekly to put slavery in our fundamental law. We confess that we are not prepared for this."[155] The paper eventually rejected the Crittenden compromise and supported an amendment that guaranteed slavery in the states where it existed—which Republicans had

always conceded was constitutionally protected—in an effort to demonstrate a
Republican willingness to do something "short of a surrender of principle."[156]
If there was a crisis, the Republican *Banner* blamed it on the South: "The North
is making no war against the South—has made no preparations for a conflict
with their brethren of that quarter—has bought no arms or munitions of war—
has organized no military companies, and has not secretly banded together
'minute men' whose sworn obligation is to take possession of property belong-
ing to the Federal Government." The South had been doing exactly these
things while "the Northern people have been quietly attending to their usual
avocations—tilling the soil—building railroads—vending merchandize."[157]

The *Banner* was similarly dismissive of President Buchanan's message to
Congress during the secession crisis, complaining that the president denied
the legitimacy of secession but conceded no power to impede it. "The President, it will be seen, is endeavoring to ride two horses at the same time. . . .
He believes the South has no right to secede, yet if they do thus act there is
no law, in his opinion, which will justify him in using coercive means to bring
them back."[158] Some Democrats agreed that Buchanan was inept. A. M. Puett
deplored that "the want of honesty of purpose & firmness off action in the
President has brought this Terible crisis on us."[159] But just as many Democrats
blamed the North for the crisis, Henry B. Pickett of Groveland believed "that
all this Trouble Could be easily settled if Northern men would just Reflect and
for a few moments Consider themselves in the situation of the south and then
think how they would like to be treated while in that Condition, and then do by
the South as they would be done by while in the same Condition." If Northerners could only empathize with the South's grievances, "the whole matter would
soon be adjusted and peace and Brotherly feeling Be again Restored and our
Country again march on to greatness and glory." He hoped that Southerners
would see that Northerners were reevaluating their actions and that Lincoln's
election would be an aberration. But if the Union should dissolve, Pickett knew
that "so long as the south or any other part of our country are only asking for
their Constitutional Rights that I will neither directly nor indirectly help to
subjugate them but will stand for them and their and my Rights as guaranteed
under That instrument."[160] Many in Putnam County viewed secession as an un-
derstandable, if excessive, reaction to the election results.

In a dramatic, long-remembered meeting in Greencastle, Democrats vowed
opposition to the new Republican administration. The occasion was a gathering of the county's Union men, although not "irrespective of party" as many

meetings that secession winter claimed to be but consisting solely of county Democrats. Lincoln had taken the oath of office, and Fort Sumter still remained in Union hands, as it would for only a few more days. But for these Democrats, the war had already begun. It was a war of abolitionists against the "rights of the people of the South," which now "inaugurated a period of terror and distrust." The Republicans had rejected compromise, enacted a sectional tariff, appointed abolitionists to posts of power, ignored the wishes of the border states, made "warlike preparations," and threatened violent coercion. The most famous—or, to Republicans, infamous—portion of the meeting was its resolution on behalf of the South:

> We deny the right of the General or State Governments to embroil us or our fellow-citizens in intestine war or internal strife with the people of the co-States of this Union; and having, time and again, warned the members of the party now in power of the fatal tendency of their insane course, and implored them to abandon the stubborn and unwise policy of anti-slavery agitation, we here take for our motto, "Not one dollar, and not one man from Indiana with which to subjugate the South and inaugurate civil war!"[161]

The declaration "not one dollar, and not one man" was a quotation from Dan Voorhees, now congressman-elect, who made a speech in sympathy with the resolutions. Voorhees blamed the "national dissentions" on antislavery "agitations," and he decried coercion, vowing to support an honorable compromise to avoid war. He insisted to his constituents "that as your Representative, I will never vote one dollar, one man, or one gun to the administration of Abraham Lincoln to make war upon the South."[162] An outraged Republican said it was a speech "just such as would be vociferously cheered in Cottonocracy, to which locality the speaker politically properly belongs." Printed words could not capture the "vehemence" with which Voorhees spoke, and, in fact, some felt the printed version was tamer than the spoken.[163] Even some Democrats felt the meeting went too far and "left the room in disgust while the resolutions were being read, and since denounce them," although others gave "unwearied attention and the most hearty applause" to Voorhees and his vow of "not one dollar, one man, or one gun."[164]

Voorhees would find such aggressive views impossible to maintain. After the firing on Fort Sumter, he backed away from them. In what an unsympathetic editor called "political special pleading," Voorhees said he had meant "that he would not vote money or men to *bring on or inaugurate the present state of affairs.*"[165] But he would be haunted by the "one dollar, one man" speech for the rest of his life. Voorhees's dilemma, however, was shared by many others. Republicans and Douglas Democrats had urged the necessity of standing up for Northern rights, and the Breckinridge followers had advocated Southern rights. But no one voiced any concern for black rights. In fact, to ward off the charge of abolitionism, Republicans had flaunted their own racism. The advent of war forced residents of the county not only to choose between North and South and whether to fight or stay home but also to decide whether to support or oppose those who fought. Putnam County residents could not foresee all the ways in which war would reshape their lives and their nation.

By the time Confederates opened fire on Fort Sumter, Ned McGaughey was as dead as the Whig party. John G. Davis, plagued with ill health, became less influential in the Democratic party, ceding much power to the younger Daniel Voorhees. Among the Republicans, John Hanna became increasingly prominent. Although Delana Eckels and other older men remained a fixture in county life for several more decades, the Civil War era saw the emergence of new issues and new leaders in the county and the United States as a whole. A younger generation would fight the war or wait on the home front for the soldiers' return. These young men and women expected to live according to the gender roles established before the war, but they would soon find their expectations challenged.

2

APPROPRIATE PLACES

During the 1860 state election, Miles Fletcher, Greenbury Mullinix's chronicler, ran as Republican candidate for superintendent of public instruction. At age thirty-two, Fletcher was finally coming into his own. For the decade since his graduation from Brown University and marriage to Jennie Hoar, he had struggled to establish a career. Miles possessed an elite background as the son of the wealthy Indianapolis banker Calvin Fletcher; he took pride in being a Fletcher, and he was absolutely certain as to the "appro[p] riate place" for men and women in society. Dependent on his father's financial resources, he asserted his dominance over his wife. When Calvin Fletcher suggested that Jennie be consulted on Miles's future career before their wedding, Miles disagreed: "A woman should decide before she marries a man, whether she is willing to leave home, friends, country prefferences and everything else, and submit all to the hands, and mind of her husband." If she could not do this, she should not marry. A woman's love, he believed, consisted in subordinating herself entirely to her husband's judgment. And Miles believed that

Jennie "loves me so well, and has so much respect for my judgement, that she will with pleasure submit to whatever I wish."[1]

In an age in which middle-class couples increasingly prized companionate marriage, Miles's overt patriarchal sentiments might have seemed unusual. He did speak of his willingness to be "influenced" by Jennie, but he claimed primacy in their relationship. Even Calvin Fletcher seems to have felt that he was too authoritarian. It is possible that Miles's continued dependence on his father contributed to his desire to feel superior in his relationship with his wife. But, in fact, Miles's insistence that men and women had appropriate places and that, in the final reckoning, men's place was in authority over women was totally in accord with the norms of nineteenth-century society. Marriage was a relationship of unequals. At best, a woman could pick her own "lord and master": this was what Miles meant when he insisted that a woman had to decide before marriage to "submit all" to her husband.[2]

Miles's assumption of women's dependence was shared by citizens of the county across the political spectrum. In the 1850s, Democratic and Republican newspapers ran articles with titles such as "WHO WILL MAKE A GOOD WIFE?" or "MAXIMS FOR MARRIED WOMEN." The former advised young men to look for a girl who rose early to prepare her father's breakfast and industriously did housework, rather than one who lay abed and read novels.[3] The latter encouraged the wife to "pass . . . over" the husband's flaws, to make the best of things rather than "reproach" him, and not to spend more than he could afford. Nor was she to make trouble for him—either by extravagance, flirting, ill temper, or argument. "It is the office of the softer sex to smooth the troubles of the other." And she should submit. "Implicit submission in a man to his wife, is ever disgraceful to both; implicit submission in a wife, to the just will of her husband is what she promised at the altar—what the good will revere her for, and what is, in fact, the greatest honor she can receive."[4]

Male independence and female dependence were considered natural and complementary. But how they were to be achieved was changing for some young men and women in the nineteenth century. In traditional society, a father's property gave him power over his dependent sons. But upon reaching adulthood, a son was expected to take over the family farm or business, perhaps providing a home for his aged parents.

The Fletchers represented the upwardly mobile middle class. Calvin Fletcher had migrated from Vermont at age nineteen with only $20. He rose to be one of the most prominent civic and economic leaders of mid-nineteenth-century Indiana, amassing a fortune worth almost $50,000 by the mid-1830s. For the elder Fletcher, independence meant not just the capability to support oneself but also industriousness, education, and temperance. Although he owned a farm in Indianapolis and all of his sons had worked on it, he expected them to achieve independence through pursuing a profession. It has been observed that as grown sons sought to separate themselves from their fathers' authority, a tension grew between "restless sons and ambivalent fathers."[5] And Miles's prolonged inability to settle on a career caused his father considerable anxiety. The younger man had tried working for the Sunday School Union but "retreated the 1st day he attempted to sell books." The elder Fletcher feared his son's tendency to give up at the first reverse.[6] On his birthday, Calvin Fletcher annually recorded his reflections about his life and family, and in 1857, he had this commentary on Miles's career:

> During the first part of the year Miles had charge of my affairs as relates to the finances of the family & in 2 years he ran us much in debt by buying everything selling nothing making debts in every store & shop in town. . . . Courted the great. Did everybodies business & neglected his own & mine. He ran me in debt several thousand dollars. He confused my papers—deranged my business & everything he undertook he failed in.[7]

Nine of the eleven Fletcher children went east to school; Miles, the fourth son, received his degree from Brown in 1852. Proud of his own early self-reliance, Calvin Fletcher lamented his sons' continued need for his support. Cooley, the eldest, expected a stipend from Calvin in order to maintain the elite standing to which he—and his wife—felt entitled. Miles also relied on Calvin's financial support, but he made periodic vows to repay his father and become free of debt. Cooley felt trade was beneath a Fletcher. Miles thought it if not an honorable calling, at least a good enough one for a younger brother, Keyes, who lived with Miles in Greencastle and clerked in a hardware store.[8]

On July 15, 1852, Miles Fletcher married Jane "Jennie" Hoar. As Jennie was originally from Rhode Island, they may well have met while he was a student at Brown. They had apparently become engaged in 1849, but Miles broke their engagement the following year. Calvin Fletcher, as usual, did not quite approve of his son's actions, and it seems he accused Miles of having made advances to a girl in Indianapolis. "Wrote Miles," Calvin entered into his diary, and "gave him my opinion of a young man who makes love to evry girl he meets." Miles

Miles Fletcher. (Courtesy of DePauw University Archives and
Special Collections)

denied the accusation. Calvin also disapproved because both the engagement
and its breaking had been "entered into without parental advice," perhaps reflecting Miles's desire to be independent of his father.[9]

Calvin worried that his son sought a rich wife. Of the broken engagement,
he wrote, "I regret this rupture. If it was in consequence of her standing so
far as relates to poverty or obscurity I am decidedly opposed to the violation
of their good understanding. He should have married her. I have not desired
my sons should seek fortunes in their marriages—no far from it. I have no
confidence in rich wives in goods &c but such as are rich in virtue in faith in
Christ."[10] Whatever the quarrel may have been, Miles and Jennie reconciled
and were married. Miles was enough of a believer in the proper lines of authority, including a son's submission to his father, to ask for Calvin's permission

before the wedding. It is not known whether the young couple sought the consent of Jennie's parents. Parental permission was no longer demanded of young couples, but the bride's family might naturally feel concern as to whether the groom could support a wife and eventually children.[11] Jennie's family may have been reassured by her father-in-law's wealth, but Miles's own career plans were unsettled.

Just before their wedding and his own graduation from Brown, Miles was offered a position at Indiana Asbury University. He consulted his father about the wisdom of accepting the post. Once again, the men differed. Calvin Fletcher served as the university's treasurer from 1848 to 1855, and because of his close involvement with the university, he opposed Miles's taking the job there; he feared that his son had been offered the newly created chair in English literature not because of his talents—he would be freshly graduated from Brown—but because of his father's importance.[12] Father and son also disagreed about Jennie's role in Miles's decision. Calvin thought she should be consulted; Miles emphatically did not. "I must certainly differ with you here," he wrote his father in the lengthy tirade on the "appro[p]riate place" for husband and wife. Only a weak husband, "a ninny," allowed the wife to see herself as "The Man" and "assume the sway." Miles foresaw no such reversal of gender roles in his and Jennie's household: "I anticipate much pleasure and happiness in my matrimonial relations." He felt well enough acquainted with Jennie "to be convinced, that she has many—no, I should say some faults, and to be assured that she is not an angel," and he expected to rule his household.[13] He apparently received from Jennie the unqualified approbation his father never provided. Perhaps Miles was right that Jennie would derive her happiness from him, despite being so far away from her family in Rhode Island. Soon after he started at Asbury, Jennie noted, "Miles is more uniformly cheerful than I have known him to be for along time. Is always busy."[14]

Marriage evidently did not soften Miles's sense of primacy. In describing their room in Greencastle in a letter to his mother, he referred to the location of "my bookcase, my table, and my bed." Even the marital bed was his, not theirs.[15] Miles's interests seemed dominant. "I yesterday took Jennie, and attended a horticultural meeting," he wrote in the spring of 1853. He and Jennie "both joined," but it was "the first society I have connectd myself with since I came here." Although he owned no property in Putnam, he vowed to "take a deep interest in this society, and do all I can to promote its interests."[16] Eventually, Miles became president of the Putnam County Agricultural Society and was active in the state society.[17] Clearly, he was the driving force—taking Jennie, connecting himself with the society, working for its interests—and Jennie the appendage to his actions. Miles was also involved with the local Sunday schools, acting as parade marshal at "a celebration of the Sabbath schools."[18] The march included "all the temperance men and women of the county," a group to which he himself belonged.[19] There was no mention of Jennie being involved in such groups, although both Sunday schools and temperance work were considered acceptable public extensions of woman's sphere. During the Civil War, Jennie taught Sunday school in Greencastle. Either she did not do so earlier or Miles failed to mention it.[20]

Even within the domestic sphere, Miles claimed superiority, asserting that he had a better idea of how to do the housekeeping. "Jennie is a good teacher and a fine seamstress," he noted, perhaps having suggested that she could instruct his younger sister, Lucy.[21] But Miles wanted his mother to teach Jennie housewifery. "Jennie does well, firstrate, yet she lacks experience in many things. She works like a slave where if she only knew how, it would be done easily, and require but a moments time." Jennie was well educated and skillful at needlework, "but her mother out of a mistaken kindness never initiated her into the mysteries of housekeeping. She needs showing in many little things."[22]

Jennie experienced bouts of ill health. Before arriving in Greencastle, she had been unwell while staying in Indianapolis with her in-laws. In a note thanking them for their kindness, she attributed her renewed good health to "the clear air of Greencastle, or the pleasure of being with Miles, and the contented feeling of being at home." Like many migrants to the Midwest, Jennie suffered from the "chill" or "ague."[23] It recurred, however, along with a "severe head ache." Miles was not a good nurse. "You know that it gives me more pleasure to delve into a history, than to delve under a bed in search of a chamber," he confessed to his father. "I fear these feelings on my part does not make me the most agreable nurse in the world."[24] Jennie continued to be in "delicate health." Miles himself suffered an attack of typhoid fever, which provoked an anxious note from Jennie to her father-in-law. Lacking confidence in the local doctor, she wanted to send Miles to Indianapolis but could not accompany him because the school where she taught was having its public examination. Fortunately, Miles began to get better.[25] Unlike her husband, Jennie confessed neither inadequacy at nor dislike of nursing, and despite the competing practical imperatives of her employment, she remained focused not on herself but on the needs of her patient.

Jennie and Miles had two children—William, born in 1854, and Mary, born in 1856. Fertility rates for white women were falling over the course of the nineteenth century. By 1860, the average white woman would bear five children. Middle-class couples, in particular, actively sought to control their reproduction. Since Jennie suffered ill health with her pregnancies, this may have been particularly true for her and Miles. Calvin Fletcher worried about Jennie during the pregnancy with Mary. When he went to see her a month after the birth, he found her "very sick." When little Mary was two-and-a-half months old, Jennie took her and young Willy to visit her family in Rhode Island. Calvin still feared that she was "rather feeble."[26] In early 1858, Willy stayed with his grandparents in Indianapolis while Jennie was ill. While conducting business for his father in Putnamville, Miles took the opportunity to consult with the local doctor, Daniel W. Layman. He wrote his father that Layman thought Jennie's ailment "a combination of milk leg and neuralgia, following from cold taken in a puerperal fever. Our Dr, however, thinks it is only an aggravated case of Sciatic Rhumatism."[27]

Whatever Jennie's illness, she was unable to care for herself and had lost the use of her limbs. Mid-nineteenth-century physicians treated gynecologic ailments with live leeches, injections into the uterus, or cauterization. Jennie was presumably spared these methods because the doctors did not seem to believe her ailments were connected to her reproductive system, although complications from childbirth could invalid women long after delivery. Some historians have seen in women's ill health resistance to patriarchal authority. A number of Jennie's symptoms, paralysis in particular, fit the diagnosis of hysteria, which male doctors often applied to their female patients. Illness allowed women to avoid domestic work and sexual relations and even to exert power within the family by forcing husband and children to accommodate to the woman's needs. There is no way to know whether Jennie's illness resulted from physical or psychological sources. Miles certainly sought to embody male dominance. Perhaps ill health was her way of resisting his authority. By fall of 1859, however, when Calvin and Keziah Fletcher visited Miles and Jennie in Greencastle, her father-in-law thought she looked well.[28]

Miles Fletcher's assertions that he would be the head of the household did not preclude Jennie's working. Since Miles was still in debt, the couple probably needed the extra income, so Jennie taught school in Greencastle, often in spite of her poor health.[29] She may also have helped him in his first year of teaching at Asbury. Miles acknowledged, "I do not know what I should have done had she not assisted me so much." "She will not teach any more," he concluded, but whether that was a mutual decision or his dictate was not clear. Perhaps he—or they—felt her health could not bear the strain. But Miles did have one regret: "I am sorry on her account that we cannot keep house." Although he blamed Asbury's stingy pay for his inability to earn sufficient income to rent a house, he acknowledged how this deprived Jennie of her sphere in the home.[30]

Miles left Asbury briefly to study law at Harvard University. He consulted with his father and an older brother about this decision. Jennie is not mentioned as having a part in these discussions, although Calvin Fletcher apparently considered her in concluding, "At present I think he being married he best choose the law &c."[31] It is not clear where Jennie lived while Miles was at Harvard. He spoke of living alone in Cambridge and concentrating on his law studies. Perhaps Jennie was with her family in Rhode Island. In any case, he was "deprived of the domestic circle."[32] When he returned to Indiana, he briefly tried practicing law in Indianapolis but gave that up. He then moved back to Greencastle, where he was admitted to the Greencastle bar at the October 1857 term of court. But there is no record that he practiced law. Instead, he resumed teaching at Indiana Asbury as professor of belles lettres and history.[33] Jennie was again so unwell that Miles had to carry her about: "Her limbs are utterly helpless & painful."[34] He sent her to his parents with the admonition, "Don't let her trouble you by hindering anyone."[35] He seemed less concerned with Jennie's illness than with others' inconvenience.

Once again, Miles's financial affairs were in disarray. He feared that his creditors might approach his father, who had already loaned him $100. For two years, Miles and Jennie had cared for a young cousin, Eliza Harper. But Miles could no longer afford to keep her. Moreover, he felt their son, Willy, did not benefit from her influence. And she required more patience than possessed by "a woman with two fretting babies," Miles complained, referring to Jennie.[36] As before, Miles and Calvin spoke of decisions as if only the men made them, but clearly women played a role. Miles might have felt obligated to help his young cousin, and his father surely would have contributed financially to her support. But the extra burden on Jennie—Eliza was reputedly "wild"—may have been the crucial factor. In addition, Calvin's second wife did not want to take the girl in, perhaps because Eliza was the niece of the first Mrs. Fletcher. So Calvin Fletcher had no choice but to send the girl back to her mother, although he considered the woman an unfit parent. Jennie does not seem to have been teaching at this time, though the family had a lodger, which provided extra income but added to Jennie's household work. A hired girl was employed to ease her burden.[37]

Jennie obviously played a role in her children's lives, but it is hard to discern exactly what it was from the documents left by the Fletcher men. During Jennie's bouts of illness, Miles's younger sister, Lucy, helped with Willy—either while he stayed at his grandfather's in Indianapolis or when she herself went to Greencastle. In this way, Lucy fulfilled the traditional role of unmarried sisters in helping with nieces and nephews.[38] But when Miles spoke of governing Willy, who could be mischievous, he gave no indication of consulting his wife, sister, or any other woman. Four-year-old Willy gave his father "much trouble and concern" because of his fearlessness. The boy did not understand, for instance, why he was not allowed to plow with the mule, Jack.

Miles does not say whether Jennie had similar problems managing her son, but his mischief would lead to injury. When Willy overheard that one tied a mule's leg in order to shoe it, he decided to try this on Jack—and was kicked in the face. A young man took the child, covered with blood, to Miles and told him the boy was dead, but Miles was able to resuscitate his son by putting Willy's head under the pump and washing off the blood. The young man was then sent for a doctor. Willy had a two-inch cut under his chin and possibly a broken nose. Miles was still distraught when he wrote his father of the accident, and it is interesting that his account includes Willy, himself, the young man, the doctor, and the mule—but not Jennie. In this slighting of the mother, Miles followed a didactic piece on "Governing Children" that appeared in the *Putnam Republican Banner.* This article apprised parents of the importance of being reasonable with children. Though the mother's role was never specifically addressed, fathers were adjured always to treat a child respectfully and never to punish in anger.[39]

The strain of Miles's debt and of his frequent changes of occupation and residence must have been trying for Jennie, although only Calvin Fletcher seemed to think that she should enter into her husband's calculations about his career. In addition, Miles apparently expected to maintain appearances as became a Fletcher, which perhaps contributed to his indebtedness. When his sister Lucy was visiting, for instance, he became upset at finding that her shoe was torn: he did not want her to appear as a "sloven." Moreover, he told his father, "she did not seem to have remembered, that when here, she was not only 'Calvin Fletcher's daughter' but was also 'Prof Fletcher's sister.'"[40] One surmises that Jennie, too, was expected always to appear—and to keep house and children—in a fashion befitting Professor Fletcher's wife.

In addition to his pride, Miles Fletcher apparently had a quick temper. Calvin frequently lamented to his diary about his son's "violence," and he prayed, "May God give my son a better temper."[41] Marriage to such "an irritable man," who was unable to settle on a career in their first years together, must have been difficult for Jennie, especially since her health was often poor and her family so far away. She, in turn, seems to have been rather timid. At one point while Miles was away, she and three-month-old Willy took refuge with her in-laws. According to Calvin, the woman who had been staying with Jennie—perhaps a hired domestic or a friend—was pregnant, and Jennie was afraid the woman would need help while Miles was absent: although a mother herself, Jennie felt unprepared to cope with another woman's medical needs.[42] But in 1853, when Billy, another Fletcher brother, lived with Miles and Jennie as a student at Asbury, he reported a scene of quiet domestic life: "Jennie and Miles are in the other room reading by windows and doors are open the cricket is chearping his meary tune."[43]

Miles did care deeply about his students. Recommending one of them to his father's notice, he wrote, "I begin to feel almost ashamed of introducing to you any more young men. But the bearer of this is a remarkable young man. He has a fine mind, and is a splendid schollar."[44] Although Miles considered himself a popular instructor, he felt unappreciated. He wanted a raise from $450 to $600, but he knew the board was made up of "poor methodist ministers who receive two or three hundred dollars a year for their services. They would think it outragious for a young man to receive six hundred. In their opinion a man should teach for nothing. Their motto is 'get the cheapest teacher,' and ' . . . yet the best.'"[45] Still, he determined to leave if he did not receive the raise. After getting an increase of $200, or some promise of it, he concluded, "I shall have to return here again. They can't do without me."[46]

At Asbury, he did not get along with the influential professor William C. Larrabee. Miles thought Larrabee disliked him, and he suspected the older man was trying to maneuver him into a confrontation.[47] Furthermore, he found life at the university monotonous: "The history of one day here is the history of all."[48]

Whether it was owing to his professorial skill or to the desirability of securing his father's influence, Miles was several times solicited to run for superintendent of public instruction. In 1854, when a number of important Putnam citizens urged him to run, believing he had the best chance of winning, Miles sought his father's advice. He explained, "I should love to aid in laying the foundation of public schools in my native state."[49] His father was not receptive to the idea, however, viewing public life as the "the highroad to insolvency."[50] Despite repeated solicitations in 1856 and 1858, Calvin Fletcher remained convinced that Miles was sure to be defeated and that elected office "was debauching & distructive of all honest ends of life."[51] Miles consequently deferred running, but he became increasingly prominent in the Indiana State Teachers' Association.

In 1860, he once again considered running for superintendent of public instruction. And once again, his father firmly asserted that he could not win and that winning, in any case, might ruin him financially.[52] But this time, Miles decided to take the chance. Father and son then entered into a friendly wager. Miles thought he would run ahead of the general Republican ticket, and Calvin agreed "to give him a bushel of corn for every vote over the average vote for state ticket."[53] In 1860, Miles traveled the state, lecturing in different places. Technically, these were academic rather than political lectures, but they served to acquaint people with the candidate and to dispel the idea that a "salaried Professor" might feel himself better than others. Miles defeated the incumbent, Samuel L. Rugg, by 11,383 votes, a margin of over 4 percent. His father paid $220 to settle their debt. On a Sunday in early 1861, Miles Fletcher delivered his farewell address to the Asbury students.[54]

Miles proved successful as a school superintendent. His school bill passed into law in March 1861. He also prevented the legislature from diverting school funds to buy war bonds. Calvin Fletcher was proud of his son. He praised Miles as "bold & determined & kept part of the [school] fund from being stole. All this I feel pleased with that is his conduct." But to his son, Calvin spoke of "the uncertainty of popularity" and cautioned against expecting reelection.[55] Although Miles, too, was proud of his success—he had, after all, "*worked* & talked and thought day & night" to get his bill passed after it suffered an overwhelming defeat in the first vote—he was worried: "I am not coining money, or laying up as I should for the future."[56] His father did not reassure him. In fact, when Miles accompanied Calvin to church during a visit to Indianapolis, "'Owe no man' was the text." He thought his father had "primed" the minister, and Calvin confessed to his diary that he had.[57] Clearly, Miles did not feel that his father acknowledged his independence. When Calvin wrote him with some political advice, Miles sent his brother Stoughton to tell their father that "he was not a child [and] needed no parental caution." Soon thereafter, he "came himself & delivered the same message." Calvin replied "that so long as I was a parent I should notify him if I thot there was danger." "If it was disagreeable to him to hear precautionary suggestions," Calvin thought, Miles should "not . . . come near but act on his own independent views." In other words, he should be truly his own man. If he persisted in consulting his father, he would have to receive unwanted advice.[58]

During the 1850s, Jennie saw her in-laws frequently. Calvin Fletcher's diary records many visits to Indianapolis by Miles and his wife and children. And for Jennie and the children, that relationship would assume greater importance than ever after a tragic railroad accident in 1862. Following the battle of Shiloh, Governor Oliver P. Morton had requested that Calvin accompany him on a trip to relieve wounded soldiers. But Fletcher declined, and Miles took his father's place. As the governor's train was negotiating the rail yard at Sullivan, Indiana, it was stopped by a freight car in its path. Miles looked out the window to see what was happening, whereupon the train accelerated suddenly, causing his head to strike a protruding plank. He died in Governor Morton's arms.[59] On a lovely Sunday morning in May, the governor's secretary informed Calvin Fletcher of his son's death. That night, Miles's body arrived by special train and was taken to the Fletcher house in Indianapolis. "We required no watch as is usually the custom," Calvin recorded. "He was safe in his fathers house, the last respect I could pay him." Jennie and the children arrived that night. Calvin Fletcher buried Miles next to Miles's sister Maria in Indianapolis and paid the fare for sixty-seven Asbury students who attended the funeral. If he consulted with Jennie about the funeral plans, he made no mention of it in his diary. The only indication of her distress at her husband's death comes from cryptic notes in letters from Miles's brothers to their father, who was by then vacationing in New England. About six weeks after her husband's death, Jennie suffered a miscarriage.[60]

Although she would remarry after the war, she was now a widow with two small children. Her dependency continued, but she would now rely on her father-in-law. Miles's older brother, Cooley, assumed that his father would care for them. "I am thinking of you, &, more, that of his wife & of those two bereaved children—that bright boy, & that dear affectionate little girl, & I bow the knee & pray for them," Cooley wrote. "I know, dear father, that you will be their earthly friend & their helper now that their earthly support is taken away." Cooley evidently did not write to Jennie, but he asked his father to send his condolences—still, his was the only condolence letter that even mentioned Jennie.[61] Clearly, Calvin kept in touch with his widowed daughter-in-law and received regular visits from her and the children.[62] Although he hoped that Willy would "make his mothers heart glad," he also wanted a male figure in the boy's life, and he confided this concern to Miles's brother Keyes, who was now a soldier in the 115th Indiana Volunteers: "I hoped he would come to the relief of his father & the charge of the farm & raise Miles' boy who wants to live on the farm 'with his uncle Kid.'"[63] In early 1864, he again spoke with Keyes, who was on leave, and with another son, Ingram, about bringing Jennie and her children to the farm in Indianapolis. Keyes was dispatched to Greencastle, evidently to speak to Jennie. Calvin was prepared to be generous, but only if Jennie did as he wanted: "My advise is to take her to the farm. Give her childrin an out door life. Put Willy thro college at proper age but give him the musctle & strength of a country boy & Mary the little girl a good education—If they will comply with my suggestions I will if God permit Educate both childrin but She must comply with my terms."[64]

Calvin Fletcher did settle some income on Jennie. After Miles's election as superintendent of public instruction, Calvin had decided to deed him some land. In November 1862, he made the deed of 900 to 1,000 acres in Martin County in trust to three of his sons "to pay Miles debts & to distribute residue to widow & heirs."[65] Jennie also tried teaching school in her house in Greencastle, but the venture must not have succeeded, for she moved to Indianapolis at the end of the war. For a time, she and her children apparently lived on Calvin Fletcher's farm or boarded with Miles's younger brother Billy, now an Indianapolis doctor.[66] She did return to Greencastle, perhaps after Calvin Fletcher's death, and eventually married William D. Allen, a Greencastle grocer and Democratic politician eighteen years her senior. Allen died in 1876, leaving three grown children from his previous marriage in addition to the six-year-old son he had with Jennie. The 1870 census listed the value of Allen's real estate at $200 and his personal estate at $2,000. His wife, however, was much better off. Jennie owned real estate worth $19,000 and a personal estate of $13,000.[67] These sums probably reflected her—or her children's—share of Calvin Fletcher's estate. When the patriarch died in 1866, his will left "twenty five thousand dollars to the wife & children of my son Miles J. Fletcher deceased, or to the survivor of them," as well as the Martin County lands.[68] This bequest finally gave Jennie independence from the Fletchers.

Miles Fletcher expected submission from his wife, and Jennie appears to have complied. Her sparse epistolary remnants speak of Miles's spirits and health. Of course, these comments were in letters to his father, but it does appear that Jennie subordinated herself to Miles, following his changing career and accommodating his temper. Calvin Fletcher commented on the pride of Cooley's wife, but he made no such comments about Jennie's personality, except to note that his granddaughter Mary resembled her mother in being "smart."[69] Jennie seems to have been a quieter counterpart to Miles and his boisterous temper.

Although Calvin Fletcher had voiced more willingness to consult with Jennie about her future—and her children's—he proved as patriarchal in his own way as Miles had been. And unlike Miles, he had the financial clout to get his way. He would help Jennie if she would "comply with my terms." Nonetheless, even if her marriage into the Fletcher family required submission, it also provided her with independence through the legacy that Calvin settled on his son's widow and children. Jennie may not have been grateful for that legacy, or perhaps she did not remember her submission to Miles and his father fondly. There is no mention that she attended the presentation of "a magnificent portrait" of her late husband to Indiana Asbury by his brothers in 1878. And she was buried not with Miles in the Fletcher plot in Indianapolis but with her second husband in Greencastle's Forest Hill Cemetery. The tombstone names the interred as "J. M. H. Allen"—there is no "F" for Fletcher.[70]

Vincent Day's rise to become the largest landowner in the county contrasted sharply with Miles Fletcher's career. The Days were migrants from the upper South. Vincent's father, Ambrose, left Maryland for Kentucky, where he probably married Vincent's mother, Joanna, and where Vincent was born. At twenty-three, Vincent Day married twenty-year-old Margaret Wilkinson, whose family had come from Ohio. As a newlywed, he owned $1,200 of real estate, probably acquired with the help of his father, who also owned a substantial amount of property.[71]

Miles Fletcher's family saw to it that he had an elite education, but it is unlikely that Ambrose Day provided his son with much more schooling than the limited education furnished by the county schools. Richard M. Hazelett, Vincent's contemporary, remembered attending school in a three-faced camp deep in the woods, warmed in cold weather by fire on its open side. There, he was taught by a succession of often untrained schoolmasters, and pedagogy featured the "blab" method, in which all the scholars "studied as loud as they could hallow."[72] A generation later, Maria Crane, wife of a Bainbridge merchant, worried about the education of her children, Caroline and Milton, noting, "I hope to find a good school some time for him. this is a bad place for children they live in the street."[73]

Miles Fletcher had displayed a certain inclination for violence, but he strove to exemplify the restraint of middle-class manhood. Although tempted, he had not helped to lynch Greenbury Mullinix but had instead protected him from the mob in the confidence that justice would be carried out. He was a temperance man and deplored the violence in the community. Vincent Day, however, was no stranger to the justice system. Several times in the 1850s and 1860s, he appeared in court charged with assault and battery and other offenses. Sometimes, he was acquitted or the case was thrown out, but on a couple occasions, he paid a fine of $20 for assault; on another, he paid James Adams over $325 in damages.[74]

The details of these cases are lacking, but assault was frequently related to alcohol. A local newspaper called a drunken man seen walking Greencastle's streets with his ear nearly cut off and blood on his face and hair "one of Charley Michael's victim's," referring to the German-born saloonkeeper.[75] Vincent Day, even as a prosperous landholder and middle-aged family man, was a drinker and brawler himself.

Yet neither his legal problems nor his fines impeded Day's rise. Within a decade of his marriage, he owned real estate valued by the census taker at $19,250. The Days lived in a frame house with other buildings, including a barn. Vincent insured the barn and its contents, including hay, grain, and fodder, for as much as he spent to insure the farmhouse.[76] Like others immersed in the farm economy, he would have keenly observed the weather and followed the crops' progress. In 1859, Keyes Fletcher noted that "corn & other things are drying up. We have had no rain for several weeks. Need it very bad."[77]

Obviously, with as extensive a farm as he owned, Day produced for the market, not just for self-sufficiency. A turn to market agriculture did not, however, mean that the old habits of self-sufficiency had entirely eroded. Farmers often still valued the hardiness of crops or livestock over their quality, and crop rotation might still be infrequent, leading to worn-out lands and contributing to westward movement. Richard Hazelett's memoirs of the pioneer period emphasized the supremacy of brawn and hand tools. Corn was ground in a handmill. Plowing was done with a bull-tongue or bar-shear plow that, when it struck the frequent roots, bucked and "often hurt the plowman fully as bad as if he had been kicked by a mule." Grain was cut with a reap hook and bound into sheaves by hand. Boys on horses rode over the sheaves, separating the straw from the wheat. Then the men, using a sheet as a fan, would separate the wheat from the chaff and dirt, but as one pioneer recalled, "there was always dirt or gravel enough left in the wheat to sharpen your teeth." Hay was cut by men with scythes: "One acre per day per hand was considered a fair days work."[78]

Interest in mechanization, however, was increasing. The hardware store where Keyes Fletcher was employed sold "harvesting mashines. . . . Self rakers, hand rakers & every other kind of rakers. . . . For this is a county where the farmers have got good farms & plenty of mony & they are bound to have mashines." But farmers "are afraid to buy until they see the things work & know which is 'The' best."[79] Small farms would not generate the surplus for such machinery, but Vincent Day could afford it. In turn, this kind of equipment increased productivity and accelerated the move onto the market. The Civil War, which reduced the supply of farm laborers, accelerated the movement away from manpower.[80]

Vincent and Margaret Day would have exhibited the products of their farm at the county fair.[81] One writer described the "neighing of horses, the braying of jacks and mules, the lowing of cattle, the bleating of sheep, the squealing of pigs and the grunting of hogs, and the long, loud hoarse crow of the Shanghai rooster" at an 1855 fair. A. C. Stevenson, a noted local breeder, won prizes for the best heifer and best sow. In addition, produce such as tomatoes and onions were displayed, and women competed for prizes in household crafts such as needlework.[82]

A young man who lacked Vincent Day's advantages in having a father able to provide him with a farm would have found it more difficult to get established in an agricultural market economy, perhaps taking half a decade or more to acquire the capital, estimated at $500, necessary to start a farm. A third of adult Putnam County men did not own real estate. Younger men rented. According to one county historian, the best land in Putnam was occupied by 1840. Solon Turman bought the last piece of government land in the county—a small tract in Cloverdale Township—in October 1854.[83] With his purchase, the Putnam frontier closed. Thereafter, land would become scarcer and more expensive. One resident, Andrew Dierdorf, described himself as landless "or nearly so." He had a "spot that answers the purpose for a home but not to make a living there from." Perhaps the high prices of land contributed to his plight. "There are thousands that would become independent farmers at a reasonable price instead of paying from $5 to $25 dollars per acre."[84] The average price of the 258 acres Day bought in the 1850s was almost $28. Philip Bence, another successful farmer, paid over $10,000 for 342 acres in 1853; the price per acre was $29.77. He, too, made purchases of less valuable, probably less improved, land—400 acres in 1859 for $7.50 per acre—but if it was difficult for the landless in Putnam County to find the capital to buy land at $5 an acre, $30 would have been prohibitive. Land was cheaper in other parts of the state and to the west.[85]

Vincent Day acquired land in his name only, although land deeds did record women's rights to their husband's property. His mother, Joanna, relinquished her dower rights to a parcel she and her husband sold Vincent in 1849. When Daniel and Elizabeth Morris sold 100 acres of land to him four years later, the deed clearly stated that James Shoemaker, a justice of the peace, had examined Elizabeth "privately, separate and apart from, and without the hearing of her said husband"—she had agreed to the transaction "of her own free will and accord, and without any coercion or compulsion from her said husband."[86] This privy examination sought to protect her from coercion in an economic transaction that might injure the family finances. Women often signed documents despite their doubts, yielding to their husbands' wishes. The law tried to protect the wife, given her subordinate status, but the man's economic will generally prevailed.[87]

No record survives of Margaret Day's activities. Historians have disagreed about whether the typical farm family in that era was patriarchal or whether women's important economic contribution gave them greater status. No one disputes that women worked very hard. John Mack Faragher estimates that women produced up to one-half the food on a farm. They also prepared it for consumption, cleaned the house, made clothes and laundered them, and helped with men's labor, especially during planting, butchering, and harvest times. Women sold surpluses of butter, eggs, and cloth on the market, in turn providing resources that allowed the family to acquire more land and move to market production. Faragher appropriately cites the "enormousness of women's workload."[88]

In the early twentieth century, John Frank Turner remembered driving a store wagon through Putnam County, where farm women would trade their eggs, butter, or turkeys for store goods. He recalled the pride women took "in their skill at making butter, which was of a lovely yellow color." The Presbyterian minister's wife, Sarah M. Hawley, made lard from hogs the family had raised and tended strawberries, grapes, peas, and green currants. Once, she supervised her daughters in making a carpet for the kitchen.[89] Margaret Day, married to a prosperous farmer, would have overseen a larger operation. One female observer in Putnam County noted, "Here in the west a womans sphere has over the cooking stove and kitchen gardens she must have from six to eight kinds of preserves on her table & hot meats . . . every meal—or else is no house keeper."[90] Such was the standard to which a matron such as Margaret Day would have been held.

Historians agree that childbearing was among the most significant aspects of women's contribution to the farm. Children constituted the labor force. Margaret Day's two oldest sons were listed as farm laborers in the 1870 census and doubtless helped their father. By the time Margaret died prematurely in her mid-thirties, she had borne at least six children, the average for white women of her generation. Jennie Fletcher, widowed twice, had only three surviving children. Minister's wife Sarah Hawley married at a somewhat later age, twenty-eight, compared to Margaret Day at twenty-one and Jennie Fletcher at twenty-three, but she still had five children. Other Putnam families were even larger: patriarchs John Lynch and Peter Applegate had ten and eight children, respectively.[91] The Days had four sons before their first daughter was born in 1854. Consequently, Vincent had more help with the farmwork than Margaret did with her chores. The 1860 census shows that Vincent had also hired a farm laborer, Robert Haney, but there was no hired girl to help Margaret and six-year-old Joanna.[92] Although Jennie Fletcher had a hired girl to help with a household of two children, Margaret did not have one for a bustling farm with at least two adult men and several children to tend.

Farmers were often criticized for insensitivity to the burdens on their wives.[93] For example, Sarah Bell McGaughey, Ned McGaughey's mother, was remembered as the butt of her husband's humor. When she was absent at church one Sunday, her husband, Arthur, who relished a good practical joke, entertained an old soldier, encouraging him to talk about the war. Just before Sarah was to return, Arthur gave the man a piece of charcoal and instructed him to "mark out on the floor the plan of the battle of Lundy's Lane, so I may know just the position of the British and American forces." The elderly veteran "was so absorbed in his work, explaining it as he drew the heavy lines on the clean, white boards, that he did not notice the exit of his host, nor the entrance of the host's wife, till he heard her indignant tones demanding the cause of his defacing her floor, and ordering him to desist at once."[94] The men remembered this as an amusing story, but Sarah McGaughey not doubt was appalled to see her floor

Sarah Hawley.
(Courtesy of Indiana
State Library)

defaced, especially since cleaning it involved hauling water before she could even begin scrubbing. Farm culture valued men's work more than women's grueling routine of cooking, cleaning, and childcare.[95] Since Margaret Day had family nearby, she was probably able to share many of the farm tasks and child-rearing duties with female neighbors and kin.

When Maria Crane, a Bainbridge merchant's wife, gave birth in 1847, she did so surrounded by local women. Having taken to bed because of jaundice, the pregnant Maria felt "stupid" and was in pain. Her husband, Thomas, "called in some neighboring women, as is usual," and they delivered her son at three in the morning. But an hour later, she began to hemorrhage. Although she appeared to rally at one point, she soon became "stupid and delirious." A day and a half after her son's birth, Maria died.[96]

When Margaret Day died, she was not surrounded by female relatives and friends. She and one of the children died of smallpox in the mid-1860s. Neighbors were so scared of infection that Vincent Day and the doctor were the only attendants at the funeral. They interred mother and child in a nighttime rainstorm and filled the grave themselves, as the gravediggers refused to do the work.[97]

Jennie Fletcher and Margaret Day seem not to have sought out the public sphere, although their husbands did. Miles Fletcher was an aspiring politician and active in many civic organizations. Vincent Day spent time in the courts and taverns, a different public environ and an even more masculine one. Women's piety made it respectable for women to enter the public sphere on behalf of moral reform, although taking a leadership role was more controversial. Thus, Jennie Fletcher could join the agricultural society, but it was Miles who became an officer.

As historians of religion have argued, evangelical denominations felt uneasy about the role of women in the churches, including female preaching, even though a majority of their adherents were women. Indeed, when a female minister arrived in Greencastle, she was unable to find a church that would allow her to preach.[98] Temperance reform revealed a similar ambivalence. In the 1850s, men in Putnam still took the leading role in that cause. The *Putnam Banner* frequently recorded the activity of temperance activists and listed the officers and leading members, all of whom were male. By 1854, the Ladies Temperance Society existed; it had a female president, distributed literature, and advocated a prohibitory law. Yet no matter how significant women were in such groups, their claims to public recognition were dismissed. When they gave a temperance supper at the courthouse, 300 to 400 people attended. One of the ladies gave a speech, and others offered and read resolutions. But when the supper was reported in the *Putnam Banner,* the newspaper omitted the women's names altogether. It then reported that the women had complained the paper was "making sport" of them. When they objected to the lack of individual recognition, the editor commented that the women only wanted their names in the paper, belittling their claim to public acknowledgment.[99]

Sabbath schools were another public activity in which women might engage, and they did receive praise and recognition in this capacity. Greencastle's first Sunday school was established in 1834. It was run by Myra Jewett, a

Massachusetts woman and local schoolteacher. Beginning with twenty ladies and children, the school grew to sixty-five pupils within a year. Minister Ransom Hawley was credited with founding many Sunday schools, but his wife, Sarah, was acknowledged as a partner in this labor as well as a "zealous co-worker in his ministry."[100] In areas such as Indiana where schools were primitive, Sunday schools often supplemented the inadequate education in the standard classroom.

There were few occupations available to women in Putnam County who did not have male providers. A woolen carding factory that opened in 1826 employed women to work on hand looms. In Greencastle, widows operated boardinghouses that often catered to the college students. In 1853, Asbury president L. W. Berry provoked a crisis by ordering students out of boarding houses, where clerks supplied them with alcohol—and he expelled those who refused to move. Public sympathy opposed this academic tyranny largely because it fell hard on the widows who depended on student lodgers for income.

Teaching was the leading occupation open to middle-class women. By 1859, 20 percent of Indiana teachers were females, and they were paid as little as 50 percent of what male teachers earned. Hiring women thus saved schools money and allowed them to extend the school term. The work was often demanding. L. H. Stowell, who taught at the Bainbridge Male and Female Academy, had forty students. Like Jennie Fletcher, she taught while suffering from chills. A whooping cough epidemic seemed almost welcome because it cut her class size in half and made her work easier.[101] Harriet Dunn Larrabee was the dominant figure in female education in the county. The wife of Miles Fletcher's nemesis, William Larrrabee, she opened her school for girls in 1844 with 4 students, received a state charter in 1848, and had over 100 students in primary through college courses by 1850. The school had three terms of fourteen weeks each, and the college course followed Asbury's offerings and had a staff of at least five teachers. Harriet Larrabee was characterized as "Christian and motherly, but equally scholarly."[102] Clearly, even an acknowledged educational leader in the state such as Larrabee had to be identified by the female qualities of morality and maternity.

Educated girls could teach either to support themselves or to add to their family's income, as did Jennie Fletcher. School attendance showed growing numbers of girls during the 1850s in the classroom. By 1861, slightly more girls than boys were attending Greencastle schools. Both of Sarah Hawley's daughters, Lucy and Emeline, became schoolteachers after completing their educations. The Bainbridge Male and Female Academy advertised that it prepared future teachers.[103]

Women's participation in the public sphere, even as an extension of their presumably pious nature, was never uncontested. Politics, however, was especially off limits. Historians generally consider the Whigs and Republicans to have been more open to women's influence in politics.[104] And the Democratic condemnation of women participating in the 1856 Republican campaign would seem to support that conclusion. During a rally at Bainbridge, Democrats heckled women in the crowd of observers, calling out, "This is no place for women." The speaker, Democratic gubernatorial candidate Ashbel P. Willard, referred sarcastically to the women and children who attended meetings for John C. Frémont. But Democratic women did participate in the campaign. Greencastle women held a pro-Buchanan meeting in 1856 that censured Frémont for having eloped with his wife.[105] Still, accounts of women's attendance at rallies were frequently cited to point out a party's lack of appeal to actual voters, that is, adult men.[106]

Not surprisingly, woman's rights fared poorly in Putnam County. One female activist wrote a scathing account of her visit there: "The men in Greencastle are rude, and do all things boldly; the women dare not do anything at all, excepting to allow themselves to be kept. The men are pleased and perfectly willing to keep them, and very angry with any one who shall come here and tell them their customs are destructive."[107]

Emma Lou Thornbrough, the leading expert on Indiana in the Civil War era, finds that "the woman's rights movement had little impact on Indiana politics." For instance, when Dr. Mary F. Thomas submitted a petition for woman's rights to the General Assembly in 1859, requesting equal political rights and an end to legal discrimination, the committee that considered it reported against legislation.[108] Even those who expressed sympathy for women merely wanted "womens duties" approached from the female perspective, arguing that this "will do more good to woman everywhere" than "all the woman rights conventions the world has ever known."[109]

Writing to a local newspaper, a reader identified as "Laura" challenged criticism of the bloomer costume and objected to the attempt, whenever a woman asserted "her rights, or a small portion of those rights," to "force us back to the thraldom of centuries gone by, make us mere scullions, and enshroud us in the ignorance of the dark ages." But although "Laura" derided efforts to turn every female deviation from traditional dress or behavior into a crisis about "treason toward man's sovereignty," she did not suggest that women should rule, and she promised that women would have the "good sense" not to "outrage . . . public sentiment."[110] She defended the bloomer costume for its simplicity, pointed out that men's fashions changed just as women's did, and asserted that woman should be man's "co-equal, a partner," not his "slave, or sycophantic waiter on man's infirmities."[111] But whether middle-class matron or farm wife, women such as Jennie Fletcher and Margaret Day were not coequal partners with their husbands.

Young men could choose their path to economic independence—be it a farm, a business, or a professional career—but women could not, and they were dependent on men's choices. Though they, too, played key roles in the economic, religious, and educational life of the county, they did not seek independence but instead aided the efforts of their menfolk. Nineteenth-century women were expected to exemplify the values of woman's sphere, which was defined as the home. Not only were they to be good housekeepers and nurturers of children, they were also to possess to the fullest the character traits of passivity, gentleness, and piety.[112]

Women's submission meant that independent men made choices and the softer sex molded themselves to the males' decisions. Wives such as Jennie Fletcher and Margaret Day adapted themselves, with more or less grace, to the decisions their husbands made about residence, livelihood, and childrearing. To the extent that women were believed to be morally superior, they might contribute publicly to church and moral reform. But their dependency kept them on the outskirts of the public realm of politics—they did not vote or hold office. The disgruntled woman's rights activist mentioned earlier compared Putnam women's subordination to men to that of African Americans in a white-dominated society. She observed that Putnam women possessed not only "the spirit of niggers, but many of their manners. . . . Their suppressed giggle; their low gutteral gabble; their tittering and snickering in outer rooms, remind one of the smart 'cutting up' of the darkies." She blamed Putnam's men for keeping women ignorant of anything having to do with the "outer life," noting how these men "flatter them that they appear more ladylike, &c., to be so ignorant that their eyes kindle never with the spark of intelligence." If asked a question, she said, the women "cannot answer; they do not know anything, except to chatter away like children about 'how well they know their place,' and never dare to get out of it, &c."[113]

This woman's rights speaker found Putnam women complacent and stifled in their sphere. Yet for all their constrained circumstances, women in the community at least had an appropriate place in county life—something that was denied to Putnam's small, marginalized African American population.

3

THE EXCLUDED RACE

On November 6, 1854, the *Euphrasia* set sail from Norfolk, Virginia, for Africa with 168 American blacks on board. Of those passengers, 151 were Virginia slaves. Also aboard were 17 free blacks from the North, including a free-born cabinetmaker, Sanders Champion, and his wife, Rosanna, who were leaving Philadelphia. But the remaining free blacks were all from Indiana, and among them was the Peters family of Putnam County. From 1820 to 1860, only 58 Hoosiers migrated to Liberia. The decision to migrate was a rare choice not just for African Americans in Indiana but also for Northern free blacks, who had long been torn between their pride at the existence of an independent black nation and their conviction that the United States, not Africa, was their home. They distrusted the American Colonization Society, regarding it as dominated by slaveowners and motivated by a racist philosophy—namely, that blacks did not belong in the country of their birth. Only about a quarter of the society's migrants were free blacks. There was, however, a surge of free black migrants during the 1850s as African Americans responded to the increasing animus manifested against their race by the Fugitive Slave Act, the *Dred Scott* decision, and the black exclusion measures taken by midwestern states such as Indiana. All these developments threatened the limited rights possessed by Northern free blacks.[1]

The Peters left no record of their deliberations, but what is known of their story deviates from historians' emphasis on black community. There were too few blacks in Putnam County in the 1850s to form the institutions that historians have long believed were key to black survival, progress, and resistance to racism. Rather, white patronage played an important role for isolated and marginalized free blacks like the Peters family.[2]

The family matriarch, Tamar Peters, was born in 1804. When she was two years old, she was purchased by James Stevenson. Stevenson, who was from Maryland originally, had served and been wounded in the War of 1812, remaining an invalid for the rest of his life. In the late 1780s, he had moved to Woodford County, Kentucky. Tamar may have married another of the Stevenson slaves in Kentucky—a man named Durham, who was a gift from James's father to James and his wife on their marriage. The Stevenson family accounts do not say who fathered Tamar's children, but that individual was not with the Peters family when it went to Africa. Tamar left the United States in 1854 with her children—George, Alexander, Priscilla, and Mary—all of whom had been born as slaves according to the emigrant list. The list also included Martha Peters and Rachel Peters—possibly the wives of George and Alexander. Martha and Rachel had been born free, as had their three small children, presumably Tamar's grandchildren: six-year-old Simon, four-year-old Charles, and two-year-old Mary.[3]

The Peters clan was unusual in the history of colonization because each member was a free black from a Northern state. As the *Euphrasia*'s passenger list reveals, blacks most often went to Liberia because they had no choice: migration was a condition of their emancipation. Forty-nine people from Fauquier County, Virginia, had been emancipated by the heirs of Col. George Love; Love's will likely ordered that his slaves be freed and sent to Liberia. Other passengers had it specifically noted that they were emancipated by will. For example, Edmund and Tabitha Wise of Princess Ann County, Virginia, and their five children had been emancipated by the will of Elizabeth Wise. Thirty-eight Virginia blacks were listed as having been born free, but their places on the list of emigrants indicated family relations to those born as slaves and emigrating. Thus, Betsy Johnson, born free, and her five children emigrated with Henry Johnson, a Baptist preacher who was one of the slaves emancipated by

George Love's heirs. Similarly, Mary Foster and her five children seemed to be accompanying William F. Foster, the former slave of Francis Foster of Manchester, Virginia. In the case of the Woodson family of Richmond, it was William Woodson who was free and who accompanied his wife, Patsy, and their five children, all emancipated by John L. Tate.

Some Southern free black families had apparently made the decision to leave on the *Euphrasia*. Thirty-year-old Ralph Curry, who had purchased himself, was the only emigrant from Sheperdstown. Pleasant Morris, also from Manchester, Virginia, had been purchased by his wife, who may have been Nancy McCridie, born free and sailing with her two sons. George and Delia Banks took their two-year-old son, George, with them to Liberia. Nineteen free blacks from Portsmouth, Virginia, also sailed on the *Euphrasia*. They included Solomon Hudley and his family, as well as several branches of the Ash family. The McCridies, Banks, Hudleys, and Ashes had all been born free.[4]

Tamar Peters, of course, had not been born free, but she had been free for a couple decades by the time she left the United States. She and her sons and daughters were listed on the emigrant roll as "emancipated by Mr. Stevenson." This would have been James Stevenson, who with his wife, Margaret Campbell Stevenson, and children had migrated to Putnam County in 1826. According to county historian Jesse W. Weik, James had left Tamar and her family in Kentucky. Before Margaret died in 1831, having been widowed, "she directed that Tamar Peters and her family be freed and brought to Indiana." Weik recalled that Tamar and her children were "cared for" in Indiana by James and Margaret's son, Dr. Alexander Campbell Stevenson. Another version of the story, told by one of James and Margaret's descendants, has "Aunt Tamer" arriving in Putnam County with the family in its 1826 migration. This family historian relates that the Stevensons' daughter, Margaretta, married a Kentuckian named William Peck on July 26, 1827. Peck had settled in Indiana as a young man with only $26 and a horse; by the time of his death about sixty years later, he had over 2,000 acres of land in Putnam County, a fine house, and twelve children. According to this account, Tamar "was a free woman in Indiana, but she preferred to stay with the family and when Margaretta married went with her to her new home, where she spent her entire life."[5] Whichever date one accepts, the *Euphrasia*'s emigrant list errs in recording that the Peters children were born in slavery. If Tamar had arrived in Indiana at the later date, then only her oldest, George, would have been born a slave. If she arrived at the earlier date, then all the Peters children were born free in Indiana.[6]

But both Jesse Weik and Margaretta Stevenson, the family historian, agree in painting a paternalistic relationship between the Stevenson and Peters families. Margaretta insisted that Tamar Peters wanted to remain with her mistress's daughter. If Tamar was already free in Indiana, though, she did not need to accompany her former owner's daughter anywhere in order to be close to her: she already lived in Putnam County by the time Margaretta and William Peck settled in Greencastle. There is no record of the Peters family in the 1840 census, which only lists the names of heads of households. A black boy younger than ten lived with A. C. Stevenson's family and a black girl under ten with William Peck's. These were probably Tamar's children, but where she and the other children lived is unknown. She evidently did not head her own household until later. If she worked as a servant for Margaretta Stevenson Peck, it was apparently not a live-in arrangement. And even though Tamar may have worked for the Pecks or other members of the Stevenson clan, we cannot know if she viewed this as a purely economic relationship or whether she felt the affection the Stevensons claimed. Even the fact that her second son was named Alexander—the name of James and Margaret's oldest son, Tamar's patron— may have been less a sign of affection than a calculated appeal for the more powerful white family's aid.[7]

Margaretta Stevenson's sentimental account describes how the white family called the older black woman Aunt Tamer out of affection and how Tamar chose to remain close to the Stevensons because "she preferred to stay with the family." But in her account, Margaretta misremembers that affection by forgetting that Tamar went to Liberia, leaving the family altogether. Interestingly, the Stevenson family genealogy contains another such sentimentalized account of master-slave relations. A. C. Stevenson's third wife, Rebecca Jane Foster, reminisced about the "warm relation" existing between her grandfather, William Nelson, and his "colored people": "Grandfather Nelson was a very kind man, never known to whip a slave. The slaves worked much as they pleased; most generally pleased to work." When the slaves took breaks from their labor in the fields, supposedly to rest the horses, they actually used the time to make baskets that they sold for pocket money. In addition to Grandfather Nelson's leniency, Foster noted that "Grandmother looked after them in sickness and made them comfortable as possible." The slaves were freed when Grandfather Nelson died but chose to stay on the family farm, and "most of the old ones died there."[8] Rebecca Foster's account did make clear that the interests of the slaves and of their master—even a benevolent one—were not the same. What

Foster depicted as the slaves taking advantage of her grandfather's kindness, in using work breaks to manufacture marketable goods, might equally be viewed as entrepreneurial drive. With profits from their labor, the slaves presumably bought goods that Grandfather Nelson did not see fit to provide. Edward Ball, in his classic account *Slaves in the Family*, relates how his family, descendants of slaveowners, erased memories of whippings, of sales that separated relatives, and of the sexual exploitation of slave women. The Stevensons may well have done the same sort of forgetting.

The story of Samuel Darnall and his slaves also cautions against too readily taking white memory at face value. Hoping to find cheaper land, Darnall had moved to Putnam County from Kentucky in 1835. He had inherited black slaves when his father died, and according to county historian Weik, he "desired to free them at once, but was forbidden." Darnall then let the slaves decide which masters they wanted and sold them to those chosen "at a very low figure." There was, however, no Kentucky law "forbidding" emancipation, although masters might have had to guarantee that freedmen would not become a burden on local charity. Sometimes, too, emancipated slaves were required to post bonds as a guarantee of self-sufficiency. In 1851, Kentucky required that emancipated slaves leave the state, but this would not have been a problem for Darnall in 1835. Whatever prohibition he faced, it was probably not insurmountable if he had truly wanted to ensure his slaves' freedom.[9]

Although the Stevensons' recollections should be treated with some care, the Peters do seem to have remained under the family's patronage. Whether this was out of affection, as the Stevenson descendants liked to believe, or out of a sense that such patronage was a necessity for survival, we do not know. Tamar may have worked for Margaretta Stevenson Peck in Greencastle, but Weik accords A. C. Stevenson the role of patron for the Peters family. A. C. was Margaretta's brother and James and Margaret's eldest son. In 1821, the family sent him to scout for land in Indiana. Upon returning, he recommended Parke County, but for some reason, the family chose not to migrate. A. C. then went to Montgomery County, Kentucky, where he studied medicine with an uncle. After graduating from Transylvania Medical College in Lexington, he would briefly practice medicine in Kentucky.[10]

In 1826, A. C. Stevenson decided to return to Indiana. This time, he chose Putnam County because its blue grass reminded him of Kentucky. According to a family story, he had so little money that he made a deal with his landlady whereby he would pay her half the proceeds of his practice for a year in return for room and board. The family liked to remember "that it was probably the most profitable year the old lady ever had."[11] Margaretta does not say why the Stevensons wanted to leave Kentucky, but her account would seem to place the family's move within the ordinary migration streams of the nineteenth century, which took large numbers of Kentuckians into Indiana and Putnam County.

However, county historian Jesse Weik maintains that A. C. chose Indiana, a free state, out of antislavery principles.[12] Like another, more famous son of Kentucky, A. C. claimed to have always been antislavery. "To the institution of slavery I am opposed, in every light in which it can be viewed," he said in 1850, "and I have been opposed to it ever since I first began to think of it."[13] Abraham Lincoln would also state, "I am naturally anti-slavery. If slavery is not wrong, nothing is wrong. I can not remember when I did not so think, and feel."[14] But Lincoln came from a family that did not own slaves and that left Kentucky for Indiana in part because of religious objections to slavery. A. C. Stevenson, by contrast, was the scion of a slaveowning family. One wonders how he came to his antislavery principles and what role his interaction with Tamar Peters and her family played in forming those convictions. Tamar was two years younger than Stevenson, and she already had a one-year-old child, George, when she named her second son Alexander.[15] Did sympathy or affection for this enslaved family move the young Stevenson? Or had he wearied of the obligations of paternalism and the care slaves required? It is perhaps worth noting that, although his language in 1850 almost exactly paralleled that of Lincoln a decade and half later, Stevenson omitted one point that Lincoln made: that slavery was wrong.

Stevenson would become one of the most notable of Putnam County's citizens—but more for his civic and agricultural attainments than for his medical career. Between 1834 and 1836, he bought substantial parcels of land in the county, totaling 440 acres in Greencastle Township. He was president of Indiana Asbury's first board of trustees, served in the state government, and ran as a Whig candidate for lieutenant governor. He also served in the constitutional convention that wrote the new state constitution of 1851. When he gave the county's first temperance lecture, he persevered despite men in the audience who mockingly drank toasts to his health. For years, he published an agricultural newspaper column—the "Farmers' Department"—in the *Putnam Republican Banner,* and he became president of the Indiana State Board of Agriculture. Putnam was one of the leading cattle-producing counties in the state during the mid-nineteenth century, and A. C. Stevenson was its leading breeder. It was he who, in 1853, first imported shorthorns directly from England to Indiana. Soon, he began breeding prize cattle. He also helped form the Indiana Shorthorn Breeders Association in the early 1870s and served as the first president of the National Shorthorn Breeders Association, which was organized at the same time. If Stevenson played a patriarchal role with the Peters family, it was a role he was rapidly learning in his own life. He married three times and had twelve children.[16]

Whatever part Stevenson played in the life of Tamar Peters and her family, close relationships with whites must have been the norm for Putnam County's small number of black inhabitants. Only about 1 percent of Indiana's population was African American in 1850, but in Putnam County, blacks made up less than one-fifth of a percent. The county's black population fell by 1860, declining from thirty-seven people to twenty-two, at a time when the county's total population grew by 10 percent. As a result, blacks then constituted only a tenth of a percent of the county's total population. The structure of that population is also revealing. In 1850, thirty of the thirty-seven blacks in the county were members of six households, including the family of "Thamar" Peters. One such black household was that of Abraham Cowell and his wife, Love, who lived in Jefferson Township. Born in Virginia, the Cowells owned real estate worth $2,500. Another black household was in Cloverdale Township, where Edward Walden lived with his wife, Julia, and their four children. Edward had been born in North Carolina and Julia in Kentucky, but they had been in Indiana at least fifteen years by 1850, as their eldest child was born in the free state. Abraham Cowell, Edward Walden, and Tamar Peters were the only blacks listed in the census as owning property: the Waldens had just $300 and Tamar Peters $700 in real estate. Those not owning property included David Pollare and his wife, daughter, and aged mother, who also lived in Jefferson Township. The elder Pollares, who had been born in South Carolina, were also illiterate. And finally, there were the two households of Luke Townsend and Sylvia Townsend.

At a time when only 6 percent of Indiana's African Americans owned property, averaging $623 in value, 8 percent of Putnam County blacks had land. Since this represented only three families and was skewed by the value of Cowell's property, the average value was over $1,000. The Peters family was slightly above average for black property owners in Indiana, but owning property was itself exceptional for blacks in both the county and the state.[17]

The remaining seven free blacks in Putnam County were individuals living in white households, such as Reuben, a twenty-year-old illiterate laborer living in the home of merchant Lewis H. Sands. Indiana Asbury professor William C. Larrabee had three black children—Mary, Jane, and John A. Jordan—living in his household. Putnam County's small black population was dominated by families whose members were scattered about as individual servants, laborers, or dependents—such as Jane Keath, Reuben, or eighty-year-old Lucy, who lived with the family of Osborne Caleb in Clinton Township. The small number of Putnam's blacks in the 1850s—and their geographic distribution through the county, with many individuals living in white households—would have made forming a black community nearly impossible.

Cato Boyd evidently lacked those ties. He had once belonged to Crawford Cole and arrived in Putnam County in the 1830s. Thomas C. Hammond remembered him "being as black as jet" and a "recluse, living entirely to himself in a hut about two miles northwest of Greencastle, where he carried on the business of charcoal burning." When so few blacks possessed their own property, economic relationships with whites would have been all the more important. At the time Hammond knew him, Boyd was about sixty years old, owned 20 acres of land, and was able to read and write.[18] Having few blacks to associate with, perhaps Boyd preferred being a hermit.

At least one other story approximates the relationship between the Peters and Stevenson families, that of the black and white Townsends. In 1850, there were two black Townsend families in Putnamville. Luke Townsend, a forty-five-year-old day laborer, and his wife, Charity, had five children, all of whom were under the age of eight. The adult Townsends had been born in Kentucky, their children in Indiana. Nearby lived Sylvia Townsend, possibly Luke's mother, who had been born in Maryland. She lived with four children, aged thirty-five to fifteen: Amy, Thomas, Hetty, and Ann—all born in Kentucky. As a day laborer, Luke Townsend would have been dependent on local whites for employment. Hiram Miller, a local farmer, hired Luke, a large man, every year at "'hog killing time,' and frequently at other work." Hetty worked in Greencastle as a housekeeper for Miles and Jennie Fletcher. More-skilled employment might have been limited for the Townsends because Luke, Charity, Sylvia, Amy, and Hetty were all illiterate. The only Townsend recorded as having any schooling was eight-year-old Lucy, who had attended school during the census year, 1850.[19]

Like the Peters family, the Townsends also had a physician as a patron. Daniel W. Layman was born in Pennsylvania. When his parents died, he was raised by grandparents who took him to Virginia. After medical school at the

University of Virginia, he briefly returned to Pennsylvania and then migrated to Putnam County in 1831. Unlike A. C. Stevenson, who quickly became more of a gentleman farmer than a practicing doctor, Layman was long the leading physician in Putnamville. It was he who first saw Martha Mullinix and testified as to the wounds that killed her, and it was he who provided medical advice to Miles Fletcher about wife Jennie's ailments.[20]

Layman had married Mary Townsend, the daughter of James Townsend. James and his wife, Catherine, were born in Maryland and moved to Union County, Kentucky, and then to Putnam County, Indiana. According to county histories, Layman met Mary Townsend while en route to Indiana. He had stopped at her father's inn in Kentucky, where he became enamored of the innkeeper's daughter, and he determined to stay in Kentucky until he could win her. James Townsend, however, decided to migrate to Indiana as well, where he would establish another inn on the National Road. In 1828, he freed his slaves and offered to take north any who wished to accompany him. Luke, then a child, was one of those slaves. The white Townsends also took Sylvia and her husband, Elam, with them. Sylvia's Maryland birthplace indicates she might have accompanied James and Catherine on their earlier migration to Kentucky as well as on their final journey to Indiana. Charity arrived in Indiana some years later, one of a party of slaves traveling the National Road from Kentucky to Missouri, where they would be sold. Their wagon flooded while crossing Deer Creek near Putnamville in a storm, and locals, including Luke Townsend, turned out to rescue them. Family accounts differ as to how Charity survived. Her female descendants claimed she made it to safety on her own; her male descendants like to say that Luke saved her. In any event, a local Baptist minister, Benjamin Jones, took pity on the slave girl, purchased her, and raised her. Several years later, Jones presided as minister at Luke and Charity's wedding. Their oldest child, Lucy Agnes, had the distinction of being the first black baby born in the county.[21]

Like the Stevensons with "Aunt Tamer," the whites apparently felt they had an affectionate, familial relationship with the black Townsends, using the honorifics of "grandmother" for Sylvia (or "Sibley") Townsend and "aunt" for Hetty and Amy. Ann Townsend, who had lighter skin than her siblings, was known as "Yaller Ann." But in reality, the relationship was more ambiguous. The accounts of the black Townsends, for example, differ as to when Reverend Jones freed Charity. One version says that he freed her immediately after purchasing her. Another holds that he freed her only just before her marriage to Luke. If the latter account is accurate, Jones owned a slave, a servant for his wife, for several years in the free state of Indiana.

A curious artifact appears in one county history: a photograph captioned "Dr. Layman slave quarters," apparently referring to the log cabins James Townsend put up for the former slaves who accompanied him to Indiana.[22] That local whites remembered them as "slave quarters" indicates they did not see the black Townsends as free or as independent of their white patrons.

This confusion about the so-called slave quarters reflects the ambiguous end of slavery in Indiana. Although the Northwest Ordinance of 1787 clearly prohibited slavery in the territory that became Indiana, French residents around Vincennes, who had held slaves since the 1700s, believed the prohibition was both an ex post facto law that could not apply retroactively to their slave property and a violation of the same ordinance's protections of the French residents' property rights. But the small number of French were not the only ones hoping to evade the Northwest Ordinance. Settlers from Virginia, including the territorial governor, William Henry Harrison, used indentures to circumvent the slavery prohibition. White Southerners would take their slaves into Indiana Territory and free them, provided that they signed contracts continuing their service—sometimes for decades. Supposedly, these indentures were freely contracted by the former slaves. Of course, the African Americans were well aware that they would be sold unless they agreed to the indenture.[23]

Many early white Hoosiers, however, did not want slavery. Their opposition stemmed not so much from antislavery impulses as from a dislike of African Americans and a resentment of aristocrats such as Harrison who could afford to keep such servants. In 1810, the indenture provision was repealed, and the state's first constitution declared in 1816 that "there shall be neither slavery nor involuntary servitude in this state." Most of the state's slaves lived in Knox County, where there was both an old French population and a newer Southern aristocracy. Knox County residents and the circuit court were slow to accept the constitution's prohibition. By contrast, when the Indiana Supreme Court heard the 1820 *Polly* case, in which a French-owned Vincennes slave sued for her freedom, the court ruled in Polly's favor, freeing her. The *Polly* case was followed the next year by the case of Mary Clark, an indentured servant. The state supreme court ruled that Clark's indenture was involuntary and freed her.

These cases supposedly meant the end of slavery and indentured servitude in the new state of Indiana. But small numbers of slaves continued to be held, mainly around Vincennes. The 1840 census showed three slaves in the state,

The "slave quarters" on Dr. Daniel W. Layman's farm. (From Putnam County Sesquicentennial Committee, *Journey through Putnam County History* [n.p., 1966], 352; courtesy of DePauw University Archives and Special Collections)

one of whom lived in Putnam County. Her identity is not known—but she lived in the household of John Davis in Russell Township and was between ten and twenty-four years old. No individual household members were listed in that census, but Jane Keath (or Keith), who would have been twenty-three in 1840, later appeared in the censuses of 1850 and 1860. Keath was a free black, born in Kentucky. She was alone in 1850, living in Jackson Township but ten years later was listed as a servant in the household of Caroline Crane, widow of merchant Abiathar Crane, in Monroe Township.[24] If Jane Keath was indeed the slave in the 1840 census, it is possible that blacks who went to Indiana from slavery first passed through a stage of quasi slavery in the free state before establishing their independence. And it may simply have taken some time for white residents of Putnam County, so many of whom had migrated from slaveowning states such as Kentucky, to accept the idea that blacks were anything other than slaves. Such factors may explain the "slave quarters" on Dr. Layman's property.

Luke and Charity Townsend lived near Ransom and Sarah Hawley in Putnamville. But relations with the Hawleys may have been somewhat strained.

As good Christians, the Townsends would surely have merited the concern of Ransom and Sarah Hawley had they been in need of aid. However, the Hawley papers contain a blank pledge form—a "Colonization Subscription"—for money to send blacks to Liberia.[25] If raising money for colonization was one of Reverend Hawley's charitable causes, the Townsends may not have been too friendly.

Luke and Charity Townsend worked hard to achieve modest wealth. A landless day laborer in 1850, Luke had within a decade acquired real estate valued at $400 and personal property of $200. It is not known how much of the Townsends' success resulted from the help of white patrons or neighbors such as the white Townsends, Dr. Layman, and the Hawleys. The Peters clan also prospered. Although the Stevenson family's descendants and the county historian tended to credit the Stevensons with the success of the Peters family, Tamar and her sons and daughters "were industrious and thrifty and by their combined labors accumulated money enough to buy forty acres of land a few miles southwest of Greencastle." This land was evidently the real estate that a census taker in 1850 valued at $700.[26]

For reasons unknown, the Peters family sold their farm in 1854 and shipped for Liberia. Sailing under the auspices of the American Colonization Society, they would find their passage longer and more eventful than that of other migrants. A few days into the voyage, the captain became paralyzed, and soon quarrels erupted between the first mate and crew, causing the ship to put in to the Cape Verde Islands, hundreds of miles off the African coast. After a new crew was hired, the *Euphrasia* sailed again for Liberia in mid-January. The Peters family would spend almost three months at sea.

According to local historian Weik, Tamar died en route and was buried at sea. However, the American Colonization Society's journal, *The African Repository*, says six deaths occurred on the passage, and Tamar Peters was not listed among them. After landing, some of the *Euphrasia*'s passengers were stricken with "the acclimating fever"—malaria. It is not known whether Tamar contracted malaria and possibly died from it, but such was a common fate among new colonists: indeed, some parties of migrants suffered mortality rates as high as 30 percent when they arrived in Liberia. Unlike slave migrants, the Peters family, as free blacks, had the advantage of superior diets and health, so they might have had greater resistance to disease. But as latecomers, they would have found lucrative commercial opportunities already monopolized by earlier migrants. The American Colonization Society provided emigrants only six months of support, insufficient for them to get established. Draft animals also succumbed to disease, leaving agriculture to be done with the hoe. Many colonists preferred to make a living by bartering with the natives, exchanging trade goods for export items such as dyewood, ivory, or palm oil.

Unsurprisingly, historian Eric Burin describes colonists' reaction to Liberia as one of "wary optimism followed by alarmed disenchantment." According to the Stevenson genealogy, Tamar's sons, George and Alexander, "honored their mother by becoming distinguished governmental officials in Liberia, Africa." Since black migrants from the United States formed the ruling elite of Liberia until the late twentieth century, this may indeed have been the case, although no record of George's and Alexander's government service has been found. In fact, aside from one dispatch indicating that the Peters family went first to Monrovia, no record of their life in Liberia has been discovered. They may have stayed in the capital: because life in the countryside was so difficult, many settlers preferred to remain in Monrovia.[27]

For white Hoosiers, colonization was one of several measures employed to minimize the state's black population. An 1831 law, for example, required black migrants to register with county authorities and post a $500 bond. Most infamously, the constitution of 1851 solidified Indiana's status as a "black law state"—a state with legal provisions against black rights—by explicitly denying suffrage to blacks. Even militia service was restricted to white men. Article 13 of the 1851 constitution forbade blacks from coming into the state. Submitted to voters in a ratification vote separate from the constitution itself, the measure was approved by an even larger margin than the constitution. At the same convention in which Putnam County Democrats avowed their belief in the "*political equality of man*," they also endorsed article 13 of the new state constitution—the black exclusion clause. And Putnam County voters were even more emphatic than other Hoosiers in endorsing black exclusion. Some 80 percent of Hoosiers voted for the constitution of 1851 and 84 percent for article 13. But in Putnam County, both the constitution and the article received even stronger endorsements, with 90 percent of Putnam voters supporting the constitution and 96 percent voting for article 13. These electoral results reveal that, however close the relationship between certain black and white families might have been, there was widespread hostility to African Americans in Putnam County. A convention of Indiana African Americans protested the black exclusion provision, but no delegate from Putnam County attended.[28]

Blacks often ignored the prohibition against migrating to Indiana, and

THE EXCLUDED RACE   87

many whites—in violation of the constitution—provided them employment and aid. One such case disturbed the county in 1859, when Tom and Agnes, former slaves of the Fisk family in Kentucky, arrived to live with Col. James Fisk in Monroe Township. The colonel's father had freed them, but because they were elderly, Fisk arranged to have them brought to his home in Indiana. Some of his neighbors "took offense at the presence of negroes in their midst," and led by William McCray, "they filed an affidavit against Colonel Fisk for violating the law which forbade the harboring of a negro." Weik maintains that "the case was tried in Greencastle and much feeling was aroused, but Tom and Agnes were not transported." He also says that Tom and Agnes lived with Colonel Fisk until their deaths, whereupon they were buried in the Brick Chapel Cemetery. Yet no account of this case appears in surviving court records or newspapers, nor is there a record of their burials anywhere in the county. The census records, however, indicate that, in 1850, an elderly Tom and Aggy Fisk lived in the household of David Bruton in Montgomery County, Kentucky. Twenty years later, Agnes Fisk was living in James Fisk's household in Putnam County.[29]

If McCray did indeed sue Colonel Fisk, he did so under the provisions of Article 13 of Indiana's 1851 constitution. That article not only forbade African Americans from migrating into the state but also provided that anyone who employed or encouraged a black who had migrated into the state could be fined up to $500. It further stipulated that fines collected from violators would be used to colonize Indiana blacks. A state fund for colonization was created by the 1852 legislature, and the state subsequently employed a colonization agent. At the end of 1853, the American Colonization Society received a payment of $2,000 "from the Indiana State Treasury, by Rev. J. Mitchell, toward the transportation and support of emigrants from Indiana."[30] Although the effort failed to persuade substantial numbers of free black Hoosiers to migrate, the state did not abandon it until the end of the Civil War. Midwestern states such as Indiana were more important to the American Colonization Society as a source of revenue than as a supplier of migrants. The Peters family's decision to migrate must have been a significant coup for the struggling Indiana colonization movement.[31]

White accounts of the migration of Tamar Peters and her children removed any agency from the black family. Both Margaretta Stevenson and Jesse Weik pointed to the constitution of 1851 as having caused the family's migration. Margaretta said "the family," meaning the Stevensons, felt the new constitution "restrained the negro[e]s of liberty," language she apparently borrowed from

A. C. Stevenson. (From
Jesse W. Weik, *History of
Putnam County, Indiana*
[Indianapolis, Ind.:
Bowen, 1910])

Weik, who wrote a half century before her. According to Weik, it was A. C. Stevenson's view that the constitution of 1851 "restrained them [the Peters family]
of liberty and he aided them to a home in the colony of Liberia." Margaretta
elaborated on the role of the Stevenson family, which "provided the means for
those who wished to return to Liberia; others to go to Canada," but whether
she was merely expounding family lore or following Weik is not known.[32] In
both accounts, however, all the decisions were made by the whites. It is not
clear whether the Peters clan wanted to migrate or not.

Margaretta also related that William Nelson Stevenson, A. C.'s younger
brother, occasionally received letters from a woman named Pearl in Liberia.
Pearl may have been a nickname for Priscilla, Tamar's oldest daughter. In one
such letter, Pearl (or Priscilla) asked William to send her shoes, size three. He
sent size nines instead because he knew her to be too proud to admit her real
size. The story served to reinforce the patronage relationship by showing how
the black family continued to seek aid from the white, and it also asserted the
power difference between them: it was, after all, the benevolent white man who
not only knew what was really best for the black woman but also had the means

to provide it. Priscilla's request also indicated the difficulty of life in Liberia. Black colonists writing for help were often reluctant to criticize their new country, for to do so would call into question their white patron's wisdom in sending them—not a politic move when help was needed. But the request itself indicated that Liberia was no paradise. Indeed, the poor reports from there would influence many blacks against migration.[33]

It is possible to know how A. C. Stevenson felt about black rights and to assess the limits of his benevolence. He was, after all, a delegate from Putnam to the constitutional convention that wrote article 13. And he did make a speech about black rights. He adamantly favored colonization, and what he said reveals that his relationship with the Peters clan may not have been as affectionate as later family historians would have liked to believe. Though he acknowledged the "obligations" of the white race to the black, he believed in "an unmistakeable inferiority, both as to physical and mental qualities in the African race," that rendered their ability to rise to the level of whites impossible and that in fact tended to degrade the whites among whom they lived. He pitied blacks and bore no ill will against white proponents of black rights. But he had a particular horror of "amalgamation," and it "pained" him to see the evidence of it in the faces of people on the streets of Indiana. (Was he thinking of light-skinned Ann Townsend?)

According to Stevenson, the "exclusive remedy" to blacks' current "degraded" condition was colonization. Still the paternalist, he insisted this was "the very best thing that can be done for their good, as well as our own." Perhaps his association with the Peters family had allowed him to witness the victimization of blacks by whites. He declared himself opposed to slavery, deploring how even free blacks were "despised in their social relations, and cheated in their business transactions. They have not the intellect to protect themselves from the white people, and, in fact, they are but little better off here than in slavery." Perhaps the Peters family had failed to be properly deferential, for Stevenson also argued that "as the blacks feel their strength, whether in numbers or in the grant of greater privileges, they are disposed to abuse them instead of being discreet and modest, and making use of those privileges to make themselves more intelligent and refined, and thus more agreeable to the dominant race." Although blacks could never rise to the level of whites in the United States, he asserted, they had enough intelligence to make a success of Liberia—to govern themselves, to become "happy and prosperous there," to Christianize and civilize "the now benighted and barbarous continent of Africa."

Unfortunately, he said, blacks—possibly including the Peters family—did not know their own best interests. "I am well aware that the blacks of this country are almost universally opposed to leaving this country, and emigrating to Liberia, but it is because they are ignorant of their real interests." As long as they had whites who advocated their rights, they would cherish their "delusive hopes" that Indiana was their home and "clamor for protection and political privileges." To convince free blacks to go to Africa, Stevenson sought the imprimatur of the convention: "To have the proper effect upon the colored population, they should be told from this chamber, by the voices of the people assembled, in the persons of their delegates, that they must emigrate to Liberia, and that they need hope for no extension of political privileges, and no amelioration of their present condition in Indiana."[34]

We cannot know whether the constitution of 1851 convinced a reluctant Tamar Peters and her family to leave for Liberia. Perhaps it was the clear evidence that their patron so badly wished to be rid of them that persuaded them. Certainly, they knew that black exclusion was merely the expression of a greater underlying racism. Even if an African American could legally reside in Indiana, he or she would not be accorded equality with white Hoosiers. State laws prohibited blacks from testifying in court cases to which whites were parties, and they also forbade intermarriage. In 1850, the Indiana Supreme Court ruled that blacks could not attend public schools, even if they paid tuition. Again, such discrimination was not always enforced. For example, the Stevenson family genealogy recalled that George and Alexander Peters had received their education in Greencastle's public schools. And Lucy Townsend, Luke and Charity's daughter, must have attended the white school, as there would have been insufficient population for a separate black school.[35] But even if these black children attended private schools such as Harriet Larrabee's, it is probable that in certain locales where the black population was small and did not excite local opposition, individual black children such as the Peters boys or Lucy Townsend could attend school with white children. A powerful patron such as A. C. Stevenson or Dr. Layman could also help. But Stevenson's support of the racist 1851 constitution made it clear he could not be relied on to look after the best interests of Tamar Peters and her children.

Black exclusion and state-sanctioned colonization were merely legal expressions of the white community's racism. A county history—written during the modern civil rights movement—records that when John Reel built a log mill on Big Walnut Creek, "the burrs were made from local boulders called 'nigger heads' and they lasted about ten years."[36] According to one reminiscence of nineteenth-century life, a controversy erupted when Ellen Verner Simpson, the wife of Asbury's president, allowed a black man to sit at the family table. The man was "Uncle" Henderson, "a good-hearted and inoffensive old negro." Henderson roomed in a wagon shop and worked for Dr. Matthew Simpson, Ellen's husband, and was well liked. "One day, being in a hurry to meet an engagement, Mrs. Simpson directed Henderson to take a seat at the dinner table with herself and the children." One of the school trustees, a Kentucky-born man, heard of this lapse in etiquette and criticized Matthew Simpson so vociferously that some mistakenly attributed his subsequent resignation from Asbury to this unpleasantness.[37]

The 1850s were fateful for free black rights, not just in Indiana but nationally. As part of the Compromise of 1850, Congress passed a new fugitive slave law. The previous law, in force since 1793, made recapturing runaways the responsibility of local law enforcement and local juries. Southern slaveowners complained that it was ineffective. But the 1850 law gave jurisdiction to federal authorities. Not only would a federal marshal aid the slaveowner in pursuing a runaway slave but a federal commissioner would hear the case without a jury. In a provision that angered many Northerners, the magistrate in such a case was paid $10 for ruling the alleged runaway a slave but only $5 for a judgment of freedom. Attempts to return fugitives provoked controversy in Boston, where federal troops were used to ensure the return of Anthony Burns to his Virginia master, and in Cincinnati, where Margaret Garner desperately cut her young daughter's throat as slave catchers surrounded her family.[38]

No such cases troubled Putnam County's peace, although runaway slaves occasionally passed through. In September 1860, two boys made a discovery in a field south of Greencastle. Their hound led them to a sinkhole and began to circle it. Inside were two young black men. They explained that they had escaped from their master near Franklin, Tennessee, and had made it into Indiana with the help of other blacks and Underground Railroad agents. Having left Mooresville, Indiana, the night before, they were headed for the farm of Parker S. Browder, an 1857 immigrant from Ohio, but they had failed to make it before daylight. One of the runaways had taken ill with chills. Awaiting nightfall, they had concealed themselves in the sinkhole. The local boys took news of their discovery to Browder. That night, the runaways were escorted to his farm, where they were "safely lodged in the garret of his wash house" for three or four days. When the sick man, Jim, had recovered, Browder decided to have some flour ground—not locally—but at a distant water mill, in Parke County. He made the 25-mile trip in a covered wagon, concealing its real cargo. The runaways eventually reached Canada.

It is not certain whether Browder was "active" on the Underground Railroad, but it is clear that his abolitionist opinions made him enemies locally. As an adult, one of the white boys involved in this incident, Joseph M. Donnohue, recalled that most people in Putnam were as "ready and anxious to pounce upon a runaway nigger" as the boys' hound had been. This may have been so. When a Putnam County jury heard the case of a runaway slave named Jane who had escaped from Tennessee in 1836, it ordered the woman returned to her owner.[39] And yet, this was precisely the kind of local jury that Southern slaveowners feared as too sympathetic to blacks—and that the 1850 Fugitive Slave Act would eliminate.

Putnam County's Whig congressman, Ned McGaughey, voted for the Fugitive Slave Act. This caused him some unpopularity in the district, but the county supported the law.[40] A post-Compromise public meeting of prominent Putnam County Whigs and Democrats discussed the necessity for the "North as well as the South, to respect the prej[u]dices and feelings of each other, and cultivate feelings of mutual forbearance and respect for the interests and rights of all." Although there was no specific mention of what the South could do to placate the North, the resolutions specifically called for "protection to the South against the negro stealing citizens of the North." In concluding, participants in the meeting resolved "that we have not permitted or countenanced the abduction of slaves from the slave States, and will not countenance negro stealing any sooner than horse stealing."[41] McGaughey considered the fugitive law popular enough in the district to quote his political opponent, John G. Davis, as having called the law "a disgrace to the American Statute book," evidently feeling that such a view might hurt Davis with the voters.[42]

The best-selling novel *Uncle Tom's Cabin*, with a runaway slave as a key protagonist, provoked a hostile reaction from some in the county. A correspondent of the *Putnam County Sentinel* condemned the "vanity and wickedness" in every chapter: "Profanity and rough uncouth language is abundant, especially in the first volume; while insubordination to the laws of our common country, is inculcated with open boldness." The writer was surprised at the novel's popularity with ministers. "If novel-reading is wrong, it is wrong to read Uncle Tom's Cabin," he asserted before suggesting that perhaps the ministers made an exception for this novel "because they prefer black heroes and heroines to

THE EXCLUDED RACE 93

white ones?"[43] Having once condemned novel reading as equivalent to drinking and gambling, the clergy now made Harriet Beecher Stowe's fiction into a holy book. The *Sentinel* agreed that this novel was different from other works of fiction, "for its mischief-making propensities, its dangerous and degrading tendencies, has had no equal in this or any other age." But even if the melodramatic novel had a local following, many settlers in Putnam County felt no pressing antislavery impulse. Many had come from the slave state of Kentucky, where some had owned slaves themselves.[44]

Nor did local churches preach abolitionism. Russell E. Richey points out that Methodism, whose antislavery sentiment "came laced with racism," "evidenced a deep ambivalence over slavery." Viewing slavery as a metaphor for satanic rule, early Methodists reached out to blacks but could not entirely bring themselves to accept them as equals. Yet Methodism was problack enough to attract black adherents and charismatic black leaders such as Harry Hosier, who, ironically, may have given his name (or a variant of it) as the nickname for the state's residents. By the 1830s, antislavery activity was becoming common in Indiana churches, and in 1841, the Methodist Indiana State Wesleyan Antislavery Society formed. Methodists were still divided, however, between those who favored withdrawing church membership from slaveowners and those who preferred to ignore the issue. But there does not seem to have been any argument about slavery within the Putnam County churches. Although the county's Presbyterians fissured in 1850, this rift was due more to disagreements about theological doctrines than slavery. Catholics were preoccupied with acquiring a church in Greencastle and countering anti-immigrant hostility. At the national level, the Catholic Church did not make slavery an issue. And though an Asbury student condemned slavery in an 1854 oration and an 1855 debate, there is no indication of a debate over slavery's morality in Putnam's Methodist or Baptist churches.[45]

The 1860 census suggests that a decade of formal as well as informal hostility to black rights had taken a toll on Putnam County's black population. Of the black families listed ten years earlier, only the Townsends remained. The Peters clan, of course, had left for Liberia, and the Cowells, Pollares, and Waldens were no longer in Putnam either. Of the twenty-two blacks remaining in the county in 1860, thirteen were Townsends. Hetty Townsend was living as a servant with Professor Fletcher's family, but Luke and Charity still maintained a household in Greencastle Township. They now owned property, and their family had grown in the past decade from five to ten children. John, their eleventh and youngest child, would be born in 1861. All but one of the black children under ten in Putnam County were Luke and Charity's, as were five of the seven young black people between ten and twenty. The other African Americans were living as individual workers or dependents in white households. Jane Keath (now listed as Keith) remained in the county, as did John Jordan, eighteen and a laborer in Greencastle. There were two other black Jordans in Putnam county: four-year-old Topy, who lived in lawyer and politician Henry Secrest's household in Cloverdale Township, and twenty-year-old Harrison, a laborer living with William H. Shields in Greencastle's Second Ward. It seems likely that Topy and Harrison were related to the other Jordans: Mary and Jane, who no longer appeared in the census, would now be young women in their twenties.

As for the other laborers in Putnam back in 1850, the aged Lucy may have died in the interim, for she was not listed in the 1860 census. Young Reuben also did not appear there, nor did Vince, a Kentucky-born black man who was forty-seven in 1850—unless perhaps he was the man listed as Vincent, now fifty-six but said to be born in Tennessee. Four single men, ranging in age from eighteen to thirty-five, worked as laborers in households headed by others. William Scott was a thirty-year-old mulatto cook at one of Greencastle's hotels. And thirty-five-year-old Henderson Kemper, an illiterate day laborer born in Virginia, lived in Luke Townsend's household.[46]

The decline in Putnam County's black population by 1860 may reflect the toll taken by Indiana's 1851 constitution as well as by the federal Fugitive Slave Act of 1850. Their results seem to have fallen harder on Putnam blacks than on other black Hoosiers. Emma Lou Thornbrough, the leading authority on Indiana's African Americans, blamed the state constitution and the federal fugitive law for the slow pace of the black population's growth in the state over the decade.[47] But even as the black population grew, albeit slowly, across Indiana as a whole, in Putnam it declined. Its composition shifted away from families and toward single laborers who lived mostly in white households. African Americans were necessarily dependent on whites for employment. And despite the fact that patronage relationships were emphasized in whites' accounts of their relations with blacks in the county, A. C. Stevenson's eagerness to expel the black population indicates that such ties may actually have been detrimental to black interests. We cannot know what motivated Abraham and Love Cowell, David and Zilpha Pollare, Edward and Julia Walden—or even Tamar Peters and her family—to leave the county, but perhaps they drew their own conclusions from Stevenson's push for colonization: that leading white patrons could not be relied on for aid and that Putnam was not friendly to African Americans. If Tamar Peters and her hard-working sons—a family that had acquired property and education—were not wanted, then perhaps no blacks could feel welcome.

The 1850 Fugitive Slave Act may also have been responsible for the disappearance of some of Putnam County's blacks. Out-migration was common in the nineteenth century, especially among those with little property or small stake in a locale. Many whites in Putnam had left the county by 1860, and new ones had come in, causing an overall increase in population. Blacks were leaving Putnam County, too, but not enough new black migrants came in to stem the overall population loss. The 1850s was a period when Northern blacks felt threatened not only by the ease with which fugitives might now be reclaimed but also by the possibility that even free blacks might be identified as runaway property and taken for a hearing before a federal commissioner who had a monetary incentive to find them slaves. This scenario might explain why the Cowells, despite their substantial property, or the Pollares, Waldens, and the laborer Reuben were no longer in the county in 1860. In fact, the Cowells, Pollares, and Waldens do not appear in the U.S. census at all. Like many Northern blacks, they may have decided Canada offered a safer home than their own country, where they were now subject to recapture or kidnapping under the Fugitive Slave Act of 1850. An estimated 20,000 African Americans fled to Canada after the act passed.[48] The fugitive law might even have played a role in convincing Tamar Peters and her family to leave for Liberia, for even free blacks were vulnerable to kidnappers.

In its racism, Indiana was very like the rest of the North. African Americans were few and seemingly unimportant. As Ned McGaughey and John G. Davis had found, however, the issues of race and slavery expansion evoked powerful emotions in a society wedded to white supremacy. Over the course of the Civil War era, a striking change in the county's race relations would occur. In the 1850s, Putnam County residents might know an occasional free black—probably a former slave, possibly someone with ties to a powerful white patron. But within a decade, this was less likely. Black families, already scarce, continued to leave, and the remaining free blacks found themselves further isolated. Ironically, as state and federal law accomplished A. C. Stevenson's goal of persuading Putnam's blacks to leave, African Americans in the abstract would assume new importance to the political life of the county, lent immediacy by a civil war that made real previously unimaginable changes in race relations.

PART 2
THE WAR

4

THE COPPERHEADS

       Dr. Daniel W. Layman, the Townsend family's white patron, was a strong Union man during the Civil War. One night in the fall of 1864, Warren Township Democrats returning from a campaign meeting at Greencastle passed by Layman's house and "very loudly and repeatedly cheered for Jeff Davis." Layman happened to be outside, unseen in the dark. Angry, the doctor "picked up a stone and hurled it with all his might in the direction of the noise." Not long after, someone arrived at the house and asked the doctor to tend a hurt man. A little way down the road, the doctor found a group "in the centre of which reclined a man who was bleeding profusely from a wound in the head which his companions explained had been caused by a fall from a horse." Layman treated the cut and pretended to believe the story of its cause. When his patient later came to pay him, he refused the money, "meanwhile reminding him of the dangerous and inevitable results of cheering for Jeff Davis."[1]

    Layman's story was rendered less amusing by the reality that the war exposed frightening rifts in the county. The ordinary high jinks of political life—fisticuffs at election rallies or the polls—became deadly serious. Democrats armed themselves to resist Republican war policy, and Republicans charged them with conspiring to aid the Confederacy. Democratic politicians such as Daniel Voorhees blamed secession on Northern "anti-slavery agitation."[2] And though Republicans had insisted in the 1860 election that they had no intention of undermining white supremacy, the Lincoln administration's policies seemed to belie that claim.

After the Emancipation Proclamation, Mary Vermilion wrote her soldier husband, William, how it was rumored among their relatives that Indiana would secede and that "great black 'niggers'" would invade the state. She quoted Judge Delana Eckels, who was a leading Copperhead, or Peace Democrat, as saying, "There are 2,000 men in Putnam County just awaiting the tap of the drum, to rise up against the Administration."[3] In addition to emancipation, Copperheads objected to the implementation of the Whig economic program of a national bank, paper currency, and a high tariff by the Republicans. Peace Democrats saw Republicans as seizing on the pretext of war to violate civil liberties by suspending the writ of habeas corpus and instituting the first military conscription in U.S. history.[4] Not just Eckels but many other local Democrats participated in antidraft mobs and election riots, among them another stalwart Democratic politician of the prewar era, Solomon Akers, and a young man who would become one of Putnam County's most prominent Democrats of the postwar period, Harrison M. Randel.

The paucity of sources left by the Copperheads themselves and the self-interest of the Republicans in promulgating a great Copperhead conspiracy that legitimized Republican actions have left historians uncertain as to whether the Copperheads merely expressed antiwar sentiments that should be permissible in a free society (although rarely tolerated with good grace during wartime) or if they actually intended to aid the Confederacy, as the Republicans often charged. In Putnam County, Republicans noted that Eckels appeared jubilant at the news of the Union defeat at the first battle of Bull Run. If they had known that he was also in correspondence with a former law student who had joined the Confederate cavalry, it would only have further confirmed their suspicions of Copperhead treason.[5] Putnam County's Copperheads were certainly antidraft and antiblack. They may have skirted the line between loyalty and treason, but one cannot say for certain that they crossed it. Instead, they opposed the war as unconstitutional, rejected the draft because it threatened to make cannon fodder of them in a war they opposed, and objected to emancipation because it overturned white supremacy.

In February 1861, a Cloverdale Union meeting endorsed the Crittenden compromise and favored a convention of border states to resolve the crisis. The meeting was described as "irrespective of party," but since the Republicans had rejected the Crittenden compromise, some saw it as the work of local Democrats. Although the final resolution promised "that we will not abandon the Union until all of the remedies and guarantees the Constitution contains shall first prove powerless for our equality and safety in the Union," it nonetheless hinted that those in the meeting might secede if they, like the South, felt the Constitution was being subverted.[6]

The lead author of the committee of resolutions was Solomon Akers. His family had been in Putnam County since the earliest settlement in the 1820s. During the prewar decade, Akers, a longtime county Democrat, regularly served as a delegate from Cloverdale to county meetings and state party conventions as well as on resolution committees at party meetings. He may have earned some of his income in the law, for he was admitted as an attorney before the circuit court, but the larger portion probably derived from "retailing" alcohol. He had held many local offices, including township trustee, township treasurer, and notary public. At Cloverdale, he was postmaster, a plum political patronage job, from 1855 until the advent of the new Lincoln administration. He had always been a Democrat and "always loved" the party.[7] In the postwar years, the Republican newspaper eulogized Akers, who was now safely dead, as

> a bold, daring, outspoken Democrat; sometimes rash and overbearing toward his political opponents, and for years . . . justly regarded as a tower of strength in his party. In some of his opinions he was an extreme man. As a friend he was true, as an enemy to be feared; a man of great force of will; an untiring worker, and no man in this County rendered more effective service to his party organization than he.[8]

Influential though he was, Akers was a controversial figure. When he ran for county sheriff in 1858, Republicans charged that he had gotten the nomination "by duplicity, trickery and bargain" and that he had thus gained "a rather unenviable notoriety in his Township." He lost narrowly. Two years later, he failed to get the party's nomination for the same position.[9] After losing the sheriff's race, Akers set out to punish his opponents, including a Cloverdale Mexican War veteran, John B. Sackett, who had voted against him. The defeated candidate threatened to get Sackett's pension revoked.[10]

During the Lecompton controversy, Akers had first sided with Congressman

John G. Davis, but then he embraced the English compromise "as being the antidote for the poisenous Lecompton fraud."[11] He objected to Davis's decision to run as an independent because it would "injure the Democratic party," and he warned the congressman that their "warm personal friend[ship]" would not stop Akers from working against him. Akers had long been a tough Democratic infighter when the war further threatened a party split.[12]

Many Democrats, often followers of Stephen A. Douglas, actively supported the war. Col. Lewis H. Sands—Greencastle storekeeper, former Indian agent, and Democratic partisan—served as a chief recruiter in the spring.[13] Even Henry Secrest gave a three-hour speech in Greencastle in support of the Lincoln administration.

> [He] insisted that there could be but two parties—patriots and traitors; that he who was not for the Government was against it; that there could be no neutral ground. He was not for subjugating any section, but for conquering a peace by crushing out the rebellion. He was for war so long as traitors were in arms, and believed it to be the duty of every loyal citizen to contribute his last dollar, and even his blood to preserve the government.[14]

Sands and Secrest cooperated with local Republicans such as Greencastle mayor Marshall A. Moore in supporting the war effort.[15]

Despite these patriotic effusions, other Democrats were less willing to give the Lincoln administration unqualified endorsement. An Illinois man regarded Putnam County as "filled with unsuppressed treason" and claimed

> that there are several hundred men in this county—this old county of Putnam— who would rejoice to see the "Rattle-Snake Banner" floating aloft from your Court-house.—Not a few of them take Secession papers and openly rejoice and gloat over the treason they have inculcated. Many of them—nearly all perhaps— declare themselves for the Union on conditions, provided, if, but, &c., but these conditions—concede all that the rebels in arms ask for.[16]

When Peace Democrats sympathized with the constitutional arguments of the Confederacy, War Democrats and Republicans condemned their scruples as treasonous.

The Southern heritage of Putnam County residents also prompted questions as to their loyalties. The *Indianapolis Daily Journal* deemed the outpouring of three companies from Putnam after Fort Sumter all the "more striking as Putnam was settled largely by Kentuckians" and as Daniel Voorhees's speech was expected to have "extinguished" support for the war. Eckels and Akers were both born in Kentucky. Many Southern-born Hoosiers harbored traditional regional prejudices, especially against New England, which they felt enjoyed too much support from the Lincoln administration, particularly in its tariff policy, whereas western farmers suffered an economic disaster brought on by the closing of the Mississippi River. Democrats of Montgomery and Putnam counties met jointly in early 1863 and condemned the draft for allegedly favoring New England.[17]

Unionists in Putnam were aware of these sectional cleavages. Participants at an 1863 Union meeting resolved that they regarded "with horror the insidious efforts which are now being made by certain politicians to disturb the good neighborhood and hearty sympathy that hitherto existed between the Great North-West and New England States."[18] Nonetheless, regional ties to the South further encouraged Putnam residents to empathize with that region. Mary Vermilion quoted John Runyan, a relative of her husband's, as saying "that 'the Northern soldiers have gone South just to steal the Southern men's property, and he didn't blame the rebels to kill them, and he would kill them if he were in their places,' and much more like it."[19]

If Union men felt menaced by disloyal sentiments, some Democrats felt imperiled by the intolerance for antiwar sentiments. At a July 1861 meeting of Democrats, for example, Arch Johnson claimed he had been threatened because he viewed the war as "positive and eternal ruin." And Col. Austin M. Puett was called a secessionist because he favored the Crittenden compromise and blamed the war on the Republicans' refusal to agree. When Puett replied by threatening to break the mouth of the person who impugned his loyalty, the Republican newspaper questioned his commitment to free speech.[20] For these Democrats, the ruling question had become not union or disunion, not loyalty or treason but "liberty or despotism." The New Maysville man who so phrased it told John G. Davis, "Since writing the above I am told by an abolitionist that if we persist in our course the state will be put under marshal law. Will the people bear it. I think not."[21]

Free speech, according to a mass meeting of Putnam County Democrats at which Davis spoke, was a constitutional right "formidable to tyrants only." Davis's themes were Republican responsibility for the war and abolition. Although the South had acted "too hastily" in his view, "the election of a Black Republican, sectional President was sufficient to show the South that their institutions were no longer safe." Davis, who saw the war's purpose as abolition, favored an armistice until compromise could be achieved.²² Participants at the convention, which met a week after the first battle of Bull Run, lamented the failure of the Crittenden compromise and condemned those, such as Governor Oliver P. Morton, "who directly or indirectly plunged us into this unnatural war with our brethren." But they were

> desirous to maintain our national Union, without the loss of a single star from the glorious national galaxy. We will therefore vote for men and money to suppress rebellion, be it North or South, so long as the military shall be needed for that purpose, but when perverted so as to interfere with the constitutional rights of any of the people of the several States, we will then vote against men and money and the prosecution of the war.

Because there was an "honest difference" about the constitutionality of slavery, these Democrats proposed to resolve the ambiguity with "an amendment to the Constitution that will expressly state the right of the people in regard to the subject, and put to an *eternal sleep* the nigger question, which has agitated our country for the last twenty years."²³ After Davis finished, someone rose and announced that Douglas Democrats such as John Osborn and Delana Williamson would speak at the courthouse. The *Parke County Republican* reported that the Democrats then "*seceded* in a body" to hear the Union speeches. A month later, at a meeting of the Putnam County Union Democracy, these Democrats endorsed Stephen A. Douglas's last speech, with its insistence that, in this crisis, there were "only patriots or traitors." The Union Democrats intended to be the former, fighting "to defend and maintain the supremacy of the Constitution, and to preserve the Union." Despite John G. Davis's suspicion that the war's whole purpose was abolition, Union Democrats insisted that "the war ought to cease" as soon as the government's authority was restored. Republicans began to call Davis's followers the "Jeff. Davis Democracy," both stigmatizing them as disloyal and setting them apart from the War Democrats.²⁴

John Davis had taken a strong stand against the war at its outset and remained a controversial figure, but he was now out of office and in poor health. He would die in 1866. Leadership of the Seventh District had passed to his controversial successor, Daniel Voorhees, who was Indiana's leading Copperhead. Voorhees would maintain his popularity in the district. Politically minded families in the nineteenth century often named their children after politicians they admired. So James and Mary Brown Miller named their first daughter, born in 1860, Eliza Voorhees Miller. Edmond Huffman named a son born in 1864

Daniel Voorhees, c. 1861.
(Courtesy of DePauw
University Archives and
Special Collections)

Daniel Voorhees (and another born in 1868 after Andrew Jackson). And William and Susanna Etcheson named their son, born in 1863, Daniel Voorhees Etcheson.[25] Elections, of course, were another measure of popularity, and Voorhees easily held on to his seat in 1862. The Republicans courted former governor Joseph A. Wright, a War Democrat, as their candidate, but he declined "the honor of being beaten." The nominee who received that honor was Harvey D. Scott, the former congressman.[26]

Unionists recognized that Copperhead sentiment rose with victory and fell with defeat, but they interpreted as pro-Confederate sympathy what was instead simple horror at the war's human costs. "Secessionists have . . . been a little saucy since the battle of Shiloh," John A. Matson reported. But he also predicted that "success at Yorktown & Corinth will silence Secessionists in Indiana."[27] Similarly, Gen. William T. Sherman's occupation of Atlanta was considered the definitive answer to Copperheads who purportedly believed the conquest of the South to be impossible.[28]

Voorhees questioned the need to sustain the terrible costs. In May 1864, he reported to Davis about nine days of "almost continuous battle between

Grant & Lee," noting that "there has been no result thus far except slaughter." Though Voorhees acknowledged that Grant might be able to wear Lee down by sheer numbers—"reinforcements are going night and day to Grant"—no end of the war seemed likely without a Democratic victory in the presidential race.[29]

Democrats also feared that continued war would fundamentally alter the United States. If abolitionists succeeded in making their cause a war aim, white supremacy would be undermined not only in the South but also in the entire nation. The Seventh Congressional District convention, which met in Terre Haute to nominate Voorhees for reelection in 1862, addressed this threat to white supremacy. Democrats insisted that they favored "a vigorous prosecution of the existing war for the sole purpose of restoring the rightful authority of the government of the United States throughout its entire territory, and when this is accomplished the war ought to cease." However, they wanted the restored Union to be identical to its prewar incarnation, promising the seceded states "all your rights as heretofore." Three of the eight resolutions from the convention—and these the lengthiest—concerned emancipation. One resolved to "resist, by all proper and constitutional means, all efforts to use the war for the purpose of emancipating the slaves under any pretext." Another professed alarm at labor competition from free blacks and called for "the most stringent legislation" to enforce article 13 of Indiana's constitution, which forbade black migration into the state. The third resolution opposed compensated emancipation and abolition in the District of Columbia.[30] Two months later, Democrats' fears were realized when Lincoln made his preliminary announcement of emancipation.

Democrats won the 1862 elections in Indiana, claiming seven of eleven congressional seats and control of the state legislature. Further success in other Northern states caused Democrats to hope that Lincoln might back away from his policies, especially the Emancipation Proclamation. But the president was determined. At a meeting held in early February 1863, Democrats from southern Montgomery and northern Putnam counties accused "this Abolition Administration" of having lied about its war aims. Despite pledging not to interfere with slavery where it already existed, the administration "with shameless impudence and perfidy changed the suppression of the rebellion and the restoration of the Union to the suppression of the constitution and the liberation of the negro."[31]

As the administration made emancipation a war aim, Democratic reservations about the conflict turned to opposing its prosecution. A few weeks later, Delana Eckels called to order a meeting of Putnam County Democrats, which would soon issue a series of resolutions. The first called for "a cessation of hostilities, for such period as may be necessary to allow the people of the North and South to express, through a national convention, their wish for peace and a maintenance of 'the Union as it was, under the Constitution as it is.'" Although Putnam Democrats insisted they remained "unalterably attached to the Federal Union," they feared that Lincoln was now waging an unconstitutional war for abolition. The Emancipation Proclamation merited particular condemnation for "pretending to liberate the slaves of the South, and inviting them to servile insurrection and deeds of a most inhuman character." The proclamation was characterized as "a disgrace to the age in which we live," and, considered in the context of the abolition of slavery in the District of Columbia and the removal of "conservative Generals" such as George McClellan, it was deemed to reveal the war's true purpose. Reiterating Voorhees's vow "that not another soldier, and not another dollar, ought to be furnished for the further prosecution of this war for negro emancipation," the Democrats asserted they opposed abolition because "we believe that our Fathers established this Government for the benefit of the white man alone; and in considering the terms of settlement of our national troubles we will look only to the welfare, peace and safety of the white race, without reference to the effect that settlement may have upon the condition of the African."

Although they condemned the war's new goal, Putnam Democrats insisted on their faith in the soldiers. In fact, they feared Indiana troops would "be subject to the control of shoulder-strapped negroes," although War Department policy did not provide for black officers.[32] Uneasy since the secession crisis about fighting against their native region, Putnam Democrats now rebelled at a war to place African Americans not just on a level equal with whites but potentially superior to them.

Mary Vermilion discovered that the proclamation resonated powerfully with her husband's Copperhead kinfolk. When she asked John Vermilion, her brother-in-law, why he opposed the government, he replied that "he always hated a nigger; and when it comes to fighting with niggers he could not stand it." Mary asked him, "Have you *seen* a negro since the Proclamation?" He had not. Although he could accept blacks as army laborers, he thought having black soldiers was not "respectable." That George Washington and Andrew Jackson had used black soldiers "staggered him."[33]

Not mentioned in the Putnam County resolutions was the nation's first conscription. States were required by the Militia Act of July 1862 to meet certain quotas of men. Any states failing to induce the required number of men to volunteer might have to resort to conscription. Then, in March 1863, Congress passed a draft law. The draft became one of the most controversial issues affecting the home front.[34] Democrats regarded conscription as an unconstitutional and tyrannical violation of individual liberty; for Republicans, however, it was the opposition to conscription that was treasonous. The draft may have made Unionists less tolerant of free speech. A Manhattan man warned Republican officials about the suspicious activities of Warren Grimwell and Jacob Etter, who were "undoubtedly Southern Sympathizers, and who on last night made a regular Secesh Speach and in the course made the remark that Hell was full of such Governments, and more on the way. They also were the direct cause of Some 4 or 5 men not vol-ing in my humble Opinion."[35] Perhaps Grimwell and Etter really did endorse the Confederacy, or perhaps it was their condemnation of Republican policies—and the effect that condemnation had on volunteering— that left them open to the suspicion of harboring Confederate sympathies.

State Democrats met in May 1863 amid growing tension. Fights involving convention delegates broke out in the streets of Indianapolis, and some Democrats were arrested for carrying concealed weapons. Ohio Copperhead Clement Vallandigham had been arrested by the military in that state for speaking against the war and hence interfering with the draft. Convicted by a military commission, he was sentenced to imprisonment for the war's duration. In an attempt to quell the political storm that followed, Lincoln had him exiled to the Confederacy. In Indianapolis, Daniel Voorhees condemned the arrest in a speech outside the statehouse. Later, armed soldiers entered the hall during Thomas A. Hendricks's speech, causing the convention to adjourn.

As trains carried Democrats home, military authorities stopped them to search for weapons, claiming passengers had fired out the windows. Hundreds of revolvers were confiscated, and in addition, so many weapons were thrown out the train windows and into a local creek that the incident became known as the battle of Pogue's Run. Republicans insisted that the Democrats had planned an uprising, as was plain from their heavy armaments. But Democrats claimed that the incident, along with the recent brief suppression of some Democratic newspapers in Indiana, proved the despotism of the Republican administration.[36] The list of Democratic delegates from Putnam County has not survived, but even if Judge Eckels and Sol Akers escaped the harassment suffered by Democratic delegates in Indianapolis, they would have doubtless heard of it and been outraged.

A month later, as Republican officials began to implement the draft, Democratic outrage was expressed in other ways. The provost marshal for the Seventh Congressional District, Richard Thompson, offered enrolling officers $3 per day for about a week's work. Yet despite the generous pay, some in Putnam County did not want the job. H. M. Rockwell declined, it not being "convenient" for him to attend to this business, and recommended another man. In a note appended to the bottom of Rockwell's letter, Thompson or a clerk wrote, "I have just understood vengeance is declared against the man that enrolls the militia of this township."[37] It is not known who threatened Rockwell, but Cloverdale Township was the home of Sol Akers, who was not one to back away from a fight.

Many Indiana counties saw draft-related violence and resistance. Historian Jennifer L. Weber says, "Indiana was the most tense and violent state in this fraught period."[38] Republicans believed that Copperheads were arming themselves in order to resist the draft. In spring 1863, the Greencastle Democratic newspaper reported that "the authorities have forbidden hardware and notion establishments to sell fire arms and ammunition."[39] Thompson heard rumors that Copperheads camped in western Putnam County intended to raid neighboring Parke County and seize the weapons of its home guards.[40] In Greencastle, Matilda Cavins wrote her soldier husband of alarming rumors "that Secessionists are threatening to burn this town" as part of the statewide draft resistance.[41] An attack on enrolling officer James Sill would be the local Copperheads' major act of draft resistance in Putnam County.

James Sill had the longest employment period of Thompson's appointees—eleven days—perhaps because he encountered trouble in conducting the enrollment. A local lawyer and member of a home guard company, Sill was the enrolling officer for Marion Township, where his family had a home along Deer Creek. In the 1850s, Sill served terms as justice of the peace and notary public, and he was a well-respected member of the community. His support for the Union, however, caused a breach with old friends and neighbors. And Sill's Baptist church, adhering to its Copperhead sentiments, expelled him even though he had been a member for twenty-seven years.[42]

In completing the June 1863 enrollment, Sill used paperwork from the previous year, entering names and ages. On the day before the enrollment was to be delivered, he noticed men watching his house and became concerned for the safety of his work. His daughter, seventeen-year-old Candace, hid his papers in a salt barrel. Unbeknownst to Candace, her mother later moved them. That evening, suitors called on Candace and her sister Harriet. Upon leaving the house, one of the young men, Lawson Fry, was startled to find men concealed in the woods near the Sills' gate. Candace remembered 300 men, but the actual number was probably about 50. Postwar reports claimed that the men had stolen lead piping from the sawmills to make bullets. Although someone in the crowd recognized Fry and called out not to shoot, a bullet struck him in the shoulder. Fry staggered back to the Sill house and gave the alarm.[43]

At the house, Elizabeth Groves Sill urged her husband to take the papers and make a run for it, but he refused. With the mob approaching the front door, Elizabeth removed the papers from where she had hidden them and slipped out the back. James then urged his children to follow their mother. Harriet complied, dashing through the men like "a hunted gazelle," as Candace later put it, fully expecting to be shot. However, the mob ignored her as she tore her way through "tangled briers and brush, over fence and brooks" to a neighbor's house. Candace, unable to persuade her father to leave, was unwilling to follow her mother and Harriet. She recalled declaring, "Father, I will not leave you; I will die by your side." The mob surrounded the house, beating on the walls and doors. Finally, the leader gave Sill an ultimatum: turn over the papers in three minutes or be shot. Candace, believing the papers were still hidden in the salt barrel, offered to retrieve them, but her father shook his head no. With his daughter at his side, he went out onto the porch. Candace berated the crowd, calling them "cowards and copperheads," and held up a lantern, hoping to see their faces. Finally, her father brought out the enrollment book and papers from the previous year. One of the crowd called out to Sill, "Throw them down or I'll shoot." Sill dropped the papers. Another pulled his coat over his head to disguise himself and took the papers, saying, "We've got them; let's go." Several men fired their guns, but the crowd left.

James, of course, did not have the papers. Elizabeth had fled with them into the backyard. About fifty yards from the house, Elizabeth's foot struck a board, under which she hastily stuffed the papers. Two men seized her and demanded to know if she had the enrollment forms. She stood on the board while they searched her. Not finding anything, they returned to the crowd banging at the front door.[44]

Local Unionists were shocked by the attack on the Sill house. A Fillmore meeting condemned it and promised to bring the perpetrators to justice. Gen. John L. Mansfield of the Indiana Legion (the state militia), accompanied by Arch Johnson, addressed the audience.[45] The *Greencastle Press* advised, "Every good citizen should endeavor to allay the commotion by minding his own business and offering no resistance to the laws, or those entrusted with their execution."[46] Since the Sills had recognized several of their attackers, soldiers helped the civil officials make arrests in Marion Township.[47] Despite the Democratic newspaper's appeal for cooperation, in Monroe Township, William T. Scott received an anonymous note threatening local "abolitionists" who had sworn charges against four local Democrats. The note demanded that the men responsible for the arrests either raise the money to pay the fines—expected to amount to the hefty sum of $500—or "have your stock poisoned your Barns burnt and lives lost."[48]

Despite the threats, the U.S. District Court at Indianapolis heard draft resistance cases from Putnam and other counties in September. Joseph Ellis of Putnam, who was tried by jury for conspiracy and obstructing the enrollment, received a $500 fine. After his conviction, the defense attorney asked John Hanna, now the U.S. district attorney, to drop the charge of conspiracy against his other clients, who would agree to accept a guilty verdict for obstructing the enrollment. Hanna consented. Fifteen men paid fines of $25, and Hanna dismissed three other cases. One of those fined was Harrison M. Randel. When Randel became a prominent county Democrat in the 1870s, Republicans liked to remember him as the leader of the mob that attacked Sill's house. But Randel was only twenty-five in 1863. Born in Monroe Township, where his parents had settled after migrating from Kentucky, he had probably known the Sills all his life. He had been a teacher and farm laborer until 1862, when he began what would be a lifelong political career by gaining election to the office of county surveyor.[49]

Although probably only a member, not a leader, of the mob at the Sill house, Randel did play a leading role in the intimidation of another draft officer, H. T. Craig, who served as the enrolling officer in Monroe Township. Craig first discovered a threatening note in his front yard: "If you dont lay aside the enrolling your life will be taken before tomorrow night and you had better take our advise as friends. we dont expect interrupt you but we have heard men a vengeous against you they say you had better stay at home and you had better take our advise and stay at home." When he continued enrolling, a committee led by Randel visited him. Randel "told him to drop the business for they would shoot him if he persisted in trying to make the enrollment."[50]

James Sill's case was unusual only in that he—or his wife—managed to keep the papers he was working on. In Cloverdale, papers were stolen from Rockwell's replacement, enrolling officer Permeneas Davis. Another man, Capt. T. H. Nance, the enrolling officer for Warren Township, was riding along the National Road when someone shot at him, the bullet passing through his clothing.[51] On the same night that Sill was mobbed, M. B. Scott, enrolling officer for Jefferson Township, also faced a mob of about fifty men who went to his house and demanded the papers. These men disguised themselves by blacking their faces. Scott, however, lacked the presence of mind—or the help of female kin—to outwit them and, finding himself outnumbered, handed over the enrollment. In Madison Township, Joseph Siddens faced not a mob but a committee of four men who informed him "that if he continued the enrollment that he would find himself a dead man before he got through."[52] The Clinton Township enrollment officer also received a threatening letter. And enrollment officer Philip Wright fled his home in Washington township for fear of attack. H. M. Rockwell, who had declined to carry out the draft in Cloverdale, later complained that the enrolling officer in Jefferson Township "has lost his Rolls & there appears to be some suspicion that he is not all right on the war question & some . . . thinks that there is a little probabilit that he might probably distroyed them him self."[53]

Equally threatening to Unionists were reports of "party drills" and "midnight assemblages" in which Copperheads met to prepare their resistance. Residents of Russell Township recalled members of the Knights of the Golden Circle drilling in the bottomlands along Raccoon Creek.[54] One drill took place not at night but during broad daylight in Greencastle, where 300 men from Parke, Putnam, Clay, and Montgomery counties camped outside town and then assembled for "battalion drill." Hundreds of mounted men rode into Greencastle in the morning, "armed with every conceivable kind of weapon from the old flint-lock 'yager' to a 'pepper box revolver.'" An unfriendly observer, who compared them to a Confederate guerrilla company in appearance, claimed that the men assembled for roll call at the courthouse and then "scattered to the groceries."[55]

Howard Eckels, the twenty-three-year-old son of Judge Delana Eckels, and Capt. William Skelton of the 21st Indiana, who was in Putnam on recruiting service, came to blows on the courthouse square. A drunken Eckels remarked that he was a John Morgan and Jeff Davis man. He deliberately repeated this to Skelton, who told him to shut up. Eckels replied with an insult, Skelton slapped him, and Eckels drew a dagger, stabbing Skelton several times on the arm and in the chest. Eckels fled pursued by Skelton, who chased him to the judge's house before fainting from loss of blood. Eckels was then arrested. His father pledged $1,000 in bail. Skelton apparently recovered from his wounds, and there is no indication the case went to trial.[56]

Republicans charged that the attacks on Sill and other enrolling officers had been organized during a committee meeting at the law office of a certain "Breckenridge candidate for Congress," that is, Delana Eckels. The Republicans knew neither the identity of the committee members nor the content of their deliberations. In fact, all they did know was that "the object was to determine the course of the Democracy in regard to the conscription, and that the committee failed to agree." But the *Banner,* which pointed to the fact that resistance had begun the day after the meeting, argued that the draft resistance originated with the Democrats' consultation. The attacks had been coordinated, some occurring on the same night.[57]

Despite Copperhead intimidation, Putnam County met its recruitment quotas, although by controversial means. The journal of Thomas V. Lyon, assigned by the army to recruit in Putnam and Owen counties, showed the lack of enthusiasm for volunteering. He faced no violence, but neither did he find many men. Occasionally, he might "sweaten," or sweeten, his day by finding one recruit, but just as often he reported, "I spent the most of this day trying to recruit. But without success." By early 1864, he had grown discouraged and was suffering from the "blues." Tired of looking for recruits and reporting to the mustering office, he lamented, "I am just here [in Greencastle] on heavy expenses for nothing."[58] And in 1864, recruiting agent Capt. W. W. Allen encountered verbal opposition as he sought men for the 100-days' service. At Bainbridge, a man named Hanks asked him what side he was recruiting for. "Not for the rebel army, of course," Allen said. Hanks answered, "By G—d, that is the army I go to when I enter the service." Allen asked if he really meant he would "bear arms with, for, and in aid of the rebels," and Hanks replied, "That is the way I intend to be understood."[59]

Reluctant volunteers could be raised by generous financial inducements. At the beginning of the war, the county commissioners refused to enact a bounty in Putnam, causing many local men to enlist in other counties. But in the fall of 1863, the county needed to raise over 250 men to avoid a draft, and offering a bounty seemed the only way to make the quota and prevent Putnam County youth from enlisting in more generous locales. Though local governments had already been competing against each other for recruits by offering bounties, the need to pay ever larger sums also indicated the depth of resistance to volunteering. Antiwar areas often required high bounties. By the end of the war, bounties were running as high as $500. As is shown by a statement of payments for the July 1864 draft call, Putnam County townships were far more likely to offer bounties than were other counties in the Seventh Congressional District. Of thirty-one townships in four counties, twelve paid bounties of $400 for volunteers. And all but three of those twelve townships were in Putnam County.[60]

The draft law itself provided an alternative to violent resistance. If not exempted for medical reasons, drafted men could also escape service by paying a $300 commutation fee.[61] Mary Vermilion reported that husband William's relatives were prepared to buy their way out of the draft: "Tom [William's brother] says he has his $300 all ready, if he is drafted. He would rather pay $1000 than be shot at one round, he says."[62] Communities often supported draft avoidance by paying the commutation fees themselves. In the beginning of January 1864, Marion Township Democrats met at Fillmore in order to raise the money to buy fellow Democrats out of the draft. Congress repealed the commutation provision six months later. No longer able to purchase exemption for $300, those who wanted to avoid service could still pay someone to take their place. The result was a steep increase in the price of substitutes. Worthington B. Williams informed his son, Josiah, that various men were procuring substitutes at prices of $950 or even $1,100. Indeed, some men were willing and able to pay more than once. When James Oneal was drafted, he hired William E. Wilson as a substitute. Wilson, however, deserted, and Oneal—"anxious to remain at home"—then provided another substitute, Alexander Halton.[63]

During the winter of 1864–1865, petitions circulated in the county asking that the county commission pass a tax to refund the money townships had spent to meet the last draft, an estimated $150,000. Some objected that the commissioners had rejected aid to soldiers' widows and orphans "contemptuously" by saying that "they were not going to ruin Putnam county by such unjust taxation."[64] But now the county wanted to reimburse townships that had had to pay to raise recruits. Nonetheless, county commissioners decided to pay those who had hired substitutes up to $400 and to give an equal amount to each drafted man who had not received a bounty. The money to do this would come from a property tax. Unionists resented a tax increase that reimbursed "the stay-at-home gentry" for buying their way out of the army. Opponents of the tax sued. The case was heard before the Indiana Supreme Court, which found that the county commissioners had acted illegally. The law that provided for county bonds had authorized them to "aid the Government," but no aid was gained in repaying men who had already enlisted or provided substitutes. As the court interpreted it, the law also forbade claims by individuals for relief from the draft. However, the court allowed the county to raise a bounty to meet future draft calls. Bounties—state, federal, and local—had become inducements to enlist, but their differing amounts created numerous inequities.

As the war dragged on, bounties increased, rewarding those who had tarried in serving their county. And richer locales could pay more, not only enabling their citizens to avoid volunteering but also draining manpower from poorer areas. Bounties cost Putnam County and its townships $441,107. The county itself paid only $10,000—ten times what it spent on relief for soldiers' families—but individual townships paid sums that varied from $54,265 to $20,818.[65]

Republican officials construed cheering for Jefferson Davis, armed resistance to the draft, and opposition to the Lincoln administration as evidence of a pro-Confederate conspiracy in Indiana. Antidraft Democrats were rumored to belong to the Knights of the Golden Circle or the Sons of Liberty. Mary Vermilion thought "the Knights of the Golden Circle are busy everywhere, in every nook and corner."[66] To uncover that conspiracy in Putnam County and elsewhere, Provost Marshal Thompson hired a detective, Leonard Shewmaker, at the cost of $50 per month from late 1863 through the end of the war.[67]

According to historian Robert Churchill, the mainstay of the Sons of Liberty were the rural men who had organized to resist both the draft and an overreaching federal government. A smaller segment of the group consisted of influential men such as John G. Davis. These men used the language of the American Revolution to condemn the unconstitutional and tyrannical actions of the government, such as suspension of the writ of habeas corpus and forced conscription. But most members were unaware of the truly conspiratorial nature of the Sons of Liberty under Indianapolis printer Harrison Dodd, the order's state grand commander. Dodd had been stockpiling arms for an uprising to free the Confederate prisoners held at Camp Morton in Indianapolis and to revolt against the state government. Not only Richard Thompson, however, employed detectives: Governor Morton's agents had infiltrated the Sons of Liberty. In September 1864, Dodd was arrested. Although he escaped to Canada, some of his associates were tried and convicted by a military commission. All were eventually released. The case of one, Lambdin P. Milligan, resulted in an 1866 Supreme Court ruling that held it unconstitutional to try civilians in a military court while civilian courts were in operation.[68]

At the Indianapolis trial of the conspirators, testimony by William M. Harrison, secretary of the Grand Council of the Sons of Liberty, implicated John Davis and Delana Eckels. According to Harrison, those two men were present at an August 1863 meeting in Terre Haute arranged by Dodd. At that meeting, Eckels was made temporary grand commander and Dodd temporary deputy grand commander, which meant that Dodd was Eckels's subordinate. Two weeks later, at another meeting, Dodd became grand commander and Eckels— along with John Davis—was elected a delegate to the Supreme Council to be held in Chicago.[69] Harrison described several meetings as involving the organization of military companies: "It was the general idea that it was necessary to arm to resist the encroachments of the Administration." Although he did not mention either Eckels or Davis specifically as being at these meetings, they both probably had a good idea that the Sons of Liberty intended to resist the draft. Both men were present, however, at a February 1864 meeting, along with Dodd, Milligan, and most of the conspirators who would later be tried at Indianapolis.[70] How much Davis and Eckels knew—and condoned—of the plot to free the Confederate prisoners is unknown. They were not among those tried in Indianapolis, and Putnam Republicans, who had a long memory for any disloyalty, did not intimate a connection between Eckels and the conspiracy in postwar years.

But Davis's and Eckels's names would be blackened with rumors that had much less foundation than their connection to the Sons of Liberty. In the spring of 1864, Gen. James A. Garfield, the future president, accused them of having written letters of recommendation for a young man, Oliver Rankin of Greencastle, to Confederate general John C. Breckinridge. Rankin, according to the Davis letter, had resigned from the 10th Indiana Volunteers and had no sympathy for the Union forces. Both Eckels and Davis promised that the young man would be "faithful" to the South. Voorhees defended his fellow Democrats as "able patriots" and pointed out the letters were not in the handwriting of either man. Garfield said they had been obtained through a spy. The Democratic *Indiana State Sentinel* denounced the letters as forgeries. Garfield had the letters read in the House of Representatives, but the *Sentinel* proved correct. Rankin was not a former soldier disaffected from the Lincoln administration but a Union spy under Gen. William S. Rosecrans. It was Rankin who had the letters prepared—unbeknownst to Eckels and Davis, both of whom knew Breckinridge—because he hoped they would strengthen his cover story. Although Rankin was now believed to be dead, the clerk of an Indianapolis hotel claimed to have seen the letters composed at a desk in the hotel. John G. Davis roused himself from a "severe illness" to deny he had written such a letter—or any letter—to John Breckinridge since the beginning of the war. He blamed the "abolition fiends in human shape" for this effort to destroy his reputation. Given the extensive documentation proving the forgery, Voorhees had little trouble "settl[ing] this atrocious calumny forever."[71]

As the incident of the forged letters reveals, Republicans did not hesitate to impugn the reputation of leading Democrats for political advantage. In fact, historians have accused Governor Morton of exploiting the Sons of Liberty conspiracy. He had Dodd arrested just before the 1864 state election, in which his own reelection was controversial. The trial reminded voters of the syllogism—despite its invalidity—that since Copperheads were Democrats and Copperheads were Confederates, then Democrats must be Confederates.[72] Such Republican tactics worked at the state level—but not in Putnam County. In 1863, the Democratic candidates for county office included Melvin McKee, Elijah T. Keightley, and Clinton Walls, all of whom had been born in Kentucky. Republicans deplored their Southern ties and pro-Copperhead sympathies. Nonetheless, all three won. James Sill, however, lost a bid for real estate appraiser by 378 votes. McKee seems to have possessed the Copperhead sympathies attributed to him by Republicans. As a member of the Democratic party's executive committee, he worked hard to elect Eckels to the circuit judgeship, embracing the candidate's Copperhead reputation: "He is an eminent lawyer, and will decide all cases without fear or favor, and if our liberties have to be preserved by the Courts, I can think of no man who would stand more firmly by his convictions of right than he, regardless of the threats of Lincolns minions."[73]

Of more importance in 1864, however, was the presidential race. A Reelsville man informed John G. Davis, who was to be a delegate to the Democratic National Convention, "that nine out of Every ten" Democrats he knew "are in favor of a Decided peace man upon a peace platform" for president. He signed himself "your friend and a friend to free Constitutional government but an enemy to Despotism."[74]

On July 20, 1864, the Democratic convention met in Greencastle. Lt. John W. Cooper, Pvt. John Lyons, and Pvt. Andrew R. Allison, who were veterans of the Indiana 43rd Regiment on reenlistment furlough, observed the Democratic rally from a vantage point near the square.[75] Allison hurrahed for "Abraham Lincoln, the best man in the United States." One of the Democrats cautioned him, "You had better not cheer for him here; this is the wrong crowd." The soldiers and the Democrat exchanged words until Lyons knocked the young Democrat down two or three times. Sol Akers, described by Republican papers as "a Copperhead bully, and a large man," then approached to help the young Democrat, who, after all, was outnumbered three to one. Lieutenant Cooper stopped Akers, telling him to stand off, his help not being required. Akers said, "I have known you a long time, my boy." "Yes," replied Cooper, "and I have known you too, and I never knew any good of you either." If Akers had intended to stop the fight, Cooper's insult changed his mind. He drew a revolver and cocked it, as did Cooper. Another man, Martin Toney, came up and cried out, "Hurrah for Jeff. Davis and the southern Con—" but Cooper cut him short by striking him several times. One observer commented, "I have seen bloody men, but he was the bloodiest I ever saw." At this, the Democrats fell on the soldiers en masse. Men and women in the courthouse yard were yelling, "Kill him, kill him, kill the soldiers." Cooper ran, throwing stones and exchanging fire with the pursuing mob, which was led by Akers. Having "retreated" up Washington Street, Cooper hid in the cellar of the Putnam House, whose owner was Nancy Walls, the widow of a Mexican War soldier. The crowd was breaking windows with stones when the landlady's daughter, sixteen-year-old Mary Louise Walls, emerged with her father's cavalry sword and began a counterattack that cut one man and slashed the sheriff's clothing. Republicans maintained that she was restrained by guns held to her head.

Although Lou Walls saved Cooper and defused the riot, attacks on soldiers persisted throughout the day. A home guard unit, the Putnam Blues, helped put down the rioting.[76] Judge Eckels also intervened. As Cooper hid in the cellar, he heard the judge move through the house, searching for him and calling his name. Cooper remained hidden and, had Eckels entered the cellar, would have attacked. Cooper subsequently learned that Eckels meant to protect him from the mob, "but his political record was a bad one and I was afraid to trust him." Cooper's regiment later presented Lou Walls with a pistol bearing an inscription on its handle: "Presented to Miss Mary Louise Walls by the officers of the 43rd Regiment, Indiana Volunteers, for her heroic defense, July 20, 1864, against a furious mob."[77] Political brawls were by no means unusual, but Republicans found the spectacle of a mob turning on a soldier who dared to cheer for the president "infamous." They used the incident to dismiss Democrats' claims to be the advocates of "peace" and "free speech."[78]

Unfortunately for Indiana Republicans, they needed the votes of War Democrats. Unlike some other Northern states, Indiana did not allow absentee ballots, and its Democrat-controlled legislature had blocked a measure to let soldiers vote in the field. Consequently, the voters would be those who had stayed at home, many of whom were Copperheads. In September when John Hanna spoke in Indianapolis, he called on his auditors to forswear the partisan loyalties of a lifetime. In civil war, he said, there were "but two parties to this issue—the Unionist and the disunionist, the patriot and the traitor." Hanna reminded them that during the nullification crisis, it was the Democrats who supported the Union. Since 1862, Republicans had co-opted the label "Union," hoping to obscure the allegedly abolitionist associations of their party name and to appeal for common ground—saving the Union—with War Democrats. But the Union label was a thin veil concealing a still vigorous partisanship.

Although Hanna acknowledged slavery as the war's underlying issue, he made only passing mention of race. He called on Democrats to "renounce your unholy allegiance to treasonable secret orders," specifically mentioning the "God forsaken bastard Sons of Liberty." Hanna denied that peace was a possibility. "What mean the men who in our midst to-day cry, Peace? . . . I tell you they mean peace and independence for rebels, but bitter, bloody, cruel, relentless war upon the men who stand by the Union. They mean disunion and dishonor." He blamed the four years of war on the deficiencies as commander of George McClellan, the Democratic presidential candidate. Hanna's tone had been largely cajoling up to that point, but in the latter part of the speech, it became threatening. The prosecutor reminded his audience, "Let me tell you there is yet room in our jails and penitentiaries for conspirators and felons; that the arm of the judiciary is not powerless; that the sword of justice has not been sheathed."[79]

Governor Morton hoped to circumvent the omission of an absentee voting law by getting soldiers home to vote. During the spring of 1864, he spoke to C. C. Matson and other officers of the 71st Indiana about having the regiment return to Indiana for the fall elections. Matson was eager to help see "that a good many Union votes could be carried into the 7th Congressional District," but the administration was wary of taking soldiers out of the field, where they might be needed. The governor persuaded Lincoln to have some

Indiana troops furloughed from Gen. William T. Sherman's army during the Atlanta campaign. In Bridgeport, Alabama, in October, Thomas Lyon noted that "several train loads of soldiers went north. Some to vote."[80]

The Republicans won in Indiana, both the state elections in October and the presidential election in November, by about 20,000 votes. It was not the soldier vote, however, that made the difference. Morton had only secured furloughs for about 9,000 men. Although Morton won reelection, he very narrowly lost Putnam County. The Seventh District went Democratic, reelecting Voorhees over Henry D. Washburn of Vermillion County, colonel of the 18th Indiana. Despite being on active duty, Washburn had returned to Indiana to campaign. Subsequently, he contested the result, and a Republican Congress awarded him the seat in early 1866.[81] As with the gubernatorial race, the congressional race was close in Putnam. Voorhees won the county by only 36 votes, whereas his margin in other counties was in the hundreds. Delana Eckels won the circuit judgeship by 26 votes. Although Republican Higgins Lane received the second-highest number of votes for state representative after Austin M. Puett, the county commissioners gave the certificates of election to the Democrats, Puett and Samuel Colliver. The state House of Representatives, which had passed into Republican hands, threw out the Democrats' claim and seated Higgins Lane and A. D. Hamrick.[82]

The *Banner* charged that the narrow Democratic success in Putnam was due to "the Cloverdale fraud." As the returns came in on election day, it became apparent that the expected Democratic sweep of the county was not to happen. Even Voorhees's majority in the county seemed in doubt. The Republicans would win the county unless the last township to report—Cloverdale—went overwhelmingly Democratic. Two Democrats, including James A. Scott, set out for that township, where they visited the inspector who had the ballot box, Arabian Davis. Davis had spent election night at Sol Akers's house, having taken the ballot box with him. Scott, as he told Greencastle Democrats a few days after the election, "arranged" the ballot box while at Akers's house. He then returned to Greencastle and told his friends to double their bets on the election's results. By some accounts, the fact that money was riding on the election was a more powerful motivator for fraud than partisanship. The next day, Cloverdale presented its ballot box, but there were only sixty-one Union tickets inside. When the county commissioners held a trial over the Cloverdale fraud, ninety-one men "of reputation and veracity" swore that they had voted the Union ticket at Cloverdale. Nonetheless, the Democratic commissioners concluded there was no fraud.[83]

A few weeks later at the presidential election, there was again turmoil in Cloverdale. Bad weather kept voters away, and the total number of votes cast fell from October's state election total. In Cloverdale, however, Democrats insulted Union men who tried to vote, whereupon a fight broke out near the polls, seriously wounding one man. The "notorious" Sol Akers and the judge's oldest son, William Eckels, were in the fray; Akers claimed he was trying to stop a gunfight between a Democrat and a Republican. After wounding the Democrat, the Republican voter fled with his brother through a hail of Democratic gunfire. In a further irregularity, the Cloverdale Board of Election took the ballot box to an ailing voter's bedside so he could vote for McClellan.[84]

Although the Democrats employed desperate measures to hold the county during local and state elections, Republicans were not entirely innocent. Democrats claimed that Republicans in Greencastle stuffed the ballot box during state elections. Puett alleged Republican fraud when he argued for his seat before the state House of Representatives. He was suspicious of men who, dressed as soldiers, went to the polls and were allowed to vote and of votes cast by Asbury students.[85] Lucy Hawley, Ransom and Sarah Hawley's daughter, told her brother that some Asbury students had committed fraud in the presidential election: "Some of the College Chaps . . . having voted illegally" had wisely left town.[86]

Despite Akers's claim to be a peacekeeper, the Republicans insisted that he was the leader of "a company of desperadoes," including deserters who terrorized Cloverdale. This "guerrilla band" had been organized as a military company of the Sons of Liberty, and it had been "drilling for a long time." Republicans accused Akers and his gang of burning Union men's houses, stealing their property, and carrying out assassinations. Having been deprived of his patronage post by Republican dominance, Akers was stationmaster for the New Albany and Salem Railroad at Cloverdale. It was in that position that he had allegedly taunted Unionist passengers by leading his sons in cheers for Jeff Davis. On a Sunday in early December 1864, Akers's gang was also alleged to have attacked Samuel Ring, a miller at Cataract in Owen County in a shootout that left Akers's son, William, dead. The gang vowed revenge against the town of Cataract. Sol Akers was said to have told his men "that the village and mills of Cataract must be burnt, as part of the Democrat programme."[87] No general attack occurred, but after the war ended, there were complaints that gangs of deserters and Copperheads had burned Unionists' houses and killed their livestock around Cloverdale and Cataract. Sent to clear out the bandits, a company from the Indiana 43rd captured six. In April 1865, Solomon Akers was the lead defendant in a civil action filed by the county auditor, Elijah T. Keightley. Among the forty codefendants was William S. Eckels, the judge's son. The court ordered that all but two of the defendants had to pay $743.77 in damages. It seems Akers paid a steep price for his Copperhead activities.[88]

War's animosities shattered county residents' faith in the power of shared political principles to transcend partisan differences. Many now regarded Delana Eckels and Solomon Akers, who were known to be fierce partisans before the war, as virtual traitors to the country. Harrison Randel was just beginning a long political career, during which his alleged Confederate sympathies would be repeatedly pointed out. Two picnics were held on the Fourth of July in 1863—just days after the attacks had been made on James Sill and other draft enrollment officers. Henry and Jane Vermilion attended the Union picnic at Fillmore, "and there wasn't a traitor there"—because the Copperheads held their own picnic in a Democrat's pasture near Mount Meridian. The Union picnic featured the usual patriotic songs and speeches but also included a military drill by soldiers. Each side accused the other of responsibility for such "exclusive celebrations" of the Fourth, but the Civil War had so divided Putnam County that its people could no longer join together even to celebrate a universally beloved holiday.[89] There is no evidence that county Copperheads ever repented of their resistance to the draft, emancipation, or Republican rule. And local Republicans never forgot—or let anyone else forget—the wartime Copperhead activities of Eckels, Akers, and Randel. But the Copperheads had been right about one thing, which they also let no one forget: Republican rule challenged white supremacy.

5

THEIR OWN CORNER

When Alice Chapin's husband, Lucius, joined the Union army in early 1862, she was a young wife with two small children: a seven-month-old boy and a toddler girl. Unlike most wives, Alice reacted with enormous distress to his decision to enlist, telling Lucius, "I do not *verily* believe I could live & bid you good bye to go in the *Army* how can you for a moment think of such a thing, can you leave *me? can* you leave our babes? *no,* no, *no.*" The thought made her weep uncontrollably. She prayed "continually for grace & patience for us both always together." Though Lucius Chapin had decided that enlisting was in the best interests of his family, his wife referred to the "precious promises," presumably their marriage vows, that were to hold them "always together."[1]

Although Lucius would later achieve considerable success in life, he was not doing well in the 1850s. By the time he entered the army, he had tried his hand at mining in Clay County, clerking for a railroad, managing a Sunday school office in St. Louis, and running a pottery business. The year 1861 found him and Alice, just two years after their marriage, renting a farm near Terre Haute. He owed a substantial amount to the local doctor, Daniel W. Layman, mostly for visits to the Chapin children. Alice also suffered from ill health, possibly related to her pregnancies.[2] She was again unwell and their baby son was also ill when Lucius joined the army. Part of her dismay was at Lucius leaving her: "*I* cant spare you long can I? though I am kindly cared for & every thing that can be thought of done, still I am not satisfied I want my own corner & family." She acknowledged that Lucius had "had the hardest time nearly any one, ever had," in part due to his care for her: "I do not forget the many hours of patient kind attention you have given me, I love you for it."[3] But Alice wanted her "own corner," the home that was the married woman's acknowledged sphere, with her husband there to provide for his family.

Alice insisted on Lucius's physical presence at home, where he could care for her and their children, but he and his father-in-law emphasized the necessity of making a living, even if it took Lucius away from home. Alice's father, John Willson Osborn, who was a longtime newspaperman in Terre Haute and Greencastle, understood this need.[4] In a note appended to Alice's desperate appeal that Lucius not enlist, her father wrote, "The idea of your going into the army breaks hir heart—But I told her you certainly would not go unless you could procure such a position, as would *pay* and enable you to resign and return home if the service was not pleasant to you."[5] J. W. Osborn spoke of the army as a new beginning for Alice and Lucius's family: "It has been said that *she tied your hands,* so that you could not make anything. For this the present arrangement has been made for her support, until you can make a start."[6] From Osborn's perspective, Alice was a burden from which Lucius needed relief, whereupon he could earn the money necessary to support her. Lucius himself wrote Alice of the practical disposition of his pay and bounty money, some of which he had hoped to save but which instead had to be spent on her bills that winter.[7] He repeatedly avowed his love for his family and asked after the children, especially their sick boy, and assured Alice, "Many times in the day my *heart* turns to the dear ones at home."[8] "Only necessity," he insisted, "can put me in the army."[9]

James M. McPherson has argued that women and men disagreed about the nature of men's duty. Lucius Chapin was not concerned with dishonor or shame if he did not enlist—the justification that many of the soldiers McPherson writes about in his study gave wives unhappy with their absence in the army.[10] Instead, Lucius was preoccupied with paying his debts and becoming an independent head of household, as was expected of a young husband and father. In many ways, absence did not alter the roles men played, and they still strove to exercise authority in the family. Many enlisted to provide for their families, just as Lucius had. In their letters, soldiers continued to advise on family matters. Sons and husbands sent money home, fathers counseled their children, and almost all the men provided opinions about life on the home front.

Alice Chapin, however, fit the mold of McPherson's wives, who were convinced that male duty meant staying home to care for the family. Nineteenth-century married women expected to have their own homes. Newlyweds might live with family while getting started, but the vast majority of young couples set up housekeeping on their own. Yet Alice's disappointment at the sacrifices war demanded of her did not cause her to question woman's sphere. Although historians have been preoccupied as to whether the war advanced woman's rights—either by encouraging women to seek a wider political role or by causing men to acknowledge women's contributions—wives on the home front concerned themselves with caring for their children, maintaining ties to absent husbands, and paying the bills.

Nina Silber has recently emphasized the obstacles to women's involvement in the civic sphere during the war.[11] One principle obstacle was that many women did not seek to use the war to gain access to the public sphere. Rather, they saw the war as an impediment to fulfilling traditional roles. Alice viewed Lucius's absence in the army as depriving her of the role of mistress in her own household. Women like her yearned for the return of the men who were bread-winners and who cared for them. The war did not change these women's relationship to male authority. The women of Putnam looked forward to the end of the war and the reestablishment of men's traditional roles within the household. For many couples such as the Chapins, the Civil War occurred as their generation attempted to make the transition to their own households, moving from the status of dependents on parents to that of providers and homemakers. The war altered the strategies they used to achieve their appropriate places, but it did not alter their perception of those places. They firmly believed that a married couple should have their "own corner," as Alice Chapin put it. The man's earnings would support it, and the woman's care would maintain it.

Lucius was still at Camp Morton when his son's condition worsened. At Alice's behest, he returned home. Their son died an hour after he arrived. A tumultuous scene followed, precipitated by the emotional turmoil surrounding the infant's death and Lucius's enlistment. Lucius's sister, Sue, turned upon Alice with accusations that cut to the heart of the Chapins' marriage.[12] She accused Alice of not truly loving Lucius, her proof being that she had not named her son after her husband, and she added that Alice was lazy and "no *fit wife* for *her Brother.*" Further, Sue insisted that the family had sent Lucius into the service in order to get him away from Alice: Sue alleged, according to Alice, "that they had got Lu to go to the Army on purpose to get him away from me & hoped he *never* would come *back* to *me.*" Although Sue "cooled down" and partially recanted her outburst, she apparently expressed a family grievance against the burden Alice had been for Lucius.[13]

Another family crisis, the death of Lucius's brother Cowgill, brought a reconciliation between Alice and her in-laws. After the funeral, Lucius's mother wrote her son, "I do not wish you to feel any uneasiness about Alice in the future as I intend to take care of her myself and see that she does not have to do her housework."[14] Alice remembered that when she first arrived at the Chapin house in Putnamville, her mother-in-law "threw her arms around me, kissed me, and said she would henceforth love me as one of her own children—and desired the past should be buried. . . . We had a real long talk and many tears were shed."[15] The good feelings resulted in part from the recognition that Lucius had incurred some financial hardship in sending his brother's body back to Putnamville. Freight for the coffin cost $15, exceeding a month's pay for a soldier, and the Chapins understood that he consequently could not send money for the support of his wife and child and that Alice had heartily endorsed his course of action.[16] Sarah Chapin's remark about relieving Alice from housework, however, was telling. In her mother-in-law's eyes, Alice had shirked her duties in the home because of her frailty.

Throughout the war, Alice vacillated between accepting Lucius's duty and making coquettish demands that he return home. On the one hand, she closed a passage about her love for him with "still my darling, my *brave,* my Soldier lad, your wife is proud to think of you standing firmly to your *duty,* a *Man,* the *'noblest work of God.'*"[17] But on the other hand, although she affirmed Lucius's rectitude and asserted her pride in him, she continued to urge him to choose family over duty: "Just tell 'Uncle Sam' you cant stay any longer *nohow.* Your woman wants you & you want her so bad." If Lucius would "come to wifey," they could "build us a little cottage home, and be *very* happy. Wifey will make good *dinners* as she can and Ally our little darling will be a great comfort, and make music and happiness for our hearts, and *wouldn't* we be a happy family?"[18] In a typical passage, she undermined Lucius's resolve even as she seemed to offer support: "I will do my *very* best to be a *woman* and to do as my dear husband would like to have me, for I love him and would not make him feel badly nor that I am not willing to bear a part of the burden of restoring our Union."[19]

Lucius Chapin was unusual in being a married man in the army. Most soldiers were single and young, on average twenty-three or twenty-four years old. Married soldiers such as Lucius, at age twenty-eight, and John Applegate, at thirty-eight, were generally older than the average. The first volunteers were young men without families, such as the students at Asbury or Lucius's brother George, who was twenty-three years old, a member of the Union Guards, and one of the first soldiers from Putnam County to enter the war. After his three months of service in the Guards, George signed up for three years as a sergeant in Company I of the 27th Regiment. By 1863, he was promoted to first lieutenant. Another unmarried brother, Elisha Cowgill (known as Cow), enlisted with Lucius in August 1862, joining Company M of the 4th Cavalry, where Lucius would become company quartermaster.[20] A student at Indiana Asbury, Courtland C. Matson, also twenty-three, joined the Asbury Guards the day after Sumter fell. When the Guards' three-months' service expired, Matson enlisted for three years in the 71st Indiana Volunteer Regiment (later the 6th Indiana Cavalry). He would rise to the rank of colonel, serving in Kentucky and in Sherman's campaign in Georgia.

The next to join were married men such as Lucius Chapin. A historian later estimated that Putnam sent 2,000 men into military service during the war. Indiana sent a total of 208,367 men, ranking it second in the North for the percentage of its men of military age who served in the Union army. According to one study, 30 percent of Union troops were husbands. Edmund J. Raus's study of Cortland, New York, found that a fifth of married soldiers had children. When Ransom E. Hawley, Jr., a single college student, joined the Putnam County Rangers, he was told that half of the company were married men.[21]

Husbands were not the only men using the war to establish their adulthood. Sons often sought their parents' consent. As the youngest child of Ransom Hawley, Sr., and Sarah Hawley, Ransom, Jr., was seventeen years old in the spring of 1861 and a student at Wabash College in neighboring Montgomery County. Finding himself in dwindling classes, young Hawley resolved to enlist. He pointed out that both his grandfathers had served their country, hoping thereby to persuade his parents to agree to his plan. Their permission may have been withheld, however, for he remained at college until the summer of 1862, finally signing on for a three-month stint with the Putnam County

Rangers, intending "to avenge the blood of Putnam Co. boys." Ransom served with the Rangers for sixty days, until he was wounded at Uniontown, Kentucky. He mustered out in early October 1862 and returned to his studies.[22] But in the summer of 1863, the war again drew him. He wrote his parents from college, "I suppose as soon as you saw Gov Morton's call for six months men you at once said to yourselves that that wayward Ransom wants to enlist. If you did you guessed it at once." His sense of duty impelled him to join. He asked, "Can I have permission?"[23] He evidently received their consent, for he served intermittently between July 1863 and his mustering out in September 1864. He returned to Wabash College the following spring.[24]

Ransom Hawley's liminal status between youth and adulthood was not unusual, for even single men were members of families and constrained by familial ties. Although aware that what they had seen in war forever separated them from those at home, they continued to act as family men, to bear their families in mind and be shaped by them. Lieutenant Matson was doubtless influenced by his father, John A. Matson, a lawyer (he had been part of Greenbury Mullinix's defense team) and a prominent local political and civic figure. The elder Matson was active in recruiting rallies after the firing on Fort Sumter. When the three-month volunteers Matson helped recruit returned home in the fall, he extolled their prowess, however brief, on the battlefield and complimented their bravery at a dinner in their honor. One of the honorees was his son.[25] In influencing Courtland, John Matson had anticipated leaders who would encourage parents to motivate their sons. Speaking at Greencastle in October, for instance, Senator Joseph A. Wright, a War Democrat and former governor, "appealed to the old men to urge their sons to volunteer. . . . He appealed to mothers and fathers to say to their sons, 'GO.'"[26]

The structure of the Union army reinforced ties to the home front. As is well known, Civil War soldiers belonged to companies and regiments that had been formed by geographic location. Consequently, they served with men from their hometowns. Often, these men were relatives. Josiah Williams, who enlisted at age twenty-two, served with his mother's brother, George W. Reed. Lucius Chapin had not just his brother Cow in his company but also Alice's uncle, Jones Seely, who was its captain. Alice Chapin hoped that Lucius and her uncle would become closer through the army, although Lucius does not appear to have had much respect for Seely.[27]

Soldiers remained tied to family and community after they mustered in. In camp in the summer of 1861, it was reported, "one of the favorite songs among the boys is, 'O! do they miss me at home?' and they sing it with visible emotion."[28] William Anderson observed how, before the troops left Indianapolis for the South, women sought to prepare the men for unfamiliar tasks such as laundry and cooking. As his regiment readied itself to leave Camp Morton in Indianapolis, many visitors came to see their menfolk before they left: "The wimen partake of washing the dishes often, and tell the boys how to do: and how to cook." When Anderson saw "the boys" "staggering around among the pots . . . I wonder if they do not think of ma—or home often." In turn, he "often saw the mother in camp wat[c]hing her sone, and [rest] of the boys cooking; and looking at them with a longing look, as if she thought that I never raised you to be a cook; and I do not think that you will soon without I could teach you for some time."[29] Another observer at camp saw one "poor fellow" drop three potatoes into the fire as he attempted to peel them. He gave up in disgust with a look that said, "I wish sister or mother were here."[30] Having been told that it was impossible for soldiers to avoid lice, which she could not even bring herself to name but termed "*Travellers,*" Alice worried about the men's cleanliness and inquired how Lucius could do laundry in camp.[31]

The soldiers' triumphs belonged to family and community. Lucius's sister, Anna, praised his "good work in clearing two countys of gurrillis." But she lamented, "Oh! I do wish you could all come home!"[32] Josiah Williams's mother took pride in the words of Putnamville's minister, "good Brother Hawley," who "congratulated me upon having a son who had acted so honorably and done such good service for his country."[33] After the victories in Atlanta and Mobile, the streets of Greencastle were illuminated, and there were speeches by local dignitaries.[34] Lt. Joseph M. Donnohue wrote a public letter about the fighting around Atlanta in which his company of the 123rd Indiana had played a role. Donnohue believed the approbation of those at home validated the troops' efforts: "It is a great satisfaction to soldiers in the field to know that their friends at home appreciate their services. We don't expect the *world* to take notice of our actions, but when our actions are worthy of the notice of our friends we like to have them know it. We are all proud of 'Old Putnam,' and hope some day to make her proud of us."[35]

Lucius Chapin felt his family obligations necessitated his war service, but others believed that they could best care for their families at home. At least a dozen home guard units, whose stated purpose was to care for the families of those who had volunteered and to protect the home front from invasion, were organized in Putnam County. A county historian recalled that home guards consisted of men too old to serve "or for some other good reason unable to leave their homes."[36] Early in the war, joining these companies was often a first step to joining the army. The Union Guards, to which George Chapin belonged, was the first home guard company to organize in Putnam. It mustered into federal service on April 26, 1861, becoming Company H of the 10th Indiana Volunteer Regiment. The home guards revitalized in 1863 after Confederate cavalry under John Hunt Morgan raided Indiana, becoming part of the Indiana Legion, the state militia.[37]

As men made their decisions about military service, women showed their support. Local women presented "a very nice flag" to the Floyd Guards and received three cheers in return.[38] When George Chapin enlisted, he noted that "the Ladies of GreenCastle presented us with a beautiful flag."[39] A Union meeting in October 1863 attracted an "immense crowd," including "the ladies . . . [who] were here to cheer their husbands, brothers and fathers, as well as friends, and to animate and encourage them in their efforts to sustain the Government, and send words of cheer to the brave sons of old Putnam now in the field for their country's honor."[40] Male community leaders such as John Matson exhorted men to join or praised their service, but it was the women who prepared the meals for celebrations or after drills. Similarly, though Josiah Williams pondered the uniform he would wear in the Putnamville Guards, it was his mother who sewed it.[41]

Much of the energy that had once gone into women's charitable work was now diverted to soldiers' aid activities. In December 1862, the Union women of Bainbridge organized a soldiers' aid society that collected, within just six months, $100 in cash and six boxes of bed linens and food. The money was used to purchase hospital supplies. Sometimes, a church's female aid society renamed itself, as happened in one of the Greencastle Presbyterian churches. Some of the women who became active in soldiers' aid had acquired administrative experience in prewar organizations. Caroline Williamson, president of Greencastle's Ladies Soldiers' Aid Society, had been president of that town's Ladies Temperance Society. During the war, she dispatched articles of clothing and hospital sheets to Eli Lilly's 21st Indiana. As Jeanie Attie has argued, the state strove to appropriate women's unpaid labor for the war effort: no one would think of not paying soldiers, yet women were expected to volunteer their services. The Greencastle ladies aid society had over 100 members who met weekly to make clothes for the soldiers.

Despite having already assumed a leading role in caring for soldiers and

Josiah Williams in his Civil War
uniform. (Courtesy of DePauw
University Archives and Special
Collections)

their families, women would find a commensurate public role emerging only
gradually. And though an account of a soldiers' aid meeting named the men
who presided over the public event, the only woman to receive notice was the
wife of a lieutenant in the 18th Indiana Battery, her music students having given
a performance. Men helped collect and distribute the goods troops needed,
but those items were the products of female labor: clothing, canned fruit, jellies, bread, and chickens.[42] When Joseph M. Sadd acknowledged goods received
from the soldiers' aid society in Greencastle, he referenced the women: "Received from the Ladies Soldiers' Aid Association of Greencastle, Ind., $42[.]15
in cash, and two boxes of fruit, cakes, and eggs, forwarded by Mrs. Willliamson,
to the care of Mrs. Sadd, to be distributed by her among the soldiers of the hospital where she has a charge."[43] Joseph Sadd handled correspondence for his
wife and conducted a ministry at the hospital, but Cosima Sadd had "charge" of
the wounded and sick at the hospital.

Troops relied on aid packages, both from the soldiers' aid societies and
from their families, partly as evidence of women's continued commitment to

the war. Josiah Williams imagined that "the ladies & daughters are manufacturing blankets, knitting stockings mittens &c for the Hoosier Boys in Dixie."[44] He himself received "a couple of nice comforts a pair of boots & shirts, drawers & stockings &c. . . . Ma of-course sent a few jellies that serve quite well to make the substantial articles of army food quite palatable; so now I am very well prepared for the 3 y'rs. or the war."[45] When Ransom Hawley became seriously ill, he diffidently asked his parents to send a boiled ham because "mess pork & beef" was too "tough to a convalescent." His parents immediately sent the ham and other goods.[46]

Unlike most soldiers, who appreciated care packages from home as signs of civilian concern for their welfare, the bachelor George Chapin thought them a waste, complaining that the food spoiled in transit.[47] But such sentiments were rare among the troops. Food from home dominated Josiah Williams's account of a Christmas feast that he enjoyed with various officers and the commissary, Simpson Hamrick: "I believe I wrote to you about the nice Hoosier supper we had of the good things that arrived in those friendly boxes from the goodly land of Hoosier."[48] They feasted on stuffed roast turkey, jelly cake, sweet cakes, large pound cakes, jellies, fruit butters, canned peaches, and cream. Even George Chapin eventually relented and asked for a box from home for Christmas 1863.[49]

In addition to visits, wives tried to maintain contact by sending "little favors," as one husband called them. Alice Chapin sent her husband goods from home such as a flannel cap, flannel shirts, and socks. Perhaps out of a desire for simple fare or as an acknowledgment of their straitened circumstances, Lucius requested plain bread and butter.[50] Yet she had no butter to send, "as every bit in the Country is bought up by those who are sending Boxes & they are *many* I assure you." When Alice did send a package, however, it was far more sumptuous, including turkey, quince pies, apples, fried cakes, bread, onions, dried corn, and stamps. Many of the items were donated: her father provided the stamps, and an aunt supplied the fried cakes. She herself made a cake, which she enclosed along with mittens, pickles, a necktie, soap, and a nightcap.[51] Alice's efforts continued throughout the war. She sent another package a year after the first, and this time, she had procured butter—as well as honey, pickled cherries, and cake. Lucius considered this box a special act of devotion to him, for he knew that his wife would have had to deny herself in order to provide it.[52] Elizabeth Applegate also sent a care package, for which her husband profusely thanked her: "The box came to hand yesterday alrite and it was a godsend sure for we was about plaid out of everything . . . the Mess past a vote of thanks to you and say they hope you may live forever it was the best box of grub that we have reciev yet."[53] Officials of the Sanitary Commission may have criticized women for often sending the wrong things or food that spoiled before it arrived, but the real purpose of these goods was not so much to supply the troops as to keep alive a domestic connection in which women cooked for and clothed their men.[54]

Gifts showed that some Putnam women emphasized personal care for their men rather than public work for the war. Eliza Daggy wrote at the beginning of the war noting that "several weeks ago we had a festival to raise means to buy clothing for our soldier boys that took most one whole week but we felt paid if we did have to work pretty hard. we cleared over two hundred dollars wasnt that doing well!"[55] Mary Vermilion felt guilty about her failure to contribute to the war effort: "I feel ashamed of the life I am living. It is not worthy of a patriotic American woman. I ought to be up and doing [something] for the cause! I shall always be ashamed of myself, I think. And I am afraid my husband will be ashamed of me too." But rather than volunteering for the soldiers' aid society, she made a bouquet while daydreaming about her husband, William.[56] A sense of public service doubtless motivated some of women's war work. But Eliza Daggy's reference to "our soldier boys" bespeaks family and community ties. Eliza's brothers were soldiers. Women's public service supported their menfolk. Other Putnam women, however, did less for the troops en masse and more for their husbands individually. By doing so, they emphasized their role as wives, not as members of the public sphere.

Women traveled to camps to visit husbands and care for relatives. Simpson Hamrick wrote approvingly of Louisa Gilmore's efforts as nurse to her husband, Robert, who was wounded at Antietam. Hamrick called her "one of the Patriotic women of Putnam."[57] Other men, such as Lucius Chapin, struggled with longing for their wives. When his train passed through Greencastle and Terre Haute as he traveled from the mustering-in camp at Indianapolis to join the army, he fretted because he was unable to see her.[58] Stationed in Kentucky, he wrote, "Wify I would be so truly glad to see you this morning and hold you close to my *heart*."[59] Alice's pet name—"Wifey"—emphasized her social role. Middle-class couples aspired to "companionate marriages" in which the partners shared an emotional and sentimental bond.[60]

But William Anderson, a bugler in an artillery regiment and a bachelor, thought female visitors interfered with work. One day, he reported, visits from the wives of the captain and lieutenant made it difficult to complete the muster roll. Such sociability made "our chance very poor to transact much business," Anderson complained, "when the quarters was full of Ladys."[61] But like George Chapin's complaint about food packages, the bachelor Anderson's lament was a solitary one.

Enlisted men found it difficult to visit their families during the war. Officers' wives often traveled from Putnam County to stay with their husbands in camp, even bringing small children. Alice visited when Lucius was at Camp Morton in Indianapolis but not when he was in camp in the South.[62] John Applegate, a sergeant in the 6th Cavalry, and his wife, Elizabeth, failed several times to arrange visits. John wanted Elizabeth to travel to Indianapolis, but she protested that she could not get there without male help. This situation caused some distress for their young daughter, Allie, who "had a good cry because she could not come to morrow."[63] Later, while serving in Kentucky, John talked of renting a house near where he was camped and of moving Elizabeth and Allie closer to him.[64] Ultimately, nothing came of the plan, probably because of the expense.

Meanwhile, the Applegates complained about each other's failure to write. John noted, "You complain of me not writing . . . I hav ritten to you twice since I receivd one from you."[65] Despite the pleasures of army life, which he called "pick Nick evry day," he confided to her that "I want to be at home wors than ever I did in my life I wish you was with me." Bad dreams about her gave him "the blues," and he longed for letters from home. He instructed her to "kiss Alli for me and 40 for your self."[66] Upon failing to hear from her, he wrote asking if she would "condesend" to write to him. But his sarcastic tone was belied by a pleading postscript: "Liz if you Love me do try and wright often."[67] Although he knew that her letters often did not reach him because of his cavalry unit's frequent moves, he continued to fear the lack of letters meant an absence of affection.[68] When Elizabeth accused John of not wanting to visit home, he explained the difficulty in getting furloughs. Even his mustering out of the army presented a problem. He wanted Elizabeth and Allie to meet him in Indianapolis. Allie was eager to see her father, but Elizabeth was unsure of how to make the arrangements. Yet unlike her resistance to traveling at the beginning of the war, she did say that if John would inform her when he got to Indianapolis, "then any time we will come."[69]

The Chapins' relationship, at least according to Alice's letters, was among the most openly sensual. Having her hair brushed, for example, caused Alice to reflect, "Now if you were here I would comb your hair—and help *you* fix up—and give you *visible* demonstrations of—what? I am sure your heart can tell." She went on to remind Lucius of how they had rested *"Heart* to *Heart.* Love answering love the feeling so hard to express can such hours be forgotten?"[70] In another letter, she described herself as "mostly *undressed* sitting beside '*Our* Bed.'" If he were there, she said, she would drop her pen and "fall to loving her *dearie.*"[71] Months later, she was still fantasizing about his *"rap* at the door that wakes me so easily!"[72]

Intimacy sometimes had costs for women. Adding to Alice Chapin's distress at the death of her infant son was the fear of pregnancy. "I am more and more convinced," she confided to Lucius, "that I am again in *trouble.*" She contemplated taking "the Wine *Mixture,*" perhaps to induce an abortion, but asked for his advice: "I love my husband and I love his *children* but this is more almost than humanity can bear."[73] Lucius recommended seeing Dr. Layman. Three months later, Alice was recovering at her father's house, but whether it was from an abortion, a miscarriage, or some other ailment is unclear.[74]

Soldiers were particularly concerned about the financial welfare of their families at home. The oldest Chapin son, Henry, had remained home with his widowed mother and younger sisters. When he became ill, George Chapin, who was owed four months' pay, promised to send money so that Henry could hire out some of his work. George sent $100 upon being paid, and he continued to send money home despite the family's reluctance to use the funds for their own needs. Henry seemed to think the money should be set aside, but George, having sent $150 in November 1863, instructed him to spend at least $50 if not the entire sum on their mother. For George, who hoped to get the family out of debt, this was preferable to having Henry work himself too hard and leaving the family in need.[75] Henry and the others may have felt constrained about taking George's pay for the larger family, but George saw himself as contributing to their welfare.

Married soldiers, especially, had an obligation to provide financial support for their families. Money was a constant concern for Lucius Chapin and John Applegate. Applegate had been a blacksmith before the war and had been married to Elizabeth Lynch for sixteen years by the time he enlisted. The couple had lost four children at young ages. Their only surviving child, Allie, was six years old in 1861.[76] With his cavalry regiment constantly on the move, John received his pay irregularly and at one point had even gone six months without compensation. Realizing that Elizabeth was feeling the straitened circumstances, he sent money whenever he got it. On one occasion, he sent $40, but he warned that Elizabeth would have "to do the best you can with as it will be sometime before I will get anymore."[77] In late 1864, after John was captured, his captain arranged for Elizabeth to draw her husband's pay.[78]

The gifts wives and husbands exchanged during the war revealed their different conceptions of their roles. Women sent food and clothes, signifying wifely care for the physical needs of their husbands. But as breadwinners, men sent money for the family's upkeep.

When the war ended, John Applegate lingered in the army. Despite his wife and daughter's desire that he return home, he saw an opportunity to make some extra money. He had expected to be home earlier but wrote, "As I hav not maid any mony yet it is as good a chance as I will ever hav to make som now I will try and stay long a nough to make us a home of our own so you must not fret but get along without me a little longer." Reiterating that he had not been paid and badly needed money, John asked Elizabeth to send stamps and instructed her "to look a round and see if you can find cheap peas of property to sell."[79] Even the officers felt John should return home, Elizabeth argued, stating, "I think you might come home as well as the rest of the folks."[80] But John tried to explain that he remained in the army for the best interests of the family: "You said in your last that you [w]as a fraid that I hav forgotten you and Alle now My Dear Wife it is on your and Alles account that I staid in the army to try to mak som[e]thing to buy you a home with."[81]

Many men had enlisted in order to receive a bounty, but these bounties proved insufficient to support their families. Even though the Indiana legislature authorized local taxes to be raised for the support of soldiers' families, many localities did not take advantage of the law. Finally, in 1865, the state legislature mandated a special levy with a stipend for wives and a set amount per child. Yet by the time the legislation took effect, the war had ended and most soldiers were already home. As a result, families who needed help during the war had to rely on private aid, rendering them recipients of charity rather than of an obligation that the community owed them because of their husband's or father's service.[82]

The community made efforts to recognize soldiers' roles as family breadwinners by helping provide for those at home. During the war, Putnam County commissioners and the township governments expended $28,260.65 in aid to soldiers' families. As the first winter of the war approached, county residents debated how to help those families. The county board of commissioners was petitioned to make an appropriation, but it did not do so for several months.

Once the appropriation was secured, however, John Matson cautioned that it was only $200 and thus insufficient to the need. Voluntary contributions from the public were still required to aid the hundreds of families who had sent men into the war.[83] During a recruiting drive in the summer of 1862, "the married men came forward promptly, and by their liberal subscriptions have put the family of every volunteer in comfortable circumstances for 60 days."[84]

The early focus was on landlords and what they could do to assist this effort; accordingly, Greencastle landlords promised to lower rents for soldiers' families. The next step was the formation of a committee and the establishment of "depots" to which goods for the families could be delivered. Stores such as that of T. W. Williamson, Caroline's husband, in Greencastle served as depositories. Appeals were made to farmers for donations of wood, flour, meal, beef, turkeys, chickens, butter, eggs, dried fruits, and other foods. Each township had an agent, who was often a community leader—such as storekeeper Tom Vermilion in Jefferson Township.[85] Donors were reminded that "God has blessed us with an abundance. Let us share it with those whose homes poverty has entered. Let the soldier in the distant field know that while he is giving his life for his country, his family is cared for and supplied with all needful comfort."[86] Others deplored how little was being done for the families of the soldiers, pointing to how "our gallant army" strove to protect civilians from those who would destroy their government.

Calls for food and aid came in late November, coinciding not only with the onset of winter but also with the season of Thanksgiving and Christmas celebrations, which tended to remind the fortunate of the need to aid those who were less well off. Efforts in Greencastle culminated in a Christmas Eve festival and dinner. Donors were asked to provide not only food but also presents to set in the branches of a Christmas tree. When the festival opened, the limbs bore everything from a diamond ring to a tin sword. Crowds filled the hall to the point "almost of suffocation." The festival took in close to $600 for the soldiers' families, and similar efforts continued throughout the winter. A stereopticon lecture after Christmas on statuary and art was held to benefit a soldiers' aid society. By early winter 1864, however, the call was not for food but for fuel, the weather being bitterly cold. Once again, the soldiers' aid societies asked farmers to take wood to local stores, where they would then be directed as to which families needed it.[87]

Even though Lucius Chapin had enlisted to solve his financial problems, Alice found herself inadequately provided for during the war. "Do you feel that

you can give me up to struggle with poverty and all the trials I am called on
to bear; and go unflinching to the Bloody field?" she queried her husband.[88]
She did not want Lucius to go without money himself, but she worried about
having "no means to keep hunger away."[89] Alice noted that the government's
failure to pay soldiers on time made soldiers' aid necessary: "Truly we need the
aid through the country of societies for relief of Soldiers families if *this* is to be
the way Uncle Sam & Abe *Lincoln* pay their hirelings." She borrowed money to
buy groceries and purchased medicine and coal oil with a dollar her father had
sent her. J. W. Osborn also sent Lucius's mother another dollar, which went
toward buying shoes.[90] By detailing the money she and her mother-in-law had
received from her father, Alice emphasized Lucius's failure to provide for his
female dependents. She asked his advice on receiving the soldiers' aid: "The
women or a *good* many of them rec the *'aid' societies* help They draw from the
time their husbands *enlisted* & many of them are in comfortable circumstances."
With the proper papers from his captain, Alice could get $1.25 per week: "Do
you not think so long as you draw us *Pay* & I am in need very much of money I
had better have it?"[91]

Although Lucius may have felt differently, Alice and many women viewed
this not as charity but as payment their families deserved because of their husbands' public service. An appeal urging donations of food and clothing for the
families asked, "Will you thus see them suffer for the necessaries of life, while
their own husbands are engaged in fighting to sustain this great government
of ours?"[92] Even though Alice went on relief, it proved not to be the solution:
"I am out almost of funds as the Relief failed me to the suit of several $."[93] The
government and community were no better providers than her husband.

Alice could have earned her own money, but Lucius forbade it. She suggested easing her financial plight by having him sell medicines of her manufacture in camp, but he apparently did not agree. In the summer of 1863, the
Chapins were particularly hard pressed for money. Having borne the expense
of returning his brother's body to Indiana, Lucius himself was now ill and in the
hospital at Nashville. Then, Alice was offered a job as a schoolteacher in Terre
Haute, which would pay $40 per term and permit Ally to accompany her.[94] But
Lucius "veto[ed]" the idea, despite Alice's repeated mention of her need for
money. "So you dont want a 'School Ma'am' for a Wifey? *Well* I suppose I'll have
to give it up though I only had to get my Certificate," she wrote. She would try
to make money "drying Corn" and "putting up Tomatoes."[95] Lucius's sisters

were also teaching and boarding, but as they were unmarried young women, this was evidently not a reflection on his ability to provide. So Alice continued to supplement her income by selling medicines in Greencastle.[96]

The war's close brought renewed concerns as to how Lucius would make a living. "Does your mind never rest on the future and our means of subsistence hereafter in the hard times to come after the desolatry influences of this war shall be felt with more force?" Alice asked.[97] Clearly sharing her worries, Lucius asked her to inquire about buying a farm on good terms at the end of the war. Land prices around Terre Haute, where Alice's family lived, seemed too high. Should he be unable to find 40 acres at a good price, Lucius toyed with the idea of moving to Illinois; Alice had come up with a plan, in consultation with one of her family members, for them to rent a farm near Chicago. But Lucius's father-in-law wrote him about prospects closer to home, where a 40-acre tract was for sale and where he could get work as a carpenter for $3 per day.[98] Meanwhile, Lucius's family hoped he would return to Putnamville, where he could contribute to his widowed mother's support. Lucius pronounced himself willing to "gladly avail myself of an opportunity to make a living," but he demurred that nothing could be done until he mustered out. Gently, he invoked his authority as head of household, cautioning Alice against getting her heart set on any one plan: "Do not become to settled in any plan as your man might have to disappointment you and he does not want to do that he loves you too much." For all his invocation of his love for her, it was clear the decision would be his and his alone.[99]

Just as couples tried to preserve traditional financial roles, so they sought to preserve the father's authority in the family. Alice Chapin reminded Lucius that he had abandoned his paternal responsibilities, and she insisted that she was striving to preserve his daughter's attachment to him. She wrote him that upon waking, Ally had been talking to herself, "Got *no Papa*—poor Papa *gone*, gone to War? Gone fight Webels.' . . . her Papa will be glad to know he has a place in her mind *early* in the morning and late at night; she always kisses me Goodnight for you."[100] Alice expressed concern about the child's development, noting that Ally was "very intelligent and sweet" but capable occasionally of "the most ungovernable fits of passion." Her shared concerns about childraising included a measure of guilt. "I do want her to grow up a good kind amiable woman. Oh how we need *home* and *Papa!*"[101] Waking up in the morning, Ally said, "I so *mad* at Papa." When asked why, she said, "Cause he no dont come *home* see *Ally.*"[102] Lucius professed to love hearing that his daughter was talking about him. He may have been more reassured, however, by his brother's report that Ally "knew your picture & kissed it."[103]

The little girl scrawled notes to her father in her mother's letters: "I must write to Papa I love my Papa Little Brother gone up heaven to God. Ally wants to see papa. Ally write papa letter."[104] Lucius, in turn, sought to mold his child from afar. "Papa sorry to hear of his little daughter having to correct Mama," he wrote Ally, but "it does not look well She *must* obey her dear Mama whom she loves very much and I am sure she will if she lives love her much soon if her faults are corrected now. But Papa thinks . . . his whiping you is only because to whip is just on all."[105] As the war continued, he worried about the separation from his family: "If I am permitted to return home in peace to my family it will take something more than I now know of to induce me to *leave* my home again Though I perhaps will not regrett the past when it is once ended. My little girl will be in her sixth year will I know her[?]"[106]

Like other fathers, John Applegate obviously missed his daughter greatly. He asked Elizabeth to "kiss Alle a thousand times for me."[107] His homesickness for Allie seemed to encompass all children, for he asked his daughter to "giv my lov to all the children in the nebor hood."[108] John was not so concerned with forming his daughter's moral character, though he did instruct her to "bee a good girl and Lov and obay your Ma and pray for your Pa."[109] He was determined that Allie be thankful that she had been spared the hardships of war that he saw around him: "I am well and hope that you and your Ma ar well and happy you ought to bee happy and thank god that you do not liv in this unhappy country I hav seen little girles like you turned out of ther homes at mid knight and thar homes and every thing they [owned] burned up that is dun every few dayes hear on both sides."[110]

Most of all, John wanted Allie to write. "I want you to bee a good girl and mind your ma in every thing and then you will pleas me I want you to wright as often as you can if it is only one line it will pleas me."[111] He asked that Allie "be a good girl and go to school every day until school is out."[112] Education would enable her to "wright to your Pa." And she could get her mother "to wright a few lines to me for you but I would rather you would wright it your self it would mak me so glad to her from My Little Daughter."[113] Perhaps because he knew she was old enough to write, John was not content to hear about Allie from Elizabeth. But Allie did not always write. On one occasion, Elizabeth said the hot weather made her "to lazy to write," and on another, she was "too sleepy."

But Elizabeth affirmed, "She wants to see you so bad."[114] Like the other fathers, John tried to regulate Allie's conduct in spite of the distance. He reported to her what he had heard from her mother—that she had been the best little girl in town—and urged her to be good all her life.[115] Although concerned with his daughter's behavior, John did not enumerate the character traits that made up goodness.

James Marten has written that men struggled to fit their ideas of duty, which took them away from their children, with the responsibilities for the daily care of the children. They reconciled these competing imperatives by "providing wide-ranging guidance and instruction." Marten noted that men provided more advice to sons than to daughters, but Lucius Chapin and John Applegate may have refrained from advising their daughters because of the girls' youth. Applegate, although he intensely desired to hear from and have contact with Allie, evidently did not subscribe to the same ideas of character formation as other, more educated Putnam men. For him, it was enough that Allie be "good" in some general and largely undefined way.[116] More than Lucius Chapin, he left the specifics of his daughter's conduct to his wife, telling Allie to "mind your Ma obay her in every thing."[117]

Despite their close involvement in home affairs, soldiers obviously could not share the civilians' experience of war. When Sarah Hamrick complained about "a Regt of Soldiers stoping in the Switch & coming in to the orchard," her brother Simpson explained, "You have but a Small idea of Soldier depredations unless you was near a camp or along the line of march of an Army I hope Indiana may Never be over run by an Army of Neither friends or enemies."[118] A soldier in the 133rd noted, "The fenceless, uncultivated farms and warlike defences everywhere visible in Tennessee, plainly show that war is abroad in the land; of which fact Indiana is scarcely aware save as her people read it in the papers."[119]

Because of the distance army life created, families worried about their menfolk's conduct. Simpson Hamrick defensively insisted upon his "steady . . . habits" in response to his family's anxious inquiries about his pastimes. Families worried that their men were indulging in drink, exposing themselves to the weather and thus risking illness, and spending too much money.[120] Concerned that John might fall into the wrong company, Elizabeth Applegate adjured him to "be a good man remember it pays well to do right."[121] That worry, together with John's participation in the fighting for Atlanta, prompted her to wish him home: "Tell me if you have plenty to eat, and take good care of yourself, and

Above all be good and may the time soon come when you will be at home to stay all the time, not quite a year and I hear you will not reenlist."[122]

The furloughs that were given to those soldiers who reenlisted after their three years of service permitted visits home that sometimes exposed the gulf between their experience and that of their families. Local politicians dominated the speeches at banquets celebrating the veterans' service. Local women, of course, prepared these banquets. If the veterans were called on to speak, it was by the audience and done extemporaneously. At such a celebration for the 43rd Indiana, D. E. Williamson, a local lawyer and state attorney general, gave a prepared speech on behalf of the soldiers, and at the end of the planned festivities, Lt. Col. Alfred Hawn was asked to speak.[123]

A Portland Mills orator also addressed the 43rd and 14th Indiana Infantries during their furloughs. Although he praised the bravery of the troops, referring to "their bronzed faces and their manly forms," much of the oration emphasized reestablishing the old order of which the soldiers themselves had been part. These men were "valiant sons," Indiana's "children" who were returning home to "fathers, and mothers, and wives, and sweet-hearts," where they were situated within a network of relationships: "Come home! After so many days of toil and nights of broken slumber, come back to the endearments of your father's house. Take your seat at the old fireside, and recount to eager listeners the story of your hairbreadth escapes, the part you have born in the defense of your country's institutions." The soldiers might be blessed and might reminisce, but they would do so within their father's households, once again being subordinates rather than independent men.[124]

Even in discoursing upon "the gallant slain," the orator placed the bloodshed within the context of familial relations: "Our loss of life in this war has been terrible. All over the land homes have been darkened; hearth stones have been made lonely, hearts have been torn, old age has been left without a prop, families have been deprived of a strong arm of support." The men who had died at Wilson's Creek, Shiloh, Gettysburg, and Fort Donelson had been sons, brothers, husbands, and fathers. The speaker noted that those on the home front had "often heard and read how our poor boys die." "Their last thoughts," he insisted, "are always of God, home and those to whom they are bound by the tenderest ties."[125] But for all his emphasis on the close connection between soldiers and home front, the orator spent little time on the men whom he addressed. Acknowledging that he was expected to say something specifically about the 43rd and 14th because the dinner was, after all, in their honor, he nonetheless excused himself, saying, "It is useless for me, my friends, to enter into the details of their history." His audience had followed their exploits and knew their roles in the campaigns, so he quickly passed over the specifics of those regiments. For all the orator's emphasis on home front gratitude, the soldiers might well have felt slighted by his inability to be specific about campaigns they had waged.[126]

The greatest example of the gulf between soldiers and civilians was in the reality of death. Josiah Williams had to inform his parents of the death of his Uncle Whit (George W. Reed) in the battle of Cedar Mountain. "The bulletts flew like hail," Josiah wrote his parents, "and I am sorry to inform you it was when Uncle Whit fell; who was killed by being shot in the left ear (or near there) as he was only about ten ft from me when he threw his hand up by his head and fell forward upon his face. As our men were falling thick & fast & the Reg't giving back I had not time to get him from the field or see to his things; we being between two fires."[127] Recovering the body was important to people at home but often impossible on the battlefield. The day after the battle, Josiah "made a diligent and fruitless search for Uncle Whit's (Lieut. Reed's) body."[128] Almost a month after his uncle's death, he reported that he had been unable to locate it.[129] The missing corpse apparently encouraged false hopes, for Josiah cautioned his parents, "I would gladly believe Uncle Whit was yet living if possible; but I saw him fall." In addition, the officers captured at Cedar Mountain had long since been exchanged and Reed was not among them, nor was there word of him from other released prisoners.[130] When his parents remained unpersuaded, Williams added the testimony of Lt. Thomas Box, who, having been wounded and taken prisoner, had just been released from Libby Prison. Box was by Reed when a bullet struck Reed in the cheek; as he started for the rear, he was felled by another shot. "If Reed had been alive & taken they would have taken him with the others & released now at the same time," Josiah concluded. "That settles all doubt with me."[131]

Another Putnam soldier, Simpson Hamrick, died at Chancellorsville. As with Josiah Williams's uncle, the body could not be recovered, this time because it was on ground held by the Confederates.[132] Other members of Hamrick's and Williams's regiment provided the family with the gruesome details of Simpson's death. J. A. Crose wrote, "*Simps is dead!* He was killed in the terrible Battle of yesterday, while bravely cheering his men. Shot through the Body by a cannon shot, which killed him instantly. . . . Simps died a brave soldier: universally beloved by the Regt. and his death is regretted by all."[133] Apparently, the

Hamricks sought more information, for Crose wrote again with further details of the battle, the wound, and Hamrick's last words: "Oh! Boyo! oh Boyo!"[134] A surgeon's letter provided even more graphic description, noting that the enemy shell "entered the left hip and passed out at the anterior Rupturing the lining membrane of the bowels also with a grape in the left hand cutting it from the arm he suffered very little and died with all the honor and glory of a brave soldier and a gallant officer."[135] Crose promised to return Simpson's possessions—his valise, belt, and hat—but was less sure about the body: "His body is within the Enemy's Lines but we will make every effort to secure it."[136] Despite Crose's good intentions, recovering the body proved impossible. Members of the regiment knew where it was and had marked it before retreating. A friend of the Hamrick family even inquired at Governor Morton's office about recovering the remains. But the army had fallen back at Chancellorsville, leaving Simpson buried within Confederate lines. An effort to recover the body under a flag of truce proved unavailing. The captain of Simpson Hamrick's company insisted to A. D. Hamrick that failure to recover the body indicated no lack of affection for his son and described their efforts at length.[137]

The Chapin family was better able to recover their son's remains. After Cowgill Chapin died on April 7, 1863, at Nashville, his body was returned to Putnam County and buried near his father's grave.[138] Although Lucius had feared that his brother's body might arrive before news of his death did, he had nonetheless sent Cowgill's corpse home. "I could not bear the thought of having his body laid where it would only be tramped upon by the worst Rebels that ever trod upon this green earth," he wrote Alice. He knew that Cowgill "loved his *home*," and he wanted him interred there.[139] Their mother, Sarah Chapin, overruled family members who wished to view the body. Surrounding the coffin, which remained unopened and was draped with a flag, were flowers arranged by Cowgill's sisters and sister-in-law. Rev. Ransom Hawley "preached a delightful sermon from the words 'Blessed are the dead who die in the Lord.'"[140]

Yet a year later, when George Chapin was killed at Resaca, Georgia, on May 15, 1864, the Chapins too were denied the consolation of a proper burial. Since Lucius had successfully returned the body of one brother, his mother expected him to care for George's remains as well. She asked Lucius to see to it that the body was dressed in a new suit of clothes, which she dispatched for that purpose, and to send her George's things lest they be lost. Before the Civil War, death had been a domestic ritual in which the women of the family prepared the body for burial; Sarah Chapin, a widow, would have cared for her husband's remains in this way. She appreciated enough of war's ravages that she refused the requests of Cowgill's sweetheart, Reverend Hawley's daughter Lucy, to view his body. But she still did not comprehend Lucius's inability to recover George's body as he had Cowgill's. The civilian Hamricks and Chapins did not understand the disorder and tumult of the battlefield. The Hamricks felt betrayed that Simpson's body had been abandoned. And Sarah Chapin assumed that Lucius could easily care for his brother's body, not realizing that he might not be given leave for such duties.[141]

At the beginning of the conflict, death had been a communal tragedy. The first Putnam man to die in the war was a member of the Union Guards, James H. McGill. Wounded at Rich Mountain, Virginia, McGill died July 27, 1861. When his body was returned home in early September, he was buried with due solemnity. The service took place on the college campus with "a very timely and eloquent" sermon delivered by Dr. Thomas Bowman, president of Asbury University: "An immense concourse of people turned out to pay their last respects to the honored dead. Several military companies were present in full uniform and escorted the remains to the cemetery."[142]

John Applegate did not die in battle, but his experiences revealed that wives could sometimes understand all too well the danger their husbands faced. At the end of July 1864, he was among a large Union cavalry force, under George Stoneman, that was surrounded and captured on a raid to Macon, Georgia, during the Atlanta campaign. Applegate was imprisoned at Andersonville.[143] Elizabeth was frantic with worry. John had not written, and she noted that "we have news here of the terrible battle you have had at Atlanta." She wanted to know if he had been in it: "John I am almost worn out with dred and anxiety. . . . may you be kept from all harm is the daily prayer of your wife."[144] When she did hear from him, the letter seemed out of date with the news of battle: "I was glad to hear that you was safe and well, but when I think it has been over a week, since your letter was written and truly we do not know what a day may bring forth. . . . I cannot help being uneasy while you are exposed to so much danger."[145] When his letters did not come, her tone became more pleading: "Why dont you write, oh if I could only know that you was safe and well what a relief it would be to me, write and tell me that you are."[146] When he was paroled in early April 1865, he wrote Elizabeth of his captivity. Unsurprisingly, he was "not very stout" after his time in the notorious prison camp. Perhaps long months of waiting to hear from John had sharpened Elizabeth's anxiety, for when a letter went astray that summer, she wrote a "mighty scold" about the worry caused by his failure to write. Her letter made John cry, and he asked her not to send any more in such a tone. It turned out that John was not at fault—and Elizabeth wrote an apology—because Capt. John Hansel had lost the letter John entrusted to him.[147] John had worried that a lack of letters revealed his wife's indifference, but when he failed to write, Elizabeth's reaction revealed how keenly aware she was of the war's risks.

What soldiers and their families received in return for risking their lives was military honor. Family connections were important to military advancement. Simpson Hamrick wanted a second lieutenancy, and to that end he enlisted his father, A. D. Hamrick, and other contacts, including Superintendent of Public Instruction Miles Fletcher. When Hamrick received a first lieutenancy, he required a loan from his father to properly equip himself.[148] John Matson interceded with Governor Morton seeking a major's position for his son Courtland and praising the young man's "capacity," "indomitable energy," and experience in the Peninsula campaign.[149]

Josiah Williams, who sought promotion as an officer in a new regiment being formed, also got the help of family and friends such as A. D. Hamrick and John Matson. "I feel quite proud of the incouragement my friends of Putnam Co. flatter me," Josiah reflected.[150] Ultimately, he failed to gain promotion because Putnam County and the Seventh Congressional District lacked sufficient political clout with Governor Morton to secure the promotion. Josiah did not reenter the service when his three-year commitment ended, despite his mother's urgings: "Why lay aside the *blue coat* that you have honored so long[?]" While appealing to Josiah's desire for advancement, Lydia Williams confessed, "*In truth si* I would like to see you wear the *Eagles* upon your shoulders."[151]

A Greencastle man who had seen George Chapin in New York told Sarah Chapin that her son "was a splendid looking man & officer."[152] Sarah took George's death hard, but she eventually became reconciled to his loss. Perhaps the "beautiful letter" from his commander, Captain Holloway, comforted her, "saying that when it came to his time he wanted to die at his post just as George did he said he had never seen any one so much Lamented as he was."[153] Condolences from friends also eased the pain: "Mary Kinsgbury wrote me a beautifull letter on the 4th remembering the mother of the fallen brave who had laid down their lives for their country," Sarah noted, and "Mr Walls, the Methodist minister at pu ville calld on us and said any woman might be proud of such a Son to be calld his mother."[154]

Perhaps there was indeed some compensation to Simpson Hamrick's family in the assurances that their son had died a "noble death. . . . a noble patriot" fighting for his government and his home and some comfort in the vow that "the proud Hoosiers yet living will avenge his death and be along the first to hoist the Stars and Stripes over the rebel Capitol."[155] When his brother George fell, Lucius Chapin consoled himself, "Oh how hard to make such sacrafices for truth and Country but God has ordered it so and let us submit to his unerring wisdom."[156]

Civilians may never have understood what the young men they sent to war experienced, but no insurmountable rift between soldiers and civilians emerged in Putnam County. Rather, both soldiers and civilians struggled to preserve their roles as providers, fathers, and community members despite the war's disruptions. War changed the men who fought it but did not estrange them entirely from those at home. Married couples strove to maintain contact and to preserve their domestic roles, either through visiting or exchanging gifts. Women continued to rely on their husbands as breadwinners. Absent fathers attempted to maintain relationships with their children, and their wives aided this endeavor. Women accepted the political or social roles assigned to them as women; they sought to accommodate the authority of even absent males. Elizabeth Applegate, despairing over her husband's failure to write, lamented, "John it is hard for me to stay at home and think that you are having such hard times and exposed to so much danger if there was only some way that I could help you, oh if I could only be with you. god grant the time will soon come that you can be with us and stay with us."[157] She did not seek to change her role in light of the war but instead sought to restore the old roles, with her family reunited and her husband at home. John, lingering in the army after his release from prison, justified his slow return by the need to provide for his family. Removed from "their own corner," men and women clung to prewar conceptions of their place.

But even if the war did little to change gender roles, it radically changed the position of African Americans in the nation. Blacks' role in the war threatened white supremacy and the racial order of prewar society. Wives such as Alice Chapin and Elizabeth Applegate did not seize on the war to assert their independence. African Americans did. In Putnam County, the Townsends were the only black family left by the time of the Civil War. They had persisted even as antiblack sentiment became codified in national statute and the state constitution. When the war came, the family's eldest son, Robert, would embody one of the greatest threats to white supremacy, becoming a soldier in the U.S. army.

6

SHOULDER-STRAPPED NEGROES

Putnam County's Copperheads opposed the war and emancipation because they feared undermining white supremacy. The image of "shoulder-strapped negroes" having command over white soldiers captured those fears. It was precisely to quell such white racism that the War Department discriminated against black troops. Not allowed to enlist until after the Emancipation Proclamation, black soldiers received less pay, initially found themselves restricted to noncombat duty, and could not become officers.[1] Although the war did bring a shift in the treatment of blacks—and the attitudes of whites toward them—the gains were incremental. Robert E. Townsend, son of the county's most stable and successful black family, served in Indiana's only black regiment, the 28th U.S. Colored Troops (USCT). Far from becoming the authority-wielding threat to white power that Copperheads dreaded, young Robert never saw a battlefield. He instead returned home, broken in health, and died while barely in his twenties. Although Robert Townsend's sad experience highlights just how exaggerated the Copperheads' fear of black supremacy was, the war nonetheless did erode white power. Not only did Robert become a soldier, however briefly, but white residents of the county also embraced some measure of black rights as a necessary war aim.

Robert was Luke and Charity Townsend's oldest son. Born in Indiana, he was only eighteen years old when the Civil War began. Some of the Townsend children could write their names, but Robert had to sign documents with his mark: given that Luke and Charity were acquiring property, hard work rather than education may have been the family's priority. As the eldest son in an upwardly mobile family, Robert was expected to go to work at an early age, which he did, helping his father in his work as a day laborer. Such help became more necessary with his father's growing age. In 1862, when Luke rented land and grew corn on Hiram Miller's farm, Robert did most of the work because Luke was crippled with rheumatism. Robert also labored for other farmers in the neighborhood, where he was considered "a steady hand at work." Most of the money he made went to his parents.[2] John C. Albin remembered Robert as "one of the best hands I ever had" and, beyond that, as "the mainstay in the support of the family" because Luke was disabled. In addition to farmwork, Robert toiled in a rock quarry south of Greencastle for a year before he enlisted. John Summers, a white neighbor of the Townsends who also worked in the quarry, remembered him as "a strong, hearty, robust young man" whose wages helped support his family.[3]

On January 4, 1864, about six months before his twenty-first birthday, Robert Townsend traveled to Indianapolis and enlisted as a private in the 28th Regiment of the U.S. Colored Troops. Although the Emancipation Proclamation had authorized black troops, Indiana had moved slowly in this regard. Historian William R. Forstchen believes that fear of a political backlash prompted Governor Oliver P. Morton to delay authorizing a black regiment until after the state elections of late 1863. Meanwhile, other states recruited hundreds of men in Indiana for their own black regiments, including the more famous 54th and 55th Massachusetts. Garland H. White, a former slave and a minister in the African Methodist Episcopal (AME) Church who helped raise the 28th, argued to Governor Morton that Hoosier African Americans wanted to serve their own state. Morton finally justified recruiting black troops on the grounds that if blacks fought, fewer white men would have to. Although members of the regiment came from many states and all parts of Indiana, most were from Indianapolis. Calvin Fletcher donated a portion of his farm for their mustering ground, which would be called Camp Fremont after the abolitionist general John C. Frémont. Except for his age—he was five years younger than the average for his company—Robert was a fairly typical soldier of the 28th. Like him, most were free-born farmers or laborers from Indiana.[4]

There are no sources to tell us what motivated Robert Townsend. Perhaps like many white soldiers, such as Lucius Chapin or John Applegate, he sought the money to make a start in life or help his family. In addition to a $300 federal bounty, the 28th's recruits were promised $100 from Marion County, to whose enlistment quota they were attributed. They would be paid $10 per month, $3 less than white troops. Such pay discrimination rankled black troops throughout the war, including the men of the 28th, but enlistment in the Union army nonetheless brought tangible economic rewards that might have been attractive to Robert and his family. Or the young man may have sought adventure. Recruiting propaganda for the 28th urged the "loyal colored" man to "cover himself with glory."[5] Of course, enlistment for a young black man carried additional meaning. That same recruiting propaganda specifically pointed out that the Confederacy "has for its basis slavery and oppression," and it exhorted, "Hereditary Bondsmen! Know you not that he who would be free, himself must first strike the blow?" Black men were urged to take part in the "great event . . . the overthrow of American slavery, and the elevation of our race to the dignity of men, and the sustaining of the General Government."[6] Although the Emancipation Proclamation removed prohibitions to African Americans serving as soldiers, it did not remove doubts about whether blacks had the manhood and intelligence necessary for combat.[7] Young black men who enlisted thus had something to prove about their race.

Whatever idealism black recruits such as Robert Townsend carried into the army rapidly eroded. By the spring of 1864, the regiment paraded through Indianapolis before its departure for Virginia, where the conflict had ground into a bloody war of attrition. Upon arriving in the east, the 28th was first stationed at Washington, D.C., and then sent to a camp near Alexandria, Virginia. But in early June, the regiment joined the Army of the Potomac south of Richmond, where it settled in to besiege Petersburg. As the siege dragged on, a former Pennsylvania mining engineer who was now a Union officer conceived the idea of tunneling under the Confederate lines and exploding several tons of gunpowder. To lead the attack that was to follow the explosion, Gen. Ambrose Burnside planned to use black troops, who had as yet seen little service in the campaign. Gen. George Gordon Meade, however, did not want to entrust the battle to green troops, so the black regiments, including the 28th, were relegated to the second wave of the attack, which was led by white troops.

Despite the spectacular explosion, which opened a hole in the Confederate lines, the Union attack was uncoordinated and badly led. Union troops waiting close to the site of the blast were temporarily stunned by its impact. Moving through the complex of trenches, they crowded one another, unable to bring large numbers of men together for the attack. Meanwhile, the veteran Confederates rallied and mounted a counteroffensive. By the time the 28th went into the attack, the Union had lost its momentum; one Union observer said there was at that point "no prospect of success." When the 28th passed to the front through the lines of wounded, it came under heavy rifle fire and case shot from the Confederate counterattack. Most members of the 28th were driven back into the huge crater that had been carved out of the earth by the explosives, where they would suffer from the broiling heat, lack of water, and diminishing supplies of ammunition. By midafternoon, Burnside finally complied with orders to retreat, but not all Union troops were able to escape "the Crater." Some African American troops trapped there were shot by white Union troops, who feared being taken prisoner with blacks. And Confederates killed other blacks whom they had taken prisoner. The brutal engagement that would be known as the battle of the Crater was a bloody loss for the Union. Two of the 28th's officers were killed, and twenty-two of its soldiers were killed or mortally wounded.[8]

Meade's decision not to use black troops to lead the assault has been criticized as racist. Although he justified his decision on the grounds that if the attack failed, the commanders would be condemned for sending black men to be slaughtered, perhaps he, like many others, doubted the manhood and courage of black men. Indeed, some would impute cowardice to the black troops at the Crater and fault them for losing the battle. But Garland White, who now served as the 28th's chaplain, rejected that charge. White described the troops as prepared and in good spirits when "the earth began to shake, as though the hand of God intended a reversal of the laws of nature. This grand convulsion sent both soil and souls to inhabit the air for a while, and then return to be commingled forever with each other, as the word of God commands, 'From dust thou art, and unto dust thou shalt return.'" The men then began to entrust White with letters for their parents and messages for their wives. Col. Charles S. Russell ordered his troops to fix bayonets, said his farewell to White, and vowed to lead the men to Petersburg itself. When White "saw our colors waving over the enemy's works," he mistakenly thought the battle had been successful. Blaming the defeat on poor leadership by the generals, he even found fault with the

1st Division of Colored Troops, who he said were mainly from the slave states: "They did not stand up to the work like those from the Free States."[9]

Petersburg would not fall until April 1865. Its abandonment by Robert E. Lee's army caused the Confederate government to evacuate Richmond. Black troops, including the 28th, were the first to enter the former capital. Garland White saw slaves liberated from the markets and families being reunited—his own mother found him after twenty years. When President Lincoln entered Richmond, the 28th paraded through the city. After the war, this unit went on to see service in Texas, where the men experienced not only homesickness and disease but also bafflement that black men who had served their country were denied the vote. Their regiment returned to Indianapolis in January 1866.[10]

But Robert Townsend did not participate in any of the regiment's defeats or triumphs. Although everyone remembered him as a strong and healthy young man, he sickened after a month or two at Camp Fremont. After purchasing some pies from one of the camp peddlers who sold food to the troops, he became "violently sick." The surgeon believed him to be suffering from food poisoning, administered an emetic, and sent him to hospital. Eventually, friends from Greencastle arrived to take him home. He never rejoined the regiment. After Robert's discharge in August 8, 1864, he lived at home but was not healthy enough to work. Although he helped his mother around the house and tended the garden, he could no longer perform the strenuous manual labor of farming and rock quarrying, with which he had helped support the family before the war. His former employer, John C. Albin, did not consider him "fit for any sort of work."[11]

On May 28, 1865, Robert died at his home in Putnam County of "enlargement of the heart." His mother described him as "lingering along in great suffering" before he died.[12] One of the 28th's white officers, Col. Henry Goddard Thomas, remembered that when the troops of the 28th learned they were to lead the attack on the Crater, they would sing every night until the battle, "We-e looks li-ike me-en a-a marchin' on, we looks li-ike men-er war."[13] Robert Townsend never became a man of war, but the Civil War did cause white residents of the county to rethink their assumptions about slavery and race.

Although the Copperheads overtly opposed Republican efforts to transform the war to save the Union into a war to end slavery, others in Putnam County were more willing to see an end to slavery. Insofar as slavery was responsible for the war, abolition offered a way to preserve the Union. Jeremiah Bum insisted to Calvin Fletcher, "I would deprive no loyal man of one single constitutional

Robert Townsend's grave. (Author's collection)

right" but added that "self preservation is the first law of nature." Preservation of the Union, for Bum, meant ending slavery: "If in the struggle [to restore the Union] . . . slavery should fall forever let it go i am for the union and constitution without slavery rather than its destruction to save slavery."[14] Bum's letter was pragmatic, not ideological, in its abolitionist sentiment, reflecting a shift in Northern opinion toward abolition as a military necessity. William Anderson agreed: "It is plainly to be seene that the slave has been the cause by going to war; if ones scull is so thick that they could never comprehend the idea before; for the whole interest is the negroe, with the wealthy people; and the poor class are led by the rich like a feather before the wind." Anderson thought "it is the best time for them to loos the damning chain of bondage that they have ever saw."[15] Like Bum, he was more interested in ending the source of conflict between the sections than in aiding African Americans.

By contrast, Mary and William Vermilion called themselves abolitionists, an unusual stance in Putnam County. Declaring herself "in favor of *immediate,* not *gradual* emancipation," Mary rejected colonization, not because she accepted blacks as fellow Americans but because "this country will need all its laborers for the next few years."[16] Yet despite her avowed abolitionism, she still identified blacks as property and their destiny as laborers. For William, it was antipathy toward Copperheads that fueled his abolitionism: "I am abolitionist full blooded. . . . I like the negro better than I like traitors. I would rather live by a loyal negro than by half of the people who are living in Putnamville."[17] W. H. McIlvaine, a soldier in the 11th Indiana, explained why the Emancipation Proclamation was required: "*Slavery is the cause of this war,* which no one will deny. It is also the *life* and *sinew* in supporting and prolonging this war. The President has the constitutional power to declare the slaves free. . . . The Proclamation is simply a *military necessity.*"[18] The proclamation did not discourse on the grandeur of human freedom, and neither did McIlvaine.

The Chapins also avowed abolitionist motives. For Lucius Chapin, slavery was a "dark blot."[19] His brother George was even willing for the carnage of war to continue until abolition was achieved. After Antietam, George wrote, "I hope the war will last until the *slave* shall be *free.* I am in for the war until liberty be established in every part of our country: till every man shall be free." But George Chapin shared with McIlvaine the pragmatic desire to end the source of national strife, writing that the country would never have peace until emancipation was achieved: "We have had war on the subject of slavery ever since our existence as a nation and more we are having bloodshed by the ocean on its account & no other. Now let us make way with the barbarous, corrupt and wicked institution and we shall be free indeed."[20] Like many abolitionists, Chapin regarded the "enormities" of slavery as a national sin: "Alas my country how thou art suffering for this sin!—And yet will *hardly* repent."[21]

Putnam whites had absorbed something of abolitionist propaganda. Mary Vermilion hoped her cousins would be converted to abolitionism by reading James R. Gilmore's 1862 novel *Among the Pines: Or, South in Secession-Time.*[22] Thomas V. Lyon's papers contained a poem entitled "The Negro Slave" that Lyon had modeled on an antislavery poem, "The Slave Ship." He presented it to some of the numerous female friends he made while on recruiting duty in Putnam County. Written from the perspective of a woman whose children were being sold, the poem repeatedly mentions the violence of slavery. Torn from their mother's arms, the children are dragged away, bound, and beaten. The girl begs to be taken away in place of her brother, whose blood stains her face: "Take me, whip me, chain me, starve me; / All my life I'll toil with Joy," she declares, if only she can save him. At the poem's beginning, the mother appeals, "Help! O help, thou God of Christians," but when no help appears, she closes by wondering, "Christians, who's the God ye worship? / Is he cruel, fierce, or good? / Does he take delight in mercy / Or in spilling human blood[?]"[23]

Similarly, the Chapin papers contain a long poem called "The Song of the Fetter," possibly composed by Alice Chapin, who did write poetry. The poem follows a chain from the forge to "the ship's foetid hold," where it binds the "dusky forms," and proceeds from auction block to cottonfield. The fetter is "rent . . . asunder" by the Civil War. The "battle's fearful clang," contrasted with the ringing of chain and shackle, makes the slaves "*free, free, free.*" For this, the poem gives credit to God rather than any action on the part of the slaves. "Let the glory ever be / *To Him who destroys but to Save!*"[24] Both poems emphasize the physical brutality and unchristian nature of slavery, while denying the ability of slaves to alter their own condition.

Whatever their exposure to abolitionist ideas, most soldiers bore with them the racial prejudices common to their homes. But as they moved south with the army, they came face to face with large numbers of slaves. For the white soldiers from Indiana, this might have been their first exposure to African Americans, and it caused some limited rethinking of their assumptions. Soldiers commonly used the word *white* to refer to that which was of better quality. Upon returning to camp from the field, John Applegate noted he was pleased "that I have got back where people live like white folks."[25] William Anderson objected to being shipped south in "some old old baggage cares that was not fit fo[r] white men to wride in."[26] Keyes Fletcher reported that Hoosier soldiers felt dismayed at being lowered in status. The camp hospital in Kentucky, he observed, "is in a large nigger jail. Our boys say they don't like the idea of being brought from Ind . . . to be put in jail & a nigger one at that."[27]

The word *nigger* was ubiquitous at that time, even among those perhaps expected to use more genteel language. Billy Fletcher referred to Samson, the African American butler at a western Virginia inn, as "the bigest blackest and politest of niggers," and in the center of his journal, he drew a stately Samson.[28] Keyes Fletcher also used *nigger* to describe his contraband servant, a man named Norris Allen. (Contrabands were runaway slaves who took refuge in Union army camps.) Again, use of the word contradicted much that Keyes said about Allen, whom he described as "a splendid nigger," a hard worker, "6 feet high and stout as an ox." He was also "about 2/3 white" according to Keyes and had been "*sold* by his own half brother, because every body knew it, & he was an eye sore to him." Keyes intended for Allen to return with him to Indiana. But despite the black man's capabilities and compelling personal story, Keyes regarded him as a possession and referred to him as "My darky," having decided that Allen would move to Indiana with no apparent regard for the man's wishes.[29] Billy's and Keyes's use of the demeaning term was at odds with their own descriptions of Samson's dignity and Norris Allen's competence, and it was equally at odds with their father's behavior. In his private diary, Calvin Fletcher used the words *colored* or *Negro*. Calvin "regret[ted]" the attitudes of soldiers in Keyes's regiment toward blacks, but he did not specifically mention his sons' attitudes.[30]

Like the Fletchers, William Anderson found black labor readily available, but he felt less comfortable exploiting it. Upon first entering Kentucky, his unit camped in the yard of a plantation. In the morning, Anderson and some others "rode to an old rich planters and called for our breakfast; and the negroes got up us one that was rite." Soon, the regiment had its own black cook "and have our meals got up in the best of stile. I find that it is a very pleasant thing to eat after negro cooks; Still I used to think I would not like to eat after they had cooked the victuals."[31] Ransom E. Hawley remembered a long night guarding a path in the Cumberland Gap: "Our reward came in the A M when a colored man came in with a basket of apples and other goods things to exchange for groceries. His basket was soon emptied."[32]

White soldiers from Indiana enjoyed watching African Americans dance and listening to their music. "At night Co. I had a real jubilee in the shape of fiddling and nigger dancing until tattoo," Josiah Williams related.[33] Another soldier described how some freedmen were persuaded to dance. As three soldiers played on fiddles and a horn, blacks gathered in the doorway to listen. "After a little coaxing," two black women and two boys "began to dance a little." When they seemed hesitant, one of the white officers "jumped up and began to pat jube." This encouragement was all that was needed to set off a performance that "beat any show." A man named John "would jump about 2 feet high and then come down on it heel & toe."[34] Observing these entertainments may not have promoted much cultural understanding, but it did allow white soldiers and black contrabands to become acquainted. In September 1862, when Keyes Fletcher passed "a great many darkies" at a saltworks near Winchester, Kentucky, he recognized "several of them [as] the very same fellows" he had seen "singing their corn songs" months earlier: "One fellow, that I saw dance the jigg . . . knew some of our boys, & seemed as glad to see them as a brother. He walked with us about a mile."[35]

White soldiers from Putnam were impressed in a different way by African American religiosity. William Vermilion heard a black man preach to their regiment, and although the minister had been a slave all his life, he was literate "and almost as white" as one of Putnam County's Baptist ministers. In fact, Vermilion thought the freedman "used better language and was undoubtedly a more intelligent man and a better preacher" than his counterpart in Indiana.[36] Although listening to a black preacher was evidently a new experience for Vermilion, there was a long tradition of black ministers appealing to white audiences. Methodist bishop Francis Asbury had found himself less popular than some black preachers, such as Harry Hosier. While stationed in Alabama, Thomas Lyon made it a habit to visit "darkey meetings," where "they had a good old fashioned time." He helped organize a Sabbath school there for black women, giving them readings in the Bible.[37]

Among the African Americans whom Putnam soldiers encountered were many contrabands. In Tennessee, Keyes Fletcher saw contraband camps that housed men, women, and children. The contrabands were "bed & clothed by the *government*," but Keyes was also aware of the labor they did. Besides building fortifications, blacks cooked for white officers, troops, and the hospitals; worked as teamsters and nurses; and performed many other noncombat tasks for the army. "I am very willing for them to take the spade & pick, dig trenches & build breastworks or cut down the timber, & to garrison Southern forts I think is a good Idea," Keyes concluded. "But the North Western army never will let them fight amongst them."[38]

The 27th Indiana, which included many Putnam County men, adopted its contraband cook, a man named Henry. When slave hunters came looking for Henry, the colonel gave him protection but was overruled by the general, who dismissed Henry's guard. Simpson Hamrick and others had to restrain the men "from just pitching into the Negro hunters for Henry had become the favorite all through the Regt every man regretted to see him go & all would have fought for him streight through." Some of the soldiers then decided to send Henry to Indiana in order to prevent his master from reclaiming him. Having smuggled him out of camp, they had him rendezvous at the railroad with an officer going north. Henry's ultimate destination was the Hamrick home in Putnam County. He was a "verry intelligent boy," Simpson reported, adding that if his father, A.

D. Hamrick, aided Henry, the whole regiment would be grateful.[39] Henry was not the only contraband with the 27th. Josiah Williams and his uncle "revel[ed] in the luxury of having a nigger man to cook."[40]

By contrast, William Vermilion was less enamored of black workers. When the army in Memphis needed to take down about 100 houses that were blocking their guns, black workers were assigned the task. After the supervising white officer went to take dinner, the workers set fire to the buildings, thinking that the quickest way to clear them. "That was Negro-like," Vermilion commented.[41]

Aden Cavins was more tolerant of the contrabands. He kept his wife, Matilda, informed of the welfare of a child named Lindsey who had attended her when she visited camp. "Lindsy is well and much flattered by your messages to him. He stood up like a man until the thickest of the fight on the first day," whereupon Aden sent him to the rear.[42] John Chapin, Lucius's brother, was also easily pleased with black servants. He had gone to the South both to be near his brothers and to preach to Union troops. The black woman who kept his room did it in "style" with fresh bouquets. "These black servants are wonderfully faithful and often times neat," Chapin wrote.[43]

Yet despite their subservient roles, contrabands could be perceived as threats to white supremacy. Considerable ire was raised by stories that blacks received preferential treatment over white soldiers. Back in Putnam County, a rumor circulated concerning Gen. Nathaniel P. Bank's retreat from Strasburg, Virginia, in May 1862. It was said that blacks had been allowed to ride in the wagons in preference to sick soldiers. Capt. T. H. Nance denied this rumor, and Simpson Hamrick attributed it to the Copperheads. Hamrick explained that accompanying the army were "quite [a] Number of . . . Negroes": some were employed as drivers, laborers, cooks, or servants, but others were slaves who had fled their masters by accompanying the Union army. These runaways had brought their masters' horses and wagons. So wounded soldiers were not forced out to make room for blacks; rather, "many a tired & Disabled Soldier ordered Negroes to Dismount & they . . . had the benefit of the Negroes horse that he had taken from his master. . . . all this Blow about Negroes being hauled is made because there is Some Sympathy yet for Rebles even in the union Army." Such soldiers then spread the rumors to their Copperhead friends at home.[44]

Putnam whites at times sensed that blacks and whites did not quite know what to make of each other. William Anderson, for one, was mystified: "We can not tell what the true sentiment of the people [is] in reference to the war: I mean the colored people. They are very pleasant and accomodating to the union soldiers."[45] In fact, slaves were assessing the changes brought by these new men. Maryland slaves told Hamrick that "their Masters was all Secesh until the union troops came there & now they are all union men."[46] Aden Cavins's contraband, Lindsey, did not know how to respond when Matilda sent him a gift. "Lindsey laughed and giggled at his present," Aden wrote his wife, "and then putting on a serious face asked me why you sent it to him, and when I told him you liked him for what he had done for you as well as for what he was doing for me, he laughed, put on a broad grin and said he was glad you liked him."[47] "Our Negraw says the Hoosiers all have the biggest & largest Whiskers that he ever Saw," Simpson Hamrick reported. Blacks, too, were seeing new people, just as Hoosiers were seeing blacks for the first time.[48] By the end of the war, blacks no longer feared to express their loyalties. Lucius Chapin related, "We asked the Darkies if the Rebels went by their in a run No Massa they didn't run 'Dey went flyn.'" The blacks took pleasure in the Confederate defeat, and beyond that, they cast their fortunes with the invading army: "The Darkies are flocking in by Hundreds," Lucius Chapin reported, and "women men young and old from the infant to the white haired are here and wanting to go along—Raged bare footed yet eager anxious to endure any hardship in order to and be free."[49]

African American Unionism helped to break down traditional prejudices. As Anderson gradually came to realize, blacks were on the Union side. Two slaves showed him and other Union soldiers a corncrib, saying that "their masy was a reble and they did not care how much corne we would take." Slaves were good sources of information: "The negroes tells us more about the rebles than we can find out any other way. They are more truthful than many of the white people that talk so much. I have all the comfidence in some of the negroes." Slaves had found that Northern soldiers treated them better than did their masters, so "they will tell all about the rebles that they know."[50] The 27th also received information about Confederate movements from a black man they rescued from drowning. He told them the Confederates had fallen back—"*skedaddled*"—20 miles.[51] George Chapin insisted, "There is not a single instance on record of the slave acting treacherously with Union soldiers, and yet the Union Soldiers curse them just because they are black. They have always proved a help to our cause by giving all the information in their power."[52] Chapin's regiment liberated black soldiers who had been captured the previous fall. One of the blacks had agreed to act as manservant for a Confederate officer, but when the Union advanced, the man grabbed the officer by his feet and held onto him until the

Northern troops came up.[53] A soldier in the 133rd, writing from Bridgeport, Alabama, referred to a "company of gentlemen of Southern birth, composed of the *loyal* men of the South, negroes."[54]

Sympathy for individual contrabands helped persuade soldiers of the need for emancipation. The threat to Henry, the contraband cook, accomplished more for the cause of abolitionism than anything else had, Simpson Hamrick said. The army was becoming abolitionist because the more white soldiers saw of slavery, "the more Detestable it appears."[55] Putnam soldiers noted the light skin of many slaves. And even though Keyes Fletcher compared the contrabands he saw in Tennessee to "a big case full of Monkeys," he acknowledged their biracial background. The contrabands were "of all Sorts, shapes & colors. Little black wooly heads, & & little white wooly heads & little yaller straight heads."[56] Of two children, four and six years old, William Vermilion observed, "The girl is full as white as many children living North, the parents of whom are always prattling about the Abolitionists bringing Negroes North to associate with white people. Poor fools that they are, talking about Amalgamation. They believe in slavery but not amalgamation, when slavery *is* amalgamation."[57] Upon visiting New Orleans, a self-proclaimed Jacksonian Democrat observed that "God Almighty seems to have changed his view in making niggers—at least three fifths of them were nearly white." "The Southern climate blackens a white man, but whites a black man," he concluded.[58]

Educated slaves surprised Putnam whites as much as light-skinned ones did. A visit to "a nigger Sunday School" in New Orleans impressed the Jacksonian Democrat. About 200 pupils were present, but the school enrolled as many as 400 to 700. Although a white teacher in one of the city high schools presided, his assistant was a black man who had graduated from one of the best eastern colleges. "The pupils were orderly, tidy, obedient and attentive. The little shavers read portions of scripture from large cards.—They sang several hymns with a hearty good will and were accompanied with the melodeon, played by a young and educated nigger teacher in one of the schools. At the conclusion they made the large building ring again with the song, 'Slavery's chain is bound to break.'" In addition to the Sunday school, this man visited a school for black children taught by a family of "educated niggers, but in a very faded condition." Again the school was large, having about 300 scholars. He reported, "One of the more advanced classes read *well* in the National Fourth Reader, and were proficient in Geography. The teaching was very thorough and accurate, and the school in every sense well and ably conducted. This is but one of fourteen similar schools in this city alone."[59] The visitor was impressed with the erudition and culture of some African Americans.

Antislavery sentiment was also encouraged by disgust with white Southerners. Lucius Chapin's in-law Jonas Seely reported that the officers and men of his command had all been proslavery until they went south. They were now repelled by white Southern fealty to slavery: "Touch their Nigger & you touch their God." He observed that white Southern women would rather lose all their menfolk than lose their slaves, the hallmark of genteel status.[60] Seely himself evidently felt little sympathy for black slaves, but he had learned the place of nonslaveowning whites. What offended him was the arrogance of slaveowners and their contempt for whites who worked, no doubt including Northern free white men.

Outrage over slavery did cause white Putnam soldiers to accept—though often with reservations—African Americans' aspirations to be soldiers. Josiah Williams, for one, believed in using "the *nigger* every way as a drudge &c but when he don's a Soldiers clothes I consider it dishonoring a noble profession."[61] Thomas Lyon provided no comment on black soldiers but merely noted the actions of "darky" regiments with neither criticism nor approval.[62] William Vermilion wrote, "We want every negro sct at liberty & if any person tried to enslave them give them a gun & let them flood the South with blood."[63] And W. H. McIlvaine thought it simple good sense to use blacks as soldiers, thus reducing the need for white troops:

> Suppose you were drowning and a big *buck nigger* would come to rescue you from death. Would you because he is black and called a negro, kick him away and allow yourself to drown? No, sir! I think not; and he who would must be a fool. So its with this government war business. Whenever a black man can serve this, his adopted cou[n]try, I am willing. If a black man can save my life, all is right, I shall not grumble."[64]

Putnam soldiers were much like other Union troops in accepting abolition and finally black troops as a pragmatic measure to punish the South and end the war.[65]

Initially, officers in black regiments were all white. This situation reflected doubts about black men's capabilities as soldiers and leaders of men. Eventually, however, some black soldiers became noncommissioned officers, and a few even gained commissions. Yet some questioned whether white officers would be willing to command black troops. William Vermilion reflected, "What little people knew when they used to say that the Government could not get white men to command Negro troops." Vermilion knew many sergeants and privates who, unable to advance because of limited opportunities, were eager to take these new commissions.[66] George Chapin considered applying for a place in a colored regiment and advised his brother Lucius to get one, too: "There is not the least doubt of the slave's being good material to work on. I believe they can be trained easier than the white men and there is no end to their faithfulness or devotion to the cause of freedom."[67]

While soldiers adjusted their attitudes, antiblack sentiment remained strong on the home front. Emancipation seemed to confirm Democratic suspicions that the war had all along been abolitionist. At the courthouse in Greencastle, the Democratic meeting of February 1863 condemned the Emancipation Proclamation and refused to further support a war for "negro emancipation." The Democrats, presided over by Delana Eckels, were indifferent to African Americans' claims to a place in the polity, asserting that the United States was a white man's nation. After the defeat at Fredericksburg, rumors circulated in the county that Lincoln would not issue the final Emancipation Proclamation.[68] But any hopes that Republicans would abandon black rights proved illusory.

In a major campaign speech at the Governor's Circle in Indianapolis in 1864, John Hanna taunted Democrats with the specter of racial equality. He asked, "Who are they so horrified by day and by night with the specter of negro equality?" His answer was, "Generally those so much lower than the negro that they can never hope to be his equal without the special interposition of the power of the Godhead." But he reassured the Copperheads that such fears of equality were "groundless." "The law of progress," Hanna explained, "forbids it. While [the black man] is going up in the scale of patriotism you are going down, and the idea that you will ever be compelled to meet on terms of social equality is utterly preposterous. The very nature of a patriotic negro revolts at such a consummation."[69] Hanna did not argue that blacks were as good as whites but rather that Copperheads were so low as to be inferior even to blacks.

When the Indiana legislature passed a resolution approving the Thirteenth Amendment, the *Banner* praised the act: "Thus one by one the States are wheeling into line and arraying themselves against the monstrous iniquity and curse to the United States, African slavery."[70] Nonetheless, Indiana's Thomas A. Hendricks would be one of only six senators to vote against the amendment. Historian Michael Vorenberg says that Indiana had "the most prolonged debate" among all the Northern states over the amendment. Democrats argued that the measure would make Indiana's black laws unconstitutional, but Republicans countered that there were different classes of citizenship: just as women did not enjoy full political rights although they were citizens, blacks, too, could still be discriminated against in law. Emancipation need not mean equal rights. This formula reconciled Hoosiers to the Thirteenth Amendment. In fact, Indiana was the only Northern state that failed to repeal its black laws during the Civil War.[71]

The war's end would not become an occasion for pondering its emancipationist meaning. Lee's surrender and Lincoln's assassination caused Putnam County citizens to reiterate their opposition to treason—but these events brought no assertion that the commitment to black rights would continue. News of Lee's surrender arrived in Greencastle at 10 A.M. on Monday, April 10. From that moment "till late in the night, the rejoicing was continual. Some manifested their joy by ringing bells, others by blowing horns, all vieing with one another in their efforts to make the most noise. The illumination at night, and the display of fire-works was grand. The students of Asbury mustered their forces, and paraded the principal streets, and with their torches made a beautiful appearance." Asbury students serenaded Daniel W. Voorhees, who was staying at a local hotel, with songs such as "John Brown" and "Rally 'round the Flag."

Such a celebration would have been incomplete without speeches. That evening, a crowd assembled to listen to D. E. Williamson, Rev. Aaron Wood, and John Hanna. Whereas Hanna used the occasion to once again denounce the Copperheads and Williamson made clear how the nation had grown in might, Wood spoke of nationalism, addressing his "FELLOW CITIZENS . . . as a part of a great Nation of freeman, . . . [I] cannot address you as citizens of Greencastle or Putnam, nor even Indiana, but as citizens connected with a great Nation, whose sovereignty extends from ocean to ocean. This sovereignty obtained by our fathers, symbolized by that flag,—has been maintained at *great sacrifice.*" Wood's theme was the triumph of nationalism over states' rights. This development had implications for Putnam County, as localities had to find a place as a small part of a larger whole. Wood also reminded his listeners of the war's cost. But apparently, none of the speakers discoursed on the expansion of U.S. liberty to African Americans. Wood's reference to freemen seems to have been nothing more than standard patriotic rhetoric.[72]

The victory celebration had its own costs. J. M. Leak lost an arm when a cannon discharged early during one of the salutes. Leak, a mechanic by trade, was ramming the gun when it fired, throwing him some distance. He suffered burns and grave damage to his left arm, which had to be amputated. The accident occurred despite the presence of "experienced artillerymen" who had warned the celebrants not to fire the cannon with "defective implements," for doing so "would probably produce accident and death."[73] The veteran soldiers' warning was not heeded.

April 20 had been declared a day of thanksgiving by Governor Morton, but he changed it to a day of mourning after John Wilkes Booth shot President Abraham Lincoln. Soldier F. M. Harris's good cheer at peace was shaken by news of the assassination. "Eve[r]y human countenance is so greatly changed," he noted, with "tottering Sad Harts."[74] In Putnam County, citizens retired to bed on Friday night, still in a celebratory mood, only to awaken Saturday to "the crushing announcement by telegraph, that Abraham Lincoln had fallen in the very midst of his work of patriotism." Word soon arrived that the president was dead. "All were astounded, and overwhelmed with grief." Churches tolled their bells, no business was conducted, people thronged the streets, and houses were draped in mourning. Women similarly adorned the churches with colors of mourning and patriotic symbols such as the flag. Even Copperheads expressed "profound grief." As usual, the occasion led to a public gathering at the courthouse, where Col. John A. Matson spoke. On Sunday afternoon, a procession from the Masonic and Odd Fellows halls moved toward campus. Church congregations joined in as it passed, each congregation bearing a flag draped in mourning. At the campus, "many stalwart faces were bathed in tears." An estimated 4,000 people assembled to listen to scripture reading, prayer, more speeches, and a choir.[75] One of the orators, Rev. E. W. Fisk, "almost Deified Lincoln," Matilda Cavins related, "and his remarks were approved by all I have heard speak of them."[76]

At that Sunday meeting on the college campus, resolutions were also approved "irrespective of party," condemning the assassination and mourning the president but asserting that "we despair not of the Republic." Although a leader might fall, the nation's institutions would prevail. On Wednesday, funeral services were held in the college yard because the crowd was too large for Asbury's chapel. Dr. Thomas Bowman, president of the university, was the speaker. Citizens of Putnam had yet another occasion to mourn the president on April 30, when Lincoln's funeral train passed through Indianapolis. That morning, a half-fare excursion train carried mourners from Greencastle for the viewing in the statehouse.[77]

Ransom E. Hawley showed interest in going to Indianapolis to see Lincoln's body, but his father strongly cautioned him against the idea: "You will see a large procession, you may see the coffin but I do not think you will the corpse. I am told the embalming is imperfect—the body is changing and probably will not be seen." (Reverend Hawley was correct; Lincoln's face had grown black and sunken before the body left the East Coast.) In addition, Reverend Hawley disapproved of a Sunday trip and warned, "There is no little danger to life, limbs, morals, & money in the immense crowds that will be in Indianapolis."[78] Genuinely anguished at Lincoln's death, Sarah Hawley wished, "Oh! That every Union man might resolve *never never* to go into a theatre for in a theatre the mighty has fallen How sad Oh! How sad."[79]

Josiah Williams was in the East, where he too witnessed obsequies surrounding Lincoln's death. "The funeral ceremonies of our much lamented and martyred President were quite grand," he reported to his parents, "but of course you have seen all in the papers. I saw the remains on the third [d]ay when lying in state in the Capitol. Thousands were constantly wending their way there. Baltimore was draped in deep morning." The funeral procession in New York City took four hours to pass.[80]

No records remain of how the fallen president was mourned by the Townsend family. Robert Townsend would have been entering his final illness when the war ended. The Lincoln that Putnam County's white residents lamented was the savior of the Union, not the Great Emancipator. Consequently, the assassination of the beloved leader did not spur his followers to commit themselves to his "new birth of freedom." In Putnam County, people instead concentrated on revenge. F. M. Harris hinted that the assassination "gives thirst for blood to all loyal people whom are for this war worn republic."[81] The *Banner* argued that the assassination made clear "the Dangers of the Hour." The joy of victory might cause the victors to forget their bitterness in "magnanimity," but important questions remained for the nation to settle: "Who shall be its citizens? What the punishment of treason[?]" The *Banner* favored an amnesty for the "bulk of the people," who had either been "duped by crafty leaders" or "been the slave of slavery": "Let them be forgiven." This generosity did not, however, extend to the elite. "But the leaders! Let them DIE! Let the government vindicate itself by branding treason as the *blackest* in the catalogue of crimes."[82] Although the *Banner*'s editorialist mentioned the question of citizenship, he concentrated exclusively on how to punish white Southerners, not on what the new status for African Americans might be.

It was not just Lincoln's death that led many in the county to predict a harsh peace but the *"great sacrifice"* described by orator Wood. "Too many widowed hearts have bled, too many orphans cried to God to be avenged, too many patriot hearts ceased to beat on the thousand bloody battle fields of the Republic, too many spirits of starved prisoners wonder through the land," the *Banner* predicted, for Confederates to receive mercy.[83] The paper expected soldiers to want vengeance against those who had caused their sufferings: "When those of our brave boys who are so fortunate as to survive all these horrors, return to their homes, with what feelings of hatred and revenge will they behold these men, who have from the beginning done all in their power to prolong the war?"[84] Many in Putnam would acutely feel the nature of this "great sacrifice": John Applegate, who returned seriously ill from his imprisonment at Andersonville; Lucius Chapin, who lost two brothers to the cause; the fathers of William Anderson and Simpson Hamrick, who lost their sons; and Luke and Charity Townsend, whose son came home to die. It remained to be seen whether the sacrifice of African American soldiers, such as the Townsends' son Robert, would be remembered in the postwar period.

Despite the sacrifices made by the Townsends and many other black families, racism still existed in the county. In the 1860s, an editorial in the *Asbury Review* considered the admission of black students. Women had been admitted recently and with controversy, and the editorial was not friendly to the idea of further widening the student body. In the words of the university's historian, admitting African Americans seemed "even more degrading than Asbury's admission of women."[85] But in the prewar period, discussions about race and slavery took place in a county that was overwhelmingly white, whereas the black population of Putnam would grow after the war. Indeed, Democrats had feared blacks would move north of the Ohio River, and they even accused the Lincoln administration of encouraging "a worthless negro population" to settle in the free states.[86] The war and emancipation "had aroused every colored person to the importance of striking for freedom, and men, women and children are generally on the move for some place beyond the reach of their late masters." The Putnam County Democratic newspaper noted that freedmen sometimes suffered the "most cruel and fiendish atrocities" at the hands of "their late owners, especially is this the case when males of families have been enlisted in our army." But recognition of the brutality inflicted on freedmen did not mean Hoosiers wanted this "black vomit" in their state.[87]

It was the war that made it possible for blacks to move out of the slave states. During the 1860s, Indiana's black population more than doubled, reaching 24,560 by 1870, and it continued to grow through the rest of the century. In addition, the pattern of black settlement in the state altered. Until the 1850s, most African Americans were located in the counties along the Ohio River, across from Kentucky. But in the 1860s, blacks began to move into the central part of the state. In Putnam County, the black population tripled, from 22 people in 1860—most of them in Robert Townsend's immediate family—to 74 in 1870. Over one-third had been born in Indiana, with just as many having been born in Kentucky, and the rest came from all over the South, including one person born in Mississippi.[88] The numbers, though, were still tiny: African Americans in 1870 were three-tenths of a percent of the county's population, up from one-tenth in 1860. But some residents of the county would take note of the new arrivals.

At the war's end, Carpentersville experienced an influx of both white and black refugees. A local commentator disliked the Southern émigrés for "their aristocratic notions and domineering principles," but a black man took even longer to earn acceptance. Jim came from Kentucky in search of his former master, who was one of the white refugees.

> For a few days the negro seemed to be in danger of life or limb, but it was finally concluded to wait a few days and see how he conducted himself. Finding that he was quiet and industrious, it was agreed that Jim might stay and enjoy a little corner in this great country. So I believe the majority of the citizens have concluded that a white man is about as good as a darkey, if he behaves himself.[89]

On the one hand, Jim faced a degree of hostility that white migrants, even former Confederates, evidently did not; on the other, he found some measure of acceptance in the altered racial climate after the war.

Unlike Jim, some of the black migrants were themselves former soldiers. Robert Townsend died without seeing combat, but his younger sister, Catherine, married a veteran, Wyatt James, a former Mississippi slave who served in the 28th USCT, where he had known Robert. James had gone to Greencastle during the war, probably as a runaway slave. After enlisting at Indianapolis, he served in the Petersburg campaign and in Texas. He had seen combat, having been wounded in the leg at the Crater. When James settled in Putnam County after mustering out in 1866, he boarded with the Townsends and worked as a laborer. James was the Mississippi-born black recorded in the 1870 census.[90]

Illness denied Robert Townsend the opportunity to prove his own manhood or that of his race, rendering him not much of a threat to white supremacy in the county. But Wyatt James's experience was different. Even though black soldiers were rarely in positions of command, he and other black men embodied the "shoulder-strapped Negroes"—men with the authority earned from having risked their lives for their country—that Copperheads feared. Veterans such as James and other freedpeople moving into Putnam County would continue to demand their new rights. When Garland H. White, the chaplain of the 28th, spoke at the regiment's mustering out in Indianapolis, he asked "that his people be favored with the full advantage of the elective franchise, as the best and only means of affording them a sure protection from their oppressors, and regretted that the very men with whom his people had contended in battle, had now more authority in the Government than those who had fought to sustain it."[91] The men of the 28th knew they needed to be "equal before the law"; otherwise, as White lamented, "we have got no home."[92] The 28th's veterans had reason to fear that Indiana would prove no home for black men. William Gibson, who spent a furlough in Parke County in spring 1865, found Hoosiers "very indifferent" to the idea of repealing the black laws, but he viewed equal rights as part of the pay due the 28th for their service. Gibson believed that men who fought for their country deserved "the rights and privileges due to other citizens." He asked:

> Shall these brave sons return home after periling their lives for several years in the storm of battle for the restoration of the Union and to vindicate the honor and dignity of that fair Western State which is classed among the best composing this great nation, but to be treated as slaves? Shall it be said by the nations of the earth that any portion of the United States treated her brave defenders thus? I hope never to see the day; yet it is fast approaching.[93]

Gibson's pessimism was not unwarranted, but the war *had* altered race relations. White soldiers and some civilians had accepted those alterations in order to remove the causes of the conflict and win the war. It remained for Wyatt James and other African Americans to remind ambivalent white Northerners of the war's emancipationist meaning.

PART 3
AFTER THE WAR

7

RADICALS AND CONSERVATIVES

In 1868, Putnam County's most notorious Copperhead, Sol Akers, was murdered at an election-year rally in neighboring Owen County. At the time of his death, Akers was quarreling bitterly with another former Copperhead, Judge Delana Eckels. Republicans made a show of mourning Akers in order to highlight Democratic divisions. But Republicans had a sincere reason to regret his death—it deprived them of living evidence of Democratic treason. Even as reconciliationists called for overlooking the war's causes and rifts, Republicans sought to keep the party affiliations of the war alive by reminding voters of local Peace Democrats' failure to support the Union. Meanwhile, economics increasingly competed with Reconstruction for partisans' attention. Republicans who had earned the title radical for their insistence on empowering African Americans increasingly advocated conservative finance, including a return to a specie currency. Democrats, always conservative on race, embraced soft money and sought support from those who were dissatisfied with conservative fiscal policy. Even though definitions of *radical* and *conservative* shifted as race gave way to finance, the economics of the postwar era remained rooted in the Civil War. The debate over specie was, after all, a debate over whether the soldiers' money, greenbacks, sufficed for a postwar economy.[1]

A week before Lee's army surrendered at Appomattox Courthouse, Daniel Voorhees spoke in Greencastle. He began by defending the Democratic party "against the common and worn out calumny that it is in favor of disunion." Voorhees now accepted abolition as a fait accompli, but he hoped to preserve white supremacy, warning "that it is the settled purpose of the republican party now in power at Washington to place the negro by legislation on an equality as a citizen with the white man." The "next great issue," he said, centered on one key question: "Shall the white man maintain his supremacy, or shall he take into partnership in the affairs of government three or four millions of Africans[?]" The stenographer transcribing Voorhees's words did not record the audience's reaction—there were no notations of laughs or hisses when the congressman made these predictions—but Voorhees told the crowd, "You look incredulous."[2] Copperheads had warned that the war would erode white supremacy. Now Voorhees predicted a future in which former slaves voted and were completely equal under law with whites.

In fact, local Republicans initially emphasized the need to punish traitors, not promote black rights. During the war, R. M. Hazelett had described the prevailing sentiment in Putnam as "to treat the common soldiers well but give the leaders the deavel if they catch them."[3] That sentiment persisted throughout Reconstruction. A decade after the war, the *Banner* urged continuation of Reconstruction policies because "we have spent too much blood and treasure on these rebellious Southerners to let them overthrow the Government now."[4] Republicans in Putnam also insisted that the traitors included antiwar Northerners. Northern Copperheads were as bad as Southern Confederates: an ex-soldier called them Siamese twins. The Copperheads, it was argued, "should share the same fate—die the same political death—as their fellow conspirators South."[5] Permanently disempowering Southern and Northern Democrats proved, however, a difficult task.

The policy of the new president, Andrew Johnson, emphasized both punishment and white supremacy. His proclamation of amnesty restored to former Confederates their property, with the exception of slaves, and their political rights, but it did not extend to the wealthy or to political and military leaders. But Johnson quickly undercut the proscriptive elements of his plan with generous pardons. A former Democrat, he broke with Radical Republicans who favored black rights, vetoing both the 1866 civil rights bill, which outlawed racially discriminatory state laws, and the Freedmen's Bureau bill, which extended the lifetime of the agency that helped former slaves adjust to free labor. Locally, Johnson passed over a Republican applicant to reinstate E. R. Kercheval, who had served as postmaster at Greencastle under James Buchanan, and he removed John Hanna as U.S. district attorney for Indiana, reputedly because Hanna refused to adopt what he referred to as Johnson's "Copperhead" program. Putnam Democrats gloated over the president's Reconstruction policy, especially his veto of "the infamous Freedmen's Bureau bill." County Democrats resolved to oppose Radical Republican measures aimed at "bringing about an equality of races before the law."[6]

In addition to overriding Johnson's vetoes, the Radical Republicans passed their own Reconstruction bill the next spring, using the military to implement their policy in the South. Putnam Democrats accused Republicans of using the power of the federal government to "put the negro above the white man." The Greencastle Democratic newspaper referred to the Radical Reconstruction measures as "the negro supremacy and military dictator bills." Further, Democrats resented the taxation necessary to pay for Radical measures. The Democratic newspaper ran a poem entitled "Taxes! Taxes!" that claimed there were taxes on every item one ate or wore or even heard, smelled, or felt. One line demanded, "AND WHAT ARE THE TAXES FOR?" The poem's answer was, "Why!— the Freedmen's Bureau to keep in repair, / so that Radical loafers can each have a chair, / and a chance for the pickings and stealings there!"[7]

As commander in chief, Johnson was in a position to replace military commanders friendly to the Radicals' policy. When Johnson fired Secretary of War Edwin M. Stanton, in violation of the Tenure of Office Act, the increasing conflict between congressional Radicals and the White House led Congress to impeach and try the president. The impeachment crisis gave new strength to Putnam County Democrats. John A. Matson broke with the Republicans over what he saw as efforts to subvert the Constitution and deprive the president of his "just powers." A respected former Whig, Matson issued a public statement accusing Radical Republican senators of acting as "a vigilance Committee" in their zeal to remove Johnson from office.[8] But Matson's position was more complicated. His speech to a Democratic meeting in 1868 revealed that impeachment was only the breaking point after protracted discontent with Republican policy. First, he disagreed with punishing the South, preferring a general amnesty to military government. In addition, he seemed uncomfortable with black rights, believing "a general amnesty . . . would place the Southern

States in the hands of the white men." The Radicals' policy of disfranchising Southern whites and enfranchising Southern blacks "would end in anarchy and war."[9]

Matson's son, Courtland C. Matson, a former Union soldier and War Democrat, agreed that the Republicans were unnecessarily interested in black rights. He now alleged that the Radicals had prolonged the war in order to shift its focus to the slaves. For the election of 1868, C. C. Matson organized the Union White Boys in Blue, which grew to 120 members. The organization accomplished two purposes. It showed that there were soldiers in the Democratic party, and it strengthened the party's association with white supremacy. Just as these Democrats had rallied as soldiers to save the Union, so would they now rally to save the country from Radical Republicanism. The White Boys opposed both the "despotism" of military reconstruction and the Freedmen's Bureau, which maintained "in vicious idleness and profligacy hordes of unthrifty and indolent negroes." They further "opposed . . . negro supremacy and the domination of an inferior, degraded race in these [Southern] States, by which one-third of our States are to be ruthlessly abandoned to the mismanagement and control of barbarism."[10] Democrats specifically asserted that the White Boys in Blue were not the Grand Army of the Republic (GAR), which admitted "colored troops" and sympathized with "negro-elevating schemes."[11] The Republican response was to organize the Grant Boys in Blue. Using Grant's name not only reminded voters that the Republicans had a genuine war hero as their presidential nominee, it also avoided the issue of race. Grant's boys could be white, but in contrast to the Democratic soldiers, race was not their defining feature.[12]

During Reconstruction, Democrats portrayed the Southern people as "disposed to accept the results of the war in good faith," the conclusion James Smiley reached after a Southern tour.[13] When J. R. F. Pilcher, principal of the Bainbridge Male and Female Academy appeared as the main speaker of the Democratic county convention of 1867, he argued that "the old harmony and brotherhood" could be achieved if the North merely "extend[ed] the hand of fellowship to them." He received "great applause."[14] Local Democrats dismissed evidence of bad fellowship, such as the Ku Klux Klan, as a Republican fabrication designed to inflame Northern opinion in support of Radical policy. During the election of 1876, C. C. Matson accused Republicans of making "the mole hill" of "Southern outrages" into a mountain for partisan purposes. Local Democrats further minimized Klan violence by labeling minor vandalism as

Klan actions. When inebriated youths took gates off hinges, released stock, and blocked roads in Putnamville, the *Press* called it the work of the local "Ku Klux." Even Republicans trivialized Klan atrocities by equating them with common political harassment. After a Democrat disrupted congressional candidate John Coburn's speech, the *Banner* called the heckler "one of the Ku-Klux." Such bandying about of the Klan's name trivialized the group's threat to Southern Republicans.[15]

Putnam Republicans themselves were uneasy about making allies of African Americans. They denied that citizenship, which the Fourteenth Amendment in 1867 defined to include African Americans, conferred suffrage rights. John Hanna dealt at length with "the Bugbear of Negro Suffrage" in an 1866 campaign speech. He pointed out that women and children were citizens but not voters, and argued that Indiana would still be able to deny black suffrage under the Fourteenth Amendment.[16] But race riots in Memphis and New Orleans that killed numerous African Americans provoked Hanna into a rare plea to protect the freedmen. African Americans, he insisted, had defended the federal government even in battle. He asked, "Will it injure you or me, degrade our social or political standing to simply shield them from wrong, encourage them in industrial pursuits, and assure them that the fruits of their toil shall be enjoyed in security and peace?"[17] Democrats pointed out that Hanna had championed the Republicans as "a white man's party" in 1860.[18] His changed rhetoric, however, indicated the claims on the nation that the war had given African Americans.

Radicals embraced black suffrage to create a Republican party in the South, where one had not existed before the war, in order to secure the policies of Reconstruction. But there would be black voters in the North as well. Silas Shucraft, an African American, had successfully lobbied Governor Oliver P. Morton to recruit black troops during the war. Later settling in Greencastle, Shucraft editorialized that African Americans were well aware of the source of their freedom and knew "to whom we will stand indebted for the ballot when it comes." If that was not clear enough, he avowed that "the colored voters, everywhere, will distinguish who have been friends indeed, and who their foes—that they will rally as one man under the Republican banner as naturally as water flows downward."[19] He wrote an eloquent treatise on the Fifteenth Amendment, in which he noted "the great disadvantages incident to servitude" but insisted that the freedmen "show the evidences of capability and adaptability to become intelligent citizens of the republic" just as immigrants had.[20]

Democrats opposed black suffrage, "believing . . . that it will be the best for both races to leave the government of the American people in the hands of the white race where our fathers placed it."[21] Democrats doubted that African Americans possessed the independence necessary for self-government; in fact, they contended, the Freedmen's Bureau demonstrated their dependence and incapacity. Judge Solomon Claypool, speaking at the Democratic county convention in June 1866, opposed "'bureaus' for 'niggers.'"[22] When Democrat Thomas Gillespie was traveling by train to Greencastle, he mistook the light-skinned and refined Shucraft for a white man and struck up a conversation with him. Gillespie was appalled to find his traveling companion not only supportive of black suffrage but unterrified by the possibility that his daughter might marry a black man. "My God, man! Would you be willing to put your child on an equality with a nigger?" Gillespie asked. "Certainly," was the answer.[23] But Democrats clung to their stereotypes, both insisting that Shucraft was illiterate and implying that he was a tool of the Republicans who wrote his letters for him, a stereotype invoked repeatedly over the years about outspoken black Republicans.[24] Democrats found it impossible to believe that local blacks had independent minds.

Democrats in Putnam and other Indiana counties strenuously opposed black suffrage. To prevent consideration of the Fifteenth Amendment in the Indiana legislature, seventeen senators and thirty-seven representatives (all Democrats) resigned their seats, including Putnam's state representative, Willis G. Neff. The mass resignations broke the quorum, necessitating the calling of special elections to fill the empty seats. Neff and his fellow Democrats were promptly reelected to a special session. Again, the Democrats were determined to resign and break the quorum. But Senator Oliver P. Morton, home from Washington, reinterpreted the rules so that a quorum equaled not two-thirds of the total house membership but rather two-thirds of those members who had not resigned. Despite Democratic protests, the General Assembly then ratified the Fifteenth Amendment. In 1870, however, the Democrats gained control of the Indiana General Assembly for the first time since 1862, sweeping the state offices, partly on the basis of the amendment's unpopularity in the state.[25]

Some local Republicans now moved to make good on Shucraft's promise of black political participation. At the first meeting of county Republicans after ratification, Milton Osborn wanted to recognize "colored Republicans" by appointing some of them as delegates to the state convention. As a member of the legislature, Osborn had worked to secure ratification of the Fifteenth Amendment, and "he asked this recognition of the 'colored brethren' as an indorsement of his course." But his request provoked a "lengthy discussion." Although the assembled Republicans were generally friendly to having blacks participate, "they seemed to entertain a lurking suspicion that it would damage the party to honor them in the manner proposed by Mr. Osborn." *Banner* editor George Langsdale offered a compromise by which Republicans celebrated ratification of the Fifteenth Amendment,[26] and he invited participation from any Republican "regardless of race, color or previous condition of servitude."[27] Black Republicans continued to participate, sometimes only as "spectators." But Allan Jones, a mulatto carpenter from Kentucky, ran in the Republican primary for city marshal, which Democrats said confirmed their charge that Republicans were putting "Negroes to the front, white men to the rear."[28] Adding to Republican qualms about blacks in politics, a Portland Mills Democrat found local Republicans "so unfortunate as not to have a sufficient number of citizens of African descent to make the thing work respectable."[29]

Despite their tiny numbers, Democrats persisted in seeing black voters as a threat. In their 1870 convention, the Democrats declared the Fifteenth Amendment unconstitutional and asked for its repeal. They began speaking of "the united negro vote" as if it were a formidable obstacle, and they worried that Republicans inflated their vote totals by colonizing black voters from Kentucky. When occasional fights broke out between white and black men, Democrats said that "the fruits of the [Republicans'] negro-equality doctrines" had made blacks less deferential. An 1872 Grant rally in Greencastle presented a disturbing scene of black agency to Democrats. With large numbers of black Republicans from Vigo County participating, two Democrats who refused to join cheers for Grant were mobbed. The *Press* cited several instances of blacks assaulting whites and blamed Radical Republicans for instigating black hostility.[30]

Because the county was still narrowly divided, black voters might have had an impact. In the 1866 congressional race, Solomon Claypool won Putnam County by two votes although the Republican, Henry D. Washburn, prevailed in the district. By narrow margins, Republicans won the two state representative seats. John Applegate was elected sheriff with 51 percent of the vote. The 1866 results in Putnam comported with those throughout the state—a Republican victory but often a narrow one.[31]

Black suffrage prompted Democrats to rally immigrants. They warned the foreign born to "Secure Your Naturalization Papers," as Radical Republicans might stiffen requirements for voting. The Democrats feared that Republicans "may disfranchise enough of the foreign born population to continue in power, with the help of the negroes."[32] Judging by naturalization records, immigration to the county had peaked in the 1850s and then declined to half its prewar level during the 1870s. And given that the population of the county was growing, immigrants made up an increasingly smaller proportion of it.[33] In addition, Democrats could no longer count on Irish fealty. The Irish organized an "independent" organization outside the political parties that nominated their own candidates for county office; eventually, that organization fused with the Republicans. Many Irish Americans felt the Democratic organization took them for granted and failed to reward their loyalty. William Cramer cited Democratic mistreatment of Irish candidates, noting that Patrick Heaney and Martin Kelley, running for offices in Monroe township, had been defeated because fellow Democrats "scratched" out their names on the ballot.[34] Cramer complained, "When the Irish ask for an office the Democrats laugh and sneer at them. 'You have but one right, and that is to walk up and vote for the men we have selected, you voting cattle,' is what they say."[35]

Republicans actively courted the Irish, but Democrats expected the Irish to be repelled by Republican "political fanaticism," especially regarding black rights. A "leading" local Republican was quoted as saying, "We put on the Irishmen to give the ticket strength, and the negro to give it color."[36] William Cramer insisted, however, "I am sorry that we haven't a colored man on the ticket."[37] In an 1880 campaign parade, Irish Republicans marched along with the Colored Republican Club and other Republican delegations.[38]

Factionalism among local Democrats helped the Republicans. The infighting involved two leading former Copperheads—Sol Akers and Judge Delana Eckels—and a scandal over the Democratic county treasurer. The treasurer, William E. D. Barnett, had placed the public money in a bank that failed, losing $15,000, for which Barnett was liable. Fortuitously, the county board—of which Barnett's father was a member—decided the county needed a new poor farm. William Barnett was appointed to find a site, and he selected land mortgaged to himself. Voting in favor of the deal, the board issued an order to pay him $15,966.14. John Hanna protested that a new poor farm was unnecessary and insisted that the purchase was a "subterfuge" to allow the county board "to do indirectly that which they cannot do directly," namely, pay the treasurer's obligation. Hanna appealed the purchase through the courts.[39] Embarrassed by the publicity, the county commissioners decided to give the new poor farm to Indiana Asbury. But clearly, Barnett had powerful friends locally, as the county commissioners' efforts to save him revealed.[40]

Sol Akers was very much outside this establishment clique. In 1866, the county Democratic convention had chosen him as one of the delegates from Cloverdale Township to the congressional convention, the kind of leadership position Akers had long held in the party. But the next year, the Democratic convention sidelined him. Akers won the nomination for county recorder by one vote, but then party leaders said there had been a mistake in the balloting. On the second ballot, Akers lost by twenty-one votes. Republicans thought Democratic leaders did not want to nominate him for recorder: "As he was a weight that they could not hope to carry, they were anxious to get rid of him. His democracy had cropped out too frequently during the war—he had the manhood to live up to the principles of his party."[41] The *Banner* speculated that party leaders feared Akers would not be "sufficiently pliant."[42]

Unlike Solomon Akers, Delana Eckels had become a grand old man of the party. After the war, he was lauded as "the able and accomplished Judge of this Judicial Circuit." He even aspired, unsuccessfully, to the state supreme court.[43] In 1878, when Eckels represented Cloverdale at the state Democratic convention, he received special notice as the only delegate to have voted for Andrew Jackson. He continued to uphold Jacksonian values, deriding the Republican gubernatorial candidate in 1880, Albert G. Porter, "as a very good man for a Republican, but he was a lawyer and for that reason did not think the people ought to put him above a farmer, merchant and hogkiller."[44] But as with Akers, Republicans never forgot Eckels's Copperheadism. When the venerable judge campaigned during the 1880 presidential election, the *Banner* recalled, "The only man in Greencastle whose face was wreathed in smiles, on receipt of the intelligence of the Bull Run disaster to the Union arms, was this same Judge Eckels."[45]

Eckels determined to fight Akers for control of Cloverdale's Democratic organization. In February 1868, the Cloverdale Township convention resolved, probably at Eckels's instigation, "that no one ought to be voted for as a candidate who will not agree to support our nominees, and we expect no Democrat of the Township to run against our nominations."[46] The resolution seemed designed to punish Akers if he bolted the party. Akers repeatedly disrupted the Democratic county convention that summer over the ballot for treasurer, which "was proceeding very quietly until Cloverdale Township was called." Eckels, chairing the township delegation, split Cloverdale's vote between two candidates. Akers rose to protest that the township convention had overwhelmingly voted for only one of those candidates and that Eckels's division of the vote misrepresented that township's vote. Akers "wanted to say that if they propose to play that game, that this was a good time to commence it. They may succeed now, but they can't come it in October." Akers meant that although the convention might be deceived, voters at the October election would not be. Many Democrats tried to talk at once—Eckels to explain, Akers to protest, another delegate to silence Akers, and many more to shout down the others. The townships were again polled, and again Eckels split Cloverdale's vote. "Instantly Mr. Akers was on his feet shouting—'Mr. Chairman, there is a trick abroad; there is some secret management about this.' (A voice—'Big swapping done.')" Once again Eckels tried to explain why he had altered the township convention's result, but his explanation only "created the wildest confusion."

On the eighth ballot, W. E. D. Barnett was nominated by one vote. Someone moved to make the nomination unanimous, and the chair announced the motion carried, despite a chorus of "noes" from Akers and his supporters. By splitting Cloverdale's vote, Eckels allowed Barnett to get the nomination despite Akers's opposition. The cost was a rancorous party split, with Akers vowing, "We will remember you next October," a threat to withhold Democratic votes at the election.[47]

On September 3, Democrats held a barbecue at Quincy in Owen County. An estimated 5,000 attended. Several beefs were roasted, and as usual, speakers held forth. As often occurred, there were fights and "cutting affrays." One of the victims was Sol Akers, who was stabbed in the left side; he died a day or two later.[48] Republicans suspected the death was not accidental, alleging the barbecue had been held near Cloverdale to ensure Akers's attendance. Given that Democratic functions included much drinking and consequent fights and given that Akers was known to be feisty, the barbecue presented an ideal opportunity to be rid of a troublemaker: "Some one engaged Akers in a dispute, and when he—Akers—asserted that he would not vote the unscratched Democratic ticket, he was denounced and cursed as being no Democrat. From this the quarrel grew fierce, blows were exchanged, the crowd pressed up and surged around Akers, and at the opportune moment, some one, it seems impossible to tell who, stabbed him in the left side with a knife."

Putnam Democrats did not mourn his passing: "When it was known in this City, one of our well-known Democrats remarked that the Barbacue had done one good thing—it had killed Sol. Akers."[49] Akers's insistence that he would scratch his ticket, marking out a Democratic candidate, earned him the enmity of the Eckels clique. Republicans reported Democrats as saying, "Vote an unscratched ticket or die."[50] The *Press* expressed no interest in finding Akers's killer, and no assailant appears to have been identified. It remains unknown whether the murder was a planned assassination or merely the consequence of the brawling common during political campaigns. But one result was clear: Judge Eckels and the Democratic establishment no longer faced rebels within their party. In the next local Democratic convention, Eckels represented Cloverdale and "ruled the convention." Despite "a good deal of suppressed ill feeling," he saw his nominees selected.[51]

The Democratic party under Eckels swept Putnam County in the 1868 elections. The party's gubernatorial and congressional candidates won the county, even though they lost their respective races to the Republicans and Grant won Indiana and the presidency. Even the tainted Barnett won reelection as treasurer, albeit only by 22 votes in an election where Democratic candidates polled 200 to 300 votes over their Republican opponents. Sol Akers's death may have permitted Republicans to expose the factionalism and skulduggery in the local Democratic party, but it also removed the most notorious local Copperhead, impeding the Republicans' ability to keep alive the memory of Democratic wartime perfidy.[52]

Putnam Republicans still sought to remind county residents of wartime disloyalty by leading Democrats. Harrison M. Randel opened himself to such an attack in the mid-1870s. An established county official by then, Randel had served as surveyor and succeeded Barnett as county treasurer. In 1874, he won the office of auditor. The *Press* praised his "unvarying courtesy, accuracy, and fidelity to duty."[53] Despite being more than a generation younger than Judge Eckels, Randel too espoused old-fashioned Jacksonian rhetoric. On January 8, 1878, the day of the traditional Democratic holiday commemorating Andrew Jackson's victory over the British at New Orleans, it was Randel who gave the address, using the occasion to enunciate Jacksonian principles of equality in the Gilded Age: "Buckskin very often covers souls as noble as silk and satin."[54]

Two years earlier, the *Banner* had made much of a story in which Randel supposedly mistook an American flag for a smallpox warning sign. He denied the story, but editor George Langsdale used it to recall Randel's part in the wartime raid on draft officer H. T. Craig. This renewed interest in his wartime role concerned Randel seriously enough to make him respond that he had called on Craig "as a friend," to warn him that the people were excited and so "it would be best to let this enrollment alone."[55] Despite the *Banner*'s effort to needle the Democrats with the flag story—the newspaper charged that "Boss

Harrison Randel. (From *Atlas of Putnam Co., Indiana to Which Are Added Various General Maps, History, Statistics, Illustrations* [Chicago: J. H. Beers, 1879]; courtesy of DePauw University Archives and Special Collections)

H.M.RANDEL.
Co.AUDITOR.

Randel" had learned "confederate tactics" on "the bloody fields of Monroe township"[56]—it was apparent that Randel's political career had not been hurt by his well-known role in draft evasion during the war. The *Banner* quoted Randel as saying, "I made up my mind not to fight in this war, and did not intend to if I could help it."[57] In an editorial excoriating him for aiding the Confederacy by "getting up a diversion in [the soldiers'] rear in favor of their enemies," the *Banner* observed that "for this crime Mr. Randel has three times been elected to office by the Democrats of Putnam county. With them, instead of treason making a man odious, it has been the passport to office."[58] Randel continued to serve the county for another decade.[59]

Harrison Randel was able to shrug off questions about his wartime draft resistance in part because voters' attention was shifting away from Civil War issues. The Grange, or Patrons of Husbandry, reflected people's disgust with Republican corruption and with Reconstruction policies that neglected the concerns of Northern whites. The first Indiana Grange had been organized in 1869 in

Vigo County; the state organization formed three years later. The group grew rapidly, and "at its height Indiana had the largest number of Granges of any state in proportion to its size."[60] In Putnam County, the first Grange organized in the summer of 1873. Within a few months, there were eight more Granges in the county, with an average of twenty-five members in each.[61] The Grangers worked together for "the mutual instruction and protection of those engaged in agricultural pursuits." One way in which they hoped to make "the labor of cultivation . . . more remunerative" was through bypassing the merchants who acted as middlemen between farmers and consumers.[62]

Farming in an increasingly uncertain economic world, the Grangers found their old parties' economic policies unsatisfactory. A postwar farm depression was followed by a fluctuating market for agricultural products and then generally bad times in the 1870s.[63] R. M. Hazelett, a moving force in forming a county council of Grangers, had become disenchanted with the Republicans, describing them as "political thieves controlled intirely by the Shylocks Corporation and monied power of the east and Europe." Hazelett was tired of Reconstruction, which had spent "billions of dollars and millions of lives" on Southern blacks, and on a policy that would "inslave the white population . . . to the plutarks and monied few." He had worked hard for these causes, participating in conventions and drafting platforms, but he acknowledged the disheartening final result when he recalled that he had only stood for office "to gratify some of his friends," on which occasions he had led "a forlone hope."[64]

But in the mid-1870s, Hazelett's eventual disillusionment was hard to foresee, as Grangers were the chief topic of county conversation. In the summer of 1874, when a farmers' convention met in Indianapolis, A. C. Stevenson, who had long written an agricultural column for the *Banner,* was elected president. Stevenson acknowledged that even though he had been absent from public life for many years, the "treachery" of corrupt officeholders had brought him out of political retirement. He noted that the great issues of previous eras— the economic issues that had divided Whigs and Democrats, the rebellion, and "the negro question"—"have passed away or been settled." Corruption was the remaining issue. Stevenson called on the assemblage to forget old partisan differences and unite in the name of reform. The convention favored abandoning the gold standard, adopting a paper currency, reducing public expenditures, and cutting taxes. "Chattel slavery has been abolished," the convention resolved, "but the rights and relations of labor stand just where they did before the emancipation. . . . Capital is now the master and dictates the terms, and thus all laborers are practically placed in the same condition of the slave before his emancipation."[65]

Two weeks later, Stevenson and others participated in a "people's convention" in Greencastle that nominated candidates for local office. The convention was crowded, perhaps with as many spectators as participants. Although the meeting was supposed to be nonpartisan, Republicans dominated. In particular, Stevenson again spoke of his disillusionment with the party: "The old parties can't get out of the old ruts. . . . [The Republicans] have promised reform and reform, time almost out of mind, but they have never carried it out." True reform would require new parties. Like Stevenson, Higgins Lane was alienated from his Republican affiliation. Lane, who played a major role in the convention, said that "farmers are not men of many words. We are here to-day for the purpose of getting up a reform movement for economy and sobriety. We want to act. We want to elect a ticket that will correct abuses. . . . It is time for the people to lay aside old party affiliations."[66]

Despite Stevenson's and Lane's emphasis on corruption, Granger candidates increasingly spoke of fiscal policy. To pay for the Civil War, the federal government had authorized private banks to issue paper currency, or greenbacks, which were backed by government bonds. The Republicans now viewed this as a wartime expedient. Congress, in fact, had pulled the greenbacks out of circulation, planning a return to the gold standard. This contracted the currency in an expanding economy, which caused prices to fall. Depreciation proved especially hard for farmers, although industrial workers also experienced wage cuts. Debtors now had to repay their loans in more valuable currency than they had borrowed. As the effects of currency contraction took hold, some suggested that currency could be expanded by monetizing silver. Others proposed repealing the planned specie resumption and retaining greenbacks. "Goldbugs," however, argued that lowering the cost of money cheated the creditor.[67]

John Coburn, the Republican candidate for Congress in 1874, insisted that the Republican party should not be abandoned, as it was still capable of achieving "great national purposes." Republicans themselves had identified and dealt with their own corruption, according to Coburn. In a speech at Greencastle, he noted, "The work of reconstruction is yet going on successfully in spite of the unavoidable blunders of its friends and of the blind and malignant opposition of its enemies."[68] Speaking with passion of his own war record, he attacked his opponent, Franklin Landers, "the democratic independent candidate," for Copperheadism. He resurrected Landers's wartime failure to support the "vigorous prosecution of the war" and even invoked "Vallandigham, Voorhees, and all those fellows" in a discussion of financial policy.[69]

Coburn and Landers both wrapped the financial issue in themes whose resonance derived from the Civil War. Copperheads such as Landers, Coburn argued, had opposed greenbacks when they were instituted. Landers, who wanted the bonds redeemed in greenbacks, accused Coburn of favoring speculators: "The soldiers were promised gold; the bond-holders, paper. But the soldiers get paper and the bondholders get gold."[70] The result of the 1874 election revealed increased disaffection from the Republicans. In the state, the Democratic ticket was victorious. Independents polled strongly, winning between 16,000 and 19,000 votes for state offices. Coburn lost.[71] The Grangers gained sufficient political power in Indiana to influence the 1874 election but failed to emerge as a distinct political entity.[72]

The Grangers' desire for a flexible national currency that was not backed by specie reappeared in the development of the Greenback Labor party. County Greenbackers began organizing in 1878, and once again, disaffected members of the regular parties led the way. The Floyd Township Greenback Club adopted resolutions that condemned the contraction of the currency "to a volume inadequate to the want and business interests of the country," thus causing bankruptcy and ruin for many. Club members called for the abolition of national banks, the remonetization of silver, and equal taxation, "including the rich man's bonds." They insisted, "We hold that the full and complete legal-tender paper dollar is the best [paper money] ever devised by mortal man; and as it was considered sufficient to pay the soldier, we think it sufficient to pay any other debt that may have been contracted by the Government of the United States."[73] The Greenbackers did not forget the Civil War, but used it to legitimate their cause, reminding the country that a flexible currency, the greenback, was the soldiers' money. In 1878, a Putnam County Greenback convention advocated replacing national bank notes with greenbacks, the currency that had "saved us as a Nation."[74] In 1880, resolutions of Putnam County Greenbackers called bondholders "the enemy of the country financially," and "not worthy of the same honor and regard as the soldier who fought to save the country."[75]

Despite its origins "irrespective of old party ties," the Greenbacker movement in Putnam threatened both Democrats and Republicans. Democrats were so worried that they evidently planted William S. "Billy" Eckels, a local lawyer and the judge's son, as a spy among the Greenbackers. Billy joined the

Greenbackers not to promote their cause—the Greenbacker candidate got no votes in Cloverdale—but to lure the Republican voters into the new party.[76] But despite the younger Eckels's manipulations, the Greenbackers failed to draw significant numbers. In 1878, Parker S. Browder ran for mayor of Greencastle, having been endorsed by the Greencastle National Greenback Club. Gaining only 33 percent of the vote, Browder lost to Lucius Chapin.

However, in another race in 1878, Gilbert de la Matyr ran as a Greenback candidate for Congress and won. He defeated John Hanna despite Hanna's desperate efforts to portray himself as "a full-fledged greenbacker." Hanna tried to rebuke Democratic claims to the issue, reminding voters that, during the war, Democrats had opposed greenbacks as "Lincoln rags."

Still, despite de la Matyr's success, the Greenbackers soon dwindled. By 1880, only "eight lonesome Greenbackers" remained, and the county Greenbacker convention that year drew just fifteen people.[77] The *Banner* told the story of a Greencastle boy who would not join the Republican band "because they allowed 'niggers' to march with them." Nor would he play with the Democratic band because he disliked its members. When his father asked, "Why don't you train with the Greenbackers?" the boy replied, "Because I don't want to march by myself."[78] Greenberry Wright ran for state representative but overwhelmingly lost, getting less than 200 votes to both his opponents' totals of 2,000 to 3,000. Concluding that the Greenbackers could not win, he urged other Greenbackers not to throw their votes away on the Greenback presidential candidate, James B. Weaver, but to vote for the Republicans in the national election.[79]

The Granger and Greenbacker movements revealed an increasing preoccupation with economic issues. Democrats argued that Republican fiscal policy had favored the "moneyed sharks" at the expense of the "independent laborer," many of whom were transformed into "slaves."[80] Dan Voorhees, campaigning in Greencastle in 1874, vividly described a bondholder "stand[ing] idly by, looking at your toils in much the same manner that a cotton planter in the olden time might have gazed on his slaves at work for him in the fields of the South."[81] Economic depression only emphasized the need for attention to fiscal issues. Although just one bank in Greencastle suspended operations during the Panic of 1873, it was reported that "business matters . . . are in an exceedingly depressed condition. Money seems to be out of the question, and working men are obligated to do what they can, for whatever they can get."[82] During another economic downturn in the late 1870s, Harrison Randel offered this dire assessment: "Some men may live through this financial ruin, while many noble, energetic business men will fall by the wayside to rise no more. The black cloud of ruin hangs above us. Business is paralyzed and still. The door of prosperity is shut. Its hinges are rusty. No bright prospects lie in the near future for labor nor its friends."[83]

Disaster revealed both the precariousness of prosperity and the resilience of the booster spirit. Natural disasters, such as tornadoes and flooding after torrential thunderstorms, were periodic occurrences and often destroyed property. Another perpetual threat in the Gilded Age was fire, the best-known incident being the Chicago Fire of 1871. Greencastle too experienced several conflagrations in the 1870s, some resulting from industrial accidents and others set by arsonists.[84] One observer worried that despite their frequency, "the heavy fires all around us do not seem to awake our citizens to a realization of our awkward condition," referring to the lack of firefighting equipment.[85] But in 1874, the common council voted down a proposal to buy fire engines from Evansville because they would be too expensive.[86]

The council quickly regretted their mistake. On the evening of October 28, 1874, an arsonist set a fire in C. J. Kimble & Son's furniture factory. High southwest winds carried the fire into the courthouse square, burning parts of the business district and nearby homes. The winds scattered burning embers for blocks, causing new fires to spring up in many different places at once. Residents in Putnamville, 5 miles to the south, could see the flames. Greencastle citizens organized a blanket-and-bucket brigade and made "almost superhuman efforts" to stop the fire's spread—tearing down buildings in its path to remove fuel, battling the flames, and carrying invalids from homes threatened by the fire.[87] Moments before the telegraph office had to be abandoned, Mayor William D. Allen wired a desperate plea for help to the Terre Haute and Indianapolis fire departments. About three hours later, a special train arrived from Terre Haute carrying an engine and five firemen, bringing a "shout for joy" from the Greencastle citizens. Thirty Indianapolis firemen, with engine and horses, arrived by train an hour later, but they found the cisterns exhausted and little that they could do. By 4 A.M. the fire had burned itself out.[88]

Gillum Ridpath calculated that the damage, in proportion to population and wealth, was greater in Greencastle than in the famous Chicago Fire. Estimates of the losses ranged from $250,000 to as high as $400,000, with only $116,381 worth of property being insured.[89] A week after the fire, Putnamville minister Ransom Hawley went to Greencastle and reported, "I saw the burnt district at Greencastle today. The sight was *appalling*."[90] Hawley was not the

Near corner Washington & Indiana Sts., Greencastle, Ind. 1894 after fire.

Greencastle after the 1874 fire. (Courtesy of Putnam County Public Library)

only sightseer. After the fire, trains brought crowds from other cities to see the damage.[91] Although no one died, the fire had left many homeless and unemployed. The common council voted $1,000 to aid those injured in the fire, and a citizens committee was formed to aid the needy. An appeal went out to other cities: "Send us money, food and clothing, anything to alleviate suffering."[92] In addition to donations for the victims, aid arrived in other forms. For a six-month period after the fire, the Louisville, New Albany, and Chicago Railroad halved their rates for freight shipped to Greencastle. Michigan City lumber dealers gave the residents of the burned town a 20 percent discount.[93]

Greencastle residents both acknowledged the destruction and called for a renewed booster spirit. Although "stately mansions and attractive business houses" had been replaced with "heaps of broken brick and stone," this was not a time for "despondency and gloom," according to George Langsdale of the *Banner*.[94] Instead, "if each man who has any capital or credit left, at once goes to work, the city will soon be restored to her former condition, and even better."[95]

On the morning after the fire, Franklin P. Nelson, a director of the local nail factory and owner of uninsured buildings on the square, was shoveling debris and preparing to rebuild. Once the bricks were cool enough to move, people began clearing the rubble. Merchants soon erected temporary buildings.[96] In fact, within a week of the fire, those who could find rooms were "already carrying on business, as of old." A jeweler sold out of a shoe store, a butcher in the back of a marble shop. One livery service moved into the stables run by a competitor, and merchant G. H. Williamson sold his spoiled goods from the less damaged Black and Daggy store. Jerome Allen's drug store moved into the clothing store owned by another family member. Professional men shared offices: for instance, the legal firm of Moore Bros. moved into Lucius Chapin's office.[97] Within the year, the citizens had rebuilt their businesses and homes, making total improvements of almost $400,000.[98]

Improvements in the fire department became an urgent priority. Days after the fire, Mayor Allen called a session of the council in C. C. Matson's office, the mayor's own office having been destroyed in the fire. The catastrophe had converted the naysayers. The council now voted unanimously to buy fire equipment, build ten cisterns, and organize a temporary fire company. By the end of December, the new fire engine arrived and was named after the mayor. It had 500 feet of hose and could throw a stream of water 268 feet.[99] (When Allen died two years later, the funeral procession included the fire department in uniform and their engine, the "W. D. Allen.")[100] In 1875, another fire broke out and spread to the block of buildings on the south side of the square, but this time, almost all the damaged property was insured. By the end of the decade, the national *Fireman's Journal* praised Greencastle's fire department for its well-kept machines, good horses, and up-to-date improvements.[101]

For some, the fire became a booster story. Gillum Ridpath recorded the number of establishments after the fire: there were seventy-five doing almost $1 million worth of business annually, including eighteen factories that employed 358 workers. A year after the fire, a correspondent of an Indianapolis newspaper found "beautiful new buildings and general appearance of thrift" in Greencastle. Merchants, including G. H. Williamson, had replaced their buildings with "larger and more costly buildings then those destroyed." Others bought lots after the fire.[102] The city turned anniversary "observances" of the fire into a promotional event with a pamphlet illustrating all the new buildings.[103]

The fire revealed that Putnam County residents responded to economic setbacks with grit and determination to succeed. But the rifts over economic policy persisted nonetheless. In 1876, Delana Williamson challenged John Hanna for the Republican nomination for Congress. The Kentucky-born Williamson had arrived in Greencastle in 1841, at age nineteen. Initially a Democrat, he joined Delana Eckels's law office. But during the Civil War, Williamson became an active Republican and was elected state attorney general three times. However, he came to oppose Republican financial policy, and by 1874, he was appearing for the Grangers and urging Republicans to vote the local Independent/ Granger ticket. There were rumors, which Williamson denied, that he had voted for Franklin Landers. In 1876, he was still opposing the Republican fiscal policy of specie resumption while challenging Hanna for the right to run against Landers.[104] Speaking at Belle Union, Williamson said, "We have no issue of the war to settle this campaign. Some may say, fraud; some may say, bloody shirt; but the question at issue is one that should engage the attention of every man, woman and child in this land: it is the money question."[105] Hanna, who as U.S. district attorney during the war had prosecuted the local Copperheads, preferred to run as the "death on traitors" candidate. In a "quite unharmonious and stormy" congressional convention, he received the nomination on the third ballot. Williamson continued to feud with other Republicans before effecting an uneasy reconciliation with the party.[106]

Hanna tried to straddle the Civil War and financial issues in campaigning against Landers. Speaking at the courthouse in Greencastle, he asserted his personal integrity: "No public money has ever stuck to my hands." "I have no fine spun theories on finance," he told the crowd. He admitted the dangers of contraction caused by specie resumption, but offered general prosperity as the solution.[107] Hanna's opposition to resumption was rooted in the connection he made between greenbacks and their origins in the Civil War. Advocating resumption's repeal, he argued that the legal-tender notes were sacred, as they were "issued to preserve the life of the only true republic on earth," and he appealed to eastern financial interests not to put themselves "in the same attitude that the ultraists of the South at one time did upon the question of slavery, and attempt to crack the lash over the millions of the West in order to make them conform to your views."[108]

Hanna embraced his reputation as a "bloody shirt" orator and vowed "to flaunt the bloody shirt . . . until every man in the South, white and black, is made secure in his life and property." And he refused to forget the treason of Democratic leaders: "The question is, shall we turn our government over to those men who, in that hour, were faithless."[109] Democrats dismissed such appeals, however, as the desperate move of a bankrupt party. The *Press* published a poem titled "The Bloody Shirt" that relates a dialogue between Morton and Ohio senator John Sherman. Morton despairs of their political chances—"The people all express belief that we're a thieving crew"—but Sherman advises patching "the threadbare old device," mustering "worn-out slanders" and "the headless bugaboo Ku-Klux" to eke out victory.[110]

The 1876 campaign coincided with one of the bloodiest attacks on freedmen during Reconstruction, the massacre of black militiamen at Hamburg, South Carolina. In condemning a fight that erupted after Hanna spoke at Fillmore, where three young Republicans dressed in uniforms that showed their support for Republican candidates Hayes and Wheeler, came to blows with a Democratic youth, the *Banner* concluded, "Putnam county is trying to imitate Hamburg."[111] When gubernatorial candidate Benjamin Harrison made a campaign visit to Greencastle, the procession featured an elaborate transparency that showed piled bodies of dead black men; kneeling over them was another black man asking, "Is this equal protection of the laws?" On another banner was an image of the Hamburg massacre, with Democrats storming an arsenal.[112]

The effort to invoke Civil War loyalties failed. Benjamin Harrison lost both the county and the state election to James D. Williams, a Democratic congressman whose suit of blue jeans famously symbolized his frugality and common man persona. Hanna lost Putnam County to Franklin Landers, but he still narrowly won the congressional seat. Fiscal questions increasingly trumped Civil War issues, prompting a Putnam County Republican to complain that replacing questions of the war with mere money concerns insulted the soldiers, both alive and dead.[113]

A similar emphasis on reform carried the Democratic presidential nominee, Samuel J. Tilden, to victory in Indiana. Tilden, a wealthy New York politician, was famous for helping defeat the Tweed ring. The *Greencastle Press*'s headline blared "REFORM TRIUMPHANT!" in announcing what initially seemed to be Tilden's election. However, the *Press* also noted "DESPERATE ATTEMPTS OF THE CORRUPTIONISTS TO CHEAT THE COUNTRY OUT OF ITS CHOICE!" Republican-controlled returning boards in Louisiana, Florida, and South Carolina had certified that Republican candidate Rutherford B. Hayes had won their states. Although Democratic majorities in those states were the result of violence that suppressed the black vote, it appeared to many that the returning boards were stealing the election from Tilden.[114] A Putnamville man reported, "For the past week we have been on the 'ragged edge' in relation to the all important question. 'Who is president,' has been asked until it is worn threadbare."[115]

Local Democrats advised patience as the country awaited congressional action. Ominously, the *Press* compared the crisis to "the memorable winter of 1860–'61."[116] In order to elect delegates to a state convention, Willis G. Neff, who was chairman of the county's Democratic central committee, called a meeting that would be held on the traditional party holiday of January 8. Neff urged "the Freemen of Putnam County, irrespective of party, who believe there is an organized conspiracy to defeat the will of the people as expressed at the ballot-box," vowing to "take such action as they may deem necessary towards preserving the purity of the ballot and maintaining the rights and liberties of the people."[117]

A large turnout at the local meeting occurred despite inclement weather. Capt. J. J. Smiley presided, with the speakers including Neff and C. C. Matson. Republicans thought most of those in attendance were old Copperheads. Having dropped the facade of nonpartisanship, Democrats resolved "that while it would be our duty to cheerfully submit to an honest defeat, it is equally our duty to resist with all the lawful means at our command any such attempt upon the part of one man, or upon the part of any combination of men, thus to revolutionize our government and set aside the constitutionally declared will of the people expressed at the ballot box." Not all the speakers were as conciliatory as the resolution indicated, however. One said, "As Democrats don't be provoked into any kind of mistake to give them a chance to call you a rebel, and give you a licking and get another chance to steal sixteen years." When peaceful means were exhausted, the crowd was told, "and still your rights are denied you—right there the fight comes in. Our forefathers fought for their rights in the Revolution."[118] Republicans would later remember that Sheriff Moses T. Lewman had "announced his readiness to raise a regiment of one thousand men in Putnam County to assist in seating Tilden in the Presidential chair."[119]

In response to the crisis, Congress appointed a commission to decide the disputed electoral results from Florida, Louisiana, and South Carolina. Greencastle Republicans believed that such efforts at compromise revived Democrats' hopes for the presidency. "The Democrats in this locality were becoming reconciled to their fate . . . believing that Tilden was elected but Hayes would be inaugurated. This plan revives their hopes—gives them another chance they are almost universally in favor of it," James F. Darnall, president of the

Greencastle Iron and Nail Company, wrote.[120] A supposedly neutral Supreme Court justice—David Davis—was to have the tiebreaking vote on the commission. But when Davis resigned to take the Illinois Senate seat, he was replaced by Justice Joseph P. Bradley, who sided with the Republicans and gave the election to Hayes. Congressional Democrats could still have blocked Hayes by preventing the electoral vote from being counted in the House of Representatives, but Southern Democrats and Republicans reached a compromise: Hayes would be inaugurated in return for allowing Southern Democrats to regain power in South Carolina and Louisiana. Although congressional Republicans extracted promises from Southern Democrats to deal fairly with African Americans in their states, Reconstruction was over. By late February, Rev. Ransom Hawley concluded, "I think we shall have a republican President. The fight has been a hard one."[121] The good reverend did not realize how hard the fight had been or how much had been lost.

When Hayes was inaugurated, Republicans in Greencastle celebrated with a salute of 185 guns—the number of electoral votes Hayes received when the three disputed states were included in his favor. Democrats may have been reconciled, but they would not forget. In 1878, the county Democratic convention resolved "that the inauguration of Hayes and Wheeler as president and vice president of the United States was a fraud upon the nation, a crime against the right of suffrage, and the aiders and abettors of the foul conspiracy which placed them there should be driven into oblivion and their crimes made odious by the people if they would remain free, sovereign and independent."[122]

But the 1876 election was merely a landmark on the road away from Reconstruction. Even on occasions specific to the memory of the war, attention shifted from those aspects that Republicans deemed central to that memory. Decoration Day waxed and waned in its observance. In years when citizens failed to have a parade and the "official tinsel" of public orations, the *Banner* tried to excuse the lapse by claiming that "gaudy pageantry" was inferior to the simple sincerity of friends and family laying wreaths on soldiers' graves.[123] Decoration Day orations increasingly emphasized reconciliation. One popular speaker on these occasions was local Democratic lawyer and politician C. C. Matson, who often touched on the memory of the war. Democrats praised not only his "eloquence" but also "his manifest fairness." The local Democratic organ found his Memorial Day address of 1881 superior to the "bloody shirt" rantings of the Republican orator due to its lack of bitterness and partisanship.[124]

The *Press* did not report the text of the speech, but surviving fragments of other Matson speeches indicate that what the *Press* found nonpartisan was essentially reconciliationist in nature. Two years earlier, in a July 4th speech in Bloomington, Matson emphasized that he would not "wound" his hearers, being aware that he spoke on subjects involving their "tenderest feelings." He attributed partisan rancor and personal political attacks to the passions raised by the war. A veteran himself, Matson acknowledged, "Here is one who less than twenty years ago laid upon the altar of his country, as a willing sacrifice, the life of a youthful and dutiful son. He feels that such an injury can never be repaired, so long as love kisses the lips of death." But as a Democrat, Matson was aware of the antiwar sentiment that existed during the war: "Here is another, who, within the same time, perhaps for the mere expression of a political opinion, was seized upon by the strong arm of military power, dragged from his home, and deprived of his liberty without writ, warrant, hearing, or trial, and he feels that such an outrage yet calls for the most indignant expression of all just people." The war left "every family, if not every individual in this community . . . some experience that serves to keep in fresh recollection the awful passions that were then excited."[125] Matson thus acknowledged the Unionist's sacrifice and the Copperhead's grievance as equally legitimate. In 1875, he told those assembled at a soldiers' meeting in Indianapolis that the sacrifices of "the honored dead" in all U.S. wars should be remembered. This remark would be unexceptionable, except that he went on to say, "This should not be bounded by State lines, but prevail throughout the country." In other words, Confederate sacrifice should be accorded equal commemoration.[126]

Even Republicans seemed prepared to concede the legitimacy of reconciliationist sentiments. Dismayed by lackluster observances of Decoration Day, prominent Greencastle citizens formed a committee to arrange future services that included former mayor Marshall A. Moore, *Banner* editor Langsdale, and C. C. Matson.[127] The committee revived the 1875 ceremony with a parade. Stretching for a mile and a half, it featured a silver cornet band, seven Sunday schools (including the Catholic and black ones), a choir, a martial band, the soldiers, city officials, the new fire department, Irish Americans, fraternal organizations, Asbury students, and citizens—all of whom wended their way to Forest Hill for the service. Oliver P. Morton gave the oration to a crowd of 8,000 to 10,000.[128] Formerly the governor and now a senator, Morton was one of Indiana's most outspoken foes of the Confederacy. Although the Democratic newspaper approved his address, calling it "remarkably free from partisan feeling or allusions," it was not free of politics. Senator Morton spoke about "the memory of the dead and the gratitude we owe to their memories, the part taken by Putnam county and Indiana in the war," yet he expressed a willingness to forgive ex-Confederates and remove the legal disabilities they suffered. He would not, though, "put the rebel upon a level with the Union soldiers, admit their cause was just, or pension them as we do disabled Union soldiers. He would forgive but not honor them for their disloyalty." Yet even so, Morton argued that slavery was not the cause of the war but a "pretext": the true cause was states' rights. These positions appealed to many Democrats. Wyatt James's family or Robert Townsend's probably participated in the ceremonies, as the Townsends were active in the black Sunday school, but if they stayed to hear Morton speak, they may not have been cheered by his sentiments.[129]

Democrats protested bitterly when orators at such events asserted the emancipationist meaning of the war. The *Greencastle Press* complained that Lieutenant Governor Thomas Hanna's 1881 speech "drag[ged] the ensanguined garment from its retreat and flaunt[ed] it for the delectation of . . . political friends and admirers." In other words, Hanna waved the bloody shirt.[130] The Reverend F. C. Iglehart, who gave the 1879 oration, openly confronted reconciliation, pointing out that it was now whispered that "the conquerors were mistaken—the conquered right." As evidence, Iglehart described at length a Decoration Day service in Louisville, where the speaker had maintained that the South fought for "personal liberty, State sovereignty and national independence." In response, he asked, "What liberty did the South fight for, unless it was the liberty to lash the slave and lynch the loyal man?" Iglehart lamented, "Patriots had hoped that the political heresy that brought on the conflict had been sent to the grave forever; that the memory of the men that wore the blue, and especially the blue stained with the red, would be kept green, the value of their lives prized, the fruits of their labors preserved for a hundred years at least." His color schema may have been overdone, but he evoked the dead to remind his audience that the cause for which they had died was in danger. Iglehart did not talk explicitly about abolition or black rights but instead appealed to reconciliationist sentiment: "Let the voices of war ever be hushed by industry's busy hum. Let the conflict of races now and forever end. Let antagonism between the different sections of the country now and forever cease."[131]

Iglehart was fighting a reconciliationist sentiment that, increasingly willing to accept Confederate memorialization, equated Southern sacrifice in the war with that of the North. The Greencastle Democratic newspaper published a poem, entitled "Blue and Gray," about a young child who innocently asks, "O mother, what do they mean by blue? / And what do they mean by gray?" The child has heard two maimed veterans—one missing an arm, the other a leg—refighting old battles. One of the men "said he fought for the blue; / The other, he fought for the gray." Although the men had been on opposing sides, the child noted that "their greeting was kind and warm." When they parted "with a friendly grasp, / In a kindly, brother way, / Each called on God to speed the time / Uniting the blue and the gray." The question reminded the mother of "two stalwart boys from her riven," who fought and died for the opposing sides. Her answer is, "The blue and the gray are colors of God, / They are seen in the sky at even, / And many a noble, gallant soul / Has found them passports to Heaven."[132] The poem evoked the way in which the war had split families, and it promoted the idea that veterans on both sides had more in common than they had differences.

Though Iglehart alluded to slavery, it was not until 1880 that a Decoration Day speaker openly discussed the role of African Americans in the war. That year, the procession was particularly lavish. The "Colored Republican Club, thirty strong, in uniforms" received special mention. And two of the Sunday schools present were "colored." C. C. Matson's law partner, Henry Mathias, gave a speech that devoted only a couple paragraphs to the war before emphasizing that "sectional hate and animosities ought to be allayed" in the name of prosperity. A second oration by Rev. W. A. Smith, a member of the GAR, was delivered. Smith described the soldier's experience of leaving home, adjusting to army life, and suffering in battle or prison. Would the soldier consider the price worth paying? Smith imagined the answer: "No, I reckon that the sufferings of that time are not worthy to be compared to the glory of dying in such a cause. Our blood was shed, but slavery's stains were washed from the country. Our bodies went down in death, but four millions slaves rose free." Thus, the veteran Smith remembered the slaves, whereas Mathias had never even mentioned slavery.[133] The increased presence of African Americans by 1880—and their larger appearance in the parade as community members—helped spark recognition of slavery's part in the war. But Smith's voice was a rare one on a holiday that celebrated the soldiers' service, and on which antireconciliationist themes were controversial. The Democratic press was sure to condemn any "politico-religious" rhetoric by Republican speakers, while praising the putative impartiality of orators such as C. C. Matson.[134]

The Reconstruction of the North, Eric Foner has written, meant the triumph of "the Age of Capital." The Grange and Greenbacker movements were both responses to the consolidation of economic power taking place during the post–Civil War period. Identification with the policies of race and Civil War were at the core of Republican identity; indeed, it was what made Republicans radical, just as Democrats' adherence to white supremacy made them conservative. But Republican radicalism did not extend to economic intervention that would aid farmers and debtors at the expense of capitalists. In this regard, the Republicans became increasingly conservative, even as Democrats more readily accepted the anticapitalist critique.[135] Ultimately, the Civil War and economic issues were not entirely separate. The war would continue to echo in the rhetoric about the "soldiers' money," and in the reality that the currency issue was rooted in Civil War fiscal policies.

Another wartime policy also continued to influence members of the Civil War generation until their deaths. During the war, the federal government committed itself to a level of financial support for veterans and their dependents that was unprecedented in U.S. history. The new standing accorded pensioners gave the Civil War generation unique economic advantages—and status as the saviors of the nation.

8

PENSIONERS

By the time Lucius Chapin died, more than half a century had passed since he enlisted in the Union army. During that time, he had served as a two-term mayor of Greencastle and achieved prominence as a local lawyer and civic figure. But his grave in Greencastle's Forest Hill Cemetery is overshadowed by monuments to the county's other political and educational leaders. Chapin's children buried him under a modest gravestone that said nothing about his postwar career but recorded that he had been first sergeant in Company M of the 4th Indiana Cavalry.[1] Another Putnam citizen, Courtland C. Matson, used his status as colonel to political advantage, becoming a prominent Democratic lawyer, politician, and eventually congressman. A frequent speaker at Memorial Day services, Matson participated in the Grand Army of the Republic, the chief Union veterans' organization. He devoted his congressional career to pension legislation and served on the House of Representative's Committee on Invalid Pensions. Referring to pension measures, Matson insisted, "I have left nothing undone that I could do to promote this."[2] One of those who benefited from such generous pensions was Wyatt James. A runaway slave who served in the 28th U.S. Colored Troops, James settled in Putnam County and married Robert Townsend's sister. Like the white veterans, James filed for a pension and joined the GAR.

During his long involvement with pension issues, Congressman Matson favored the generous treatment of widows. In the case of a Fort Wayne woman, he argued that the pension from her first husband, who was a Civil War soldier, should be restored after she divorced her second husband. Matson cited two grounds for restoration: one was the widow's indigence, the other that "the husband of her early youth went into the war and in one of the earliest battles fell at the head of his regiment."[3] Just as pensions were intended to preserve gender roles for men, so were they intended to reflect a woman's proper role as dependent on a man. In practice, however, a Civil War pension could allow women independence they might not otherwise have achieved. Widow Elizabeth Applegate never remarried, and although she made money sewing and taking in boarders, the steadiest portion of her income came from a pension. Charity Townsend eventually received a mother's pension based on Robert's Civil War service, which may have made her less reliant for support on her surviving children. Civil War veterans claimed to have made unprecedented sacrifices to save the Union, and the nation accordingly gave them and their dependents an unprecedented level of financial support. A generation of young men and women, who previously had struggled to establish themselves in their respective spheres as breadwinners and housewives now reestablished their households after the war, often with help from the federal government. They did not intend to challenge traditional gender roles, but their demands for recognition changed their generation's experience of adulthood.

As Civil War soldiers returned to civilian life, they embarked on careers and occupations far removed from their military experiences. Whatever the successes and failures of their lives, however, they clung to their identity as veterans. The Civil War had been fought on a scale Americans had never seen before, and the veterans would have it memorialized on a scale greater than for any previous war. They justified their demands for recompense, including a generous pension system, because they had suffered—and in fact believed they still suffered—for their Civil War service.

These veterans have been criticized for their readiness to accommodate a postwar reconciliationism that sought to rehabilitate ex-Confederates and ignore the freedmen. Certainly, the emphasis placed by Putnam veterans on monuments, celebrations of their service, and pensions often slighted or ignored the war's larger meanings, especially in regard to race.[4] The war's emancipationist meaning might be clear to black soldiers such as Robert Townsend and Wyatt James, but young white men such as Lucius Chapin and C. C. Matson had other motivations for fighting. Although they had accepted and in some cases even welcomed the turn to emancipation, the war for them had been the first steps in their careers, not an abolitionist crusade. The Civil War gave young men striving to become independent breadwinners a sense of worth, which Decoration Day services and monuments affirmed. Pensions linked their military service with their role as family breadwinners.[5]

Lucius had chafed at the delays that prevented him from mustering out of the army until mid-1865. And though he longed to be home, to hold Alice in his arms, and to see his family, much uncertainty attended the return to civilian life. Unable to make a living for his family before the war, he had no immediate prospects.[6] He went home sick, later describing himself as "a mere shadow of my former self." He had spent five months of 1863 in the hospital, suffering from "chronic camp diarrhoea," and he would endure bouts of diarrhea the rest of his life. By the spring of 1866, he felt well enough to move to Greencastle. His brother Henry had the contract for street improvements there, and Lucius worked for him. That he earned only $6 for that job when the average pay was $23 indicated that he did comparatively little labor, perhaps because of his health. In the summer of 1867, John M. Knight, a physician who boarded at the same house with the Chapins, was called "in haste" to attend Lucius, whom he found lying on the floor of his room. His pulse weak, Chapin remained unable to speak for several hours but then regained consciousness, recovering sufficiently to resume work in a few days. Knight's diagnosis was that he had succumbed to the heat. Chapin apparently believed himself prone to such collapses because he had suffered sunstroke during his army service. For the next several years, Knight continued to treat Lucius for intermittent but extremely painful attacks of diarrhea.[7]

After recovering from sunstroke, Lucius realized that he could not make a living at manual labor or farming. Knight later affirmed that he could do "writing and clerical work but cannot do anything of a heavier nature."[8] Consequently, Lucius entered the law office of Judge Solomon Claypool, who was married to Alice Chapin's older sister, and was admitted to the bar in 1869. Active in the Republican party, he began to hold more public positions, such as deputy clerk of the city council and an appointment from the city commissioners to lay out streets and watercourses. In 1876, he was elected mayor of

Greencastle and reelected two years later, earning the substantial annual salary of $400.⁹

After the war, elevation to political office was seen as a way for communities to repay their volunteers. The *Banner* listed political candidates' regiments and ran military biographies of them, continuing to highlight their military careers long after the war was over.¹⁰ Lucius Chapin's career fell into the soldier-candidate tradition. When Chapin ran for reelection as mayor, Republicans supported his campaign as much because of his military service, even inflating his rank, as on his record in office:

> Capt. Chapin, candidate on the Republican ticket for re-election to the office of Mayor, was one of the men who went to the front during the war, and did efficient service in the Fourth Indiana Cavalry. He has filled the bill as Mayor of the city during the past two years. In every respect he is worthy [of] the support of the people, and it will be only an act of simple justice to continue him two years longer in an office which he has filled so well.¹¹

Following the firing on Fort Sumter, C. C. Matson abandoned his studies at Asbury to join the 16th Indiana. When its enlistment expired, he joined the 71st Indiana (which became the 6th Cavalry) in July 1862, serving as adjutant. Matson received promotion to colonel in the summer of 1865 and mustered out just two months later; he would forever after be known as "Colonel."¹² His father, John A. Matson, was a longtime Whig who turned Republican during the war only to abandon the Republicans for the Democratic party some time later. Courtland Matson appears to have thought of himself as a war Democrat but never a Republican.¹³

After the war, Matson enjoyed a successful legal career. He entered Solomon Claypool's law office (the one Lucius Chapin had joined), and after Claypool moved to Indianapolis, he went into partnership with Henry H. Mathias. Matson gained a reputation as an effective defense attorney. In one high-profile fraud case, the Indianapolis Democratic newspaper predicted that Matson would "pull him [the defendant] through if such a thing be possible." In fact, Matson and the defendant's other attorneys got the case thrown out by finding a flaw in the indictment. Courtland rose steadily in politics, always as a Democrat.¹⁴

Being a soldier-candidate was both a liability and an asset for Matson. Many Putnam Democrats were not inclined to honor the soldiers. In the summer of 1866, a Fillmore man insulted grieving relatives by protesting against "honoring the soldier," saying that "the honor was due the boys who *staid at home,* as the *soldiers* only 'fought to free the nigger,' for which they *deserved no honor.*"[15] Altercations involving veterans occasionally occurred. A year after the war, there was an election day fight in Putnamville between former Union soldier Kemp Clearwaters and one of the town's leading Copperheads, Jacob Etter, who had been taunting Clearwaters by "halloing" for Jeff Davis.[16] The Democrats who insulted fallen soldiers and halloed for Jeff Davis were Matson's constituents. In an effort to turn antiwar sentiment against Matson, Republicans claimed that he had been involved in the battle of Pogue's Run, a confrontation that erupted when soldiers stopped a train carrying Indiana Democrats, who were returning home from an abbreviated convention in 1863, and confiscated their weapons. The Democratic press quickly denied that Matson had had anything to do with disarming the Democrats at Pogue's Run.[17]

Republicans also tried to impugn C. C. Matson's military credentials. The *Banner* equated his Democratic leanings with service in the Confederate army, asking, "Well, which army did he belong to . . . the Union army or the Confederate?"[18] When Colonel Matson made a campaign trip to Martinsville, Republicans claimed he brought along several disabled men from Putnam whom he "passed off" as crippled Union soldiers who favored his nomination. According to reports, "One of them, a one-armed saloon-keeper, had an arm shot off while hunting. The others never served in the Union army, but one was in the rebel army."[19] But such political attacks proved unsuccessful. Indeed, Matson became powerful enough locally for the *Banner* to refer to the Democratic party as the "Matson Ring." In 1880, he was elected to Congress, where he served four terms before receiving the nomination for governor. Defeated in that campaign, he resumed his law practice in Greencastle; spent four years as an attorney for the Louisville, New Albany and Chicago Railroad; and held appointed office.[20]

By contrast, Wyatt James was markedly less successful in life than the two white men, Chapin and Matson. After the 28th USCT mustered out in Indianapolis, James returned to Putnam County, where he stayed with Luke and Charity Townsend for several months while recovering from wounds suffered at the battle of the Crater. Like Lucius Chapin, James had contracted diarrhea in camp and suffered from it both during and after the war. While boarding with the Townsends, he was hired to chop wood, but when he found that the labor caused "severe pain" because of his wounds, he resolved to find "lighter work" in Greencastle.[21] Chapin had found "lighter work" by becoming a lawyer

C. C. Matson. Image has been slightly cropped. (Courtesy of Indiana State Library)

and officeholder, but such options were not available to James. Not only was his race a liability, he also lacked Chapin's education, signing some forms with his mark. Consequently, he remained a laborer for the rest of his life. He married Catherine Townsend in 1879, and they had seven children.[22] James received statements from doctors, family members, and friends testifying that he was "practically disabled for the performance of manual labor." Similar documentation had benefited Lucius Chapin. But the Pension Bureau did not think James "totally incapacitated for the performance of manual labor" even when he was about seventy years old.[23] And despite the fact that Wyatt James had served as honorably and suffered as grievously as many white veterans, he would find that the postwar commemoration of the Civil War—though not entirely excluding black veterans—gave less precedence to the emancipationist memory of the conflict than to other aspects of its legacy.

Before the war ended, residents of the county had begun to ponder how it should be properly commemorated. Worthington Williams proposed that the citizens of Putnam County should "erect in the new cemetery at Greencastle a lofty column on which shall be inscribed the names of those that have or will die in this war." The column would record the dead and also serve as a source of pride to later generations.[24] Shortly after the war, the *Banner* published a sentimental poem entitled "Soldier's Monuments." "That little town its willing score / Of patriots had sent," the poem asserted, but although "the soldiers's resting place was made / On red field far away," the town could nevertheless "consecrate" a place at home to the memory of those absent men.

> So let the soldiers' monument
>   In every grave yard stand—
> Although their buried forms be blent
>   With distant sea or sand—
> To keep their memory for aye
>   Within a grateful land.[25]

The city council donated a lot in Forest Hill Cemetery, the new cemetery to which Williams had referred. The bipartisan Putnam County Soldiers' Monument Association was formed to raise the funds and solicit a design.[26] Women quickly took a prominent role in the fund-raising effort. The ladies of Greencastle organized a grand festival for which the women of the county would donate "edibles of all kinds" and "all articles of manufacture, both useful and fancy," to be sold to raise money for the monument. The township committees boasted that the wives and daughters of prominent men—both Republicans and Democrats—were among their members.[27]

The monument association accepted the plans of a prominent sculptor, Thomas D. Jones of Cincinnati, and raised $10,000 for his design through subscriptions.[28] On Saturday, July 2, 1870, the monument was dedicated in Forest Hill Cemetery. With businesses closed, 4,000 or 5,000 attended the ceremony. An Indianapolis band led the parade from the city to a nearby grove, where a picnic dinner was served. President Thomas Bowman of Indiana Asbury offered a prayer. The day's orations were given by Col. Richard W. Thompson and Gen. Lew Wallace, who was one of Indiana's foremost military figures. After the speeches, the audience proceeded to the monument for the unveiling. Governor Conrad Baker, with help from Delana E. Williamson, attorney general of the state, dedicated the monument. Williamson made a last-minute fund-raising plea, as the monument association still needed $150, and collections were taken from the crowd. Around the monument, a tableau of young ladies represented all the states; everyone wore white except for Janie Black, "representing Indiana, who was in deep mourning" for her "fallen heroes."

Forest Hill monument.
Author's collection.

The monument listed the names of the dead on its 8-foot-high pedestal. The name of Robert Townsend, who died after his discharge, was omitted, although the monument recorded the names of Lucius Chapin's two brothers. Above the pedestal stood a 6-foot-tall marble statue of "the gallant volunteer."[29]

The *Indianapolis Journal* praised Jones for capturing the epitome of American manhood, the "young Northwest." As Kirk Savage has noted, when communities represented the "typical" soldier in statuary, they selected white men as the true American type. After the Civil War, such "common-soldier" statues became a fixture in communities in both the North and the South. The first Civil War memorials were funereal shafts put in cemeteries, signifying the war's unprecedented mortality. Later monuments depicted the soldier at "parade rest," standing straight with rifle held upright, and they were placed in public spaces such as the town square. The Greencastle monument differed from these norms. It was placed in the cemetery rather than a more public location, yet it was not a shaft but a statue on a pedestal. And unlike the typical common-soldier monument, it showed the soldier in a more relaxed posture, leaning against a wall without a rifle, albeit with his foot resting on a cannon. Savage has suggested the parade rest pose was meant to indicate the continuing independence of the white citizen, despite his willingness to subordinate—even enslave—himself to the mastery of the national government in service of the war effort. If so, the sitting western soldier Jones sculpted was even further removed from lockstep obedience to military authority. As a "universal" type, the common-soldier monument was meant to represent the black soldier as well as the white, yet African Americans, Savage claims, often felt excluded because the carved soldier was unquestionably a white man. Putnam citizens thus created an enduring tribute to the Civil War soldiers that included young white men, such as Chapin and Matson, but excluded young black men such as Wyatt James.[30]

Once erected, the soldiers' monument in Forest Hill served as the focus of an annual rite of Civil War remembrance—Decoration Day (later renamed Memorial Day). Over the years, the veterans who remained in Putnam County took an active role in such rituals of remembrance; Lucius Chapin, for one, served frequently on the committee to organize the ceremony. Decoration Days involved rituals typical of other nineteenth-century civic gatherings in Putnam, with a parade and speeches. On Decoration Day, however, the parade was to the cemetery, and it featured the soldiers. And just as women had been expected to support men's service during the war, they were expected to acknowledge it in the postwar period as well. Accordingly, women gathered flowers, with which young girls such as Lucius's daughter, Ally, decorated the soldiers' graves.[31] On some occasions, the girls dressed in a mix of virginal white and mournful black: "When fair hands had bestowed the wreaths of evergreen and fragrant flowers thereon, their appearance was beautiful. As we looked upon them, we felt that the honors then being paid to the departed, were some compensation for what they did for us while living."[32] Instead of sewing flags, women now placed flowers. Mature women sometimes collected the flowers for those who might have been their sons, but the actual placing on the graves was often reserved for young women in order to honor the young men who would never be husbands.

Veterans did not solely rely on others to commemorate their service but soon began to form their own organizations. A year after the war, a county soldiers' association was formed in Greencastle. Lucius Chapin and C. C. Matson were among the leaders, but it does not seem to have been a very active group.

James H. Madison has argued that soldiers had little desire to remember their battlefield experiences immediately after the war: that impulse developed only as they aged. In addition, these men were busy establishing their careers. Not until September 1879 did the Grand Army of the Republic, Greencastle Post No. 11 organize in Putnam County. George J. Langsdale, an Indianapolis veteran who became editor of Greencastle's Republican newspaper, was chosen commander, and Lucius Chapin was quartermaster.

Founded in Illinois, the GAR had spread to Indiana where it had been promoted by Oliver P. Morton, who recognized its potential as a political vehicle. The Greencastle post soon had fifty applicants for membership. Wyatt James joined and served with Chapin as a delegate to a department encampment. Though the GAR differed from other fraternal organizations in allowing black members, African Americans were often marginalized in the organization. James seems to have played a larger role in his GAR post than was typical for black veterans. Black GAR members commanded the respect of whites, but they nonetheless expressed "proper" deference. With his battle scars and ties to the black and white Townsends, James was well qualified for such a role. Although county historian Jesse Weik insisted that C. C. Matson had "long been an active member" of the GAR, he was not listed as an officer in its early days, whereas prominent Republicans such as Langsdale and Chapin played a greater role.[33] (The Democratic newspaper suspected that the GAR's true purposes were political, and it warned Democratic soldiers away from it.)[34]

Greencastle Post No. 11 held meetings every Tuesday evening, affording "comrades" an opportunity to relate their army stories. In addition to excursions taking veterans to special events, such as General Grant's appearance in Indianapolis, the post arranged public entertainments, with "guns and sabers, tableaux representing camp life, war songs and reminiscences, etc."[35] At one such event in 1880, a large audience was entertained at the opera house with military songs, a bayonet exercise by men in Zouave costume, speeches on the battles of the western theater, and a tableau with two scenes representing "slavery and emancipation." Miss Lou Ward, embodying Justice, "struck the chains from the manacled limbs of the bondsmen," sending "a thrill" through the audience.[36] Perhaps the participation of a black veteran encouraged more open acknowledgment of the war's emancipationist aims. Or perhaps, unlike civic events such as Decoration Day, there was less need to appease local Democrats on such occasions.

Just as they were slow to become active in GAR functions, veterans did not begin to organize reunions until some time had passed. In 1875, Lucius Chapin helped form a Putnam "regiment" to attend the state soldiers' reunion in Indianapolis.[37] And a decade later, Greencastle held a gala reunion of the 27th Regiment. Josiah Williams, who now lived in Missouri, was unable to attend, but his sister Edistina went. She reported:

> The hall was decorated beautifully . . . the citizens of Greencastle exerted themselves in decorating, and Greencastle never looked as pretty as on Friday and Saturday of last week, the entire square was a mass of red, white and blue. The national Bank looked lovely, above the door in the three colors, was "Welcome to the 27th Ind Regiment" and on each side, in red, white & blue, the battles that the Regiment participated in.

Edistina's host had not seen Greencastle so bedecked since the war.[38]

The nation did remember the "gallant volunteers" of the Civil War through unprecedented pension benefits. A Putnam County Union convention resolved that "the Nation owes a debt of gratitude to the soldiers and sailors who fought to sustain the integrity and unity of the States, and that the liberal provision made by Congress for the wounded, the widows and the orphans, are right and proper."[39] John S. Jennings, a longtime pension agent, kept Putnam veterans apprised of what they might be awarded. By 1900, the average Civil War pensioner received $139 per year, the average wage earner $375. The pension bureaucracy did not discriminate by race: Wyatt James was drawing $204 in 1904 as compared with Lucius Chapin's $144. Black soldiers, however, sometimes found it difficult to provide the required documentation.[40]

Because pension laws were initially based on disability caused by military service, the corresponding files show an outpouring of information about men's wartime suffering. Chapin claimed to have incurred a number of health problems during the war, starting with diarrhea but expanding over the years.[41] Dr. Daniel W. Layman—who had treated him during his wartime furlough—insisted, "I have no doubt the exposure in the service of his country was the cause of his sickness."[42] Lucius's former captain, S. J. Dickerson, remembered that Lucius still suffered from diarrhea even after returning from the hospital: "It was at times of a violent character and sufficient to relieve him from duty had he asked it but he preferred to perform his duty although harassed continually by his said disease."[43] Jonas Seely, another former captain and also Alice's uncle, called Lucius a "faithful soldier, always when able at his post and only left the line when compelled by disease."[44]

Lucius's own affidavit intermixed a chronicle of his military service, assertions as to its medical consequences, and testaments to his faithfulness. His diarrhea began in March 1863, and he noted that he "used such remedies as I had with me not answering sick call." Growing "much worse," he was first sent to a hospital in Nashville and then given a thirty-day furlough. "My health improving, I determined to join my Regt," but after a hard campaign, he reported, "my disease became chronic and remained my hair dark, came out, and come in white." In July 1864, he "was prostrated at Chattahoochie River while on duty by sun or heat was unconscious," but he returned to his company within a week. After more service, he recorded, "My hearing was affected and remains so." In the final campaign of 1865 in Alabama, he noted, "I suffered all the time with the disease hardly able to keep along, but those last days kept many a man going who was not able."[45] The summary in Lucius's pension file stripped away these testimonials to his patriotic service, concentrating instead on the essentials as the pension bureaucracy saw it: that Lucius had been healthy when he enlisted, that he had been in the hospital and treated for diarrhea, and that he continued to suffer from it. Dr. Hiram R. Pitchlynn described Lucius in 1881 as "emaciated"—at 6 feet 2 inches, he weighed only 150 pounds—and incapable of any but "light" work. Pitchlynn predicted that Lucius would be afflicted by diarrhea the remainder of his life.[46]

In June 1865, Lucius began receiving a pension of $4 per month for chronic diarrhea. That sum was doubled years later as the condition worsened—as graphically described in his file—into bouts lasting up to three days. In these later years, Lucius's ailments expanded, but he considered them linked to his war service. He enlisted the help of Dr. Knight to describe his 1867 collapse and link it to the sunstroke he had suffered during the Atlanta campaign. Lucius also believed that a case of malaria during the war was responsible for episodes of vertigo. To pension officials who might suspect intemperance, Laban H. Dickerson insisted, "I will say that Sergt Chapin was noted for his temperance and honesty while in the Service and still has that reputation."[47] By the 1890s, old friends were testifying that the fifty-nine-year-old Chapin's hearing was quite bad, which Lucius also blamed on that bout of malaria.[48]

In 1890, Chapin received $12 per month for the diarrhea and "nervous debility res of sunstroke." However, the government rejected his claims that the sunstroke had caused impaired hearing—the government found his hearing to be fine—or that he had suffered malaria poisoning.[49] A decade later, Lucius claimed that he was losing his teeth because of scurvy during the war, but the Medical Division of the Pension Bureau insisted that for loss of teeth to be legally allowable, it had to have followed "immediately after incurrence of scurvy."[50] In response, Lucius filed another affidavit, describing his 1863 hospitalization and recalling that the surgeon "burnt his mouth with caustic on account of said scurvy." During the next two months, he stated, "his mouth was very sore, gums swollen and bleeding, and his teeth began to come out, and break off"; even after returning to his regiment, he continued to lose teeth and suffer from gum disease.[51] In response, the board recommended a payment of $24 per month. But Chapin now developed pains about the heart. He got his pension raised in 1907, and again five years later to $30 per month. Finally, Lucius's pension envelope was stamped "DEAD." The Chapins were not yet done with the government, however. Lucius's younger daughter, Hannah Lee Chapin Pettyjohn, requested government aid with her father's burial expenses, for which she was reimbursed in April 1915.[52]

Wyatt James's claim upon the government was more straightforward than Lucius Chapin's. At the battle of the Crater, James had taken a bullet in the left leg and a piece of shell in the left side, leaving visible scars. He, too, had entered military service "a healthy man" and left disabled. James also had contracted diarrhea in camp, causing him to miss duty.[53] It was to such wartime sufferings that he attributed the ailments plaguing his old age. His rheumatism and respiratory problems derived from a "severe cold" contracted at Petersburg "from exposure and sleeping on the wet ground." From rheumatism, he had developed heart disease; from chronic diarrhea, "piles," or hemorrhoids, that led to disease of the liver and spleen. All this resulted in "general debility."[54] As happened with Lucius Chapin, James's physicians affirmed that his ailments were not related to "vicious habits," although there was in his case an additional notation stating that there was no sign of "Venereal Disease." James's Townsend in-laws and his doctor testified to the difficulty he had in doing manual labor. His file, like Chapin's, contained gruesome descriptions of his ailments—bloody hemorrhoidal tumors, bouts of diarrhea, heart attacks, and eventually blindness and paralysis. By the time Wyatt James died of a cerebral hemorrhage in 1927, he was receiving a pension of $90 per month.[55] With its affidavits from fellow soldiers and physicians, his pension file resembled Lucius Chapin's. The accounts of James's old comrades were direct, however, lacking the testimonials to his character as a dedicated soldier that Chapin's former officers provided. But both pension files shared an insistence that the problems of old age—rheumatism, loss of teeth, bad hearing, and heart problems—had been caused by the veterans' wartime service.

Stuart McConnell has detailed how pension law evolved to accommodate the aging veteran population. Legislation passed during the war stipulated that a disability had to be related to one's service, but as the aches and pains of aging veterans grew over the decades, that law was revised so that old age itself was considered sufficient disability.[56] Still, Lucius Chapin and Wyatt James firmly believed that their infirmities resulted from hardships they had endured for their country. In their later years, they remained convinced they were suffering because of the war.

As a congressman, C. C. Matson was in a position to affect the pensions other veterans received, and he agreed that these disbursements were based on suffering. Being a Democrat, he was mindful of keeping government frugal, yet he "cheerfully" voted for a pension bill that he admitted would take more money from the Treasury than any measure since the Civil War. This was "no charity," in his opinion, but a "sacred debt" created by the war, and it was fitting to share the "bounty of the Government" with those who suffered "helplessness brought upon them in its military service."[57] In 1887, Congress passed a bill Matson introduced, whereby any honorably discharged veteran with a disability would receive a pension of $12 per month. But although President Grover Cleveland had expressed sympathy for disabled veterans, he vetoed the dependent pension bill. Matson was then in the awkward position of seeking to overturn a veto by a president of his own party. The president not only feared the cost, which Matson insisted was affordable, but also objected that the recipients were not required to be propertyless. Matson countered that his bill—like all pension bills—was based on disability. In the end, Matson was unsuccessful and the veto stood.

Three years later, under a Republican president from Indiana, Benjamin Harrison, Congress passed the Dependent Pension Act. Matson was no longer a member of Congress by that time, but the bill did essentially what he had envisioned—providing a pension to any disabled veteran who had been honorably discharged. Because it neither required the veteran to be poor nor stipulated that the disability be war-related, the 1890 bill became, in effect, a pension for anyone who had served. By 1900, three-quarters of surviving veterans were receiving pensions, and by the next decade, over one-quarter of Indiana's population consisted of pensioners—a proportion typical of the North.

At the turn of the twentieth century, the federal government would spend over 25 percent of its money on Civil War pensions.[58]

The generation of young men who had fought the Civil War believed they deserved recognition not just because they had saved the nation, but also because their sacrifices for the Union had rendered them physically unable to be independent men. The federal government owed them pensions so that they could provide for their families as they otherwise would have as healthy wage earners. Black veterans such as Wyatt James benefited as much as white soldiers in this regard, making pensions in that way a radical break with white supremacy. In another way, however, pensions were fundamentally conservative. Their purpose was to allow men to continue their accustomed roles despite physical disability incurred during the war. Those roles included providing for their dependents.

Elizabeth Applegate had anxiously awaited her husband's return from the war. In an effort to provide for his family, John had stayed in the army after his release from Andersonville.[59] The Applegates did not intend the war to change gender relations but merely disagreed on how best John might fulfill his obligations as breadwinner. By the time he returned home, he had survived not only three years of war, but eight months of imprisonment and the explosion of the steamboat *Sultana*.

When Applegate arrived at the Andersonville stockade, it held three times as many men as it was designed to accommodate. Rations were measured out by the spoonful, and even these might be denied as punishment for infractions of the rules or escape attempts. Many of the prisoners had no cover, but some dug holes in the ground for sleeping. Applegate contracted chronic diarrhea in prison and emerged a mere "skeleton." The same conditions that caused soldiers such as Lucius Chapin and Wyatt James to become ill—contaminated food and men passing bacteria between themselves—were exacerbated by the crowded, unsanitary conditions of the prisoner camps.[60] From Andersonville, Applegate was transported to Vicksburg, where he was placed among the sick on the *Sultana*. As it drew near Memphis, the steamboat exploded. Applegate awoke from sleep to find himself in the water. He seized a floating board, but others did as well and their weight soon pulled him under water. Applegate then swam to a bale of hay and, along with three others, clung to it as it floated downstream. The current carried them downstream for 7 miles before they were rescued by men in a boat. He had spent four hours in the water, providing another shock to his "prostrated system." Rejoining his regiment in Pulaski,

Tennessee, Applegate was commissioned a first lieutenant, "but his health was broken." He spent seven weeks in a hospital before returning to his regiment and mustering out in September 1865.[61]

When her husband returned home, Elizabeth now had to care for a chronic invalid. John Applegate affirmed, "I have never saw a well day since I was discharged from Prision." Having once hoped to make money through his army service, he now found himself unemployed after the war and so sick that "he has not been able to do anything." John recovered for periods but was "subject to constant relapse" that left him "confined to his bed—apparently in as bad a condition as ever."[62] County Republicans elected him sheriff in the fall of 1866, as recompense for "what he had done and suffered for his country." Applegate alternated periods of work with bed rest, but by the next autumn, it was clear that he grew worse with each relapse: "Kind friends did what they could to render his short stay on earth as pleasant as possible." He died in November 1867 at the age of forty-four.[63]

The circuit court held a solemn ceremony to memorialize Applegate's death. With the courtroom draped in mourning, a committee drafted resolutions in a meeting presided over by Judge Delana Eckels. "He lived an active life and discharged faithfully the duties of the Patriot soldier and of his civil position," the court concluded. "He was a kind, affectionate husband and father, and a true hearted friend."[64] Five days after he died, the government judged Applegate's disability total and awarded him an invalid pension of $17 per month, backdated to his date of discharge. Applegate's pension requests had been filed by John S. Jennings, who now refiled on behalf of his survivors. "She is a worthy woman," Jennings asserted of Elizabeth Applegate.[65]

Jennings's characterization of Elizabeth encapsulated much of the prevailing philosophy about pensions for female dependents. The women had to be worthy—in other words, they had to follow the gender norms for their period. John Applegate had joined the Union army to be a breadwinner for his family, but the war left him incapable of fulfilling that role. Pensions for dependents recognized that military service might have that result, and reassured men considering service that the government would care for their families if they were killed or crippled. The Civil War, however, was unprecedented in the number of family members who qualified as dependents and in the amounts they could receive; the widow's monthly pension, for example, doubled from $4 to $8. And just as disbursements for men were based on the assumption that the war had deprived them of their ability to be breadwinners, Civil War pensions were predicated on a belief in women's "intrinsically dependent nature." Although this justified denying women political or legal rights, it also gave them a right to men's wages. The federal government would step in where it had deprived a woman of her wage earner. In addition to generous pensions for widows, the 1862 pension law made mothers of dead soldiers eligible for pensions if they had been dependent on the son's earnings. This provision made it possible for Charity Townsend to claim a pension based on Robert's service.

Despite the fact that such pensions were based on the assumption of female dependence, they actually allowed women unusual independence. Historically, the lack of a male wage earner had often meant a widow had to live with a son or married daughter or endure a lonely poverty.[66] Civil War pensions helped women avoid turning to others for help. In Essex County, Massachusetts, 88 percent of pensioned widows were heads of households, as opposed to only 60 percent of nonpensioned widows.[67]

Elizabeth Applegate was forty-four years old when her husband died. Perhaps without the pension, she would have had to remarry or to rely on male relatives. Instead, she maintained an independent household until old age made it impossible for her to live alone. Early on, friends had wondered how she would provide for herself and her daughter, Allie. One such friend, Irving E. Showerman, wrote that he and his wife would "do anything in our power to assist you or to make your trouble lighter." He asked to know "how you are situated" and assured Elizabeth, "You no doubt find no lack of friends ready to see that your necessities are provided for, or to help you to provide for yourself." He hoped such measures would be successful and closed with "good wishes for your prosperity."[68] Elizabeth's in-laws were evidently loving and kind. John's father, Peter Applegate, closed a letter to Allie with "our Love to your kind Mother and be sure to Kis her from us."[69] But Peter was elderly and had suffered business reverses.[70] He may not have been in a position to aid Elizabeth and Allie with anything more than good wishes, affection, and urgings to rely on divine help.

Elizabeth owned her house in Greencastle, and widows in that town traditionally earned money by renting rooms to students. In fact, being a boardinghouse keeper was a common occupation for widows everywhere. Elizabeth did rent out part of her house to an Asbury student, and when her father, John Lynch, died in 1872, her share of his estate was valued at over $1,000. In addition, she owned some shares in a savings and loan, and she loaned out money. Elizabeth did a lot of sewing—stockings for her granddaughter and gifts for friends—but she was also sent work and presumably received pay for it. But her steadiest source of income was her widow's pension of $8 per month, awarded March 4, 1868, and backdated to September 15, 1865. She had enough to live independently if she kept her eye on costs.[71]

Elizabeth had sufficient resources to see to her daughter's education. Allie Applegate attended school in Greencastle, including the women's college, and normal school in another county. She then taught school for seven years, two of them at a public school for African American children. In a state where the average teacher stayed for only two years, this made her quite experienced.[72] As before the war, education remained a contested issue in Putnam County, where its advocates deplored the public's unwillingness to pay school taxes and indifference to education. Teachers were often unqualified, having gotten licenses through their friends' recommendations. Some were even abusive. In one instance, a Bainbridge jury acquitted a female teacher of assault and battery after a three-hour deliberation but probably did so because jurors feared undermining instructors' authority in the classroom. As was true statewide, Putnam teachers were poorly paid, which some felt led to incompetence in the classroom.[73]

Nonetheless, improvements in education continued in the postwar period. The number of children in school, as well as teacher pay and the length of the school year, all increased in the decades after the war. Attendance rose to 60 percent but still lagged behind the state norm. Greencastle residents especially took pride in their school system. In 1880, the Greencastle high school graduated four students, two men and two women. Despite the small number, it was a gala affair with floral decorations and orations by the graduates. State legislation became more supportive of schools. By 1873, a new school law required that teachers attend a township institute or model school. Such institutes included lectures on topics such as arithmetic, geography, grammar, penmanship, reading, drawing, and spelling. Putnam County held its first teachers' association meeting five years before the law was enacted. And Greencastle obviously benefited from the involvement of Asbury professors and local teachers.[74] Ultimately, Allie Applegate, like many female teachers, left the profession for marriage. She wed a Methodist minister, J. S. White, in 1881, and bore a daughter, Esther.[75]

Even though Elizabeth Applegate lived alone as an independent woman and encouraged Allie's schooling and work, she did not seek to challenge women's roles. Writing to Allie about an auction she attended, she demurred,

"You will begin to think I live on the street,"[76] a reference to woman's proper place being in the home. She longed to see Allie and Esther but confided that when she thought of traveling alone, "my courage almost fails me."[77] Perhaps it was advancing age that inhibited her, but during the war, she had also been reluctant to visit her husband without an escort. Elizabeth's letters always had fond words for her granddaughter, but she did not emulate her father-in-law in passing on affectionate wishes for Allie's husband, whom she never mentioned in letters to Allie. Perhaps Reverend White expected to play a more patriarchal role in the family than the long-widowed Elizabeth was prepared to accept.

In her old age, Elizabeth busied herself with sewing, baking bread, and caring for the sick. Allie had moved away with her husband, but she returned for visits with Esther, on whom Elizabeth doted. Elizabeth also regularly attended lectures at DePauw (as Indiana Asbury was now known), concerts, and church. She sometimes heard female speakers, including a lecturer and preacher, and she went to a "big democrat rally" to "see the show." She visited the "old cemetery" where John was buried. Allie worried about her mother living alone, but Elizabeth professed an inability to find anyone to live with her. However, after years of independent living, the thought of a caretaker may not have been appealing. Nonetheless, at the beginning of 1890, Allie prevailed and moved her mother in with her own family. Perhaps Elizabeth's health had deteriorated to the point where she simply could not live alone. For several years, Elizabeth had suffered from pains in the side that sent her from one Greencastle doctor to another in search of succor, and she also had symptoms of diabetes. She died in April 1890, a few months after moving in with Allie.[78]

Before her death, Elizabeth Applegate applied for an increased pension. Her grounds were that although John had been commissioned as a first lieutenant on January 1, 1865, his imprisonment in Andersonville had prevented him taking that commission until May 1, 1865. She asked for $17 per month, the amount awarded the widow of a first lieutenant, with the back pay that was due John. While she waited for the pension office's decision, she noted the help she was receiving in obtaining "my money." She did not view the pension as a gift from a grateful nation or as John's income but simply as her money, which she had not yet received. In the end, she was awarded $161.34, but the sum was not paid out until after her death. Reverend White made inquiries about how his wife could receive the last payment from the government for her father's service. Allie received $145.21 after the fee of $16.13 for the pension attorney, Jesse Weik, was deducted.[79]

Allie's motives were not mercenary. She ordered an impressive crystal granite monument, at the cost of $115, to be placed in Forest Hill. She buried Elizabeth there but also disinterred her father's remains from the Old Cemetery, reinterring them at Forest Hill. After her long widowhood, Elizabeth Applegate was at last reunited with her husband. The marker also bore the names of John and Elizabeth's dead children—Oscar, Eva, and Augustus—so perhaps Allie had them buried with their parents as well.[80] The cost of reinterring her father and siblings probably consumed the balance of the government's final check.

As independent as Elizabeth Applegate remained until her final days, she, like all women, received her pension benefits based on her relation to a Civil War soldier. Elizabeth needed witnesses to swear that she was still a widow; otherwise, she would have lost the pension. Similarly, in order for Charity Townsend to receive a mother's pension for her son Robert, she needed to show not only that she had depended on him for support but also that there was no one else to provide for her: her husband had been unable to support her, and her other children had left home.[81]

Although Luke Townsend did not die until four years after his son, he had been too old and incapacitated with rheumatism to "earn much by his labor." Dr. Layman estimated that Luke had earned only about $100 per year in the last years of his life. Robert's farmwork and employment at the quarry had, as Charity insisted in her pension application, gone "toward the support of herself and family." Layman reported that he "attended [Robert] for near two years but made no charge for my attentions and medicines for the reason that himself and mother was poor—and not able to pay." Like Elizabeth Applegate, Charity was required to prove that she had not remarried after Luke's death in order to keep her dependent status. Her own indigence and age were further aids to receiving the pension. Lucy Moss and Emma Williams swore "that said Charity Townsend is poor, and has no income save what is contributed by friends, or earned by her own labor; and they believe her unable to earn her subsistence by reason of Advanced age and feebleness."[82]

After Luke died, Charity and the children sold their "little home" at Greencastle Junction for $800, Charity's share of which was the widow's third, and bought a house in Greencastle. But the house was mortgaged to pay a debt of $250, and it was foreclosed on when the Townsends could not repay. By the time Charity applied for a pension, almost twenty years after Robert's death, she was propertyless.[83] She earned a living "by doing all kinds of work . . . such as washing & ironing," with some assistance from her seven surviving children. But once grown, those children were "going out to do for themselves" and, by implication, leaving their mother to fend for herself. Charity now had just the washing and ironing to provide income, and she had "only managed to obtain, by hard work, a very meager subsistence."[84]

Charity applied for a pension in 1871 as a "dependent mother." Luke had died by then, and she was "dependent upon herself for support." The application was denied. She had specified that she had not remarried, but the Pension Bureau wanted assurance that Robert had neither wife nor child who might claim his benefit. Robert's brother William had provided an affidavit to that effect, but it was apparently overlooked. According to Donald R. Shaffer, only 36 percent of black parents made successful pension applications, compared to 70 percent of white parents. In 1885, Charity was finally awarded a pension of $8 per month, with back payments due from May 1865, the date of Robert's death. The twenty years of benefits totaled the astonishing sum of over $1,900 for "one of the most worthy colored ladies" of Greencastle.[85]

Pension law required Charity Townsend to exaggerate both her dependence on Robert and her independence from her surviving children. She lived for years after the war with her daughter Lucy and son William, who were old enough to contribute to the family income, as well as with her younger children. Even as they grew up, many of Charity's children stayed in Greencastle, so even though she was no doubt poor and did work hard, it was unlikely she had no support from her offspring. Nonetheless, her lump-sum payment must have provided a far more secure old age than she might otherwise have had.[86]

Government pensions offered women such as Elizabeth Applegate and Charity Townsend some independence, yet they did not view themselves as woman's rights advocates. Elizabeth went to hear female speakers and preachers without commenting on her views of women's status. Female roles had changed since the prewar period, but women's claims to an equal place with men still provoked controversy. When Asbury admitted five women students in 1867, male students felt they had lost their elite status, as schools such as Harvard and Yale did not admit women. Meanwhile, the women were regularly snubbed: they were left off the commencement program and denied participation in the literary societies' performance. This "morbid" contest between men and women at Asbury came to a head in 1875, when Flora S. Turman and Newton L. Wray tied for top place in the class standing. Forced to choose a valedictorian, the faculty chose Wray, leading to accusations that women at Asbury suffered "persecution." The uproar caused a reversal of the decision, and Turman was awarded the top honor.[87]

Mary Frances Donnohue and Elizabeth Ames, both graduates of female seminaries, organized the Woman's Reading Club in Greencastle, one of the oldest women's clubs in the state. Donnohue and Ames sought a "more expansive life" through study. Anne Ruggles Gere argues that educated women found the clubs an outlet for their intellects that their ordinary lives did not provide. What began as a book club might became a forum for discussing public questions. The Greencastle group grew rapidly, having about thirty women in the 1870s, and meeting twice a month. As was true of many clubs, membership was reserved for the elite, and the meetings reflected the traditions of upper-middle-class entertaining. Most homes where they met had a piano, so they had music as well as recitation and debate. Before the Civil War, the Greencastle newspaper editor had found temperance women presumptuous in wanting their work acknowledged in their own names, but the newspaper now regularly reported on women's doings.

Scholars have argued that women's clubs could lead women to challenge the precepts of their society, but the Greencastle club appears not to have been terribly subversive. On the one hand, some of the county's leading intellectuals participated, including professors from Indiana Asbury, and Mary E. Langsdale, wife of the *Banner*'s editor and a woman suffrage advocate, was a founding member. But on the other hand, judging by the records that have survived, the talks at their meetings were not particularly controversial. Martha Jane Ridpath, an Asbury graduate and local teacher, gave many club talks on teaching Sunday school. Her 1911 address was a meditation on the importance of reading.[88]

Woman's rights, including suffrage, had been condemned in Putnam County before the Civil War. But even though the topic remained controversial, it received more support in the later decades of the nineteenth century than in the past. In 1870, Elizabeth Cady Stanton lectured in Greencastle "on the woman's rights question," and woman suffrage was the topic of a debate in Putnamville a few years later. "The ladies seemed to enjoy the occasion grandly," it was reported, "especially while the affirmative were speaking."[89] George Langsdale, editor of the *Banner* and onetime president of the local woman suffrage association, relied on traditional arguments about U.S. republicanism and woman's sphere: "It has always been the boast of the American that, in this country since the Declaration of Independence, all are endowed with certain inalienable rights. We believe in making this declaration good, and if any woman wants the right to vote, let her have it." Langsdale was dismissive of notions of women's physical and mental incapacity for political rights: women, too, were capable of walking to the polls. He conceded, "There may be a difference of mind in men and women," but he added, "So there is between man and man."[90] Someone identified only as "J. F. L." wrote to the paper and argued that women could be liberated from slavery to their "tyranical lord[s]" and given political rights without endangering their essential natures.[91]

Not everyone agreed. A correspondent identified as "Nemo" believed that "the ballot in the hands of woman, entitling her to all the privileges and responsibilities of political citizenship, would be a calamity hurtful to herself and disastrous to the Nation." If women wanted political influence, they should exercise it through their sons. Nemo pronounced woman's role in the home—inculcating "virtue and religion"—a paramount support of the government.[92] Meanwhile, "Adam" denied that women were equal to men in nature and asserted that suffrage would lead to marital discord and divorce.[93] "A WOMAN" agreed that her sex might have an "abstract right" to the vote but argued that in exercising it, a woman neglected her duties as "presiding genius of the family circle": "[The] woman is as really represented in politics by her husband as though casting the vote herself." Even though she adhered to a strict definition of woman's sphere, A WOMAN cautioned men such as Langsdale, who "flatter themselves that they are to go down to posterity as the Phillipses and Garrisons of the crusade for woman's rights. We refuse to consider ourselves enslaved."[94]

The plight of widows influenced the debate. Opponents of woman suffrage, such as A WOMAN, had portrayed marriage as an organic whole in which the natures of the two genders complemented each other—man as breadwinner, woman as housekeeper. Yet what if the husband died? Some argued that widows had certain political rights that alleviated the supposed oppression women suffered. From this viewpoint, the widow's guarantee of a share of her husband's property was a benefit women received. They also had a limited suffrage, having the vote in school elections. Langsdale pointed out that widows incurred lawyers' fees in administering estates that widowers did not. Another prosuffrage writer argued that if widows could exercise political rights, "of course, wives whose husbands are on a 'journey,' or, peradventure, are asleep and can not be waked, will ask the same privilege."[95]

Other political rights, such as holding office, seemed acceptable provided that the occupant was a worthy woman—a Civil War widow. In 1868, a controversy arose in Bainbridge over the removal of the postmistress, Mrs. Darnall, "the widow of Dr. Darnall, who lost his life in the service of his country." Republicans were outraged that her replacement was to be a supposedly less worthy widow, Mary Ellis. Mary was deemed less estimable because her deceased spouse, F. M. Ellis, had been a Copperhead.[96] When the position of state librarian opened in 1880, one correspondent in the *Banner* put in a plea for Emma A. Winsor of Greencastle, whose husband, Capt. Samuel H. Winsor, had served for three years in the 8th Indiana Battery. A shell injury to the head at the battle of Stones River had paralyzed him and rendered him mentally unstable. Subsequently, he was confined to the Indiana Hospital for the Insane, leaving his wife with no breadwinner. The correspondent wrote, "It is hoped that the wife and children of Captain Winsor . . . will not be overlooked."[97] Advocates promoting Emma Winsor for the open position based their claims not on any special competence she had as a librarian, but on her political connections and—most important—on her husband's service in the Union cause.

J. F. L. believed that women had earned the suffrage for their work in support of the Union. If the Civil War could broaden the suffrage to include African Americans, it could also do so for women. Once the Fifteenth Amendment had passed, giving black men the vote, Indiana congressman George Julian proposed a sixteenth amendment to extend the suffrage to women, and in 1869, the Indiana Woman's Suffrage Association endorsed Julian's proposed amendment. J. F. L. argued that just as African Americans had educated themselves on political issues once they achieved suffrage, so would women.[98] A Democrat doubted whether ladies would want to sit "in the legislative halls with Sambo and Dinah" and in fact suspected that woman suffrage was a movement to increase the black vote for Republican purposes.[99] But even though Indiana's General Assembly considered woman suffrage on several occasions in the 1870s, it was consistently defeated. The suffrage movement lapsed in the state until World War I. Women's contribution to the war effort finally cemented passage of the Nineteenth Amendment, giving women the vote. Even then, Indiana woman suffragists had to persuade Governor James P. Goodrich to hold a special session. Indiana ratified in January 1920.[100]

Their role in public life having expanded, women now appeared by name as officers in organizations such as the missionary society. But these organizations still revolved around women's traditional charitable roles. When Putnam County organized a society for the relief of the poor in 1877, the officers were women, and the instructions were to leave contributions at "Mrs. Chapin's on

Jackson street."[101] It was the mayor's wife, not the mayor, who would oversee this public philanthropy because it was based on women's traditional role as caretakers. Temperance work was still the most common public role for women. Prosuffrage writers argued that women voters would use their moral influence to enact antialcohol measures.[102] After state law changed to require voters' signatures in order to obtain a liquor license, some noted that woman suffrage would make it difficult for liquor sellers to get the necessary majority of local voters' signatures. Jonathan Birch, speaking at a Greencastle temperance meeting, pointed out that woman suffrage "will almost absolutely dry up the liquor business."[103] In the 1870s, the liquor industry helped defeat state constitutional amendments for both prohibition and woman suffrage.[104]

What is generally referred to as the women's temperance crusade was actually a joint effort by antialcohol men and women to eradicate liquor from the community. Temperance was popular among small-town white Protestants, who believed it possible to morally perfect their society. Before the Civil War, moral reform was seen as a natural extension of woman's moral virtues and the need to protect the domestic sphere, even when it took women into the public sphere. Elizabeth Applegate, who spoke apologetically of appearing in public, joined the Women's Christian Temperance Union (WCTU). And Alice Chapin, a woman who had longed for her own home, pledged to stay in public until the liquor sellers were driven out of Greencastle. After all, women also suffered when alcohol abuse impeded men from being good breadwinners or made them a threat to their families.[105] Even the Democratic newspaper lamented the plight of "the worse than widowed and fatherless ones" victimized by "the demon of intemperance."[106]

As they had before the war, temperance groups struggled to find a tactic that would successfully close the saloons. In the early 1870s, they opposed licenses for saloonkeepers. Some objected that this strategy would not work, because the county board would grant the licenses and the courts would uphold those grants. Others believed that the county commissioners could be lobbied into denying licenses. Members of the Putnam County Temperance Alliance hired lawyers to fight applications for liquor licenses. The alliance gathered signatures to remonstrate against granting licenses to six establishments, and it also retained three law firms, including Claypool, Matson and Chapin, to represent the remonstrators before the commissioners' court. Further, the alliance invited all the ministers in Greencastle to urge their congregations to attend the court session. When the commissioners met, the courtroom was filled to capacity, the ladies of Greencastle having turned out en masse. The commissioners, however, deferred the remonstrance, causing "great disappointment" to the women present.[107] Meanwhile, the saloonkeepers formed their own association "for our mutual protection," boycotting the businesses of temperance men.[108] But the liquor sellers were already feeling the pressure. Shortly before the commissioners' court met, Michael Maloney gave up and withdrew his application for a license.[109]

When the commissioners reconvened, people crowded the courtroom to hear the application of John Cawley for a license to retail alcohol. Judge Eckels, one of Cawley's attorneys, claimed the packed room was intended for "overawing the Court." Yet the *Banner* praised "the courteous conduct of the ladies, and those who accompanied them," as they quietly witnessed the efforts of men to obtain the legal right "to lead their sons and relatives into the habit of intemperance, and . . . blight the fondest hopes of some of those who sat there."[110] In fact, just a few weeks later, the twenty-nine-year-old son of Dr. Thomas Bowman, president of Indiana Asbury, was shot in a drunken saloon brawl. John Durbin Bowman died early the next morning in the arms of his mother, to whom "he said that if he could be permitted to live he would lead a different life to what he had in the past."[111]

Cawley's application turned on his "good moral character." His witnesses included prominent Democrats such as Howard Briggs, editor of the Democratic newspaper; two other saloonkeepers; Fr. J. Clements, the Catholic priest; and Henry Wilmes, a Catholic schoolteacher. Wilmes forthrightly announced, "I ask where I can get good beer, and I always get good fresh beer at Cawley's, and he keeps good liquor, too."[112] Cawley's supporters revealed that the political and ethnoreligious divide on alcohol that had existed before the war remained in force. Antialcohol reform was a Republican and native-born Protestant cause.

The remonstrators summoned witnesses who testified that Cawley had broken the law in several ways: gambling occurred at his saloon, where customers played billiards and wagered on the games; alcohol was sold to minors and drunks; and liquor was sold on Sunday. The unusually lengthy proceedings— over sixty witnesses were called—required a night session and three hours the next morning for the lawyers to make their closing arguments. The courthouse was crowded throughout, with "a large proportion of ladies" attending.[113] In the end, the county commission awarded a license to only one applicant, John L. F. Steeg, who ran an establishment at the railroad junction outside Greencastle. Two liquor sellers withdrew their applications and gave up the fight, but

John Cawley and William McCoy appealed to the common pleas court. Cawley's appeal for his license went to trial in October. After a week of arguments,
the jury was unable to reach a verdict. By the end of 1871, the *Indianapolis Journal* announced, "The last saloon in Greencastle closed last week, and the City
Marshal says he will have to saw wood to make a living." But Cawley remained
in business.[114]

The campaign for total prohibition accelerated after the license fight. Prohibition forces advocated a constitutional amendment requiring that all state
officers take an oath not to drink while in office; they also discussed whether to
form a third party, and in the 1872 elections, they ran a prohibition ticket that
got a small vote. The next year, the state legislature passed the so-called Baxter
bill, which required a petition of support from the majority of voters in a ward
or township to sell liquor.[115] Rev. Ransom Hawley wrote his minister son, "The
new Temperance law gives much encouragement to work. . . . The present is
the best Temperance law we ever had."[116]

Temperance forces rallied to make sure the law was enforced. Professor J.
S. Gillespie reported that the law was already having a dampening effect in
Greencastle, where a "respectable grocery store" had opened in place of a saloon that had shut down. Gillespie believed "that no one can get his license renewed in Greencastle according to this law."[117] A Bainbridge man, however, saw
things differently, lamenting, "Either the new temperance law is no account,
or the authorities of the town are afraid to enforce it. We notice a good deal
of drunkenness on the streets, even in the day time. There is no use having
any law unless it is enforced."[118] The results were also mixed in Cloverdale,
where "the new liquor law has been enforced here in a few cases of drunks,
but there appears to be too much drinking, and the venders are escaping the
law so far entirely."[119] After initially being intimidated by the law, residents of
Manhattan, in Putnam County, also found it less than effective: "Our drinkers
are not so timid about getting drunk as they were at first, and unless some of
them are indicted by the Grand Jury, they will continue to get drunk as they did
before the new law passed."[120] Even in Greencastle, the law did not fully eradicate the saloons. Robert L. Higert and William McCoy procured the signatures
necessary to apply for licenses in the First Ward, although some of the signers
subsequently asked that their names be removed, fearing that "more than one
expulsion from church membership" might follow becoming known to have
signed a saloonkeeper's petition.[121]

Lucius Chapin took a prominent role in the temperance movement.

Interior of Higert's saloon. (Courtesy of Putnam County Public Library)

Appointed to the executive committee of the antialcohol forces, Chapin prepared the legal case against granting liquor licenses to Higert and McCoy, finding numerous technical faults with the petition and its signatures. Despite his efforts, however, the commissioners overruled all objections and granted the license. A Terre Haute judge denied the remonstrators further remedy in the courts. Chapin nonetheless received praise for his efforts: "L. P. Chapin devoted about two weeks of his time, without fee or reward, to preparing the cases against the applications for liquor license, and deserves the thanks of the entire community for his work. That his efforts were unsuccessful was no fault of his."[122] Meanwhile, antilicense efforts continued. Searching for irregularities, a committee of the Greencastle Temperance League examined signatures on saloonkeepers' license applications that had been filed at the auditor's office. But inability to drive the saloonkeepers away caused one Greencastle observer to despair, "The Baxter law is a perfect failure with us."[123]

Disappointment with the Baxter law set the stage for the women's crusade of 1873–1874. It began in Fredonia, New York, when temperance lecturer Diocletian Lewis advocated that women should go into the saloons and pray there until proprietors agreed to close their doors. Husbands endorsed this expansion of woman's sphere, the women took up the cause, and the crusade was launched, spreading to twenty-one states, including Indiana, which was second only to Ohio in the level of participation. Greencastle women adopted the crusade and seem to have had one of the more vigorous movements in the state. Barbara Leslie Epstein believes the crusade was more successful in smaller towns because peer pressure and organization were more effective in such settings.[124] The women's crusade at first evoked a humorous response from the saloonkeepers:

> It was reported yesterday that ladies would call last evening at the various saloons of the city to engage in prayer for the saloon keepers and their patrons. The ladies failed to make their appearance, in lieu of whom, the proprietor of one of the saloons said he hated to have his customers disappointed, and called upon his negro "Bill" to lead in prayer. Bill took a strong glass, knelt before a chair and prayed fifteen minutes. They call it a powerful prayer.[125]

As the crusade proceeded, it became less of a laughing matter. The *Banner*'s editor interviewed some of the saloonkeepers who were its targets. Several of them asserted the lawfulness of their business. "In a very courteous manner," for example, William McCoy "informed the interviewer that he is selling liquor under the Baxter law." McCoy "does not think it right, as long as he has commenced his business under, and in accordance with a law of the State," that the women should now try to circumvent the law.[126] Other liquor sellers emphasized that women had interfered in an area outside their proper sphere. P. M. Layton said, "I think the women would better stay at home and tend to their own affairs." But he allowed that he would treat the women "respectfully" because he "couldn't hardly get along without them," one of many insinuations that women drove men to drink. Higert also felt that the women could do more good through traditional means of persuasion. "If they want to affect this business morally," he said, "let them go to the men who drink. I tell lots of men every day that they ought not to drink so much." Richard McMannis emphasized that he would treat the women as ladies but not let them interfere with his lawful business. And John Cawley, who also disapproved of the crusade, "doesn't intend that they shall pray in his house."[127]

The crusade began in Greencastle, where there were church services and meetings whose principal speaker was William Baxter, author of the law. Despite the wind and rain one dark night, a crowd turned out for a temperance prayer meeting at the Christian Church in Greencastle. Lucius Chapin chaired the gathering, and his wife was one of the female leaders reporting to the assembly. Alice Chapin endorsed the sentiment of another woman, who "proposed to continue in the work until their object is gained."[128] After a "probationary season of prayer on the part of the ladies," necessary for "nerving them up to the work," the women began picketing saloons, including those of Cawley and Higert, in early April. They arrived in pairs when the saloons opened, were given seats near the proprietors, and stayed until closing. The *Press* accused the women of pursuing a mission "not . . . of prayer, but of espionage," for the ladies noted all who visited the establishment. For the women's part, although they disliked inhaling tobacco smoke all day, they reportedly were offered no "indignity" except for one attempt to drive them out by throwing red pepper on the stove. In addition to the women's vigil in the saloons, the crusade also featured daily prayer meetings.[129] Alice Chapin was a leader in this aspect of the crusade, making speeches and presiding over temperance meetings where Lucius sometimes spoke. At a Mount Meridian church, Alice led the religious exercises and then "made some remarks, giving something of her experience in the work of the crusade, during the spring and summer, and closed by briefly stating the object of the meeting."[130]

Not all women found it easy to take so public a role, however. Hester M. Downey quoted one woman as saying, "I feel like it would kill me to go to the saloons." Downey insisted that all the women felt so at the beginning, "but those who have gone, prompted by a sense of duty, have not lost one particle of the purity and virtue of their hearts." She urged men to encourage their wives to participate.[131]

Editor George Langsdale went to a Greencastle saloon to see the crusade's effects. He found one drinker who said, "as he complacently wiped the lager froth from his mouth, that the business was never respectable before, but now the countenances of the ladies had made it eminently so." Langsdale thought the billiards players were less profane with five ladies sitting in the bar. And when he complimented the owner for being the most civil of all proprietors to the ladies, the man "replied in a reflective, half sorriful, half puzzled manner: 'I don't know; I'm afraid they don't give me credit for anything respectable or even decent.'"[132]

Patience soon grew thin, however. One morning, the women found they were denied entry into the saloons. In response, they camped on the sidewalks. The *Banner* reported, "The doors of the saloons are guarded constantly; and every effort is being made to detect violations of law and to prevent by their presence customers from entering. To-day they sit in the cold rain, well provided with umbrellas, warming stoves and wrappings, feeling, as they say, not one whit like giving up the battle."[133] At a Greencastle city council meeting with many of the ladies in attendance, the council (controlled by Republicans) adopted ordinances permitting "all sober adults," regardless of sex, to visit the saloons, and prohibiting obstruction of the view from the street into the saloons. But the saloonkeepers tired of their female guests and began to order them out regardless of the ordinance. Parnell M. Layton was fined $25 for a "rude assault" on Ruth Tingley, who was standing picket duty outside his saloon. John Cawley asked a group of women to leave his saloon, but when Eliza J. Nelson refused, he placed his hand on her arm to escort her out. She then struck him with her umbrella, giving him a cut over his left eye, until being restrained by the marshal.[134] Cawley's trial for expelling a woman from his saloon in violation of the city ordinance resulted in a hung jury. When the retrial a month later appeared likely to bring the same result, Mayor William D. Allen ruled against the city to expedite an appeal, which was later dismissed.[135] By that time, it was clear the crusade would have limited effects.

The crusaders turned out to see the trial of Robert L. Higert for selling to a habitual drunkard. His acquittal was regarded as a portent of how the remaining liquor cases would be decided. After this defeat, attendance lagged at temperance meetings.[136] The decline of the temperance crusade coincided with the depression that followed the Panic of 1873. Ultimately, "hard times closed many more rumholes than high morals," according to one historian.[137]

Democrats called the women's presence in the saloons "so glaring an innovation" that it helped turn public opinion against the crusade. As before the war, temperance was an issue that divided the political parties. The *Banner* said that the Democratic organization manufactured votes "in the rum shops, and other haunts of ignorance and vice."[138] And the Republican county convention unanimously adopted a resolution bidding "God speed to the noble and heroic women engaged in the movement against intemperance."[139] By contrast, the *Press* saw the women as motivated by moral if "ill-judged zeal" and stated that "the men who stood at their backs" had political motives and used the women as "catspaws."[140] Lucius Chapin was chairman of the Republican Central Committee at that point, and his partisanship led to discord among the temperance advocates. At one meeting, two ministers protested "mixing politics and temperance" and threatened to withdraw if such proceedings were taken over by "political speech-making." Alice Chapin, presiding over this meeting, adjourned it, "counseling the brethren to love one another."[141] Although there were temperance Democrats, such as Lucius Chapin's law partner and brother-in-law, Judge Claypool, most Democrats continued to insist that following "moral law," rather than modifying state law, was the proper way to counter the evils of intemperance.[142]

Republicans who were now courting immigrant voters insisted "there are some Germans and Irish citizens that are firm friends of the temperance movement, and it is all wrong to heap epithets upon them."[143] Fr. Denis O'Donovan of Greencastle's Catholic church favored prohibition. But immigrants were still associated with alcohol. Temperance advocates believed German voters had provided the signatures qualifying Greencastle saloonkeepers for licenses under the Baxter law.[144] And when Father O'Donovan spoke of "the sin of drunkenness" during the women's crusade, his message was mixed. "While women were the greatest sufferers," according to Father O'Donovan, "they were also largely responsible for the spread of intemperance." Whether women actively drove men to drink or merely failed to inculcate temperance principles the priest did not specify. Nonetheless, Father O'Donovan seemed to echo the saloonkeepers' taunt about women's responsibility for male vice.[145]

After winning control of the legislature in 1874, Democrats replaced the Baxter bill with a new liquor law that gave county commissioners the power to license liquor sellers. Remonstrations were possible, but the burden had shifted from the applicant to those who would seek to deny the license. The women's crusade, however, sparked the formation of organizations such as the Women's Christian Temperance Union.[146] When the WCTU formed in Putnam County in September 1874, it resolved to resist the liquor trade "in every way which law-abiding, Christian women may appropriately and justly do."[147] In the early 1880s, the WCTU endorsed woman suffrage, its leaders having concluded that only the vote would give women the power to enact prohibition.[148] The temperance movement also continued in the form of "Blue Ribbon" clubs. The Blue Ribbon movement had been founded by a reformed eastern alcoholic, Francis Murphy, and it had spread to Indiana by the late 1870s. The ribbon symbolized that one had taken the pledge not to drink. In an atmosphere of religious revival, the movement featured reformed alcoholics testifying at its meetings. Jack Stevens, an alcoholic cited in John Cawley's license case, had reformed and now delivered a testimonial entitled "The Life That I Did Live; or, the Life of a Drunkard."[149] By the late 1870s, estimates indicated there were nearly 1,000 "Blue-ribbonites" in Greencastle. There, the temperance movement opened its own building, with a reading room, a library, and a main hall for the meetings of the Blue Ribbon club. At the opera house, the Blue Ribbon Dramatic Club put on a performance of the classic temperance melodrama *Ten Nights in a Bar-Room*. Ninety-five percent of Bainbridge's drinkers were said to have signed the pledge renouncing liquor.[150] Temperance advocates persevered but shifted their focus from shutting down the saloons to personal redemption.

Lucius and Alice Chapin's partnership in the temperance movement revealed something of how gender roles had changed since their marriage twenty years earlier. Lucius had struggled to become a breadwinner; Alice had insisted on her desire for her "own corner," the home sphere promised to wives. Civil War pensions allowed men such as Chapin and Wyatt James to have a steady source of income. And although predicated on a belief in women's traditional dependence, pensions gave widows and mothers such as Elizabeth Applegate and Charity Townsend some income, liberating them from reliance on family members or the need to remarry. Elizabeth Applegate enjoyed this independence but never became a woman's rights advocate. Alice Chapin, unlike many other female temperance leaders, does not appear to have been an advocate of woman suffrage.

The changes in gender roles had been incremental. Men still saw themselves as breadwinners, even if they achieved that role with some help from the government. Women still believed in the values of the woman's sphere as they themselves took a more public role in reform causes, in some cases using the necessity of reform to argue for the vote. Putnam County, however, would confront a more abrupt change when North Carolina African Americans abandoned that state for Indiana. And Wyatt James and Charity Townsend would welcome these migrants into a revivified black community.

9

EXODUSTERS

      A year after Robert Townsend died, his brother William, Wyatt James, and four other black men testified in mayor's court in Greencastle. William Tally had been brought before Mayor Milton A. Osborn for harassing black youths playing ball in a pasture. The prosecutors introduced the six black men as witnesses. Tally's attorney, Willis G. Neff, objected that their testimony was inadmissible because Indiana's constitution forbade blacks testifying against whites. Mayor Osborn overruled the objection, in part because "the law known as the civil rights bill, enacted by Congress, was supreme . . . and such being the case, the negroes were unquestionably competent witnesses in the cause before him."[1]

Reconstruction would bring enormous changes not only for African Americans in the South but also for those in the North. Leslie A. Schwalm argues that emancipation affected Northerners' concepts of race. In the upper Midwest, many found black migrants out of place on a "white frontier," and Indiana, of course, had both southern roots and a strong tradition of antiblack hostility. Given those facts, the challenge to white supremacy revealed by Tally's conviction was extraordinary, as were the changes in race relations brought to the county by the Civil War. Local African Americans, such as the Townsends and their in-law Wyatt James, now had status formerly denied them as citizens before the law, as voters, and as veterans. In the postwar period, Putnam County's growing black population allowed for the formation of a black community where none had previously existed. Active in the community's creation, the Townsends welcomed a surge in black migration into the county as Reconstruction came to an end in the South. Although many local whites resented and feared the Exodus, others welcomed the migrants either as cheap laborers or as potential voters. But no one contested the right of African Americans to move into Indiana, despite the fact that black exclusion had been a cornerstone of white supremacy before the war. Although the North Carolina Exodusters did not find what they expected in Indiana, having been promised a paradise of equal rights by the migration's promoters, they did find Putnam County much changed from the white supremacist frontier that the Townsends had encountered two generations earlier.[2]

When the war ended, Indiana's black laws were still in force, including its constitutional prohibition on black in-migration. Consequently, there was some doubt about whether veterans of the 28th USCT, such as Wyatt James, could return to the state because many had entered Indiana in violation of article 13. It was not until two years after the war that the enforcing legislation was repealed. But just as James had made his way from the Deep South to Indiana, so did many others, with the number of African Americans in Putnam County more than tripling between 1860 and 1870. Yet they never exceeded one-third of a percent of the county's total population.

The Exoduster migration of 1879–1880, however, caused a dramatic surge in the county's black population. The 1880 census counted 547 blacks and mulattoes in Putnam County, which not only was seven times the number in the previous census but also represented an unheard of 2.4 percent of the county's population. The migration also changed the composition of Putnam's black population. In 1870, almost 80 percent of the local African American population had been born in Kentucky or Indiana. But in the next census, this was no longer true as 48 percent of the county's black population were now North Carolina–born. When Minnesota senator William Windom reminded a Democratic politician from Putnam that a few hundred black migrants in a population of over 20,000 was not a great number, the politician replied that the migration had caused "a good deal of excitement."[3] Indeed, the North Carolina Exodusters threatened the county's established labor relations and politics.

Between 1850 and 1880, manufacturing in Indiana had increased eightfold, although it was still dwarfed by agriculture. Food-processing operations, including distilling, were important early industries in Indiana. The trend in the state reflected that in the country at large. Before the Civil War, one in four jobs had been in manufacturing; by 1900, it would be one in two. Although Putnam was not among Indiana's most industrialized counties, local boosters hoped to promote manufacturing there.[4] Greencastle boasted that its location on two railroads and two turnpikes, with two more roads planned, made it an attractive location for industry. "We have a foundry and machine shop, a large pump factory, two flouring mills, two planing mills, wool, furniture and carriage factories, and many other establishments of less importance," a Greencastle resident noted. By 1878, a nail factory employed 200 people and was one of the three largest such factories in the state.[5] Greencastle nails—"made of the best of iron" and comparable in "quality and finish" to any on the market—won a red ribbon at an exposition in Indianapolis.[6] In addition, Cloverdale possessed a steam stave machine that turned out 18,000 staves per day, Putnamville some limestone quarries, and Bainbridge a sawmill and two flour mills.[7]

Some considered such early boasts of industry overdone. One observer still found "mud and bad sidewalks" in Greencastle, where "the spirit of rural repose" prevailed, not "the clatter of machinery, the bustle of the populace, and the prevalence of flying coal, smoke and cinders."[8] Although gravel and stone walkways eventually replaced the mud that had passed for Greencastle's sidewalks and although an "elegant stone front block" opened in the town, roads and bridges remained in poor condition and the courthouse was increasingly outdated.[9] Boosters were quick to deplore a tendency of local residents to regard Greencastle as "rather a quiet town," demurring at any suggestion that its nails, pumps, and buggies made it "a place of some importance—a live, flourishing town."[10]

Agriculture was still the county's major economic sector. Agricultural fairs, which had been suspended during the Civil War, resumed in 1868. Numerous stock entries of "fine cattle and good horses" were featured at the 1871 county fair. There were also plenty of mules, hogs, and sheep. However, Putnam farmers tended not to emphasize pure breeds, and the ensuing crossbreeds perplexed at least one observer. Despite "meager premiums," there were displays of corn, potatoes, sweet potatoes, yams, and beets. The next year, the fair fea-tured imported Norman and English draft horses, but the floral hall—filled with women's products—continued to be the most attractive and well filled of the exhibit venues. The description of the 1874 fair praised the "fine horses and mules," the 800-pound hogs, and the variety of domestic fowls. One of the highlights was Simpson Lockridge's Canadian bull.[11]

Putnam County was recognized for its fine stock. T. C. Hammond, presi-dent of the First National Bank, had established a herd with "good pedigreed females, selected from the best herds of Kentucky" and a bull called Earl of Putnam. The county was paid a visit in 1879 by a commission from the Royal Agricultural Society of England. Having hastily organized a reception commit-tee, Mayor Lucius Chapin met the commissioners at the railroad station and escorted them to the city offices, where they were welcomed by local leaders. The commissioners, consisting of two English members of Parliament and a Canadian, visited Asbury and then the farms of Simpson Lockridge, Thomas Hammond, A. C. Stevenson, and other leading Putnam agriculturalists. The commissioners were particularly interested in talking to Stevenson, who was "widely known as one of the best informed and most successful stock-raisers in the Western States."[12]

Although Putnam was in the wealthier part of Indiana, its average yields were smaller than those of other nearby counties. This situation may have reflected a continued adherence to soil-depleting practices: many farmers still failed to use "all the modern improvements" or see the benefits of agriculture "conducted on scientific principles." The *Press* condemned "dreary farm houses" shaded by "scraggy trees . . . or no trees at all," with chickens scratching in the front and pigs wallowing in the back.[13] By the post–Civil War period, small farmers could no longer compete. Only commercial farmers with large operations selling on the market could hope to prosper, and they would be tied to the vagaries of the larger economy. A speaker at a Grange convention deplored the large numbers of mortgaged farms in the county.[14]

Elmer Thomas remembered his boyhood on a farm near Parke County in the 1880s. Farmers were still clearing land in those days, and small game was plentiful. Thomas financed his college education by trapping opossum, skunk, mink, and raccoon as well as raising pigs. He recalled splitting rails for fences as Abraham Lincoln would have done a half century earlier. His father, however, had more modern equipment—a thresher that was first powered by a horse and later by a steam engine.[15] Thomas's family still bartered for most of its goods.

In the fall, they exchanged turkeys for winter boots and clothes. Livestock was raised to pay the taxes. And they traded eggs and butter for groceries such as coffee, brown sugar, and spices. Although the goods traded on both sides were priced in dollars and cents, "little real money changed hands."[16]

Land had become considerably more expensive. By borrowing money from life insurance companies and buying out mortgages, Vincent H. Day acquired real estate throughout the Civil War era until he was the largest landowner in the county (indeed, one of the largest in the state) by 1881, with over 1,600 acres. When Day first began buying in the 1850s, prices averaged $28 per acre. By the 1870s, he was acquiring smaller parcels at higher prices, averaging almost $200 per acre. Higher prices doubtless reflected the improved nature of the land as well as its scarcity. For labor, Day relied on hired hands until his sons were old enough to work on the farm.[17]

Difficulty getting land had been driving young men westward or into tenancy since the 1850s. The Civil War had brought Northern farmers high prices for their products and a shortage of farm laborers. Both developments encouraged investment in improved technology such as the McCormick reaper. Better plows, steam tractors, and other machines became available during the era as well. The large capital investment such machinery required, however, increased the difficulty of moving from tenant to independent farmer. The surpluses produced by better machinery also lowered prices, hurting all farmers. Although small holdings still typified the state in 1880, Putnam was among the few Indiana counties with sizable large farms worked by tenants. In fact, the county demonstrated the class diversity taking hold in Northern agriculture in that period: there were wealthy commercial farmers such as Stevenson, small subsistence producers such as Elmer Thomas's family, and tenants such as those who worked Stevenson's and Lockridge's lands.[18]

In addition to admiring the fine cattle Lockridge and Simpson were breeding, the British commissioners noted that both men rented out their land. Lockridge's tenants paid him half the wheat and a third of the corn and oats produced. Tenancy rates were higher in the Midwest then in the East, according to the 1880 census, which was the first to record farm tenancy, and Indiana's tenancy rates were slightly higher than average for the Midwest. Of states in the Old Northwest, Illinois led the pack with almost a third of its farmers renting by paying in cash or shares, Indiana was next with 23 percent, somewhat higher than in Ohio and much higher than in more recently settled states. As was true of all the midwestern states, two-thirds or more of the tenants rented on shares.[19] Doubtless, the hard times of the 1870s made it even more difficult for young men to establish farms.[20] Consumer spending also dropped, "for every man that has a dollar thinks that if he spends it he may never see another one, and so he hangs on to it."[21] New Albany industrialist Washington C. DePauw, one of Asbury's trustees, rescued the university financially, for which he was rewarded by having it renamed after him in 1884.[22]

The depression affected the labor market. A Democratic rally in the 1876 election featured a wagonload of men dressed as paupers bearing a banner declaring, "We Want Work."[23] Homeless men, or tramps, wandered the countryside. Now, the transportation network carried "beggars of almost every description and nationality" through the county.[24] In cold weather, they became more visible as they sought places inside to sleep. One beggar, a blind man who played a French harp on the streets, also wore a red ribbon, eliciting donations from the temperance ladies.[25] Democrats complained that Republicans dismissed the unemployed as shiftless and unwilling to work, when, in fact, "we turn our eyes and look across this broad land of ours and see the thousands without employment traveling from place to place hunting for labor, but all in vain."[26] The Gilded Age may have brought fortune to some, but it was often a period of hardship for laborers who struggled not only with the difficulties of an industrializing workplace but also with a fluctuating business cycle that created depression and unemployment as well as prosperity.[27]

Heather Cox Richardson has argued that Northern attitudes toward black workers evolved from the prewar period. Before the war, white Northerners believed blacks were lazy and would not work. During and after the war, however, they came to accept that blacks were actually willing to work and that, if they followed the free labor model of the North, they would prosper. But the labor strife of the 1870s disillusioned many Northerners who, now seeing black demands for help in the context of labor unrest, dismissed the freedmen as merely wanting continued dependence on the federal government.[28]

Putnam County whites accepted southern stereotypes of black indolence. The Putnam Democratic newspaper, for example, spoke dismissively of "those that will work," establishing shiftlessness as a norm.[29] Demeaning portrayals of black labor abounded. The *Greencastle Banner,* a Republican paper that was friendly to black rights, published an advertisement for Dobbin's Starch Polish. In the illustration, a stout black woman holds up a white shirt to a stern-looking white lady and asks, "How Da Shine[?]" The image reinforces the notion of blacks as laborers subordinate to white standards, and the expression on the white woman's face leaves no doubt that the black woman will have difficulty measuring up. The woman's menial work was indeed representative of the jobs held by some blacks in the county, such as Ruben Harney, "the boss rat killer" of Putnamville, who killed forty rats at one time. Meanwhile, racist language remained common. A. M. Hodge of Cataract sent in his subscription "for that wooly nigar paper of yours": that, at least, was the portion of Hodge's letter the *Banner* deemed fit for publication. And antiblack activity had little social stigma. After Solomon Akers's twenty-year-old son, John C. Akers, led a crowd of rowdy young men in heckling a Freedmen's Aid Society speaker, employing "the foulest language and most insulting epithets," Cloverdale citizens promptly elected young Akers constable.[30]

Despite these circumstances, Putnam County possessed a stable core of black citizens. In 1876, Greencastle's Colored Hayes and Wheeler Club had forty-six members. These men included Allan Jones, the president, who had testified against William Tally in 1866; J. K. Hart, a minister; and Samuel Hutto, secretary of the black Sunday school. Several members of the Townsend family also belonged, including Robert Townsend's brother-in-law Wyatt James, and three of Robert's younger siblings, William, Jay, and Enos.[31] Of the members of the Colored Hayes and Wheeler Club who could be traced in the 1880 census, half had stayed in the county. Those who left tended to be younger men in their twenties or older men over fifty. Three-quarters of those who remained in Putnam County lived in their own households. Their occupations, however, were for the most part unskilled. They worked as laborers, janitors, and servants, and thus, their independence as householders was compromised by their dependence on white employers. Old patronage ties remained strong. Enos Townsend had moved to Indianapolis and was working as a servant in the household of James T. Layman, the doctor's son.[32]

Children in Putnam's black families had access to education. Although Indiana law provided for segregated schools, few communities had enough black children to justify a separate school.[33] As in many towns, therefore, black children in Putnam went to school with whites. William Ecton, who migrated to Indiana in 1867 with a family of eleven, pointed out, "My children go to the white school, and receive the same treatment that white children do."[34] In the spring of 1879, a black youth won a volume of Lord Byron's poems as the prize for being the best scholar at a school west of Greencastle.[35] North Carolina migrants were drawn, in part, by opportunities to educate their children. William Croom noted that Putnam County offered "good schools for our children."[36]

And Lewis Taylor concluded enthusiastically, "Indiana is the place to educate poor children. School houses are plenty, with good teachers, and the schools run from six to nine months each year, white and colored children going together the same."[37] Although Northern school reformers saw many deficiencies in Indiana's schools, to southern blacks these schools were "better and of longer duration than schools in the South."[38] Ironically, the Exoduster migration would lead to school segregation. With the increased African American population, black students were often taught in a separate room. By 1894, the black population had fallen enough so that the students were reintegrated, attending school with the white children once more.[39]

A growing population also allowed local blacks to form their own churches. For decades, the Townsend family had worshipped with whites. But Christian fellowship did not create social equality, even inside church walls. A correspondent of the *Banner* described something he observed on a Sunday at one of Greencastle's "popular churches." An elderly freedwoman, known for nursing white soldiers, had seated herself in the front. With a "deep sense of shame," the correspondent watched as the usher conducted her to the back of the church.[40] Such incidents doubtless contributed to the desire for separate institutions.

Luke and Charity Townsend presided over the founding of the Bethel African Methodist Episcopal Church at their home in 1872. The church's site moved over the years, but the Townsends remained involved.[41] When Catherine Townsend James died in 1939, she was the oldest member of "her beloved church," the one her parents had helped found. There was also another black Methodist church. This church, however, was governed by white bishops, whereas the Bethel AME Church was "controlled by the colored people exclusively." The black Methodist church survived from 1876 until 1910, by which time the congregation had fallen to eight members; they probably joined the AME church.[42]

But even these black churches needed good relations with whites. During the 1870s, the black community struggled to find funds for their church. "Of course their white friends will assist them in this laudable undertaking," the *Press* announced, urging attendance at a fund-raising "entertainment."[43] When local blacks bought the lot for the Methodist church from the Democratic sheriff Moses T. Lewman, Republican editor George Langsdale asked them to return his $5 donation, evidently feeling they had sold out to the Democrats. To make up for the loss, Lewman gave the black Methodist church another $5.[44] The black Methodists were caught between hostile patrons.

Bethel AME Church, which Luke and Charity Townsend helped
found. (From R. T. Jones, H. A. Mills, and T. J. Bassett, *Souvenir of
Greencastle, Indiana* [Greencastle, Ind.: M. J. Beckett, 1892]; courtesy
of DePauw University Archives and Special Collections)

Even the AME church had to struggle with white control. Mayor Lucius
Chapin presided over a meeting to help the black congregation find money to
finish its building. Several black men spoke of their community's "anxiety" for
a church of their own. But white help meant white control: the meeting established an executive committee to which each church in the city would appoint
a member. Lucius Chapin would serve for the Presbyterians. This white executive committee worked with the AME church trustees in controlling the money
raised and erecting the church building, turning over full control to the AME
church when the project was completed.[45] Although benevolent whites credited the black population with wanting "to improve their moral and religious
condition," they clearly believed the blacks needed their help. An article in the
Greencastle Banner reported, "Having to depend on their white friends for the
funds, they are willing to leave the entire management to them, and we are assured will have a lively appreciation for whatever may be done in their behalf."
Not only would Greencastle blacks have a limited say in whatever the "white

friends" did for them, but they were expected to be properly grateful as well, much as slaves were once expected to be grateful to paternalistic owners.[46]

A flurry of fund-raising did ensue, including a "colored concert" and a dinner and festival. The new minister, Rev. John H. Clay, continued to rely on white aid. A former Georgia slave who had escaped into Union lines during the war, Clay traveled to Indianapolis and went to school while working as a molder, starting in the "infant class" at age eighteen. He became an AME minister and in 1877 took over the Greencastle district.[47] "The condition of the colored people of Greencastle is bad," Clay noted. They still lacked their own church and were "struggling" to raise the funds to finish building. In appealing to the white community for funding, Clay underscored the black community's poverty, affirmed that blacks would be grateful for help, and tried to reassure white patrons that black recipients would properly handle the money they provided, which would be placed in the hands of a white treasurer. Deferentially, the minister concluded his appeal to Greencastle citizens, "I hope and pray that God will bless you with both a willing ear and a helping hand." The fundraising campaign evidently succeeded. In August 1878, the cornerstone for the new church was laid.[48] Like the black Methodists, Clay found that patronage relations intersected with politics. But his dedication to his church had limits. When a Democrat offered to make a donation in return for the pastor's vote, Clay replied that before he would sell his vote, "he would worship out doors, without any shelter."[49]

Booker T. Washington's subordination of black political rights to economic advancement has been attributed to the precarious position of southern blacks after Reconstruction's failure, yet Northern blacks also faced a similar dilemma. As workers and churchgoers, they could gain a measure of acceptance denied them as voters. A Bainbridge correspondent boasted, "Our town is entirely free from the fifteenth amendment, the last shadow of it disappeared last week."[50]

A picnic east of Greencastle in 1878 drew blacks from all over central Indiana, especially Terre Haute and Indianapolis. The *Press*'s account emphasized the festivity of the occasion, noting its games of croquet and baskets of food. Its brief summary of the speeches portrayed them as exhortations for African Americans "to eschew politics and secure respect for their race by making themselves useful citizens." This goal could be achieved by learning "useful trades," farming, and pursuing other economic endeavors. Judge Solon Turman complimented the assembled crowd on their "orderly behavior, the ability and culture displayed by their speakers, and bade them godspeed in their efforts to educate and elevate their race."[51] The *Banner* gave a fuller account of the address by Rev. E. R. Bagley of Terre Haute. Since the Fourth of July was approaching, Bagley noted Americans' "favorite saying . . . that this is the freest land on the globe." He held this to be true for whites but false for blacks and Asians. To correct this, Bagley advocated education, access to jobs, and land-ownership, rather than politics and voting.[52]

A far more political vision for elevating the black race emerged as Reconstruction came to its bloody end in the South. In an editorial entitled "Will They Come North?" the *Banner* argued, "The colored men of the South are practically disfranchised while living in that section, but those of the North have the privilege of the ballot the same as their white neighbors." Accordingly, it was the duty of southern black men to move north: "Let them come to this side of the Ohio river and assist in making a 'Solid North' against a 'Solid South.' Their own interest and that of the men who set them free demands that they do this." Not only would southern blacks be safe from violence and able to exercise their rights, they would also ensure that the Republican party, "their friends," remained in power. By going north in time to be counted in the 1880 census, they could increase the North's electoral vote and power at the South's expense.[53] The *Banner* compared black migration into Northern Democratic states to military service during the Civil War: "The charging of a rebel fortification by colored troops, during the war, was not a more necessary or gallant action than would be that of moving on the Democratic stronghold in Indiana in time to carry their works at the next election."[54] In late April 1879, the *Banner* implored,

> "**To the Union Men of the South:**
> *Come up out of Egypt!*"[55]

George Langsdale of the *Banner* would become the voice of the Exoduster movement in Putnam County, and Reverend Clay probably influenced him. During the summer of 1879, Clay attended a convention in Nashville that formed committees to encourage migration. Though convention participants acknowledged the existence of discrimination in the North, they deemed the "outrages" in the South were worse and thus decided in favor of migration.[56]

But the Exodus could not have occurred if southern blacks had not desired a new life. For years, North Carolina freedmen had been considering migration. Samuel L. Perry, one of the Exodus organizers, had distributed brochures from Nebraska in 1872. In the late 1870s, the idea of moving west would revive after a bad crop year, when "there was a terrible cleaning up of the colored people" as tenants were evicted. Now, those interested in migration turned their attention to Kansas. Perry organized a society, with himself and Rev. Peter C. Williams as agents.[57] Traveling to Washington, Perry and Williams sought help from the National Emigration Aid Society. From there, they traveled to Indianapolis, where they received a letter from Clay causing them to go to Greencastle and meet with Clay and Langsdale. Clay told them that there would be homes for the migrants in Putnam County. Perry and Williams had rejected Indianapolis because "these people that we represented wanted to farm and not to hire out."

Perry found Clay unwilling to open his church for a fund-raising meeting to support migration to Kansas. Instead, Clay pointed out that he and other blacks had moved from the South and settled in Putnam County, where they "owned property and things looked splendidly, and . . . they were getting good wages."[58] In early April 1879, Clay did preside over a meeting at the Bethel church of the black citizens who had assembled to help black migrants to Kansas who were stranded in St. Louis. Church members formed a committee not only to raise money for these Exodusters in St. Louis but also "to find locations for such farmers and their families as desire to come to Putnam county."[59]

Although Perry later insisted that he had learned little and liked less about Indiana, he took the circulars Clay had written back to North Carolina and distributed them. Indiana soon became an attractive destination because not only was it closer than Kansas, and thus less costly to reach, but also it reputedly had more work available. Julius A. Bonitz, editor of a Goldsboro, North Carolina, newspaper, said that in the spring and summer of 1879, Perry and Williams held meetings in North Carolina at which "incendiary speeches were made; the unpleasant features of life in North Carolina were dwelt upon and exaggerated, while Indiana was pictured as a perfect paradise for colored men." Perry and Williams also read letters attesting that blacks were treated just like whites in Indiana—eating at the same table with employers and going to school with white children. Migrants were told they could earn at least a dollar per day in wages and, incorrectly, that their fare would be paid.[60] One of the Exodusters, G. McMerrick, said Perry and Williams had told North Carolina blacks "dat the farmers of Putnam county would give each of us a cow and calf, a garden patch and a potato patch and $15 per month." Indiana was depicted as "a land a flowin' wid milk and honey. From what was told us we thought dat dere was no end to de money here."[61] Clay's circular promoted black life in Indiana with the enthusiasm of a booster document. It praised the state's fertile lands, healthy climate, good schools (while acknowledging that city schools were often segregated), "church privileges," equality before the law, job opportunities, and "remunerative wages." Moreover, Clay promised that "colored men already here will assist those who come in obtaining work or situations."[62]

The words extolling Indiana's attractions fell on receptive ears: an estimated 2,000 to 3,000 blacks left North Carolina in 1879.[63] P. C. Williams recalled that "after laboring and economizing for fourteen years . . . my people find themselves as poor and ignorant, and despised as they were at the close of the war—a condition differing from absolute slavery only in this, that they are now at liberty to emigrate without being hunted down by bloodhounds."[64] Other North Carolina blacks complained that "they could not get money for their work, and had to take their pay in orders out of the stores."[65] Although Democrats insisted that life in North Carolina was fine for blacks, it was Klan violence in the early 1870s that helped their party regain control of the legislature. Further, resurgent North Carolina Democrats had not only impeached and removed the Republican governor but also amended the state constitution to end the elected county governments that had been created under Reconstruction and that gave blacks control in counties with large black populations. The legislature would now appoint county officials.

The Exoduster counties in east-central North Carolina had precisely such large black populations. Exoduster Willis Bunn had been a member of the North Carolina legislature for eight years, and he had served in his own county as justice of the peace for ten years. Bunn had concluded that life in North Carolina was "intolerable." Clay's circular exploited a fear that the Reconstruction amendments would be repealed and slavery reinstated. Democrats in North Carolina also mandated school segregation, gave landowners control over the crops, and required men to work on the roads. Combined with falling prices for tobacco and cotton, all these factors contributed to despair among North Carolina blacks.[66]

Politics may have mattered less to many Exodusters than the desire to make a living. When a *Chicago Tribune* reporter asked a ragged North Carolina migrant why he had left his home state, the reply was, "Because times is so hard there. . . . We couldn't live. 'Pears as if we were gwine to starve."[67] Questioned about the reason for the Exodus, Langsdale said, "The invariable answer [the Exodusters] give is, that they come to better their condition." They told him "that in all their lives that they had lived in the South they had been able to accumulate nothing, and they believed that if they got to Indiana they would be able to accumulate property and enjoy it the same as the white man."[68] Migrant Samuel Jackson said that blacks were going north because white landlords in the South cheated them. Thomas Bynum recalled the story of a black man who had rented a farm for three bales of cotton. He had raised eleven bales and lived frugally but still found himself short after "settling day," when the landowner claimed that the black man's expenses encompassed everything— all eleven bales of cotton as well as his corn and pea crops. It was this kind of treatment, Bynum pointed out, that had caused the Exodus.[69]

By the beginning of 1880, there were 700 black migrants reported in Indiana, with 150 in Putnam County alone. As was true with the influx of Exodusters in Kansas, this massive migration of blacks from the South required a practical response from the areas where they settled. As on the Kansas-Missouri border, the black community organized to help the migrants. When the Exodusters reached Indianapolis, they were housed and fed in local churches and their thin clothing, suitable to the southern climate but inappropriate for Indiana in winter, was replaced. From Indianapolis, smaller parties dispersed to other parts of the state, including Putnam, Vigo, Montgomery, and Miami counties.[70]

A similar philanthropic pattern occurred when migrants reached Putnam County. When the first party of over fifty Exodusters arrived in Greencastle in October 1879, Clay and Langsdale met them at the station and led them to the black church, where they stayed until finding homes. Alfred Newbern lived in the church for three days until he found work.[71] The *Banner* praised the black citizens of Greencastle, led by Clay, as Good Samaritans "caring for and entertaining their brethren who have arrived from the South."[72] Handling the influx strained the resources of Greencastle's small black community. The *Banner* solicited money, food, and clothing for the North Carolina immigrants. P. C. Williams described a partnership in which Clay did the hands-on work while Langsdale acted as "philanthropist."[73]

Resistant to seeing that blacks led the migration, local Democrats called Langsdale "de boss of de emigrashun." They caricatured him and his philanthropy with the face of a black man labeled "Massa Lambtail's Pet Lambs," an image that appeared in the Democratic newspaper. Some of those opposed to the migration blamed "shyster politicians" rather than "the poor deluded negro," reinforcing ideas of blacks' basic inferiority: being "ignorant," blacks were easy victims of crafty whites such as Langsdale. Lured north with promises of nonexistent labor, African Americans were "poor dupes" and "catspaws" whose votes were what the Radicals truly wanted. Sheriff Lewman insisted that the famous Clay circular had been written in Langsdale's hand and only signed by Clay. Langsdale admitted to acting as Clay's "ameneunsis" in writing the circular but said that Clay could write and had composed the document himself. By claiming that African Americans were deluded, Democrats could blame the migrants' suffering on Republicans rather than acknowledge the inhospitality expressed by some Hoosiers to the new arrivals.[74]

Republicans and Democrats made competing claims about black refinement and worth. At the Putnam County Democratic convention in early 1880, H. M. Randel, outgoing chairman of the county's central committee, told the story of a man whose son was trying on clothes at a shop. Some of the North Carolina migrants came in to buy winter clothes. When the clerk went to help them, the man made his son take off the clothes, saying, "We will go where we can trade among gentlemen!"[75] But for the Exodusters and their white supporters, it was these racists who lacked gentility.[76] Lewis Taylor found Indiana whites unlike "any I have ever been among before. They have all treated me with the greatest kindness, except once I met with some Democratic loafers at the water tank on the railroad just North of town. They called me all sorts of names, but I thought too much of myself to stop and talk with such fellows. I prefer to associate with gentlemen."[77] The *Banner* avoided dialect in its interviews with Exodusters and emphasized the refined speech and writing of those with education, but the Democrats mocked the migrants' language, proving the point of Randel's outraged shoppers.[78]

A Cloverdale man composed a poem entitled "Massa Lambstail's Pets," which captured the Democratic view of the Exodus. Written from the perspective of the freedmen (the "pets"), the poem asks if Massa Lambstail would "hunt us all a home, and feed us niggers too?" if they went north. The "pets" expect to receive "clothes and food / About de 'lection spell" from Massa Lambstail. Conscious of Langsdale's income from his federal patronage job as postmaster, the poet states, "Now Massa Lambstail mighty rich, / His pension mighty fat, / It makes de berry muscles twitch, / To think we may git dat." The "pets" are glad to be free of cotton: "We cullud gemmen work no more, / We Massa Lambstail's pets." These "gemmen" were also conscious of their "rights": "De Copperheads shan't talk to us / Upon de 'lection day, / Or den we make a mighty fuss, / And vote as massa say." Relying on stereotypes of black indolence, the poet expresses not just resentment at black pretensions to gentlemanly status and political rights but also fear of black political power. The depiction of Langsdale as "Massa" denies the reality of blacks' freedom and ability to act on their own.[79]

At first, Democrats took little notice of the Exoduster movement. Sheriff Lewman initially dismissed the *Banner*'s "Appeal" as one of Langsdale's "foolish ideas." But after the first group arrived, Lewman was worried enough to spend $7 to buy a copy of the Clay circular from an Exoduster.[80] Unable to believe that there were reasons for North Carolina's African Americans to be dissatisfied, Putnam Democrats attributed the migration entirely to Republican political motives. The Exodusters, they said, were "coming to vote the Republican ticket" and thus "change the political complexion of Indiana":[81] the Exodus would "Africanize the State in the interest of the Republican party."[82] Sheriff Lewman accused Langsdale, whom he called "Mr. Nigger Boss," of trying "to ship into Putnam county a few hundred negroes—enough to change the politics of the county."[83] In short, Langsdale was engaged in the old political fraud of importing voters.[84] It was for this reason that C. C. Matson and other Democrats at the county convention condemned the Exodus: "This county was made the initial point of attack by those now engaged in the importation of colored voters into the State of Indiana; and we now declare upon this subject that we believe, from evidence undisputed and indisputable, that the scheme is one which originated with Republicans, and was intended to benefit the Republican party in the coming election." Matson and other county Democrats did not oppose "natural immigration," but they fiercely objected to this "forced one." It was "an outrage perpetrated upon our community by Republicans, in a desperate attempt to seize political power at the coming general elections."[85]

Local Republicans denied that the migration had been organized for political purposes. J. F. Darnall, chairman of the county's Republican central committee, said, "I know of no organized effort in Putnam county by the Republican party to aid or encourage the immigration of colored men." Darnall affirmed that anyone, "without regard to color," would be welcome in Putnam County. "A great many of the best citizens of this county immigrated from the South," he noted. "Certainly all who desire to come have the right to come."[86] M. A. Moore suggested that Democrats who opposed the migration should vote against their party, which had made the South "so intolerable for the colored man, that he flees the land of his birth, the home of his childhood, and the graves of his ancestors to find political liberty in the land of strangers."[87] Langsdale, of course, had been open about the political motivations for migration.

But aside from Langsdale, Indiana's Republican party did nothing to actively stimulate the migration. Republicans were certainly happy to welcome the migrants and their votes, but they did not organize the Exodus.[88]

The Exodusters themselves denied that they were recruited to vote. Thomas Bynum of Wilson County, North Carolina, recalled, "I never heard anything about politics until I got to Indianapolis." A Democrat there asked him if Republicans had taken him north to vote. "I told him, no, that I brought myself."[89] One North Carolina migrant dismissed the voting question by referring to economic need. "Lord, boss! we don't keer about voting. We wants something to eat. We wants to get these rags off, and wants some good warm clothes."[90] Adult black men, however, could be expected to be Republicans. Sheriff Lewman asked P. C. Williams how the Exodusters would vote. "I don't know," answered Williams, "but I suppose they will continue to vote as they have been doing; those who are Democrats will vote the Democratic ticket, and those who are Republicans will vote the Republican ticket. I don't think that a change of climate will change their politics."[91] Williams, of course, must have been just as aware as Lewman that there were very few black Democrats.

For all their denials that politics motivated their migration, the Exodusters were glad to recapture their political rights. Lewis Taylor said, "I thank the Lord that I was able to come here where I can have my rights, and get what my labor is worth, and be treated like a man."[92] Taylor had been a slave until freed by the Union army, but he never felt "really free until I struck the State of Indiana."[93] During the spring 1880 elections, Willis Bunn spoke at the Republican headquarters in Greencastle, where he and other black speakers were described in the Republican press as "intelligent colored men . . . who denounced the shotgun policy of the South in an emphatic manner."[94] One Exoduster, G. McMerrick, claimed to be disillusioned about Republican motives. "We wouldn't come up here if we'd thought dey only wanted us to vote," he told a reporter.[95] The Colored Republican Club, which had existed before the arrival of the Exodusters, no doubt received a fresh infusion of members.[96]

The migration may have had some influence on local elections. In April 1880, Republicans carried townships that had gone Democratic two years earlier, and they gained votes in other Democratic townships as well. Black voters, however, faced hostility. His ballot snatched from his hand, a black man in Clinton Township was dragged from the polls and told that "no d—d nigger should vote in that township."[97] In the state elections of 1880, two black men in Madison Township were told they could not vote unless they cast a Democratic ticket. They subsequently got three men to accompany them to the polls, where, despite threats of trouble, they voted "unmolested." Cloverdale Democrats objected to a black man named Maston Johnson giving a political speech; they retaliated by overturning outhouses, defacing signs, and perpetrating other acts of vandalism against local Republicans. Although the Democratic candidates, including congressional candidate C. C. Matson, won the county, Marion Township Democrats cursed the effects of "d—d Niggers and money."[98]

The black migration did not translate into a straight gain of Republican votes. Indeed, Democrats gained 300 votes in Greencastle Township, which was not enough to win the normally Republican stronghold but did indicate the unpopularity of the migration. C. C. Matson claimed that the Irish—some of whom had defected to the Republicans in the late 1870s—had now returned to the Democratic organization because of the black migration. Democrats even claimed that Republicans were disaffected by the Exodus. Bainbridge residents said that their only black voter was driven out of the county by "Republican bulldozers" angered by the Exodus.[99]

Republican leaders such as Langsdale welcomed the Exodusters, yet many Republicans as well as Democrats feared the competition for labor.[100] Daniel E. Shoemaker, a tenant farmer, surveyed the difficulty of getting work despite his reputation as a "successful corn-raiser." He argued that Republicans who claimed a labor shortage merely disliked paying a man a wage "sufficient to keep body and soul together." He also thought employers liked the idea of black labor because they believed it would be more easily controlled. Shoemaker claimed that he had heard E. H. Wilkinson, who was dissatisfied with his white tenant, declare, "By Jacks, he would get him a black man, and he could make him do." Shoemaker insisted, "I am not a man of prejudice," but he added that "as a Republican, I always liked a white sheep better than a black one." He thought many "honest, laboring Republicans will winter their votes" by staying home rather than going to the elections "or vote the Democratic ticket on account of the exodus business." Shoemaker saw the labor situation as a zero-sum game: "Every dollar that is payed out for colored labor is taking that much from the poor white man."[101]

Putnam County Democrats agreed, maintaining that the migration violated "the great law of supply and demand, and has, therefore, unduly disturbed the employment of our resident laborers."[102] Lewman insisted that Putnam County had little demand for any but skilled labor. Men stood idly on street corners, loafing for lack of work, and "tramps" passed through. Lewman even opened the jail at night so homeless men would have a place to sleep out of the cold. Local Democrats argued that there was no reason for blacks to leave North Carolina, where they had "work, wages, food, clothing and shelter." On the one hand, Democrats worried that black "pauper laborers" would displace white workers by driving down wages; on the other hand, they feared that if the blacks did not work, they would become a burden on the taxpayers (despite the fact that all the relief had been privately provided). The Indianapolis Democratic paper compared "the importation of cheap colored labor" to that of "Chinese cheap labor" in California, which had threatened the jobs of white workingmen.[103]

The *Banner* defended the migration in economic terms: "We need their labor." Just as in an earlier period, southern poor whites had gone to Indiana and prospered through hard work and frugality, so too should southern blacks—fleeing greater "evils"—be allowed this opportunity. These migrants would enrich Indiana: "Our farms will be better tilled; uncultivated fields will find tenants; forests will be cut down and new farms opened; in the wet regions ditches will be made and the land reclaimed from the water which now covers it." Those who opposed this migration were deemed "too ignorant or lazy to compete with black workers in the labor market."[104] Langsdale cited the state board of agriculture's pamphlet, which was intended to recruit emigrants to Indiana, as showing there was demand for labor,[105] and numerous Republicans provided testimonials as to their need for workers. Dr. A. C. Stevenson said that "his own farm has been running down for want of labor for several years." Franklin Township farmer W. D. Barnes reported that farmers in Putnam County, regardless of their political party, "had hired negro harvest hands, and he has no doubt they would be glad to hire them for steady farm work."[106] Fences needed repair; land needed to be cleared of brush, and pastures of logs. As the *Banner* pointed out, leading Democrats such as C. C. Matson, Russell Allen, and Tarvin C. Grooms "have had Negroes in their employ for years, and it seems a little queer that Democratic farmers in the country should not be allowed the same privilege."[107] Democrats did hire North Carolina migrants. John Vermilion said, "Let the darkies come; they make excellent hands."[108]

Democrats insisted that Republican employers were firing white employees and replacing them with North Carolina blacks. Isaac Browning was accused of turning out "a poor white girl," whom he replaced as cook with "a big buck negro." In a speech to the Democratic county convention, H. M. Randel attacked the Exodusters' economic threat. Black labor was displacing white, Randel claimed, and the poor would soon lose their employment "and see Starvation blanch its haggard form on the faces of their dear ones." He condemned those who would "blacken our fields with pauper Negro laborers."[109]

Even some local blacks disliked the Exoduster movement. Luther R. Monroe, "a workman at the rolling mill" who characterized himself as a "citizen and laborer," contested Langsdale's claim that there was plenty of work in the county. Monroe feared that immigration would drive down wages. Although he was a Republican, he protested, "I don't like to see men come here to starve to death."[110] Similarly, a "Colored Citizen of Greencastle" wrote the paper to suggest that Clay's circular exaggerated wages and the demand for labor. Having seen Clay leading women and children who had arrived from North Carolina, the observer described it as "pulling and shipping them around like cattle."[111] Exoduster Mingo Simmons reported that local blacks were divided about the migration: "There is one party among the colored folks out there that do not want us to come and one party that does."[112] T. C. Grooms insisted, "The resident negroes there complain very bitterly against these new-comers. . . . They say it will cut down wages and increase the number of laborers."[113]

At least initially, the Exodusters felt they had improved their condition. Squire Nobles said, "We get more work than we can do, and have the offer of a job every day." Cornelius Harrison was cutting wood at $.85 per cord and had "plenty of work."[114] Other migrants reported wages of $12 to $18 per month, about average for a farmworker, all with room and board.[115] For Henry Bolden, it was less the wages than the method of payment: "I find that here they don't pay for work in orders, but pay the hard cash." Like other Exodusters, Alfred Newbern praised not only the high pay and amenities—milk cows, firewood, and gardens were commonly mentioned—but also the fair dealing by employers. Newbern had left North Carolina "because wages were so poor, and I was cheated so much that I could not make a living."[116] William Croom felt he had found in Indiana the place where African Americans could be "free and have the same chance in everything that white men have." Croom said all the blacks were getting work at wages twice what they received in North Carolina, and what they had to buy cost less than in the South. By the beginning of 1880, Croom was living near Russellville in a "good brick house," "all nicely plastered inside." He had plenty of meat, three bedsteads, bed covers, and a cookstove provided by his employer. He expected to be furnished with a cow and to put in a garden.[117] Robert O'Hair, a white resident of Brick Chapel, considered such upward mobility possible for blacks in Putnam. He cited a Kentucky man who earned money to become a landowner and gained the respect of even initially hostile neighbors. Another black man whom O'Hair employed made enough money to buy his own home in another part of Indiana.[118]

The Exodusters seemed surprised to be treated well by whites. Louis Ricks had moved his wife and five children to the farm of Dr. A. C. Stevenson. His wife lost a baby in childbirth, and Ricks stated that "Dr. Stevenson has waited on my family in their sickness, and treated us with great kindness; as has his family." The Stevensons' kindness had persuaded him that "white people and colored people are all one here; there ain't any difference."[119] Alfred Newbern said of his employer, Riley Springer, "[He] treats me well. No white man in the South ever treated me so well."[120] William Hill, who worked for James Torr west of Greencastle, commented, "I am treated about the house the same as though I was a white person. There seems to be no difference here because of color."[121]

Putnam Republicans affirmed both the right of laborers to change residence and the right of employers to hire whomever they wanted. Formerly a black law state that forbade African American in-migration, Indiana now had a substantial number of Putnam citizens who insisted that mobility was an attribute of freedom.[122] G. C. Moore said, "Negroes are citizens of the United States and have the same rights to come to Indiana as any other citizens." William Trail of Franklin Township thought that blacks "are a free people, and have the same right to come here that the whites have."[123] President Alexander Martin of Asbury University concurred, "We are a free people to move around in this country, and I don't see why the colored people should not do so too."[124] Whites accepted that the disabilities once imposed on Indiana's black population were no longer legitimate. Col. John A. Osborn felt that once the blacks were in Indiana, they should "be permitted to enjoy all the rights that whites do without question."[125]

The Exodus reminded Putnam residents of the evils of slavery. W. H. Ragan, a former senator from the district including Hendricks and Putnam counties, said, "Remembering their long years of bondage, we are under obligations, as the friends of humanity, to give them kindly treatment and remunerative employment."[126] Even the Exodusters' appearance confirmed slavery's horrors. The *Greencastle Banner* described Exoduster Nathan Wade as a blonde who looked white. Wade's complexion reminded those who met him of the sexual exploitation that had existed under slavery.[127] Exoduster bodies bore the marks of other kinds of violence as well. During the Great Depression, a white Works

Progress Administration interviewer heard Exoduster Spear Pitman recall seeing a slave man ripped to pieces by dogs as punishment for getting into a fight. He remembered the casual cruelty of slave patrols and overseers, who sometimes "whipped for nothin' at all" but merely because some "just liked to see blood." "I've got marks on my back," Pitman said, "growed over by now but still plain."[128] Doubtless, other Exodusters had similar stories, reminding Putnam whites that the horror of slavery was no abstraction.

Not all Putnam County residents were moved by sympathy for former slaves, however. A popular humorist satirized the panicked reaction of Indiana whites to the black migration. Petroleum V. Nasby paid a visit to Indiana "to assist in keeping that state from being Africanized." Signing himself "Cawcashen," Nasby related, "I come to Plugville [Indiana] the minit I heerd that a dozen uv niggers, wich hed got the noshen uv leevin ther nateral homes in the sunny South, perposed to settle here." Nasby came "to aid the strugglin whites uv this seckshun to repel this invashun, that Injeany shood be saved from the horrors uv nigger dominashen." Precisely because the Exodusters had not come as servants but rather as "free men," Hoosiers found the migration "altogether too disgustin."[129]

Local Democrats did try to stop the Exodus. Sheriff Lewman received word that A. M. Heath, an "advance agent" of the Exodusters, would be arriving late at night at the Greencastle depot, so he met him there at about 1 A.M. Heath inquired about the location of the post office, as he was carrying a letter of introduction to Postmaster Langsdale. Lewman told him the postmaster was not in at that hour and then found Heath lodging at a hotel and pretended to be friendly to the migration, gaining his confidence. Lewman claimed Heath admitted that the purpose for getting enough blacks into Indiana by May 1, the date for the census taking, was "to carry the State for the Republican party." Though Lewman denied telling Heath that "he had better get out of town pretty quick or the ku-klux would get after him," Heath did leave suddenly the next morning. The sheriff maintained it was because M. D. Bridges, who was sympathetic to the Exodusters, had told Heath that he had fallen into the Democrats' hands. But according to Republicans, Harrison Randel played a decisive role in speeding Heath's exit. Randel appeared at the hotel the next morning and gave the hotelkeeper $10 to buy Heath a train ticket. He then had a "short, sharp, and decisive" conversation with Heath that left Randel "a little amused" by its effect.[130] Perhaps Randel, determined to think the best of southern whites, failed to appreciate the alacrity with which a black man would respond to a white man's threats.

The efforts to expel Exodusters by Democrats such as Lewman and Randel intersected with the desire of some disappointed black migrants who genuinely wished to return to their native state. C. S. Wooten, a white farmer in North Carolina, received letters from Sarah Smith and Frank Jones in Belle Union and Greencastle, who asked for help in getting home. Sarah claimed to be out of clothes, homeless, and without food. As a single woman with children, she found it difficult to find work. As Frank Jones confirmed, a "woman that is got children can not get a place to stay." Her brother Allen would let her stay with him, she noted, but his employer did not want him to take in another family. Sarah asked Wooten to send her money to return. Jones, too, had been unable to find work and wrote, "I is not sadfied heare and wont to come home." "These pepel hare don't not like black pepel as well as the whit pepel do hare," Jones explained, and he wrote repeatedly to ask for money to return, promising to work for free until he had paid it back.[131] Greencastle lawyer and Democrat T. C. Grooms saw Chloe Smith, who was Sarah and Allen's sister, at the courthouse trying to find someone to write a letter for her, which she intended to send to her former employer, requesting money to return to North Carolina. Sheriff Lewman said he made inquiries about railroad fares for Chloe, Sarah, and their children. Meanwhile, F. B. Fields, a North Carolina Republican, testified that two of his former hands, including Nathan Wade in Greencastle, had written him that they wanted to return to North Carolina. They told Fields they could not get enough work to make a living; one had been "husking" (or "shucking," as the North Carolinians called it) corn.[132]

Republicans maintained that Lewman was coercing the Exodusters. Chloe Smith, the *Banner* insisted, had written no appeals for aid. Lewman summoned Chloe and other Exodusters to a meeting at the courthouse, and told them "that their old masters had sent for them to come back, and if they would do so money would be sent to pay their way." Chloe evidently told her employer that she would have to leave: "She seemed to think that whatever the High Sheriff of the county advised must be done without question. When told that this was a free country for her as well as for the whites, and that she could do just as she pleased about going or staying, she was greatly relieved." Langsdale claimed Nathan Wade returned to North Carolina because of news that his mother was sick.[133]

Mingo Simmons did accept the sheriff's offer to pay his passage back to North Carolina. Republicans thought Simmons was unhappy because his wife had refused to join him in Indiana. But he was also dissatisfied that his pay was only about $10 per month after board was deducted, and he felt he could have done better in North Carolina. Langsdale tried to discredit his account by reporting that other blacks called Simmons a wandering, dissatisfied man. Exodusters Henry C. Roundtree and William Croom similarly stigmatized some returnees as being "lazy and wont work," or as whiskey-drinking "loafers." The *Banner* accused Lewman of pursuing blacks "worse than a Southern blood hound," accelerating his efforts to chase them out of the state before election time. But Lewman viewed himself as a humanitarian, aiding destitute migrants—deceived by Republican promises—to return to homes and employers in North Carolina.[134] One Exoduster whose wife and six children had remained in North Carolina vowed to return home. Insisting he and others had been promised "work all de time" at good wages, he lamented, "We's been he'ah nine days and hab only made $1.50. I's a Republican, but dat won't make a nigger a libin."[135] Although Republicans depicted Lewman as a villain, one North Carolina Exoduster remembered that he could get no aid in Greencastle until he met the sheriff.

Just as migrants had gone to Putnam County to better their condition, they left it when it did not meet their expectations. Alfred Newbern, who had originally praised Putnam's high wages and fair treatment, became disillusioned in a short time: he found wages less than half what he had been promised, and prices for lodging and food were high. G. McMerrick also found that work could not be had at a living wage. He went to "Bainbridge, Brazil, and all around, trying to get work, but was offered only a few cents a day above de support of myself. I could do bettah dan dat in North Carolina."[136] Robert Quinn upset a Republican meeting at Brick Chapel because, when called on to speak about why he had left North Carolina, he complained that he had been misled about wages in Indiana. He had expected $1 to $1.50 per day but found instead that one earned only $.50 a day and had to pay house rent. Having hoped to "better [his] condition" he was now told to wait for good times to return, and he was worried: "I don't think us poor darkies will ever see it."[137]

Exodusters and their employers also faced intimidation and violence. A longtime black resident of Greencastle said that the North Carolina blacks were refusing to take work in the countryside because Democrats had warned them "they would be mobbed, that they would be cheated out of their wages, and treated just as badly as they had been in the South."[138] Some blacks were being intercepted in Indianapolis and told that they would be "kukluxed" if they went to the countryside. Posters went up throughout Putnam County warning farmers not to employ black laborers. A Republican county convention condemned arson directed at black laborers as "a crime against liberty and humanity."[139]

A mob in Shelbyville intercepted a train, determined to keep "the damned niggers" from getting off. Aboard that train, Elias Churchwell was in a party from Greene County, North Carolina. The mob "didn't do us any harm," he reported. "All they did was to shoot off their mouths at us. They acted like drunken Democrats, and I guess that is what they were." The incident merely convinced his party to go on to Indianapolis rather than stop in such a "hole" as Shelbyville. A group of fourteen Exodusters who arrived from North Carolina during the Christmas holidays had to remain at the depot overnight because the black church was having a festival. Drunken young white men disturbed their rest by throwing firecrackers into the room, then stealing and cutting up the Exodusters' clothing. Four youths, including William Eckels, Jr., Delana Eckels's grandson, were arrested and tried before Mayor Chapin, with C. C. Matson defending them. Eckels and two others were found guilty of malicious trespass and were fined $10 each and ordered to pay costs. Eckels paid, but the others went to jail. The North Carolinians were astounded "that at last they had got to a land where there was a law to protect them."[140] The *Banner* used the incident to show the difference between Southern and Northern justice. Henry Bolden agreed "that we [the Exodusters] have the same protection by the law."[141]

As such incidents grew more serious, however, Exodusters may have lost faith in legal protection. Henry Whited was fired on three times when going to Limedale to get the mail. His employer told him Democrats did it, but he later found out it was his employer's son. Someone cut a tree down so that it fell on a cabin for black laborers on Riley Springer's farm. J. C. McCoy of Cloverdale, who had hired a black worker, had his hay barn burned. Another case involved J. H. Wilson, a Russell Township farmer who had employed Sanders Jones, a "quiet, inoffensive, hard-working man." Jones was cleaning up a house on Wilson's farm for his own family to live in when someone burned it down. Wilson condemned the "Ku-klux Democracy." Meanwhile, Langsdale received a note with a drawing of a man hanging from a scaffold and the legend: "Langsdale hung for shipping niggers." Two drunken whites attacked some black men on their way to a meeting at Bethel Chapel, but it seemed the black men got the better of the fight, hitting one of their assailants in the face with a brick. And in September 1880, Elijah Ecton and his son George were walking home from their jobs when they were attacked by a party of Democrats heading to a meeting in Bainbridge. The Ectons also fought back.[142]

When locals resorted to violent means to stop the migration, some wondered whether the violence of Reconstruction had moved north. The *Banner* headline asked, "IS THIS A FREE COUNTRY, OR ARE WE ALL THE SLAVES OF DEMOCRATIC HATE? WILL REPUBLICANS SUBMIT TO THE DESTRUCTION OF THEIR PROPERTY?" More plaintively, an editorial asked, "Is this Indiana or Mississippi?"[143] The *Indianapolis Journal* called the Christmastime prank on the Exodusters at the depot "lawlessness of the Yazoo type."[144] But not everyone was sure Democrats were the sole culprits. For instance, Democrats blamed the arsons in Russell Township on local Republicans. T. C. Grooms noted that the township was a Republican stronghold where residents opposed the emigration.[145] Sheriff Lewman told an investigating congressional committee that he believed some Republican laborers had made threats against the migrants, although he admitted Democrats may have been involved in some of the arsons: "I was not claiming that the Democrats out there in Indiana are saints."[146] The Democratic newspaper reported that a neighbor boy from a Republican family got drunk and decided to "kill a nigger." He fired into the house of an Exoduster family on the farm of Clay Darnall, a Republican. Darnall was adamant about finding the perpetrator of this act until the boy's father threatened to vote Democratic if Darnall did not "dry up."[147] Mingo Simmons, another one of the Exodusters, believed that Republicans might indeed be complicit in the attacks, as many said the Exodusters "take away their labor, and cut down their wages, and they are against it."[148]

National Democrats were concerned enough about the migration to Indiana to mount an investigation. In early 1880, a congressional committee headed by Indiana senator Daniel Voorhees looked into the Exoduster movement. Sheriff Lewman and George Langsdale were among the 153 witnesses who testified from Alabama, Georgia, Kansas, Louisiana, Mississippi, Missouri, North Carolina, Texas, and Indiana. Although most scholarly attention has focused on the migration to Kansas, which the committee did examine, the entire rationale for the investigation was to discern whether the Exodusters were going to Indiana from North Carolina in order to swing Indiana to the Republicans. The very resolution that Voorhees submitted elicited a challenge from Minnesota Republican William Windom, who demanded that if testimony showed blacks had been driven out of the South by "cruel and unjust treatment, or by the denial or abridgment of personal or political rights," the committee should follow up with recommendations about how to secure the freedmen's rights. Windom later pointed out that although the numbers going to Kansas dwarfed those going to Indiana, the Indiana Exoduster movement was considered more important because of its "alleged political purposes."[149]

The Democratic majority on the investigating committee concluded that the North Carolina migration to Indiana was induced by politicians who used aid societies' circulars to spread discontent among North Carolina blacks. The majority report, submitted by North Carolina Democrat Zebulon Vance, found no cause for blacks there to be unhappy. Their economic conditions were good, there had been no "outrages" against their voting rights, they had equal justice in the courts, and they had control of local schools. Furthermore, the majority claimed that North Carolina's conditions pertained all across the South. Yet even as it extolled the fairness with which the freedmen were treated, the report openly called them "the subject race" of the South.

The majority concluded that the migration was a plot by Republicans to move blacks from the South, "where their votes could not be made to tell, into close States in the North, and thus turn the scale in favor of the Republican party."[150] The Republican minority, in contrast, blamed attacks on black political and civil rights in the South for the migration. Windom's report said that blacks themselves had conceived of the Exodus, in some cases having spent years gathering information and making plans. The aid societies were charitable organizations that had sprung up to meet the migrants' needs. Although Windom conceded that conditions in North Carolina were relatively good, he enumerated murders in other parts of the South, condemned the sharecropping system as "peonage," and concluded that blacks had fled because of "political persecutions, whippings, maimings, and murders committed by Democrats and in the interest of the Democratic party." Windom estimated that only a few hundred voters had migrated to Indiana, hardly enough to turn the state. But as Emma Lou Thornbrough has argued, Democratic and Republican reports both failed to acknowledge the economic aspirations of the Exodusters.[151]

In December 1880, the North Carolina Exodusters met at the Greencastle courthouse to consider their situation "as it relates to our future welfare, and to decide whether or not it will be beneficial to our race in the South for them to continue to come to Indiana."[152] Willis Bunn presided, and Rev. A. A. Burleigh, Clay's replacement, was secretary. Many speakers contrasted life in North

Carolina with that in Indiana, "the sentiment being that they had never really enjoyed the blessings of freedom until they came here." The convention urged southern blacks to choose Indiana as their destination rather than Kansas or Liberia. The delegates deplored that the Civil War had made them only "nominally free." In the South, they were returning to a state of "servitude," in which legal discrimination made it impossible to rise out of poverty, schools were rendered worthless, and fraud and violence deprived them of their political rights. As slaves, they had had value; yet as free men and women, their lives were worth nothing. For these reasons, they had left their homes and moved to Indiana. "Nor have we been disappointed": in Indiana, they were not treated differently because of their color; they received equal protection from the law, education for their children, and fair wages for their labor; and they had "the same chance in life" as the white man. Although they acknowledged that Indiana was not a "paradise" and that they had not always been treated well, they described their adopted state as a "fertile country" offering "the industrious husbandman a rich reward." The Exodusters concluded, "We feel that our real freedom dates only from the day we entered Indiana."[153]

Nonetheless, many of the Exodusters would leave Putnam County by the late 1880s. Of the Exodusters who were in the county in 1880, only seventeen have been traced in later censuses. The 1890 census does not survive, and many Exodusters may have died before the next census was taken. Of those found in the 1900 census, five were still in Putnam County, seven had moved to other parts of Indiana, four had returned to North Carolina, and one had gone to Kansas. Some went to Indianapolis, presumably seeking better economic opportunities. Twenty years had passed, but they apparently had not improved their economic status greatly over their lives in North Carolina. In the 1870 census, most of the Exodusters had been farm laborers. Those in Indiana in 1900 were mostly day laborers or farm laborers. Bennet Haywood was a teamster in Indianapolis, where Squire Nobles worked as a whitewasher. Dow Whitaker was a quarryman in Putnam County. Only Adam Edmonson, who thirty years earlier had been a farm laborer in North Carolina, had his own farm in Putnam County. Meanwhile, Putnam's black population fell from a high of 576 in 1880 to 357 ten years later.[154] As some disillusioned Exodusters had discovered, "Our welcome soon wore [out]." A Greencastle man composed a poem based on the testimony of a North Carolina Exoduster before the Voorhees committee; it contrasted the promises about Indiana as a land of "milk and honey" with the reality he found there: "Dar wus col'ness in de a'ir out dar, /

And de folkses looks dey froze us; / And de darkies die dar ebery day / From the chillin' winds dat blows; / ain't no work to get an' do, / No pay for what yer's done; / And yer begs all day for a bone ter eat, / An' starves from sun to sun." The lament concludes, "I'm exodustin' back ter de lan' / Dat's bes' on earf for me!"[155]

Emma Lou Thornbrough calls the Exodus "a pathetic chapter in the history of Negro migration," but this seems too harsh a conclusion.[156] The migrants certainly suffered, and moving to Indiana clearly brought little upward economic mobility. But those who had returned to North Carolina had not prospered. Three were day laborers, and another, Albert Phillips, appeared in the 1900 census as a "bum."[157] Although Indiana had proved less open to black rights than the Exodusters expected, African Americans there could nonetheless vote and exercise political rights denied them in the "redeemed" South. And those Exodusters who stayed in Putnam County joined its black community. When Stan Pittman arrived in the county in 1880, he met Wyatt and Catherine James. He knew them "intimately ever since," his family intermarrying with theirs.[158]

For two generations, the Townsends had been the only stable black family in the county. As the black population grew in the postwar period and as a black community emerged, the Townsends remained a constant. They helped found the black AME church, participated in Republican politics, and welcomed Exodusters such as Pittman. The Exodusters' migration revealed the dramatic changes that the Civil War had brought to Putnam County. Black mobility itself, forbidden by the constitution of 1851, was now universally conceded to be one of the rights of freedom. Republicans even encouraged the migration. A. C. Stevenson, who may have once urged the Peters family to leave the United States, now welcomed black laborers. Whether Republicans such as Langsdale and Stevenson were motivated by a desire for cheap labor (or black votes) or an altruistic belief that the nation owed the freedmen, their encouragement of black migration into the county marked a revolutionary change from the attitudes of the prewar period, in which antiblack racism had been universally accepted.

Conclusion

The Monument Builder

George J. Langsdale was a man of causes. Fiercely partisan as editor of the Republican party's organ, the *Banner,* advocate of woman suffrage, recruiter and philanthropist for the Exodusters, he would become the driving force behind the design and construction of the Soldiers' and Sailors' Monument in downtown Indianapolis. Like many settlers in Putnam County, Langsdale had grown up in Kentucky before returning to his birthplace, Indianapolis, where he worked for a Democratic newspaper. During the Civil War, he became a lieutenant in the 3rd Indiana Cavalry. After mustering out, he settled in Greencastle, purchasing the *Putnam Republican Banner,* which he owned until 1890. A "stalwart Republican," Langsdale was active in the Grand Army of the Republic, serving as commander of the Greencastle post upon its founding. As zealous about honoring the veteran as about any other cause he undertook, he became the leading proponent of constructing a soldiers' monument for the state capital.[1]

As Kirk Savage has written, monuments are deeply contested expressions of public sentiment. The visions of sculptors, monument commissioners, and interested segments of the public often clash over design, location, or other important features. Visibility, permanence, and expense characterize the public monument, raising the stakes as to its content. What a monument represents for future generations is the meaning of the event it commemorates *as understood by the generation that erected it.*[2] Rising from the center of the state capital, the Indianapolis monument eventually surpassed the height of the city's other structures. At its dedication, Governor Winfield T. Durbin accepted "this noble shaft" as a testament that the people of Indiana remembered "the blood and treasure expended in upholding principles upon which human liberty rests and upon which constitutional government is founded."[3] It had taken over a decade to complete, and the story of its erection revealed the continuing debate over the war's meaning for the generation that fought the battles and insisted on an appropriate commemoration of their deeds.

In 1867, the same year that Langsdale bought the *Banner,* Governor Oliver

George Langsdale. (From *Atlas of Putnam Co., Indiana to Which Are Added Various General Maps, History, Statistics, Illustrations* [Chicago: J. H. Beers, 1879]; courtesy of DePauw University Archives and Special Collections)

P. Morton suggested that the state should have a Civil War monument. Morton wanted to place it in Crown Hill Cemetery in Indianapolis, reflecting the common assumption that a graveyard was the appropriate place for a monument to the war dead. Nothing came of the idea until nearly a decade later, when George Langsdale brought it up with a group of Greencastle veterans and Republicans, including Lucius Chapin, who met in the *Banner* office at night to talk politics. Langsdale then approached a soldiers' reunion in Indianapolis with the proposal. Soon, $1,000 was collected and the GAR took up the cause, raising money over the next decade. B. F. Havens recalled that Langsdale "entered the work with great spirit and organized the movement to raise the money by appeals to the public, camp fires, and through subscriptions from counties" for several years. But the proposal languished until the legislature appropriated

$200,000 and appointed a monument commission, selecting Langsdale as its first president. Langsdale opposed the cemetery site and persuaded the legislature to specify the Circle, formerly the location of the governor's mansion.[4]

Construction began in 1888, and the cornerstone dedication was held the next year. The former lieutenant governor, Thomas Hanna, was among the delegation representing Putnam County, and over eighty veterans from Greencastle's GAR Post No. 11 marched in the day's procession. Langsdale rode with the other commissioners in a carriage following that of President Benjamin Harrison. Delivering a short speech, Langsdale stated that the monument would

> honor the citizen soldiers and sailors of the State who gave their lives for the preservation of our liberties, the maintenance of the government and the vindication of the national honor. And as men of every creed and color and of every political faith and practice were true to their country in the hour of her peril, and shed their blood for her protection so, too, every man in the State who has worn the national uniform can join hands around this monument.[5]

Here, Langsdale explicitly construed the monument as including black soldiers, such as Wyatt James and Robert Townsend. For the next decade and a half, workers toiled to erect the almost 300-foot structure. The Exodusters who had moved to Indianapolis would have seen it going up.[6]

The monument's story captures many aspects of the Civil War era in the North. Although art historians note the influence of Egyptian and Greco-Roman styles, the monument commission sought to balance foreign influence with Americanness. A design competition was held, and the winning entry was *The Symbol of Indiana* by Bruno Schmitz of Berlin. But when the figures in the relief groups representing "War" and "Peace" were finished, they were deemed too Germanic. Sculptor Rudolf Schwarz had rendered them with beards, but the monument's regents, who remembered American Civil War soldiers as clean-shaven, ordered the beards removed. (Putnam County's Civil War statue of a bearded man, however, had been praised as a representation of the typical westerner.) Commissioners also rejected a Medusa head as insufficiently American, preferring instead of snakes an olive-wreath crown. Animal figures—mountain lions, bears, buffalo, and the bald eagle—gave supporting elements of the monument a uniquely American cast. Ironically, despite this emphasis, not only had an immigrant designed the monument, but immigrants played a prominent role in its dedication. In addition to a performance by a

German American singing group known as the Liederkranz, members of the Turner societies (German American cultural and physical clubs), "clad in their gymnasium suits," marched to the monument and laid an evergreen wreath at its base.[7]

The monument's purpose was to honor the state's participation in the war. As such, it is a fiercely martial creation: statues at each corner represent the branches of military service; two bronze astragals depict the army and navy; and statues on the periphery honor Indiana's war heroes, including Oliver P. Morton. Inside the cornerstone is a large copper box containing, among other documents, the Indiana adjutant general's report in which appear the names of all soldiers from Indiana who fought in the war. By contrast, only the names of the war dead appear on the Putnam County statue, located in Greencastle's Forest Hill Cemetery: that monument commemorates Lucius Chapin's brothers Cowgill and George and Simpson Hamrick, who died in battles from Tennessee to Virginia, but omits Lucius, John Applegate, Josiah Williams, and Robert Townsend, all of whom served but survived. In Indianapolis, even though the names are hidden under a "majestic mass of masonry," the monument indeed speaks for "every man" of the Civil War generation who wore the uniform.[8]

The monument also commemorates the contribution of women. In the decades since Martha Mullinix's murder, attitudes toward women had changed. Indeed, Langsdale was such a vocal president of the Woman Suffrage Association in Greencastle that detractors labeled him "Granny" Langsdale. Newspapers such as his *Banner* routinely carried stories of divorces, seduction cases, and "outrages" against women, revealing a new openness in discussing these issues.[9] Indiana's permissive divorce laws resulted in an exchange between Langsdale and North Carolina senator Zebulon Vance, who during the Voorhees committee hearings, clashed over an Exoduster alleged to be a bigamist. Langsdale ventured that if the charge was true, "probably he has learned that from the example set him in the time of slavery." Taking umbrage at that remark, Vance defended North Carolina's morality by insisting that Indiana had forty divorces—"dissolutions of the highest social tie"—for each one in North Carolina. Langsdale replied, "Well, in Indiana our people don't submit to anything of the kind; they get divorces." To his way of thinking, neither women nor men should submit to "anything of the kind" but should instead be free to dissolve their marriages if needed—a principle that would liberate a woman from a husband who made the woman's sphere a misery.[10] Langsdale was also more vocal about violence against women, and in his columns, he advocated greater penalties for such crimes and excoriated local officials inclined to deal lightly with male offenders.[11]

In depicting women's contributions to the war, the Soldiers' and Sailors' Monument reflects the increasingly public role women assumed. The cornerstone, for example, contains the roster of the Women's Relief Corps, and a crowned woman's head surmounts a plaque reading "To Indiana's Silent Victors," which lists the numbers of Hoosier volunteers in the Civil War and Spanish-American War. The War group at the monument's eastern base features Bellona, the Roman goddess of war, with a fierce countenance leading troops into battle while an angel carrying the flag flies overhead. On the opposite side of the monument, the Peace group also possesses a female angel and a goddess, this one more serene. Behind the goddess, a soldier embraces his wife. In front of this group is another set of sculptures called "The Return Home," in which a mother welcomes her soldier son. Topping the monument is a 30-foot-tall statue of "Victory." A martial figure like Bellona, she carries a sword to symbolize the military might with which the North won the war. Overlooking the discontent of wives struggling on the home front or the ways in which pensions had inadvertently liberated women, the monument stresses traditional roles that no one had intended the war to upset. The female sculptures support the war effort and welcome the men home.[12] Monument commissioner Gustavus V. Menzies, however, felt women were insufficiently commemorated in the work. At the dedication, he praised "the womanhood of Indiana, who gave husbands, sons and sweethearts to the cause" and worked for sanitary commissions and in hospitals. He called them "ministering angels." But even though he felt there were not enough women represented in the monument, he did not quarrel with the traditional representation of their roles.[13] The monument embodies the incremental change in rights and status the war brought to women.

The most revolutionary change that occurred in Putnam County concerned not women but race. Republicans there initially denied that their cause would challenge white supremacy. And many Putnam County residents accepted a war to save the Union. But antiwar Democrats suspected from the outset that the war would undermine white supremacy. Although the Copperheads may have been wrong in accusing Republicans of having abolitionist intent all along, they proved correct in asserting that the Civil War would permanently alter race relations. More and more Putnam citizens accepted a greater degree of black rights, and young black men such as Robert Townsend and Wyatt James

The Peace group on the Indianapolis Soldiers' and Sailors' Monument. (Courtesy of Indiana State Library)

did their part to gain them for all African Americans. The Civil War ended Indiana's black laws and opened the state to a previously forbidden black migration. Enough Southern blacks took advantage of their new freedoms to allow longtime Putnam County blacks, such as the Townsend family, to participate in creating a black community where one had never existed before. Nonetheless, it was clear even during the Exoduster movement that not all racial attitudes had changed, prompting many North Carolina migrants to leave, either to find better jobs or because of their disappointment with Indiana. What is perhaps more remarkable is that so many white Putnam County residents had welcomed the Exodusters, a consequence of Civil War idealism and political pragmatism—but also a brief moment of racial egalitarianism.

It is unusual for a Civil War memorial to represent emancipation. James H. Madison has pointed out that the markers Hoosiers erected on battlefields throughout the South and in the cemeteries and town squares at home neglected race in favor of celebrating the common soldier and his fight to save the Union. In the Soldiers' and Sailors' Monument, however, a slave holds up his broken shackles to the goddess Peace. Although emancipationist in its message, the monument is typical in its representation of the helplessness of the slave and his need for outsiders to liberate him. The slave sits rather than stands, holding up his chains to a goddess who seems indifferent to his presence. The slave's degradation is represented not just by the chains but also by his lack of shoes and a shirt while surrounded by well-clothed figures. The monument fails to tell the story of a Robert Townsend or a Wyatt James, men who actively sought freedom for their race.[14] Yet when it was erected, Indianapolis's black newspaper, the *Recorder,* used the opportunity to assert, "The monument is for Indiana's loyal sons, both white and black. The Negro was a good soldier, for oftimes his comrades in arms were his bitterest enemies still he fought for 'a new birth of freedom.'" Black veterans played a role in the dedication. When the Martin Delaney Colored Post from Indianapolis passed by, third in the ranks of the marching veterans, a reporter described the scene: "As the colored men appeared renewed cheers broke forth. From the windows and the balconies around Monument place flags and banners were waved. The colored post had a large number of men in line and made a fine showing. 'They are the boys who went into battle shouting, "Remember Fort Pillow,"' called out a veteran, and again there were cheers and a waving of flags."[15]

During the development of the monument, Langsdale resisted the reconciliationist tendencies of his age. Commissioners disputed which direction Victory should face. Some wanted her to look westward, toward the statehouse. But Langsdale prevailed in having her face south, toward the land Hoosier soldiers had conquered for the Union. And Victory would not only hold a sword but also lift a torch aloft to shine the light of civilization, implying the South was in need of such illumination.[16] The principal orator at the 1902 dedication apparently felt uneasy about such imagery. John W. Foster insisted that Victory was not standing "in exultation over a fallen foe" and was glad that all "bitterness" was gone and that all were part of a "common country."[17] The marching veterans, however, had sung "Marching through Georgia," along with other Civil War songs and hymns, in a triumphal spirit that belied Foster's sentiments.[18]

Although bipartisanship prevailed during the dedication ceremony, where

Republicans and Democrats shared the stage, conflict between the parties characterized much of the monument's construction. B. F. Havens, who served on Langsdale's committee in the early days, felt that fund-raising lagged because Langsdale failed to include Democrats. Havens recalled his first meeting as a committee member, when Langsdale outlined his fund-raising plan for public appeals. Having suggested approaching the political parties for an appropriation, Havens then secured the support of the Democrats, despite the potential cost to taxpayers, by telling them that the Republicans would certainly back the monument and welcome any opportunity to denounce the Democrats for failing to do so. Ultimately, both party conventions endorsed an appropriation, and the legislature passed it.[19]

Friction on the monument commission resulted in part from Langsdale's dictatorial style, which irritated even fellow Republicans, and in part from the scheming between Republican and Democratic members. William H. English, a Democrat on the commission and a former Copperhead from southern Indiana, even claimed the idea for the monument as his own, supposedly originating in a Memorial Day speech he made at Indianapolis's Crown Hill Cemetery in 1872.[20] English was the principal advocate of a westward-facing statue, and when veterans supported some of his ideas for the monument, Langsdale was dismayed. "He never did anything for a soldier, or for his cause, that I ever heard of," he lamented.[21] It may have particularly wounded Langsdale that his old Greencastle GAR post, No. 11, sided with English in opposition to placing the dates for the U.S.-Mexican War on the monument.[22] In a mix of the martial language central to the veteran's identity and the social language of the era, one Democratic commissioner observed that "Langsdale is a sly old chap to form a line of battle, but he is a failure on the field, as he is not a good mixer with men."[23] Of the many men who had served on the monument commission over the decades, three were cited at the dedication ceremony in 1902 as "conspicuous" in their work for its completion: Langsdale, Mahlon D. Manson (another Democratic congressman), and English. Only Langsdale had survived to attend the dedication.[24]

On a sunny, pleasant day in mid-May, thousands gathered to observe the dedication of the Soldiers' and Sailors' Monument. Festivities began in early morning and continued into the evening. Women were conspicuous in the crowds, waving their handkerchiefs when the aged veterans marched into view. The governors of Indiana and Ohio were there, along with the widows of Senator Morton and President Benjamin Harrison. (A decade earlier, President

Harrison had spoken at the cornerstone ceremony.) Lew Wallace, Indiana's foremost Civil War hero, appeared as one of the speakers, and James Whitcomb Riley recited a poem, "The Soldier," composed for the occasion. Many veterans who marched in the morning parade were seen in tears, as were members of the crowds. Perhaps the most emotional moment of the ceremony came at its end. On the morning of the dedication ceremony, veterans had gathered at dawn in the statehouse to receive the battle flags kept in storage there. They had carried their regimental flags in the parade, placed them on stands at the monument to be watched by National Guardsmen throughout the day's services, and then returned them to the statehouse after the vespers service. As the tattered banners were returned to their cases, the veterans struggled unsuccessfully to hold back tears. It is likely that putting the banners away reminded them not just of the flags' glory waving in battles long ago but also of the many comrades they had laid to rest then and in the forty years since the war.[25]

The speakers would send a mixed message about the meaning of that sacrifice. Chaplain D. R. Lucas evoked "the martyred boys in blue": "They bled to purify the nation from the stain of slavery, they died to redeem it from secession, they trod the wine press of agony in battle, in prison, in hospital to keep their country an undivided heritage for future generations." But Commissioner Gustavus Menzies, in his presentation of the monument, praised Lincoln for adhering to the purpose of saving the Union "no matter what might happen to the dark institution of slavery," rendering the emancipationist goals of the Civil War distinctly secondary.[26] As David W. Blight has written, reconciliation caused Americans to forget the emancipationist vision of the war.[27] By casting the freedman in stone, however, the monument preserved that vision for later generations.

W. E. B. DuBois famously said of Reconstruction, "The slave went free; stood a brief moment in the sun; then moved back again toward slavery."[28] The history of the Civil War era in Putnam County, Indiana, demonstrates that it was the entire nation that experienced that moment in the sun. Just as it was a fleeting and incomplete moment for the slave, so the effect of the Civil War was partial and incomplete but immensely consequential for the North. The Civil War era brought many changes. As immigrants became more and more accepted, a debate over the meaning of true Americanness persisted. Partisanship continued, and although issues shifted over time, alcohol remained a constant source of conflict. Some industry grew up, but Putnam County remained largely agricultural, with Greencastle forever being not a "Milltown" but a college town.[29]

As women moved increasingly into the public sphere, they retained their preference for distinctive and largely separate gender roles. And veterans, regardless of their accomplishments in civilian life, prized military service as central
to their identities. Oliver Wendell Holmes, Jr., said of the Civil War generation,
"Our hearts were touched with fire,"[30] and in Greencastle, thirty years after the
war, Union veterans still recalled the intensity of that blaze:

> There are more in Post No. 11 who were with Kimball at Winchester, were at
> Antietam, when their comrades melted away like April Snow; were at Marye's
> height—at Fredericksburg when the nation gave up her fourteen thousand
> men. The crack of their rifles went to make up the din and the roar of the battle
> at Chancellorsville; they Stood shoulder to shoulder with the heroes who saved
> the day perhaps the nation at Gettysburgh, who struggled at Spotsylvania and
> Cold Harbor in the Wilderness; and were in the columns at Appomattox.
>
> Others there are in Post No 11 who were at Donelson and Shiloh, at Stone-
> river, Champions Hill and Chicamauga; who scaled the giddy heights of Look-
> out Mountain; who were with the hosts that sent Bragg flying in disorder from
> Missionary-ridge; who were in the charge and amid the carnage at Resaca; who
> Stormed the Solid buttress at Kenisaw Mountain; who followed the bugle be-
> yond the Chattahoochie and were at Peach Tree Creek with forty rounds and
> bright bayonets; who fought where McPherson fell, and shouted with the thou-
> sands when Atlanta Surrendered; and later, marched with Sherman when he
> went down to the Sea. Others went with Pap Thomas in pursuit of Hood, fought
> at Franklin and Nashville, where the rebel army of the west was wiped from off
> the face of the earth.
>
> This is only part mention of the Services of the membership of GreenCastle
> Post No 11.

With these searing recollections as "only part mention" of their sufferings for
the nation and with no acknowledgment of the civilian lives they had lived for
thirty years, these veterans affirmed, "We are true soldiers."[31] At the dedication
ceremony in 1902, the same was said of an aged George J. Langsdale, "a gallant
Indiana soldier" who was honored for his commitment to the Soldiers' and
Sailors' Monument. He died a year and a half later, this part of his life's work
completed.[32]

Notes

Introduction: The Murder of Martha Mullinix

1. *Putnam Republican Banner,* April 15, December 23, 1857; *Indiana State Journal,* May 4, 1857; *Indiana Daily State Sentinel,* April 30, 1857; State of Indiana v. Greenberry O. Mullinix, Circuit Court, Complete Record D, 1843–1862, Clerk's Office, Putnam County Courthouse, Greencastle, Ind., 371–376; Indiana Marriage Collection, 1800–1941, AncestryLibrary.com.

2. *Indiana State Journal,* December 21, 1857; Mullinix Family, Boatwright Collection, Cyril Johnson Room for Local History and Genealogy, Putnam County Public Library, Greencastle, Ind.; Putnam County Sesquicentennial Committee, *A Journey through Putnam County History* (n.p., 1966), 241; *Biographical and Historical Record of Putnam County, Indiana* (1887; reprint, Chicago: Lewis Publishing, 1975), 492; Probate Record F, 1853–1855, Clerk's Office, Putnam County Courthouse, Greencastle, Ind., 13–19, 515–518; Circuit Court, Complete Record D, 1843–1862, ibid., 98–103; U.S. Census, 1850, AncestryLibrary.com. The Greenbury Mullinix in this census record was listed as having been born in Maryland, but he is the right age for the future murderer. Record of Official Bonds, 1844–1911, Clerk's Office, Putnam County Courthouse, Greencastle, Ind., 11, 21, 27, 31, 33, 38, 50, 53, 66; State of Indiana v. Greenbury O. Mullinix.

3. *Indiana State Journal,* December 21, 1857; U.S. Census, 1850; Henry Secrest v. David Sublett and Mary Ann Sublett, Order Book, Comm Pleas 3 Civil, 1857–1859, Clerk's Office, Putnam County Courthouse, Greencastle, Ind., 195, 206–207; James M. Sloan and Josephus L. Fordyce v. David Sublett, ibid., 235; William H. Comstock and Jacob S. Asher v. David Sublett, ibid., 241; John P. Usher, William S. Eckels, Dillard C. Donnohue v. David Sublett, ibid., 510; Delana R. Eckels v. David Sublett, ibid., p. 510.

4. *Indiana State Journal,* May 4, December 21, 1857; *Putnam Republican Banner,* April 22, October 21, December 23, 1857; Jesse W. Weik, *History of Putnam County, Indiana* (Indianapolis, Ind.: Bowen, 1910), 228; Circuit Court, Order Book 4 Civil, 1857–1862, Clerk's Office, Putnam County Courthouse, Greencastle, Ind., 18, 28–29, 37, 39, 45–46; State of Indiana v. Greenbury O. Mullinix.

5. *Putnam Republican Banner,* April 22, October 21, 1857; Weik, *History of Putnam County,* 228. Throughout the volume, italics in quotations reflect the original emphases, either italics or underlining, in the original document. I have also refrained from changing or indicating with *sic* misspellings or grammatical mistakes except where they might render the meaning unclear.

6. *Putnam Republican Banner,* November 18, 25, 1857; *Indiana Daily State Sentinel,* November 24, 1857; *Indiana State Journal,* November 23, 1857; State of Indiana v. Greenbury O. Mullinix; Ashbel P. Willard, "Postponement of Execution," Pardons and Remissions, vol. 1, Indiana State Archives, Commission on Public Records, Indianapolis.

7. *Indiana State Journal*, November 23, 1857. For the 1841 murder, see Weik, *History of Putnam County*, 227–228; *Greencastle (Ind.) Dollar Press*, May 12, 1880; *Indiana State Journal*, November 23, 1857.

8. Miles J. Fletcher to Father, November 26, 1857, folder 9, box 8, Calvin Fletcher Papers, William Henry Smith Memorial Library, Indiana Historical Society (hereafter cited as IHS), Indianapolis; Miles J. Fletcher to Father, November 24, 1857, ibid.; Miles J. Fletcher to Father, Greencastle, November 26, 1857, ibid.

9. *Putnam Republican Banner*, December 23, 1857; *Indiana State Journal*, December 19, 1857; *Indiana Daily State Sentinel*, December 21, 1857; Weik, *History of Putnam County*, 228; State of Indiana v. Greenbury O. Mullinix.

10. Louis P. Masur, *Rites of Execution: Capital Punishment and the Transformation of American Culture, 1776–1865* (New York: Oxford University Press, 1989), 5–6, 113; Miles to Lucy, October 17, 1857, folder 9, box 8, Fletcher Papers, IHS; Miles J. Fletcher to Father, November 12, 1857, ibid.; *Indiana State Journal*, December 19, 1857.

11. *Putnam Republican Banner*, December 23, 1857.

12. Ibid., January 17, April 18, 25, 1861; *Indianapolis Daily Journal*, January 9, April 12, 1861; Putnam County Sesquicentennial Committee, *Journey through Putnam County History*, 114–115; Weik, *History of Putnam County*, 228, 231–234; *Daily State Sentinel*, April 27, 1865.

13. *Putnam Republican Banner*, January 17, April 18, 1861; *Indianapolis Daily Journal*, January 9, April 12, 1861; Putnam County Sesquicentennial Committee, *Journey through Putnam County History*, 114–115; U.S. Census, 1850; Indiana Marriage Collection, 1800–1941.

14. *Indianapolis Daily Journal*, April 10, 12, 1861.

15. Randolph A. Roth, "Spousal Murder in Northern New England, 1776–1865," in *Over the Threshold: Intimate Violence in Early America*, ed. Christine Daniels and Michael V. Kennedy (New York: Routledge, 1999), 65–93; Jenifer Banks, "'A New Home' for Whom? Caroline Kirkland Exposes Domestic Abuse on the Michigan Frontier," ibid., 135–147.

16. *Indiana Daily State Sentinel*, December 19, 1857.

17. *Putnam Republican Banner*, November 25, 1857; *Indiana State Journal*, November 23, 1857. It was reported that Jonathan Mullinix also had to pay $200 to the governor's private secretary and another "good fee" to a member of the governor's council. *Indiana State Journal*, November 23, 1857; *Indiana Daily State Sentinel*, November 24, December 21, 1857.

18. Mark W. Summers, *The Plundering Generation: Corruption and the Crisis of the Union, 1849–1861* (New York: Oxford University Press, 1987), 239–260.

19. *Indiana State Journal*, December 21, 1857.

20. *Putnam County Sentinel*, January 15, 1852; *Indiana State Journal*, December 21, 1857.

21. *Putnam Republican Banner*, April 15, 1857.

22. *Putnam Banner*, May 31, 1854; Miles J. Fletcher to Father, May 17, 1858, folder 10, box 8, Fletcher Papers, IHS; *Putnam Republican Banner*, June 22, 1853, June 27, 1855, August 12, 1857; D. W. Daniels to J. G. Davis, November 22, 1852, folder 4, box 1, John Givan Davis Papers, William Henry Smith Memorial Library, IHS; Miles J. Fletcher to Father, May 17, 1858, folder 10, box 8, Fletcher Papers, IHS.

23. "Pencil by a Prep," 1850, folder 5, p. 134, Elijah Edward Evans Papers, Manuscripts of the Indiana Division, Indiana State Library (hereafter cited as ISL), Indianapolis.

24. State of Indiana v. Greenbury Mullinix, Civil Order Book D, 1848–1853, Clerk's Office, Putnam County Courthouse, Greencastle, Ind., 266; Petitions of May 1835, December 23, 1837, Petition for Pardons and Paroles, Indiana State Archives, Commission on Public Records, Indianapolis; James Rankin to David Wallace, February 2, 1839, ibid.; W. Whitcomb,

March 20, 1845, ibid., State of Indiana v. Martin L. Mullinix, Circuit Court, Order Book 7, 1867–1871, Clerk's Office, Putnam County Courthouse, Greencastle, Ind., 23, 113–114, 520, 535, 626; State of Indiana v. Martin L. Mullinix, Circuit Court, Order Book, Civil 9, 1873–1874, ibid., 71; State of Indiana v. Martin L. Mullinix, Opinion of Supreme Court, ibid., 379–380; *Greencastle Banner,* February 5, 1874.

25. *Indiana State Journal,* December 19, 21, 1857; *Putnam Republican Banner,* November 18, December 23, 1857. On the link between Baptists and Democrats, see Bertram Wyatt-Brown, *The Shaping of Southern Culture: Honor, Grace, and War, 1760s–1890s* (Chapel Hill: University of North Carolina Press, 2001), 106–135; *Indianapolis Daily Journal,* January 9, April 10, 1861; Ed Hatton, "'He Murdered Her Because He Loved Her': Passion, Masculinity, and Intimate Homicide in Antebellum America," in *Over the Threshold: Intimate Violence in Early America,* ed. Christine Daniels and Michael V. Kennedy (New York: Routledge, 1999), 111–134.

26. *Indiana State Journal,* May 4, 1857.

27. *Putnam Republican Banner,* November 18, 1857.

28. *Indiana State Journal,* November 23, December 19, 21, 1857.

29. *Putnam Republican Banner,* October 21, 1857; Masur, *Rites of Execution,* 34–35. Carole Shammas, *A History of Household Government in America* (Charlottesville: University of Virginia Press, 2002), 112, says criminality was often blamed on poor parenting.

30. Hatton, "'He Murdered Her,'" 111–134.

31. *Indiana Daily State Sentinel,* November 24, 1857.

32. *Indiana State Journal,* December 19, 1857.

33. Ibid.

34. Ibid., May 4, December 19, 21, 1857.

35. Ibid., May 4, 1857; Hatton, "'He Murdered Her,'" 122.

36. Gillum Ridpath, "Putnam County, Ind.," *Atlas of Putnam Co., Indiana to Which Are Added Various General Maps, History, Statistics, Illustrations* (Chicago: J. H. Beers, 1879), 5; John J. Baughman, *Our Past, Their Present: Historical Essays on Putnam County, Indiana* (Greencastle, Ind.: Putnam County Museum, 2008), 2, 9–10; George Pence and Nellie C. Armstrong, *Indiana Boundaries: Territory, State, and County* (Indianapolis: Indiana Historical Bureau, 1967), 37–40, 43, 119; *Indiana State Journal,* March 18, 1852; Carl A. Zenor, "Putnam County in the Civil War: Local History of a Critical Period" (master's thesis, DePauw University, 1956); Putnam County Sesquicentennial Committee, *Journey through Putnam County History,* 162; "Pencillings of a Prep," folder 1, pp. 18, 22–41, Evans Papers, ISL; Weik, *History of Putnam County,* 66–68, 139; *Weekly Indiana State Sentinel,* June 13, 1860; W. H. Durham to David, February 2, 1859, box 3, folder 13, Davis Papers, IHS.

37. Weik, *History of Putnam County,* 38–41; A. M. S. Harrah to Husband, June 27, [1847?], folder 3, box 1, Almira Maria Scott Harrah Papers, William Henry Smith Memorial Library, IHS.

38. Emma Lou Thornbrough, *Indiana in the Civil War Era, 1850–1880* (Indianapolis: Indiana Historical Bureau, 1965), 615; Lewis H. Rudisill to John G. Davis, April 4, 1858, folder 2, box 3, Davis Papers, IHS; *Putnam Republican Banner,* August 30, 1860; *Indianapolis Journal,* March 2, 1870.

39. Putnam County Sesquicentennial Committee, *Journey through Putnam County History,* 25–27; Weik, *History of Putnam County,* 112; Thornbrough, *Indiana in the Civil War Era,* 617; Ridpath, "Putnam County, Ind.," 5, 8.

40. Weik, *History of Putnam County,* 66–68; *Biographical and Historical Record of Putnam County,* 187–188, 313–322; "Pencillings of a Prep," folder 1, pp. 18, 22–41, Evans Papers, ISL; *Putnam Banner,* August 24, 1853; *Indiana State Journal,* October 7, 1853, September 3, 1873.

41. Edward L. Ayers, *In the Presence of Mine Enemies: War in the Heart of America, 1859–1863* (New York: Norton, 2003). Stephanie McCurry, *Confederate Reckoning: Power and Politics in the Civil War South* (Cambridge, Mass.: Harvard University Press, 2010), brilliantly examines how women and slaves became political actors in a Confederacy predicated on these groups' non-political nature. Brian Steel Wills, *The War Hits Homes: The Civil War in Southeastern Virginia* (Charlottesville: University Press of Virginia, 2001), emphasizes the military campaigns that affected civilians; Daniel W. Crofts, *Old Southampton: Politics and Society in a Virginia County, 1834–1869* (Charlottesville: University Press of Virginia, 1992), concentrates on class, political, and racial divisions; LeeAnn Whites, *The Civil War as a Crisis in Gender: Augusta, Georgia, 1860–1890* (Athens: University of Georgia Press, 1995), focuses on women; and Martin Crawford, *Ashe County's Civil War: Community and Society in the Appalachian South* (Charlottesville: University Press of Virginia, 2001), is interested in how the Civil War altered the county's relationship with the outside world. Many southern home front studies seek the reasons for the Confederate defeat. Daniel E. Sutherland, *Seasons of War: The Ordeal of a Confederate Community, 1861–1865* (New York: Free Press, 1995), blames the war's destructiveness that made its continuation impossible rather than any failure of Confederate nationalism. William Blair, *Virginia's Private War: Feeding Body and Soul in the Confederacy, 1861–1865* (New York: Oxford University Press, 1998), acknowledges internal dissent and class division but blames defeat on military losses. David Williams, Teresa Crisp Williams, and David Carlson, *Plain Folk in a Rich Man's War: Class and Dissent in Georgia* (Gainesville: University Press of Florida, 2002), unequivocally argue that the southern yeomanry concluded the war did not serve their class interests and that their opposition contributed to Union victory. Jonathan Dean Sarris, *A Separate Civil War: Communities in Conflict in the Mountain South* (Charlottesville: University of Virginia Press, 2006), 2–5, believes "local power and influence" was more important to the internal civil war in northern Georgia than was ideology. Although many southern home front studies look at Virginia, two works on different regions of Tennessee emphasize its uniqueness. Robert Tracy McKenzie, *Lincolnites and Rebels: A Divided Town in the American Civil War* (New York: Oxford University Press, 2006), studies Knoxville, which had many Confederate supporters, although eastern Tennessee was strongly Unionist. Looking at middle Tennessee, Stephen V. Ash, *Middle Tennessee Society Transformed, 1860–1870: War and Peace in the Upper South* (Baton Rouge: Louisiana State University Press, 1988), 251–253, reaches conclusions similar to mine: that changes in race relations were the war's greatest transformation. In middle Tennessee, whites regressed, retreating to the rural areas and embracing tradition, whereas blacks moved forward, building institutions and claiming identities as citizens and free laborers.

42. J. Matthew Gallman, *Mastering Wartime: A Social History of Philadelphia during the Civil War* (Cambridge, Mass.: Cambridge University Press, 1990), one of the best studies of the home front North, argues that the war's changes were rooted in prewar institutions. Edmund J. Raus, Jr., *Banners South: A Northern Community at War* (Kent, Ohio: Kent State University Press, 2005), follows Cortland, New York, soldiers through the war. In addition to Gallman's work, studies of urban areas include Ernest A. McKay, *The Civil War and New York City* (Syracuse, N.Y.: Syracuse University Press, 1990); Thomas H. O'Connor, *Civil War Boston: Home Front and Battlefield* (Boston: Northeastern University Press, 1997); and Theodore J. Karamanski, *Rally 'Round the Flag: Chicago and the Civil War* (Chicago: Nelson-Hall, 1993). Other works include Michael H. Frisch, *Town into City: Springfield, Massachusetts, and the Meaning of Community, 1840–1880* (Cambridge, Mass.: Harvard University Press, 1972), which focuses on urbanization; Grace Palladino, *Another Civil War: Labor, Capital, and the State in the Anthracite Regions of Pennsylvania, 1840–68* (Urbana: University of Illinois Press, 1990), on labor unrest; and Kerry A. Trask, *Fire*

Within: A Civil War Narrative from Wisconsin (Kent, Ohio: Kent State University Press, 1995), on ethnic divisions. Like Trask, Don Harrison Doyle, *The Social Order of a Frontier Community: Jacksonville, Illinois, 1825–70* (Urbana: University of Illinois Press, 1978), emphasizes that the war strengthened community. Some Civil War studies have been particularly concerned with the emergence of northern nationalism. See Melinda Lawson, *Patriot Fires: Forging a New American Nationalism in the Civil War North* (Lawrence: University Press of Kansas, 2002), and Susan-Mary Grant, "'The Charter of Its Birthright': The Civil War and American Nationalism," in *Legacy of Disunion: The Enduring Significance of the American Civil War,* ed. Susan-Mary Grant and Peter J. Parish (Baton Rouge: Louisiana State University Press, 2003), 188–206.

43. Peter S. Carmichael, *The Last Generation: Young Virginians in Peace, War, and Reunion* (Chapel Hill: University of North Carolina Press, 2005), similarly uses a generational focus but looks only at men who served in the Army of Northern Virginia to see why the last slaveholding generation came to support secession and war. Carmichael concentrates on the prewar and wartime period, devoting only one chapter to Reconstruction.

44. Jill Lepore, "Historians Who Love Too Much: Reflections on Microhistory and Biography," *Journal of American History* 88 (June 2001): 129–144; Richard D. Brown, "Microhistory and the Post-modern Challenge," *Journal of the Early Republic* 23 (Spring 2003): 1–20; J. Matthew Gallman, *The North Fights the Civil War: The Home Front* (Chicago: Ivan R. Dee, 1994); Phillip Shaw Paludan, *"A People's Contest": The Union and Civil War, 1861–1865* (Lawrence: University Press of Kansas, 1996). Adam I. P. Smith, *The American Civil War* (New York: Palgrave Macmillan, 2007), is more interested in how civilians perceived the war, not how they experienced it. Eric Foner, *Politics and Ideology in the Age of the Civil War* (New York: Oxford University Press, 1980), 3.

45. U.S. Census Office, *Population Schedules of the Eighth Census of the United States, 1860* (Washington, D.C.: National Archives, 1967); U.S. Census Office, *Population Schedules of the Ninth Census of the United States, 1870* (Washington, D.C.: National Archives, 1965); U.S. Census Office, *The Statistics of Wealth and Industry in the United States* (Washington, D.C.: Government Printing Office, 1872), 81; Thornbrough, *Indiana in the Civil War Era*, 365n6, 370–371, 383; Putnam County Sesquicentennial Committee, *Journey through Putnam County History*, 168–169; D. R. Eckels to J. G. Davis, February 16, 1854, folder 9, box 1, Davis Papers, IHS; *Indianapolis Daily State Sentinel,* February 23, 1856; *Putnam Banner,* March 15, 1854; U.S. Census Office, *Agriculture of the United States 1860: Compiled from the Original Returns of the Eighth Census* (Washington, D.C.: Government Printing Office, 1864), xxix, xlvi, cvii, 42–45.

46. Thornbrough, *Indiana in the Civil War Era*, 417.

47. U.S. Bureau of the Census, *Historical Statistics of the United States: Colonial Times to 1957* (Washington, D.C.: Department of Commerce, 1965), 684–685, 688–689; Marc Egnal, *Clash of Extremes: The Economic Origins of the Civil War* (New York: Hill and Wang, 2009), 52–53.

48. Putnam County Sesquicentennial Committee, *Journey through Putnam County History,* 32; *Putnam County Sentinel,* December 6, 20, 1849, February 7, July 25, 1850; Solomon Akers to John G. Davis, November 30, 1857, folder 8, box 2, Davis Papers, IHS; *Putnam Republican Banner,* October 5, 1859; Danl A. Farley to John G. Davis, November 1, 1858, folder 10, box 3, Davis Papers, IHS; U.S. Census Office, *Population of the United States in 1860: Compiled from the Original Returns of the Eighth Census* (Washington, D.C.: Government Printing Office, 1864), xxxiii; Richard K. Vedder and Lowell E. Gallaway, "Migration and the Old Northwest," in *Essays in Nineteenth Century Economic History: The Old Northwest,* ed. David C. Klingaman and Richard K. Vedder (Athens: Ohio University Press, 1975), 159–176. During the 1860s, twice as many Hoosiers left the state as new migrants moved in. The following decade, slightly more

migrants went to Indiana than left it. U.S. Census Office, *The Statistics of the Population of the United States Census Compiled from the Returns of the Ninth Census* (Washington, D.C.: Government Printing Office, 1872), 328–329; U.S. Census Office, *Statistics of the Population of the United States at the Tenth Census* (Washington, D.C.: Government Printing Office, 1883), 480–481. On out-migration, see John Mack Faragher, *Sugar Creek: Life on the Illinois Prairie* (New Haven, Conn.: Yale University Press, 1986), 50; Doyle, *Social Order of a Frontier Community*, 95–118; George B. Manhart, *DePauw through the Years*, 2 vols. (Greencastle, Ind.: DePauw University, 1962), 1:167.

49. U.S. Census Office, *Population Schedules of the Seventh Census of the United States, 1850* (Washington, D.C.: National Archives, 1963); Nicole Etcheson, *The Emerging Midwest: Upland Southerners and the Political Culture of the Old Northwest, 1787–1861* (Bloomington: Indiana University Press, 1996), 2; Gregory S. Rose, "Hoosier Origins: The Nativity of Indiana's United States–Born Population in 1850," *Indiana Magazine of History* 81 (September 1985): 201–232.

50. Ann L. Skene and Denise DeBoy, *Putnam County, Indiana Naturalization Records, 1854–1929* (Indianapolis: Indiana State Archives, 1999); James J. Divita, "Without Tenement: The State of Indiana Ethnic History," in *The State of Indiana History 2000: Papers Presented at the Indiana Historical Society's Grand Opening*, ed. Robert M. Taylor, Jr. (Indianapolis: Indiana Historical Society, 2001), 91–124, esp. 100–102; Thornbrough, *Indiana in the Civil War Era*, 545–551; Gregory S. Rose, "The Distribution of Indiana's Ethnic and Racial Minorities in 1850," *Indiana Magazine of History* 87 (September 1991): 224–260; U.S. Census Office, *Population Schedules of the Seventh Census*. For an economic analysis of antebellum immigration, see Joseph P. Ferrie, *Yankeys Now: Immigrants in the Antebellum United States, 1840 to 1860* (New York: Oxford University Press, 1999). For the rise of nativism, see Tyler Anbinder, *Nativism and Slavery: The Northern Know Nothings and the Politics of the 1850s* (New York: Oxford University Press, 1992), 3–51. Although Anbinder acknowledges the deep anti-Catholicism of the nativists, he argues political nativism waxed and waned with antislavery. Civil Order Book, D, 1848–1853, Clerk's Office, Putnam County Courthouse, Greencastle, Ind.; *Putnam Banner*, May 31, 1854.

51. *Putnam Republican Banner*, January 17, 1855.

52. *Putnam County Sentinel*, July 14, 1853; Putnam County Sesquicentennial Committee, *Journey through Putnam County History*, 192; Jack W. Porter, *The Catholic Church in Greencastle, Putnam County, Indiana, 1848–1979* (Greencastle, Ind.: Saint Paul the Apostle Church, 1979), 18–20; Bainbridge Cemetery, Bainbridge, Ind.; Lynn Rainville, "Hanover Deathscapes: Mortuary Variability in New Hampshire, 1770–1920," *Ethnohistory* 46 (Summer 1999): 541–597, esp. 559–560.

53. James M. McPherson, *Battle Cry of Freedom: The Civil War Era* (New York: Oxford University Press, 1988), 859–862; George M. Fredrickson, "Nineteenth-Century American History," in *Imagined Histories: American Historians Interpret the Past*, ed. Anthony Molho and Gordon S. Wood (Princeton, N.J.: Princeton University Press, 1998), 164–184; J. Matthew Gallman, "Afterward," in *An Uncommon Time: The Civil War and the Northern Home Front*, ed. Paul A. Cimbala and Randall M. Miller (New York: Fordham University Press, 2002), 345–351.

Chapter One. A Northern Party

1. *Biographical Directory of the American Congress, 1774–1971* (Washington, D.C.: Government Printing Office, 1971), 1374; Jesse W. Weik, *History of Putnam County, Indiana* (Indianapolis: Bowen, 1910), 708–714.

2. *Putnam Republican Banner,* November 1, 1860.

3. Michael F. Holt, *The Rise and Fall of the American Whig Party: Jacksonian Politics and the Onset of the Civil War* (New York: Oxford University Press, 1999), is the definitive study of the Whigs. Marc Egnal in his economic interpretation of the coming of the Civil War shows Putnam County, formerly a Whig enclave, as unaligned in the 1856 election as it made the transition from Whig to Republican; see Egnal, *Clash of Extremes: The Economic Origins of the Civil War* (New York: Hill and Wang, 2009), 222–223. The best studies of the rise of the Republican party are Eric Foner, *Free Soil, Free Labor, Free Men: The Ideology the Republican Party before the Civil War* (New York: Oxford University Press, 1995), and William Gienapp, *Origins of the Republican Party, 1852–56* (New York: Oxford University Press, 1987). Foner emphasizes a northern free labor ideology seemingly threatened by slavery expansion. Gienapp highlights the emergence of the antislavery movement rather than nativism as the salient issue of the 1850s. For the role of nativist politics in the political realignment of the 1850s, see Tyler Anbinder, *Nativism and Slavery: The Northern Know Nothings and the Politics of the 1850s* (New York: Oxford University Press, 1992). Foner's *Free Soil, Free Labor, Free Men* did not explore the meaning of the North for Democrats. Susan-Mary Grant examines northern nationalism, but like Foner's, her North is primarily that of the Republican party and its ideology; see Grant, *North over South: Northern Nationalism and American Identity in the Antebellum Era* (Lawrence: University Press of Kansas, 2000). Democrats prided themselves on being a national party, in contrast to the Republicans with their northern sectionalism, as detailed by Jean H. Baker in *Affairs of Party: The Political Culture of Northern Democrats in the Mid-Nineteenth Century* (Ithaca, N.Y.: Cornell University Press, 1983). David M. Potter, *The Impending Crisis, 1848–1861* (New York: Harper & Row, 1976), and Eric Walther, *The Shattering of the Union: America in the 1850s* (Wilmington, Del.: SR Books, 2003), are good overviews of the events that led to the Civil War. Michael A. Morrison shows slavery expansion increasingly divided the United States in *Slavery and the American West: The Eclipse of Manifest Destiny and the Coming of the Civil War* (Chapel Hill: University of North Carolina Press, 1997). William C. Freehling, *The Road to Disunion,* vol. 2, *The Secessionists Triumphant, 1854–1861* (New York: Oxford University Press, 2007), details the crafting of southern nationalism, and Charles B. Dew, *Apostles of Disunion: Southern Secession Commissioners and the Causes of the Civil War* (Charlottesville: University of Virginia Press, 2001), examines its nature at the point of secession. Russell McClintock examines why northern leaders would not allow secession in *Lincoln and the Decision for War: The Northern Response to Secession* (Chapel Hill: University of North Carolina Press, 2008).

4. "Biographical Sketch of the Hon. D. R. Eckels, Judge of the Seventh Judicial Circuit of Indiana, Prepared by W. C. Larrabee L.L.D., Professor of Mathematics in Asbury University, for the United States Law Magazine, at the Instance of Members of the Putnam County Bar, February, 1852," in D. R. Eckels to J. G. Davis, February 2, 1853, folder 5, box 1, John Givan Davis Papers, William Henry Smith Memorial Library, Indiana Historical Society (hereafter cited as IHS), Indianapolis; Gillum Ridpath, "Putnam County, Ind.," *Atlas of Putnam Co., Indiana to Which Are Added Various General Maps, History, Statistics, Illustrations* (Chicago: J. H. Beers, 1879), 7; Weik, *History of Putnam County,* 66–68; Delana R. Eckels to J. G. Davis, February 28, 1853, folder 5, box 1, Davis Papers, IHS; *Putnam County Sentinel,* January 16, 1851, September 30, October 14, 1852; Delana R. Eckels to H. S. Cauthorn, December 6, 1852, folder 11, box 1, Cauthorn-Stout Family Papers, William Henry Smith Memorial Library, IHS.

5. D. F. Farley to J. G. Davis, December 22, 1853, folder 6, box 1, Davis Papers, IHS.

6. James H. Madison, *The Indiana Way: A State History* (Bloomington: Indiana University Press, 1986), 83–86; "Biographical Sketch of the Hon. D. R. Eckels."

7. *Indianapolis Daily State Sentinel,* February 23, 1856; Margaretta Stevenson, comp., *Stevenson Family History from the Eastern Shore of Maryland to Woodford County, Kentucky to Putnam County, Indiana with Allied Families* (New York: privately published, 1966), 99–100; A. G. Cavins to Father, October 22, 1847, Aden G. Cavins, Alumni Files, Archives and Special Collections, DePauw University, Greencastle, Ind.; A. M. S. Harrah to Husband, June 21, 1847, folder 3, box 1, Almira Maria Scott Harrah Papers, William Henry Smith Memorial Library, IHS.

8. J. Richard Beste, *The Wabash: Or Adventures of an English Gentleman's Family in the Interior of America,* 2 vols. (London: Hurst and Blackett, 1855), 1:311–312.

9. *Putnam County Sentinel,* February 27, 1851.

10. Ibid., March 27, 1851.

11. Ibid., April 10, 1851; Ridpath, "Putnam County, Ind.," 7; *Biographical and Historical Record of Putnam County, Indiana* (Chicago: Lewis Publishing, 1887; reprinted 1975), 310–311; Beste, *Wabash,* 1:313. Indiana's railroad mileage grew from 212 miles in 1850 to 2,163 in 1860. Emma Lou Thornbrough, *Indiana in the Civil War Era, 1850–1880* (Indianapolis: Indiana Historical Bureau, 1965), 332.

12. Weik, *History of Putnam County,* 38–41.

13. *Putnam Republican Banner,* November 23, 1855, February 27, 1856, September 6, 1866; Sarah Seller Wright and Minetta L. Wright, *The Seller Family in Putnam County, Indiana* (n.p.: Putnam County Historical Society, 1956); (Greencastle) *Indiana Press,* February 12, 1859.

14. *Putnam Republican Banner,* February 16, 1859; Thornbrough, *Indiana in the Civil War Era,* 431.

15. George B. Manhart, *DePauw through the Years,* 2 vols. (Greencastle, Ind.: DePauw University, 1962), 1:31–33, 75–77; Delana Eckels v. The Comm Council of the Town of Greencastle, p. 439, Civil Order Book, Putnam Com. Pleas Court, 4, September 5, 1859–May 7, 1862, Clerk's Office, Putnam County Courthouse, Greencastle, Ind.; *Putnam County Sentinel,* August 9, 1849; *Putnam Republican Banner,* March 18, 1857; Putnam County Sesquicentennial Committee, *A Journey through Putnam County History* (n.p., 1966), 198.

16. Thornbrough, *Indiana in the Civil War Era,* 466–468.

17. D. R. Eckels to J. G. Davis, December 25, 1854, folder 16, box 1, Davis Papers, IHS.

18. Thornbrough, *Indiana in the Civil War Era,* 462–465.

19. *Putnam Republican Banner,* May 13, 1857; Thornbrough, *Indiana in the Civil War Era,* 461–462.

20. Weik, *History of Putnam County,* 86–90; Thornbrough, *Indiana in the Civil War Era,* 490.

21. Miles to Father, June 5, 1853, folder 2, box 7, Calvin Fletcher Papers, William Henry Smith Memorial Library, IHS.

22. *Putnam Republican Banner,* May 23, 1855.

23. D. to John G. Davis, August 24, 1854, folder 5, box 1, Davis Papers, IHS; Daniels to Jno. G. Davis, October 12, 1854, folder 16, ibid.; *Indiana Daily State Sentinel,* May 24, 1855; *Weekly Indiana State Sentinel,* June 14, 1855; *Indiana Sentinel,* July 12, 1855.

24. M. J. Lynch to J. G. Davis, February 15, 1853, folder 5, box 1, Davis Papers, IHS.

25. Patrick Rigney to [John G. Davis], [February?], 1853, ibid.; Jno. C. Turk to [John G. Davis], February 8, 1853, ibid.; John S. Jennings to John G. Davis, February 16, 1853, ibid.

26. Civil Order Book, 6, 1863–1866, Clerk's Office, Putnam County Courthouse, Greencastle, Ind., 29, 267; Patrick Heaney tombstone, Bainbridge Cemetery, Bainbridge, Ind.

27. *Greencastle Sentinel,* quoted in *Putnam Banner,* July 20, 1853.

28. *Putnam Republican Banner,* March 31, 1858, May 18, 1859.

29. *Putnam Republican Banner,* January 16, 1856; Miles to Father, March 14, 1853, folder 1, box 7, Fletcher Papers, IHS; Miles to Father, March 15, 1853, ibid.

30. *Putnam Banner,* November 2, 1853.

31. Ridpath, "Putnam County, Ind.," 6. The classic text on economic development and its social ramifications is Charles Sellers, *The Market Revolution: Jacksonian America, 1815–1846* (New York: Oxford University Press, 1991). The essays in Steven Hahn and Jonathan Prude, eds., *The Countryside in the Age of Capitalist Transformation: Essays in the Social History of Rural America* (Chapel Hill: University of North Carolina Press, 1985), seek to understand economic change in rural areas, although the emphasis is on the Northeast and the South rather than the Midwest. For the transformation of the United States into "one of the world's great drinking countries" and the pervasiveness of alcohol, see W. J. Rorabaugh, *The Alcoholic Republic: An American Tradition* (New York: Oxford University Press, 1979). Ian R. Tyrrell, *Sobering Up: From Temperance to Prohibition in Antebellum America, 1800–1860* (Westport, Conn.: Greenwood Press, 1979), details the development of the temperance movement that grew as a response to the "alcoholic republic." Reformers saw temperance not just as a solution to excessive drinking but also as a cure for many social evils linked to drinking, including poverty and crime. Tyrrell also discusses the movement from moral persuasion to legal coercion to enforced abstinence. Temperance was most successful in New England and least successful in the South. The Midwest's plentiful corn and its heavy settlement by Southerners limited temperance's appeal. Only Indiana, Michigan, and Iowa passed the Maine law. See Tyrrell, *Sobering Up,* 1–12, 244. Tyrrell acknowledges that industrialists wanted a sober labor force. Paul E. Johnson shows the intersection of industrialization, temperance, and evangelical religion in *A Shopkeeper's Millennium: Society and Revivals in Rochester, New York, 1815–1837* (New York: Hill and Wang, 1978).

32. Thornbrough, *Indiana in the Civil War Era,* 57–58.

33. *Putnam County Sentinel,* July 22, 1852.

34. Thornbrough, *Indiana in the Civil War Era,* 29–34, 57–58, 67–69; Samuel Landes to James [Embree], February 18, 1855, folder 1, box 5, Lucius C. Embree Papers, Manuscripts of the Indiana Division, Indiana State Library (hereafter cited as ISL), Indianapolis.

35. Thornbrough, *Indiana in the Civil War Era,* 67–69.

36. *Putnam Republican Banner,* May 14, 1856; Miles to Father, June 14, 1853, folder 2, box 7, Fletcher Papers, IHS.

37. *Putnam Republican Banner,* November 18, 1857, January 27, October 27, 1858, February 2, April 6, 1859; (Greencastle) *Indiana Press,* July 10, 1858.

38. Delana R. Eckels to H. S. Cauthorn, December 6, 1852, folder 11, box 1, Cauthorn-Stout Family Papers, IHS.

39. *Putnam Banner,* April 26, 1854; Delana R. Eckels to John G. Davis, April 23, 1854, microfilm, Davis Papers, IHS.

40. *Putnam County Sentinel,* August 9, November 8, 1849; Wm. H. Durham to John G. Davis, February 15, 1855, folder 2, box 2, Davis Papers, IHS.

41. H. B. Pickett to John G. Davis, May 31, 1854, folder 12, box 1, Davis Papers, IHS.

42. *Putnam Republican Banner,* August 20, 1856.

43. Weik, *History of Putnam County,* 707–710; Putnam County Sesquicentennial Committee, *Journey through Putnam County History,* 259–260; Ridpath, "Putnam County, Ind.," 5; *Biographical Directory of the American Congress,* 1374.

44. *Congressional Globe Appendix,* 29th Cong., 2nd sess. (Washington, D.C., 1847), 233–238.

45. Weik, *History of Putnam County,* 709; Morrison, *Slavery and the American West,* 75; *Congressional Globe Appendix,* 236.

46. *Congressional Globe Appendix,* 237–238; Donald F. Carmony, *Indiana, 1816–1850: The Pioneer Era* (Indianapolis: Indiana Historical Bureau, 1998), 629.

47. Dorothy Riker and Gayle Thornbrough, *Indiana Election Returns, 1816–1851* (Indianapolis: Indiana Historical Bureau, 1960), 116.

48. Thornbrough, *Indiana in the Civil War Era,* 41, 709; Carmony, *Indiana, 1816–1850,* 548; Riker and Thornbrough, *Indiana Election Returns,* 157, 284, 295, 307, 318, 329, 340, 351, 360, 300, 334, 364; *Putnam Republican Banner,* April 22, 1857.

49. Riker and Thornbrough, *Indiana Election Returns,* 57, 61, 66, 107–108, 112, 116, 120, 124–125; Kenneth C. Martis, *The Historical Atlas of United States Congressional Districts, 1789–1983* (New York: Free Press, 1982), 82–113; Holt, *Rise and Fall of the American Whig Party,* 441.

50. *Indiana State Sentinel,* November 7, 1850, June 19, 26, 1851.

51. Ibid., November 7, 12, 1850, June 19, 26, 1851; *Indiana State Journal,* June 13, 1851; *Putnam County Sentinel,* June 19, 1851.

52. Holt, *Rise and Fall of the American Whig Party,* 559, 662; *Putnam County Sentinel,* July 24, 1851.

53. *Indiana State Journal,* June 13, 1851; *Indiana State Sentinel,* November 7, 1850, June 19, 26, July 10, 1851; *Putnam County Sentinel,* June 19, 1851.

54. E. W. McGaughey to A. Crane, July 21, 1851, Abiathar Crane Papers, William Henry Smith Memorial Library, IHS; A. Crane to J. G. Davis, July 30, 1851, folder 4, box 1, Davis Papers, IHS.

55. *Indiana State Journal,* June 14, 1851.

56. Thornbrough, *Indiana in the Civil War Era,* 3.

57. Ibid., 47.

58. *Putnam County Sentinel,* September 26, October 3, November 21, 1850; *Indiana State Sentinel,* August 14, 1851.

59. *Putnam County Sentinel,* July 24, 1851.

60. McGaughey objected to the boundary bill because the federal government assumed Texas's debt in return for that state relinquishing its claims to eastern New Mexico, territory to which McGaughey felt Texas had no right. *Putnam County Sentinel,* July 13, September 26, October 3, November 21, 1850; *Indiana State Sentinel,* August 14, 1851.

61. *Putnam County Sentinel,* August 7, 14, 1851.

62. *Indiana State Sentinel,* November 25, 1852; *Indiana State Sentinel,* October 21, 28, November 25, 1852. The Democratic candidate, Franklin Pierce, got 52 percent of Indiana's vote in 1852 versus 46 percent of the county's vote. The Whig Winfield Scott got 44 percent of the state vote but 54 percent of the county's. The Free-Soil candidate, Hale, won 4 percent of the state vote but less than 1 percent of the county vote.

63. Holt, *Rise and Fall of the American Whig Party,* xiii, 699–700, 760–761.

64. Gayle Thornbrough, Dorothy L. Riker, and Paula Corpuz, eds., *The Diary of Calvin Fletcher,* 9 vols. (Indianapolis: Indiana Historical Society, 1972–1983), 6:428.

65. *Biographical Directory of the American Congress,* 833.

66. Nicole Etcheson, *Bleeding Kansas: Contested Liberty in the Civil War Era* (Lawrence: University Press of Kansas, 2004), 9–27; *Speech of Hon. Jno. G. Davis, of Indiana, against the Admission of Kansas into the Union under the Lecompton Constitution,* Pamphlet Collection, William Henry Smith Memorial Library, IHS, 1.

67. Delana R. Eckels to J. G. Davis, February 16, 1854, folder 9, box 1, Davis Papers, IHS.

68. D. R. Eckels to John, May 16, 1854, folder 12, ibid.

69. Delana R. Eckels to H. S. Cauthorn, December 6, 1852, folder 11, box 1, Cauthorn-Stout Family Papers, IHS.

70. *Putnam Banner,* March 1, 1854.

71. Robert Mann and A. Graydon to John G. Davis, April 6, 1854, folder 11, box 1, Davis Papers, IHS.

72. R. S. Hamilton to J. G. Davis, February 13, 1854, folder 9, ibid.

73. *Putnam Banner,* March 15, 1854.

74. John S. Jennings to Davis, May 8, 1854, folder 12, box 1, Davis Papers, IHS; James Ricketts to John G. Davis, May 10, 1854, ibid.; D. A. Farley to John G. Davis, March 20, 1854, folder 10, ibid.; Lewis H. Sands to Davis, July 26, 1854, folder 14, ibid.

75. Thornbrough, *Indiana in the Civil War Era,* 55–67; Martis, *Historical Atlas,* 82–113; *Indiana State Sentinel,* October 26, 1854; *Biographical Directory of the American Congress,* 1668. Scott is listed as a Republican in the congressional biography, but local Democrats called him a Know-Nothing. Daniel A. Farley to John G. Davis, September 24, 1854, folder 15, box 1, Davis Papers, IHS; Harvey D. Scott, *Letter of Harvey D. Scott to His Constituents of the Seventh Congressional District of Indiana* (Washington, D.C.: Buell & Blanchard, 1856).

76. Thornbrough, *Indiana in the Civil War Era,* 55–67; Martis, *Historical Atlas,* 82–113; *Indianapolis Daily State Sentinel,* March 27, April 7, 1856.

77. Weik, *History of Putnam County,* 599–601; Record of Official Bonds, 1844–1911, Putnam County, Clerk's Office, Putnam County Courthouse, Greencastle, Ind., 19, 28, 47; Richard M. Hazelett, "'Little Black Book': Memoirs of Richard M. Hazelett," William Henry Smith Memorial Library, IHS, 14–17; *Putnam Republican Banner,* July 18, 1855; Michael F. Holt, "Making and Mobilizing the Republican Party, 1854–1860," in *The Birth of the Grand Old Party: The Republicans' First Generation,* ed. Robert F. Engs and Randall M. Miller (Philadelphia: University of Pennsylvania Press, 2002), 29–59. Anbinder argues that the Know-Nothings dominated Indiana's anti-Democratic fusion movement and that Indiana's anti-Democratic vote in 1854 contained elements of temperance and antislavery adherence as well as anti-Catholic and anti-immigrant sentiment. Anbinder, *Nativism and Slavery,* 71–73.

78. *Putnam Republican Banner,* February 24, 1858. See Holt, *Rise and Fall of the American Whig Party,* 862–865, on the importance of the Whigs in the Indiana Republican party.

79. *Putnam Republican Banner,* February 29, 1860; E. W. McGaughey to Henry L. Lane, Rockville, June 20, 1848, box 1, H. S. Lane Manuscripts, Lilly Library, Indiana University, Bloomington; *Atlas of Putnam Co.,* 57.

80. *Putnam Republican Banner,* September 3, 17, 1856.

81. Thornbrough, *Indiana in the Civil War Era,* 76; *Indianapolis Daily State Sentinel,* November 8, 1856.

82. *Putnam Republican Banner,* May 14, June 25, 1856; *Indiana State Journal,* July 1, 1856; Martis, *Historical Atlas,* 82–113; *Indianapolis Daily State Sentinel,* October 31, 1856. Davis received 54 percent of the total vote in the Seventh Congressional District.

83. Etcheson, *Bleeding Kansas,* 139–167.

84. *Speech of Hon. Jno. G. Davis,* 1–3, 9, 11.

85. *Congressional Globe,* 35th Cong., 1st sess., p. 1372, A Century of Lawmaking for a New Nation: U.S. Congressional Documents and Debates, 1774–1875, Library of Congress, available at http://memory.loc.gov.

86. Danl Sigler to [John G. Davis], April 8, 1858, folder 2, box 3, Davis Papers, IHS.

87. Etcheson, *Bleeding Kansas,* 168–189; James L. Huston, *Stephen A. Douglas and the*

Dilemmas of Democratic Equality (Lanham, Md.: Rowman & Littlefield, 2007), 140; *Congressional Globe*, 35th Cong., 1st sess., p. 1906.

88. D. Sigler to J. G. Davis, May 6, 1858, folder 5, box 3, Davis Papers, IHS. See also D. E. Williamson to John G. Davis, May 8, 1858, ibid.

89. A. Bowen to J. W. Davis, February 14, 1858, folder 16, box 2, ibid.

90. (Greencastle) *Indiana Press,* June 5, 1858.

91. *Indiana Daily State Sentinel,* May 25, 1858; John S. Jennings to John G. Davis, May 29, 1858, folder 6, box 3, Davis Papers, IHS; Order Book 6, May 1964 [*sic*]–October 1867, Clerk's Office, Putnam County Courthouse, Greencastle, Ind.

92. *Indiana Daily State Sentinel,* June 24, 25, 1858.

93. *Indiana State Journal,* June 25, 1858.

94. Lewis H. Sands to Jno. G. Davis, March 28, 1857, folder 5, box 2, Davis Papers, IHS*; Putnam Republican Banner,* July 29, 1857; J. Forney to J. S. Black, May 26, 1858, roll 9, Jeremiah S. Black Papers, Library of Congress, Washington, D.C.; J. Forney to J. S. Black, June 25, 1858, ibid.; J. Forney to J. S. Black, May 1, 1858, ibid.

95. (Greencastle) *Indiana Press,* April 9, 1859.

96. H. Secrest to John G. Davis, January 14, 1858, folder 13, box 2, Davis Papers, IHS; A. J. Smedley to John G. Davis, February 5, 1858, folder 15, ibid.

97. (Greencastle) *Indiana Press,* June 19, 1858.

98. *Terre Haute Journal,* quoted in *Indiana Daily State Sentinel,* June 7, 1858.

99. *Speech of Hon. Jno. G. Davis,* 14–15.

100. D. A. Farley to John G. Davis, June 18, 1858, folder 7, box 3, Davis Papers, IHS; *Weekly Indiana State Sentinel,* July 21, 1858.

101. (Greencastle) *Indiana Press,* June 5, July 16, October 9, 1858.

102. M. J. Fletcher to Father, February 1858, folder 10, box 8, Fletcher Papers, IHS.

103. Worthington B. Williams to J. G. Davis, January 10, 1859, folder 12, box 3, Davis Papers, IHS.

104. James McMurry to J. G. Davis, July 12, 1858, folder 8, ibid.; William Aldridge to John G. Davis, August 10, 1858, ibid.; *Indiana State Journal,* July 13, 1858.

105. D. A. Farly to John G. Davis, July 27, 1858, folder 8, box 3, Davis Papers, IHS.

106. Thornbrough, *Indiana in the Civil War Era,* 82–83; (Greencastle) *Indiana Press,* October 23, 1858.

107. D. A. Farly to John G. Davis, October 20, 1858, folder 9, box 3, Davis Papers, IHS; John Hanna to John G. Davis, October 30, 1858, ibid.

108. "Speech at Chicago, Illinois, March 1, 1859," in *The Collected Works of Abraham Lincoln,* ed. Roy P. Basler, 8 vols. (New Brunswick, N.J.: Rutgers University Press, 1953), 3:367; C. W. Brown, John A. Matson, D. C. Donnohue to Jno. G. Davis, June 29, 1859, microfilm, Davis Papers, IHS; Wm Tn Byerley, R Slavens Jr., William Knowles, Robt Spencer Jr., J P Alexander, Corresponding Committe, to John G. Davis, December 24, 1859, folder 17, box 3, ibid.; Henry B. Pickett to John G. Davis, February 13, 1859, folder 13, ibid.

109. John Cowgill to Jno. G. Davis, November 7, 1859, folder 16, ibid.

110. A. M. Puett to J. G. Davis, January 15, 1860, folder 1, box 4, ibid.; *Weekly Indiana State Sentinel,* January 18, 1860; Andy Grimes to John G. Davis, January 30, 1860, microfilm, Davis Papers, IHS.

111. *Putnam Republican Banner,* November 16, December 7, 1859, January 25, 1860; Potter, *Impending Crisis,* 417; Thornbrough, *Indiana in the Civil War Era,* 87; Doris Kearns Goodwin, *Team of Rivals: The Political Genius of Abraham Lincoln* (New York: Simon & Schuster, 2005), 245.

112. Speech at Greencastle, February 25, 1860 [typescript], box 1, H. S. Lane Manuscripts, Lilly Library, Indiana University, Bloomington.

113. Harold Holzer, *Lincoln President-Elect: Abraham Lincoln and the Great Secession Winter, 1860–1861* (New York: Simon & Schuster, 2008), 149; *Putnam Republican Banner,* May 31, 1860.

114. Potter, *Impending Crisis,* 419; William B. Hesseltine, ed., *Three against Lincoln: Murat Halstead Reports the Caucuses of 1860* (Baton Rouge: Louisiana State University Press, 1960), 161–166.

115. *Putnam Republican Banner,* August 22, 1855.

116. (Greencastle) *Indiana Press,* November 20, 1858.

117. A. Bowen to J. W. Davis, February 14, 1858, folder 16, box 2, Davis Papers, IHS; (Greencastle) *Indiana Press,* May 29, 1858.

118. Emerson David Fite, *The Presidential Campaign of 1860* (1911; reprint, Port Washington, N.Y.: Kennikat Press, 1967), 132.

119. *Putnam Republican Banner,* January 25, 1860.

120. Speech at Greencastle.

121. *Putnam Republican Banner,* November 2, 1859, January 25, 1860.

122. Ibid., October 26, 1859.

123. Ibid., December 21, 1859.

124. Ibid., January 25, 1860.

125. Ibid., February 29, 1860.

126. *Indiana State Journal,* July 14, 1860.

127. *Putnam Republican Banner,* July 19, 1860.

128. Ibid., October 4, 1860.

129. Ibid., February 13, March 26, April 9, 1856, May 24, 1860; *Biographical Directory of the American Congress,* 1063; *A Biographical History of Eminent and Self-Made Men of the State of Indiana,* 2 vols. (Cincinnati, Ohio: Western Biographical Publishing, 1880): 1:69; Civil Order Book, D, 1848–1853, Clerk's Office, Putnam County Courthouse, Greencastle, Ind., 261; Weik, *History of Putnam County,* 86–90; "Official Roster of Kansas, 1854–1925," in *Collections of the Kansas State Historical Society, 1923–1925,* vol. 16, ed. William Elsey Connelley (Topeka, Kans.: B. P. Walker, 1925), 658–745; John Hanna to John G. Davis, October 30, 1858, folder 9, box 3, Davis Papers, IHS; John Hanna to John G. Davis, January 25, 1859, folder 12, ibid.

130. *Indiana State Journal,* August 20, 1860. See Foner, *Free Soil, Free Labor, Free Men,* on the Republicans' free labor ideology.

131. On the investigations into efforts to influence votes on Lecompton, see Etcheson, *Bleeding Kansas,* 223.

132. Wm. S. Durham to Jno. G. Davis, May 19, 1860, folder 5, box 4, Davis Papers, IHS; Wilton A. Osborn to John G. Davis, May 21, 1860, ibid.

133. John Cowgill to Davis, November 7, 1859, folder 16, box 3, ibid.

134. A. M. Puett to J. G. Davis, December 22, 1859, microfilm, ibid.

135. A. M. Puett to J. G. Davis, January 3, 1860, folder 1, box 4, ibid.

136. Hesseltine, *Three against Lincoln,* 4–5; Potter, *Impending Crisis,* 407–414; "Speech, July 9, 1860," in *The Works of James Buchanan,* ed. John Bassett Moore (New York: Antiquarian Press, 1960), 10:457–460.

137. *Putnam Republican Banner,* January 4, May 17, 1860; Puett to Davis, January 15, 1860; Lewis H. Sands to Davis, May 8, 1860, folder 5, box 4, Davis Papers, IHS.

138. *Putnam Republican Banner,* June 28, July 12, 1860.

139. Ibid., August 16, 30, September 20, October 4, 1860.

140. Ibid., October 5, 1859, June 28, 1860; Thornbrough, *Indiana in the Civil War Era,* 88–89.

141. *Indiana Daily State Sentinel,* August 1, 1860.

142. *Indiana State Journal,* July 18, 1860.

143. *Indiana Daily State Sentinel,* August 1, 1860; Hesseltine, *Three against Lincoln,* 271.

144. Sean Wilentz, *The Rise of American Democracy: Jefferson to Lincoln* (New York: Norton, 2005), 758–766.

145. *Putnam Republican Banner,* June 28, July 5, August 2, 9, 1860; *Indiana Daily State Sentinel,* August 1, September 18, 1860; Manhart, *DePauw through the Years,* 1:150.

146. *Putnam Republican Banner,* September 27, October 4, 1860; *Indiana Daily State Sentinel,* July 21, 1860; Commencement program, July 18, 1849, folder 3, John W. Ray Papers, William Henry Smith Memorial Library, IHS; *Biographical Directory of the American Congress,* 1861; Putnam County Sesquicentennial Committee, *Journey through Putnam County History,* 220; *Indiana State Journal,* July 21, 1860; *Putnam Republican Banner,* September 6, October 18, 1860; *Indiana Daily State Sentinel,* July 26, 1860; Thornburgh, *Indiana in the Civil War Era,* 90–91. The Constitutional Union party had no ticket in Putnam County, and its state leader, Richard W. Thompson of Terre Haute, endorsed Lincoln, whom he considered acceptably "conservative." *Putnam Republican Banner,* September 6, 1860; Thornburgh, *Indiana in the Civil War Era,* 90–91.

147. *Indiana Press,* quoted in *Putnam Republican Banner,* October 18, 1860.

148. *Putnam Republican Banner,* October 18, November 15, 1860; Thornburgh, *Indiana in the Civil War Era,* 86–87, 95–96, 101; James E. St. Clair, "Henry S. Lane," in *The Governors of Indiana,* ed. Linda C. Gugin and James E. St. Clair (Indianapolis: Indiana Historical Society Press, 2006), 136.

149. Thornburgh, *Indiana in the Civil War Era,* 86–87, 95–96, 101; St. Clair, "Henry S. Lane," 136.

150. Quoted in *Putnam Republican Banner,* October 25, 1860.

151. Ibid., August 2, November 1, 8, 1860; Putnam County Sesquicentennial Committee, *Journey through Putnam County History,* 219; "Voting for America: United States Politics, 1840–2008," http://americanpast.richmond.edu/voting; Thornbrough, *Indiana in the Civil War Era,* 95–96; Potter, *Impending Crisis,* 437. Lincoln won 46 percent of the county's vote, Douglas 42 percent, Breckinridge 9 percent, and Bell 3 percent.

152. Byerley et al. to Davis.

153. Wilentz, *Rise of American Democracy,* 780–781; *Putnam Republican Banner,* December 27, 1860.

154. A. M. Puett to J. G. Davis, January 14, 1861, microfilm, Davis Papers, IHS.

155. *Putnam Republican Banner,* December 27, 1860.

156. Ibid., February 28, March 7, 1861; Potter, *Impending Crisis,* 533.

157. *Putnam Republican Banner,* January 17, 1861.

158. Ibid., December 13, 1860.

159. Puett to Davis, January 14, 1861.

160. Henry B. Pickett to John G. Davis, December 26, 1860, microfilm, Davis Papers, IHS.

161. (Indianapolis) *Daily State Sentinel,* April 15, 1861.

162. Ibid., April 13, 1861.

163. *Indianapolis Daily Journal,* April 12, 1861; *Indianapolis Journal,* April 26, 1870.

164. *Indianapolis Daily Journal,* April 12, 1861; *Greencastle Press,* April 17, 1861, quoted in *Parke County Republican,* May 1, 1861.

165. *Parke County Republican,* May 1, 1861.

Chapter Two. Appropriate Places

1. Miles to Father, June 1, 1852, folder 6, box 6, Calvin Fletcher Papers, William Henry Smith Memorial Library, Indiana Historical Society (hereafter cited as IHS), Indianapolis.

2. Nancy F. Cott, *Public Vows: A History of Marriage and the Nation* (Cambridge, Mass.: Harvard University Press, 2000), 61–62; Miles to Father, June 1, 1852. Daniel Scott Smith, "Family Limitation, Sexual Control, and Domestic Feminism in Victorian America," in *Clio's Consciousness Raised: New Perspectives on the History of Women,* ed. Mary S. Hartman and Lois Banner (New York: Harper & Row, 1974), 119–136, esp. 120–122; Rachel Filene Seidman, "A Monstrous Doctrine? Northern Women on Dependency during the Civil War," in *An Uncommon Time: The Civil War and the Northern Home Front,* ed. Paul A. Cimbala and Randall M. Miller (New York: Fordham University Press, 2002), 170–188. Classic works on woman's sphere have emphasized its connection to an emerging middle class in which women functioned less as productive members of a household economy and more as consumers reliant on male breadwinners. Scholars have debated the degree to which a separate sphere empowered or disempowered women. Nancy F. Cott, *The Bonds of Womanhood: "Woman's Sphere" in New England, 1780–1835* (New Haven, Conn.: Yale University Press, 1977); Mary P. Ryan, *Cradle of the Middle Class: The Family in Oneida County, New York, 1790–1865* (Cambridge: Cambridge University Press, 1981).

3. *Putnam County Sentinel,* April 25, 1850.

4. *Putnam Republican Banner,* July 20, 1859.

5. The transition from dependence to independence is a theme in studies of the passage to adulthood. Joseph F. Kett, *Rites of Passage: Adolescence in America, 1790 to the Present* (New York: Basic Books, 1977); J. M. Opal, *Beyond the Farm: National Ambitions in Rural New England* (Philadelphia: University of Pennsylvania Press, 2008), ix, 18–26, 43. E. Anthony Rotundo, *American Manhood: Transformations in Masculinity from the Revolution to the Modern Era* (New York: Basic Books, 1993), describes the importance of "self-made manhood" for middle-class Northern males. Although Rotundo argues the father's role declined in the nineteenth century, this was not the case with the Fletcher family. See ibid., 3, 25. Ironically, independence often came earlier to poorer youths than to middle-class youths such as the Fletchers, who relied on paternal resources to gain the professional training necessary for independence. This situation could result in a "jarring mixture" of freedom and dependence. See Kett, *Rites of Passage,* 29, 31. See also Daniel Walker Howe, *Making the American Self: Jonathan Edwards to Abraham Lincoln* (Cambridge, Mass.: Harvard University Press, 1997), 1–17, on self-making and character development, and Timothy R. Mahoney, *Provincial Lives: Middle-Class Experience in the Antebellum Middle West* (Cambridge: Cambridge University Press, 1999), for how the frontier could undermine patriarchal authority. Lorri Glover sees certain differences between Northern and Southern sons. In the South, evangelicalism was considered effeminate and race defined manliness, but in other regards, her account of Southern sons' need to balance deference with growing autonomy sounds much like the experience of Miles Fletcher. See Glover, *Southern Sons: Becoming Men in the New Nation* (Baltimore, Md.: Johns Hopkins University Press, 2007). On Calvin

Fletcher, see John H. Wigger, *Taking Heaven by Storm: Methodism and the Rise of Popular Christianity in America* (New York: Oxford University Press, 1998), 103.

6. Gayle Thornbrough, Dorothy L. Riker, and Paula Corpuz, eds., *The Diary of Calvin Fletcher,* 9 vols. (Indianapolis: Indiana Historical Society, 1972–1983), 4:105–106.

7. Wigger, *Taking Heaven by Storm,* 103; Thornbrough, Riker, and Corpuz, *Diary of Calvin Fletcher,* 6:21–22.

8. George B. Manhart, *DePauw through the Years,* 2 vols. (Greencastle, Ind.: DePauw University, 1962), 2:538; Miles to Father, February 2, 1860, folder 3, box 9, Fletcher Papers, IHS; Thornbrough, Riker, and Corpuz, *Diary of Calvin Fletcher,* 5:151, 6:xvi, 295, 344n80, 459.

9. Thornbrough, Riker, and Corpuz, *Diary of Calvin Fletcher,* 4:232, 229.

10. Ibid., 229.

11. Miles to Father, June 1, 1852; Opal, *Beyond the Farm,* 31; Karen Lystra, *Searching the Heart: Women, Men, and Romantic Love in Nineteenth-Century America* (New York: Oxford University Press, 1989), 161; Ellen K. Rothman, *Hands and Hearts: A History of Courtship in America* (New York: Basic Books, 1984), 119, 160.

12. Manhart, *DePauw through the Years,* 2:534; Thornbrough, Riker, and Corpuz, *Diary of Calvin Fletcher,* 4:105–106, 437n111; Wigger, *Taking Heaven by Storm,* 103.

13. Miles to Father, June 1, 1852.

14. Miles to Mother, September 25, 1852, folder 7, box 6, Fletcher Papers, IHS.

15. Ibid.

16. Miles to Father, March 15, 1853, folder 1, box 7, Fletcher Papers, IHS.

17. Thornbrough, Riker, and Corpuz, *Diary of Calvin Fletcher,* 6:xiii–xiv, 277, 290–291; *Indiana American,* quoted in *Putnam Republican Banner,* February 15, 1860.

18. Miles to Father, September 20, 1852, folder 7, box 6, Fletcher Papers, IHS; Miles to Father, June 26, 1854, folder 6, box 7, ibid.

19. Miles to Father, June 23, 1854, ibid.

20. Matilda to Aden, January 11, 1865, copy of letter in the author's possession.

21. Miles J. Fletcher to Father, August 31, 1853, folder 3, box 7, Fletcher Papers, IHS.

22. Miles J. Fletcher to Father, October 14, 1853, folder 4, ibid.

23. Miles to Father, September 20, 1852; Miles to Mother, September 25, 1852.

24. Miles to Father, October 5, 1852, ibid.

25. Thornbrough, Riker, and Corpuz, *Diary of Calvin Fletcher,* 5:102; Jennie to Father, December 15, 1862, folder 7, box 6, Fletcher Papers, IHS; Miles to Father, October 5, 1852; Miles to Father, December 21, 1852, folder 7, box 6, Fletcher Papers, IHS; Miles to Father, October 5, 1852.

26. Smith, "Family Limitation, Sexual Control," 121–123. For women's fertility, see also Paul Bourke and Donald DeBats, *Washington County: Politics and Community in Antebellum America* (Baltimore, Md.: Johns Hopkins University Press, 1995), 125; Thornbrough, Riker, and Corpuz, *Diary of Calvin Fletcher,* 5:513, 517, 526, 538.

27. Miles to Father, April 24, 1858, folder 10, box 8, Fletcher Papers, IHS.

28. Miles J. Fletcher to Father, May 17, 1858, ibid.; Ann Douglas Wood, "'The Fashionable Diseases': Women's Complaints and Their Treatment in Nineteenth-Century America," in *Clio's Consciousness Raised: New Perspectives on the History of Women,* ed. Mary S. Hartman and Lois Banner (New York: Harper & Row, 1974), 1–22, esp. 2–4; Sally G. McMillen, *Motherhood in the Old South: Pregnancy, Childbirth, and Infant Rearing* (Baton Rouge: Louisiana State University Press, 1990), 79–92; Carroll Smith-Rosenberg, "The Hysterical Woman: Sex Roles and Role

Conflict in 19th-Century America," *Social Research* 39 (Winter 1972): 652–678; Thornbrough, Riker, and Corpuz, *Diary of Calvin Fletcher*, 6:427–428.

29. Miles to Father, October 5, 1852.

30. Miles to Father, June 6, 1853, folder 2, box 7, Fletcher Papers, IHS; Miles to Father, June 14, 1853, ibid.

31. Thornbrough, Riker, and Corpuz, *Diary of Calvin Fletcher*, 5:147.

32. Miles to Dear Friend, March 3, 1857, folder 7, box 8, Fletcher Papers, IHS.

33. Thornbrough, Riker, and Corpuz, *Diary of Calvin Fletcher*, 5:354, 6:xiii–xiv; Order Book, 4 Civil, 1857–1862, Clerk's Office, Putnam County Courthouse, Greencastle, Ind., 13; Manhart, *DePauw through the Years*, 1:39.

34. Miles to Dear Friend, March 3, 1857; Miles to Father, April 27, 1857, folder 7, box 8, Fletcher Papers, IHS.

35. Miles J. Fletcher to Father, June 7, 1857, ibid.

36. Miles to Father, September 10, 1857, folder 8, ibid.; Miles to Father, September 21, 1857, ibid.; Miles J. Fletcher to Father, November 11, 1857, folder 9, ibid.; Miles J. Fletcher to Father, November 24, 1857, ibid.; Thornbrough, Riker, and Corpuz, *Diary of Calvin Fletcher*, 6:142–143.

37. Thornbrough, Riker, and Corpuz, 6:526; Miles J. Fletcher to Father, January 6, 1857 [1858], folder 7, box 8, Fletcher Papers, IHS.

38. Thornbrough, Riker, and Corpuz, *Diary of Calvin Fletcher*, 6:220, 277.

39. M. J. Fletcher to Father, June 6, 1858, folder 11, box 8, Fletcher Papers, IHS; Miles J. Fletcher to Father, June 23, 1858, ibid.; *Putnam Republican Banner*, December 27, 1860.

40. Miles J. Fletcher to Father, May 2, 1858, folder 10, box 8, Fletcher Papers, IHS.

41. Thornbrough, Riker, and Corpus, *Diary of Calvin Fletcher*, 6:631.

42. Ibid., 5:315, 6:50; Miles J. Fletcher to Father, December 13, 1856, folder 6, box 8, Fletcher Papers, IHS.

43. Wm. Fletcher to Mother, September 17, 1853, folder 4, box 7, ibid.

44. Miles to Father, March 13, 1854, folder 6, ibid.

45. Miles to Father, June 6, 1853, folder 2, box 7, ibid.

46. Miles to Father, June 14, 1853, ibid.; Miles to Father, July 17, 1853, folder 1, ibid.

47. Miles J. Fletcher to Father, January 13, 1853, folder 1, box 7, ibid.; Miles to Father, January 20, 1853, ibid.

48. Miles to Father, January 23, 1854, folder 5, ibid.

49. Miles to Father, My Birthday [June 15], 1854, folder 6, box 7, ibid.

50. Thornbrough, Riker, and Corpuz, *Diary of Calvin Fletcher*, 5:238–239.

51. Ibid., 5:526, 6:202.

52. Ibid., 6:460n215, 464, 486; Miles J. Fletcher to Father, July 4, 1858, folder 11, box 8, Fletcher Papers, IHS.

53. Thornbrough, Riker, and Corpuz, *Diary of Calvin Fletcher*, 6:603.

54. *Putnam Republican Banner*, April 12, November 29, 1860, February 7, 1861; Thornbrough, Riker, and Corpuz, *Diary of Calvin Fletcher*, 6:603n154.

55. Thornbrough, Riker, and Corpuz, *Diary of Calvin Fletcher*, 7:60, 122.

56. Ibid., 61–62.

57. Ibid., 68.

58. Ibid., 171.

59. Ibid., 6:181–183, 7:422–425, 427n232, 428–429, 9:276.

60. Ibid., 7:423–425, 427–429, 437; Ingram to Father, June 23, 1862, folder 3, box 10, Fletcher Papers, IHS; Elijah to Father, June 27, 1862, ibid.

61. Thornbrough, Riker, and Corpuz, *Diary of Calvin Fletcher*, 9:276; *Indianapolis Journal,* December 23, 1876; Cooley to Father, May 12, 1862, folder 2, box 10, Fletcher Papers, IHS.

62. Thornbrough, Riker, and Corpuz, *Diary of Calvin Fletcher*, 7:555, 570.

63. Ibid., 8:263.

64. Ibid., 8:339, 342, 343.

65. Ibid., 7:31, 78, 579, 607.

66. *Putnam Republican Banner,* July 30, 1863; Matilda to Aden, January 11, 1865; Thornbrough, Riker, and Corpuz, *Diary of Calvin Fletcher*, 8:299, 9:11–12, 16, 149.

67. Thornbrough, Riker, and Corpuz, *Diary of Calvin Fletcher,* 9:276; *Indianapolis Journal,* December 23, 1876; *Greencastle Banner,* December 21, 1876; Jennie Fletcher Allen, U.S. Federal Census, 1870, AncestryLibrary.com.

68. Thornbrough, Riker, and Corpuz, *Diary of Calvin Fletcher*, 9:259–262.

69. Ibid., 8:306.

70. *Indianapolis Daily Sentinel,* October 17, 1878; Jennie M. Allen, 1-7-7, Forest Hill Cemetery, Greencastle, Ind..

71. 1850 U.S. Census, AncestryLibrary.com; Indiana Marriage Collection, 1800–1941, ibid.

72. Vincent H. Day Family Collection, William Henry Smith Memorial Library, IHS; Richard M. Hazelett, "'Little Black Book': Memoirs of Richard M. Hazelett," William Henry Smith Memorial Library, IHS, 2–6.

73. Maria to Brother A., October 14, 1847, Abiathar Crane Papers, William Henry Smith Memorial Library, IHS.

74. State of Indiana v. Vincent Day, Order Book, Comm Pleas, 3 Civil, June 1857–November 1859, Clerk's Office, Putnam County Courthouse, Greencastle, Ind., 564–565; State of Indiana v. Vincent Day, Civil Order Book, Putnam Com. Pleas Court, 4, September 5, 1859–May 7, 1862, Clerk's Office, Putnam County Courthouse, Greencastle, Ind., 258, 259, 262–263; Civil Order Book, Putnam Common Pleas Court, 5, June 3, 1861–February 3, 1863, Clerk's Office, Putnam County Courthouse, Greencastle, Ind., 228, 230–231; James Adams v. Vincent H. Day, Civil Order Book, 6, February 1863–September 1866, Clerk's Office, Putnam County Courthouse, Greencastle, Ind., 337–338.

75. *Putnam Republican Banner,* February 18, 1857.

76. 1860 U.S. Census, AncestryLibrary.com; Policy No. 4964, Ohio Farmers Insurance Co., folder 7, box 1, Day Family Collection, IHS.

77. S. K. Fletcher to Father, July 16, 1859, folder 1, box 9, Fletcher Papers, IHS.

78. Clarence H. Danhof, *Change in Agriculture: The Northern United States, 1820–1870* (Cambridge, Mass.: Harvard University Press, 1969), 49–52; Richard M. Hazelett, "'Little Black Book,'" IHS, 6–9; "Reminiscences of James Shoemaker," *Indiana Magazine of History* 1 (December 1905): 173–176.

79. S. K. Fletcher to Father, May 29, 1859, folder 1, box 9, Fletcher Papers, IHS.

80. Stephen K. Fletcher to Father, June 26, 1859, folder 2, ibid.; Emma Lou Thornbrough, *Indiana in the Civil War Era, 1850–1880* (Indianapolis: Indiana Historical Bureau, 1965), 362; Barbara J. Steinson, "Rural Life in Indiana, 1800–1900," *Indiana Magazine of History* 90 (September 1984): 203–250; John Mack Faragher, *Women and Men on the Overland Trail* (New Haven, Conn.: Yale University Press, 1979), 43.

81. Fairs were held from 1853 to 1862, when the Civil War interrupted them. They

resumed in 1868. Jesse W. Weik, *History of Putnam County, Indiana* (Indianapolis, Ind.: Bowen, 1910), 148; Gillum Ridpath, "Putnam County, Ind.," *Atlas of Putnam Co., Indiana to Which Are Added Various General Maps, History, Statistics, Illustrations* (Chicago: J. H. Beers, 1879), 7; *Biographical and Historical Record of Putnam County, Indiana* (Chicago: Lewis Publishing, 1887; reprinted 1975), 309.

82. *Putnam Republican Banner*, November 14, 1855.

83. Danhof, *Change in Agriculture*, 78, 88; Weik, *History of Putnam County*, 26; U.S. Census Office, *Population Schedules of the Seventh Census of the United States, 1850* (Washington, D.C.: National Archives, 1963); U.S. Census Office, *Population Schedules of the Eighth Census of the United States, 1860* (Washington, D.C.: National Archives, 1967).

84. Andrew Dierdorf to John G Davis, April 21, 1860, John Givan Davis Papers, William Henry Smith Memorial Library, IHS.

85. Deed from Ambrose and Joana Day to Vincent H. Day, April 7, 1849, folder 1, box 1, Day Family Collection, IHS; Deed from Daniel Morris & Wife, Elizabeth Morris, to Vincent H Day, April 2, 1853, ibid.; Deed from Isaac M. Day and Mary E. Day to Vincent H. Day, May 19, 1855, ibid.; Deed from John W. and Rachel Estep to Vincent H. Day, May 7, 1859, ibid.; Paul Salstrom, *From Pioneering to Persevering: Family Farming in Indiana to 1880* (West Lafayette, Ind.: Purdue University Press, 2007), 113.

86. Deed from Ambrose and Joana Day to Vincent H. Day, April 7, 1849; Deed from Daniel Morris & Wife, Elizabeth Morris, to Vincent H. Day, April 2, 1853.

87. Stacy Lorraine Braukman and Michael A. Ross, "Married Women's Property and Male Coercion: United States' Courts and the Privy Examination, 1864–1887," *Journal of Women's History* 12 (Summer 2000): 57–80.

88. Joan M. Jensen, *Loosening the Bonds: Mid-Atlantic Farm Women, 1750–1850* (New Haven, Conn.: Yale University Press, 1986), argues rural women's work "loosened the bonds" of authority over them. Nancy Grey Osterud also sees women's farm labor as contributing to "mutuality" rather than separate spheres. See Osterud, *Bonds of Community: The Lives of Farm Women in Nineteenth-Century New York* (Ithaca, N.Y.: Cornell University Press, 1991), 9. John Mack Faragher, however, finds little evidence that women's undoubted contribution brought them equal status. See Faragher, "History from the Inside-Out: Writing the History of Women in Rural America," *American Quarterly* 33 (Winter 1981): 537–557; *Women and Men on the Overland Trail*, 48–57, 59; and *Sugar Creek: Life on the Illinois Prairie* (New Haven, Conn.: Yale University Press, 1986), 104–105. Jensen, *Loosening the Bonds*, 79.

89. John Frank Turner, "The Hoosier Huckster," *Indiana Magazine of History* 50 (March 1954): 51–60; Ransom Hawley to Father, December 8, 1851, box 3, Ransom Hawley Papers, Manuscripts of the Indiana Division, Indiana State Library (hereafter cited as ISL), Indianapolis; Sarah M. Hawley to Henry Martyn Hawley, May [1853], ibid.

90. "A Wife and Mother" to Gail Hamilton, August 29, 1855, Abiathar Crane Papers, William Henry Smith Memorial Library, IHS.

91. 1870 U.S. Census, AncestryLibrary.com; Jensen, *Loosening the Bonds*, 20–21; Faragher, *Women and Men on the Overland Trail*, 57–58; *Greencastle Banner*, April 5, 1877; *Indiana Press*, April 3, 1872.

92. 1860 U.S. Census, AncestryLibrary.com.

93. Faragher, *Women and Men on the Overland Trail*, 61.

94. Weik, *History of Putnam County*, 707; Ridpath, "Putnam County, Ind.," 5.

95. Faragher, "History from the Inside-Out," 551–554; Osterud, *Bonds of Community*, 11–13.

96. A. H. Crane to Abiathar, December 16, 1847, Abiathar Crane Papers, William Henry Smith Memorial Library, IHS.

97. *Greencastle Times,* October 22, 1885, folder 14, box 1, Day Family Collection, IHS.

98. Wigger, *Taking Heaven by Storm,* 151–157, 171–172; *Putnam Banner,* December 7, 1853.

99. *Putnam Banner,* April 26, May 3, 31, 1854. Scott C. Martin writes that temperance was women's favorite reform cause and was "a primary site for production and dissemination of new and reconfigured ideas about women and gender," especially the division between public and private spheres that was increasingly important to the middle class. But there was a misogynistic strain in the temperance movement that blamed women for men's drinking and failed to give women credit for temperance work. Scott C. Martin, *Devil of the Domestic Sphere: Temperance, Gender, and Middle-Class Ideology, 1800–1860* (DeKalb: Northern Illinois University Press, 2008), 3–14. Women who solicited aid for Kansas settlers did not have their full names given in the newspaper, although men did. The only woman to appear under her own name was Agnes Lee, the sole unmarried woman in the aid society. *Putnam Republican Banner,* September 17, 1856.

100. Weik, *History of Putnam County,* 117–119; *Greencastle Banner,* April 30, 1874; Grover L. Hartman, *A School for God's People: A History of the Sunday School Movement in Indiana* (Indianapolis, Ind.: Central Publishing, 1980), 10–11. Anne M. Boylan acknowledges Sunday schools as a forum in which women could speak on controversial religious issues. See Boylan, *Sunday School: The Formation of an American Institution, 1790–1880* (New Haven, Conn.: Yale University Press, 1988).

101. Hartman, *School for God's People,* 32–36; Ridpath, "Putnam County, Ind.," 5; Putnam County Sesquicentennial Committee, *Journey through Putnam County History,* 211; Jennie M. Allen, U.S. Federal Census 1880, AncestryLibrary; Thornbrough, *Indiana in the Civil War Era,* 502–505; Weik, *History of Putnam County,* 86–90; L. H. Stowell to C. A. Crane, July 1, 1860, Abiathar Crane Papers, William Henry Smith Memorial Library, IHS.

102. A. M. S. Harrah to Husband, June 27, [1847?], box 1, folder 3, Almira Maria Scott Harrah Papers, William Henry Smith Memorial Library, IHS; A. M. S. Harrah to Husband, May 19, [1847], ibid.; Manhart, *DePauw through the Years,* 1:75–77. Harriet Larrabee's female seminary became part of Asbury in 1867; ibid. Arthur W. Shumaker, *A History of Indiana Literature* (Indianapolis: Indiana Historical Society, 1962), 186–188.

103. Weik, *History of Putnam County,* 86–90; Sarah M. Hawley to Henry Martyn Hawley, May [1853], box 3, Ransom Hawley Papers, Manuscripts of the Indiana Division, ISL; Ransom Hawley to Father, March 2, 1857, ibid.; Father to Ransom, September 19, 1870, box 4, ibid.; *Putnam Republican Banner,* October 12, 1859. Mary Kelley, *Learning to Stand & Speak: Women, Education, and Public Life in America's Republic* (Chapel Hill: University of North Carolina Press, 2006), argues that women's education in this period was useful, not merely ornamental.

104. Elizabeth Varon, *We Mean to Be Counted: White Women and Politics in Antebellum Virginia* (Chapel Hill: University of North Carolina Press, 1998); Michael D. Pierson, *Free Hearts, Free Homes: Gender and American Antislavery Politics* (Chapel Hill: University of North Carolina Press, 2003).

105. *Putnam Republican Banner,* August 13, September 3, 1856.

106. *Indiana Press,* September 18, 1872; *Greencastle Banner,* October 12, 1876.

107. *Putnam Republican Banner,* June 9, 1858.

108. Thornbrough, *Indiana in the Civil War Era,* 36–37.

109. "A Wife and Mother" to Gail Hamilton, August 29, 1855.

110. *Putnam County Sentinel,* July 24, 1851.

111. Ibid., August 7, 1851.

112. Cott, *Bonds of Womanhood.*

113. *Putnam Republican Banner,* June 9, 1858.

Chapter Three. The Excluded Race

1. *The African Repository* 30 (December 1854): 376–381; Eric Burin, *Slavery and the Peculiar Solution: A History of the American Colonization Society* (Gainesville: University Press of Florida, 2005), 16, 172; Mary E. Anthrop, "The Road Less Traveled: Hoosier African Americans and Liberia," *Traces of Indiana and Midwestern History* 19 (Winter 2007): 12–21; Claude A. Clegg III, *The Price of Liberty: African Americans and the Making of Liberia* (Chapel Hill: University of North Carolina Press, 2004), 3–4, 34–36, 70, 173–174, 197–198; D. Elwood Dunn and Svend E. Holsoe, *Historical Dictionary of Liberia* (Metuchen, N.J.: Scarecrow Press, 1985), 17.

2. Much of the literature on northern free blacks concentrates on urban centers such as Philadelphia or New York and emphasizes the formation of organizations and communities. Although such studies note the dependence of blacks on white abolitionists and the worsening climate of the 1850s, the black populations they study had much more autonomy than the isolated rural blacks of Putnam County. Leon F. Litwack, *North of Slavery: The Negro in the Free States, 1790–1860* (Chicago: University of Chicago Press, 1961), 40, 103–112; Jane H. Pease and William H. Pease, *They Who Would Be Free: Blacks' Search for Freedom, 1830–1861* (New York: Atheneum, 1974). Joanne Pope Melish notes that New England free blacks established strong ties to their former owners. Although freedpeople saw this patronage as compensation for former service, whites viewed it as dependence. Most of all, white New Englanders were uncomfortable with their history of slavery, so they erased blacks from their history and marginalized them. Joanne Pope Melish, *Disowning Slavery: Gradual Emancipation and "Race" in New England, 1780–1860* (Ithaca, N.Y.: Cornell University Press, 1998), 1–10. Bruce Laurie has also emphasized the importance of paternalism and the relationship between "white patrons and black clients" in New England. But Laurie acknowledges that the situation for rural blacks was different from that of blacks in cities, where they had greater anonymity and population. See Laurie, *Beyond Garrison: Antislavery and Social Reform* (Cambridge: Cambridge University Press, 2005), 87–89, 99, 254. One free black, Amos Webber, benefited from connections to a white employer. See Nick Salvatore, *We All Got History: The Memory Books of Amos Webber* (New York: Random House, 1996). See also David H. Watters, "'As Soon as I Saw My Sable Brother, I Felt More at Home': Sampson Battis, Harriet Wilson, and New Hampshire Town Memory," in *Harriet Wilson's New England: Race, Writing, and Region,* ed. JerriAnne Boggis, Eve Allegra Raimon, and Barbara A. White (Durham: University of New Hampshire Press, 2007), 67–96. Harriet E. Wilson, a black New Englander, chronicled the marginalization of that region's free blacks in *Our Nig,* the first novel by a black woman, which shows how an abandoned biracial child, Frado, is treated as the property of the white family that takes her in, the Bellmonts. Mrs. Bellmont exploits Frado's labor and beats her as if she were a slave. See Wilson, *Our Nig or, Sketches from the Life of a Free Black* in *Three Classic African-American Novels,* ed. William L. Andrews (New York: Mentor, 1990). See also Mary Louise Kete, "Slavery's Shadows: Narrative Chiaroscuro and Our Nig," in *Harriet Wilson's New England: Race, Writing, and Religion,* ed. JerriAnne Boggis, Eva Allegra Raimon, and Barbara A. White (Durham: University of New Hampshire Press, 2007), 109–122. Another novel, *The Garies and Their Friends,* describes the job segregation, prejudice, and hostility against northern free blacks in Philadelphia. The

climax is an antiblack riot in which the Garies—a white slaveowner and his wife, who was his mulatto slave—are killed. One of the book's themes is that the North was as hostile, or perhaps more so, to blacks than the South. But black material success is also described and colonization rejected as predicated on the false premise that all free blacks were destitute. See Frank J. Webb, *The Garies and Their Friends* (1857; reprint, New York: Arno, 1969).

3. *The African Repository* 30 (December 1854): 376–381; Margaretta Stevenson, comp., *Stevenson Family History from the Eastern Shore of Maryland to Woodford County, Kentucky to Putnam County, Indiana with Allied Families* (New York: privately published, 1966), 71, 73, 77; Jesse W. Weik, *History of Putnam County, Indiana* (Indianapolis, Ind.: Bowen, 1910), 200–201.

4. *The African Repository* 30 (December 1854): 376–381.

5. Ibid.; Stevenson, *Stevenson Family History,* 77–78, 99.

6. *The African Repository* 30 (December 1854): 376–381.

7. 1840 U.S. Federal Census, AncestryLibrary.com; Weik, *History of Putnam County,* 200–201; Stevenson, *Stevenson Family History,* 99.

8. Stevenson, *Stevenson Family History,* 89.

9. Edward Ball, *Slaves in the Family* (New York: Ballantine Books, 1999); Weik, *History of Putnam County,* 444–446; Marion B. Lucas, *A History of Blacks in Kentucky,* vol. 1, *From Slavery to Segregation, 1760–1891* (Frankfort: Kentucky Historical Society, 1992), 52–53.

10. Weik, *History of Putnam County,* 200–201; Stevenson, *Stevenson Family History,* 77–78.

11. Stevenson, *Stevenson Family History,* 77–78.

12. Nicole Etcheson, *The Emerging Midwest: Upland Southerners and the Political Culture of the Old Northwest, 1787–1861* (Bloomington: Indiana University Press, 1996), 2–3; Weik, *History of Putnam County,* 696–697.

13. *Reports of the Debates and Proceedings of the Convention for the Revision of the Constitution of the State of Indiana,* 2 vols. (Indianapolis, Ind.: Brown, 1850), 1:247–249.

14. Abraham Lincoln to A. G. Hodges, April 4, 1864, in *The Collected Works of Abraham Lincoln,* ed. Roy P. Basler, 8 vols. (New Brunswick, N.J.: Rutgers University Press, 1953), 7:282.

15. David Herbert Donald, *Lincoln* (New York: Simon & Schuster, 1995), 29; *The African Repository* 30 (December 1854): 376–381; Stevenson, *Stevenson Family History,* 78–79.

16. Lauralee Baugh, Jinsie Bingham, Marilyn Clearwaters, and Rita W. Harlan, comps., *Putnam County, Indiana, Land Patents* (Evansville, Ind.: Evansville Bindery, 2003), 96, 100–101; Stevenson, *Stevenson Family History,* 78–79, 83–84; *Putnam Republican Banner,* April 27, 1859, December 27, 1860; Weik, *History of Putnam County,* 698–699; Emma Lou Thornbrough, *Indiana in the Civil War Era, 1850–1880* (Indianapolis: Indiana Historical Bureau, 1965), 383, 386.

17. U.S. Census Office, *Population Schedules of the Seventh Census of the United States, 1850* (Washington, D.C.: National Archives, 1963); U.S. Census Office, *Population Schedules of the Eighth Census of the United States, 1860* (Washington, D.C.: National Archives, 1967); Putnam County Sesquicentennial Committee, *A Journey through Putnam County History* (n.p., 1966), 32; Emma Lou Thornbrough, *The Negro in Indiana before 1900: A Study of a Minority* (1957; reprint, Bloomington: Indiana University Press, 1993), 133–135, 139–142.

18. U.S. Census Office, *Population Schedules of the Seventh Census;* Weik, *History of Putnam County,* 200–201. Boyd does not appear in any census.

19. Affidavit of John R. Miller, October 8, 1884, Robert Townsend Pension File National Archives, Washington, D.C.; 1850 U.S. Federal Census, AncestryLibrary.

20. *Biographical and Historical Record of Putnam County, Indiana* (Chicago: Lewis Publishing, 1887; reprinted 1975), 494.

21. Ibid.; Putnam County Sesquicentennial Committee, *Journey through Putnam County History*, 352; Weik, *History of Putnam County*, 200–201; Murray L. Townsend, Jr., *Townsend-Pittman Family Reunion* (privately published, 2005), 10–11. Townsend says that James Townsend only brought men and boys with him from Kentucky, but he also includes "Silvey" and Elam's free papers, dated November 10, 1830, and stating they "are now residents of Putnam county." See Townsend, *Townsend-Pittman Family Reunion*, 10–11, 23, 40, 205–206. For a description of the Townsend House Inn in Putnam County, see J. Richard Beste, *The Wabash: Or Adventures of an English Gentleman's Family in the Interior of America*, 2 vols. (London: Hurst and Blackett, 1855), 1:316–318.

22. Weik, *History of Putnam County*, 200–201; Townsend, *Townsend-Pittman Family Reunion*, 10–11, 23. Charity Townsend's obituary credits Benjamin Jones with rescuing her from the creek. Ibid., 205–206; Putnam County Sesquicentennial Committee, *Journey through Putnam County History*, 352.

23. James H. Madison, "Race, Law, and the Burdens of Indiana History," in *The History of Indiana Law*, ed. David J. Bodenhamer and Randall T. Shepard (Athens: Ohio University Press, 2006), 37–39. John Craig Hammond, *Slavery, Freedom, and Expansion in the Early American West* (Charlottesville: University of Virginia Press, 2007), 96–149, describes the efforts of Harrison and his allies to institute slavery in Indiana.

24. U.S. Census Office, *Population Schedules of the Sixth Census of the United States, 1840* (Washington, D.C.: National Archives, 1967); U.S. Census Office, *Population Schedules of the Seventh Census*; U.S. Census Office, *Population Schedules of the Eighth Census*.

25. *Biographical and Historical Record of Putnam County*, 494; Daniel W. Layman Account Books, Manuscripts of the Indiana Division, Indiana State Library (hereafter cited as ISL), Indianapolis, 74; T. M. Oviatt to Brother Hawley, June 30, 1853, box 3, Ransom Hawley Papers, Manuscripts of the Indiana Division, ISL; "Colonization Subscription," ibid.

26. U.S. Census Office, *Population Schedules of the Seventh Census*; U.S. Census Office, *Population Schedules of the Eighth Census*; Weik, *History of Putnam County*, 200–201.

27. Weik, *History of Putnam County*, 200–201; "The Ship Euphrasia," *The African Repository* 31 (May 1855): 133; Abeodu B. Jones, *Grand Cape Mount County: An Historical and Cultural Study of a Developing Society in Liberia* (Monrovia: Tubman Centre for African Culture, 1964), 18–20; Clegg, *Price of Liberty*, 64; Bell I. Wiley, ed., *Slaves No More: Letters from Liberia, 1833–1869* (Lexington: University Press of Kentucky, 1980), 6–7; Burin, *Slavery and the Peculiar Solution*, 146–148; Stevenson, *Stevenson Family History*, 99; W. McLain, November 1854, Records of the American Colonization Society, Library of Congress, Washington, D.C.; Tom W. Shick, *Behold the Promised Land: A History of Afro-American Settler Society in Nineteenth-Century Liberia* (Baltimore, Md.: Johns Hopkins University Press, 1980), 26–27, 37.

28. Thornbrough, *Indiana in the Civil War Era*, 14–16; Madison, "Race, Law, and the Burdens of Indiana History," 43–44; *Putnam County Sentinel*, January 15, 1852; Dorothy Riker and Gayle Thornbrough, *Indiana Election Returns, 1816–1851* (Indianapolis: Indiana Historical Bureau, 1960), 389–390. The *Indiana State Sentinel* has different election results for Putnam County's endorsement of the constitution, which show 92 percent of Putnam County voters in favor and 8 percent opposed. The *Sentinel*, however, has the same figures for Putnam County's ratification of Article 13. *Indiana State Sentinel*, August 14, 1851. Thornbrough, *Negro in Indiana before 1900*, 145–156.

29. 1850 U.S. Federal Census, AncestryLibrary.com; Weik, *History of Putnam County*, 200–201. Since modern records of burials are based on twentieth-century readings of surviving

gravestones, it is not uncommon for African American burial sites to be lost. Jennie Regan-Dinius to the author, October 21, 2008, e-mail in the author's possession; Lynn Rainville, "Hanover Deathscapes: Mortuary Variability in New Hampshire, 1770–1920," *Ethnohistory* 46 (Summer 1999): 541–597, esp. 566.

30. Charles Kettleborough, *Constitution Making in Indiana,* vol. 1, *1780–1851* (Indianapolis: Indiana Historical Bureau, 1971), 360–363; *The African Repository* 30 (January 1854): 30.

31. Thornbrough, *Indiana in the Civil War Era,* 18; Clegg, *Price of Liberty,* 151; Thornbrough, *Negro in Indiana before 1900,* 89; *The African Repository* 30 (December 1854): 376–381.

32. Stevenson, *Stevenson Family History,* 77–78; Weik, *History of Putnam County,* 696–697.

33. Stevenson, *Stevenson Family History,* 77–78; Clegg, *Price of Liberty,* 185. For samples of such correspondence, see Wiley *Slaves No More.*

34. *Reports of the Debates and Proceedings,* 1:247–249.

35. Thornbrough, *Indiana in the Civil War Era,* 14–16; Madison, "Race, Law, and the Burdens of Indiana History," 43–44; Stevenson, *Stevenson Family History,* 99.

36. Putnam County Sesquicentennial Committee, *Journey through Putnam County History,* 396.

37. Weik, *History of Putnam County,* 200–201. A history of the university, however, cites a disagreement over Harriet Larrabee's school or bouts of ill health as reasons why Simpson resigned from Asbury in July 1848. George B. Manhart, *DePauw through the Years,* 2 vols. (Greencastle, Ind.: DePauw University, 1962), 1:30.

38. James M. McPherson, *Battle Cry of Freedom: The Civil War Era* (New York: Oxford University Press, 1988), 79–80, 119–120; Steven Weisenburger, *Modern Medea: A Family Story of Slavery and Child-Murder from the Old South* (New York: Hill and Wang, 1998).

39. Weik, *History of Putnam County,* 197–200; *Greencastle Daily Banner Times,* December 16, 1895; Putnam County Sesquicentennial Committee, *Journey through Putnam County History,* 291.

40. *Putnam County Sentinel,* May 8, 1851.

41. *Indiana State Sentinel,* November 12, 1850.

42. *Putnam County Sentinel,* July 17, 1851.

43. Ibid., September 9, 1852.

44. Ibid., February 10, 1853; Weik, *History of Putnam County,* 196.

45. Russell E. Richey, *Early American Methodism* (Bloomington: Indiana University Press, 1991), 54–60; John H. Wigger, *Taking Heaven by Storm: Methodism and the Rise of Popular Christianity in America* (New York: Oxford University Press, 1998), 126–128; Stephen H. Webb, "Introducing Black Harry Hoosier: The History behind Indiana's Namesake," *Indiana Magazine of History* 98 (March 2002): 31–41; Thornbrough, *Indiana in the Civil War Era,* 20–22; George Born Manhart, *The Presbyterian Church, 1825–1950* (Greencastle, Ind.: Graphic Press, 1950), 12–13; Jack W. Porter, *The Catholic Church in Greencastle, Putnam County, Indiana, 1848–1978* (Greencastle: Ind.: Saint Paul the Apostle Church, 1979), 18–20; Daniel Walker Howe, *What Hath God Wrought: The Transformation of America, 1815–1848* (New York: Oxford University Press, 2007), 479; Manhart, *DePauw through the Years,* 1:63.

46. U.S. Census Office, *Population Schedules of the Eighth Census;* Affidavit of Charity Townsend, October 1884, Robert Townsend Pension File, National Archives, Washington, D.C.

47. Thornbrough, *Indiana in the Civil War Era,* 541–543.

48. Litwack, *North of Slavery,* 256.

Chapter Four. The Copperheads

1. Jesse W. Weik, *History of Putnam County, Indiana* (Indianapolis, Ind.: Bowen, 1910), 183–184.

2. (Indianapolis) *Daily State Sentinel*, April 15, 1861.

3. Dollie to [William], January 14, 1863, in *Love amid the Turmoil: The Civil War Letters of William and Mary Vermilion*, ed. Donald C. Elder III (Iowa City: University of Iowa Press, 2003), 45; Dollie to [William], January 27, 1863, ibid., 47–48.

4. For an overview of the political history of the Civil War, see James M. McPherson, *Battle Cry of Freedom: The Civil War Era* (New York: Ballantine Books, 1988), esp. 591–625. The leading interpretations of the Copperheads are Frank L. Klement, *The Copperheads in the Middle West* (1960; reprint, Gloucester, Mass.: Peter Smith, 1972), and Jennifer L. Weber, *Copperheads: The Rise and Fall of Lincoln's Opponents in the North* (New York: Oxford University Press, 2006). Klement believes Republicans exaggerated the Copperhead threat for political advantage, whereas Weber argues that Copperheads were a real danger. For Indiana, see Kenneth M. Stampp, *Indiana Politics during the Civil War* (1949; reprint, Bloomington: Indiana University Press, 1978).

5. For a good discussion of the problem with the sources, see Weber, *Copperheads*, 10. *Greencastle Banner*, September 2, 1880; Henry to Mother, January 4, 1864, folder 13, box 3, Henry Smith Lane Papers, William Henry Smith Memorial Library, Indiana Historical Society (hereafter cited as IHS), Indianapolis.

6. *Putnam Republican Banner*, February 7, 1861.

7. Ibid., April 13, 1859, February 7, 1861; *Greencastle Press*, July 12, 1876; *Putnam County Sentinel*, August 5, 1852; *Weekly Indiana State Sentinel*, December 20, 1855, March 31, 1858; Circuit Court, Civil Order Book, Putnam Com. Pleas Court, 4, 1859–1862, Clerk's Office, Putnam County Courthouse, Greencastle, Ind., 527; Circuit Court, Order Book, 4 Civil, 1857–1862, ibid., 442–445, 482, 493, 500, 511; 1860 U.S. Federal Census, AncestryLibrary.com; Record of Official Bonds, 1844–1911, Clerk's Office, Putnam County Courthouse, Greencastle, Ind., 24; Record of Official Bonds, No. 1, ibid., 299; Putnam County Sesquicentennial Committee, *A Journey through Putnam County History* (n.p., 1966), 83; Solomon Akers to John G. Davis, November 18, 1857, folder 8, box 2, John Givan Davis Papers, William Henry Smith Memorial Library, IHS; Solomon Akers to Jno. G. Davis, January 25, 1858, folder 14, ibid.

8. *Putnam Republican Banner*, September 9, 1868.

9. *Indiana Daily State Sentinel*, June 29, 1858; *Putnam Republican Banner*, August 17, 1859; (Greencastle) *Indiana Press*, July 24, 1858; H. R. Pitchlynn to John G. Davis, May 13, 1860, folder 5, box 4, John Givan Davis Papers, William Henry Smith Memorial Library, IHS.

10. Jno. B. Sackett to Jno. S. Jennings, December 24, 1858, microfilm, roll 2, John Givan Davis Papers, William Henry Smith Memorial Library, HIS; John S. Jennings to John G. Davis, December 28, 1858, folder 10, box 3, ibid.

11. Solomon Akers to Jno. G. Davis, January 25, 1858, folder 14, box 2, ibid.; Solomon Akers to John G. Davis, April 12, 1858, folder 3, box 3, ibid.

12. Solomon Akers to John G. Davis, July 8, 1858, folder 8, ibid.

13. *Indianapolis Daily Journal*, April 17, 1861; *Putnam Republican Banner*, April 18, 1861.

14. *Putnam Republican Banner*, September 5, 1861.

15. Ibid., April 18, 1861.

16. Ibid., June 27, 1861.

17. *Indianapolis Daily Journal,* April 17, 1861; Klement, *Copperheads in the Middle West,* 6–11; William B. Hesseltine, *Lincoln and the War Governors* (New York: Knopf, 1948), 311–315; *Putnam Republican Banner,* February 19, 1863.

18. *Putnam Republican Banner,* January 29, 1863.

19. Dollie to [William], April 16, 1863, in *Love amid the Turmoil: The Civil War Letters of William and Mary Vermilion,* ed. Donald C. Elder III (Iowa City: University of Iowa Press, 2003), 78.

20. *Putnam Republican Banner,* July 25, August 29, 1861.

21. Wm. Danley to J. G. Davis, July 29, 1861, microfilm, John Givan Davis Papers, William Henry Smith Memorial Library, IHS.

22. *Putnam County Republican,* August 15, 1861.

23. *Daily State Sentinel,* July 31, 1861; Weik, *History of Putnam County,* 238.

24. *Parke County Republican,* July 31, 1861; *Putnam Republican Banner,* August 1, 29, September, 11, 1861.

25. Weik, *History of Putnam County,* 301, 304–305; Indiana Works Progress Administration, comp., *Index to Marriage Records, Putnam County, Indiana, 1850–1920* (Indianapolis, Ind.: n.p., 1965), 188; Etcheson, Boatwright Collection, Cyril Johnson Room for Local History and Genealogy, Putnam County Public Library, Greencastle, Ind.

26. (Indianapolis) *Daily State Sentinel,* August 16, September 25, 1862.

27. J. A. Matson to H. S. Lane, May 1, 1862, box 1, H. S. Lane Manuscripts, Lilly Library, Indiana University, Bloomington.

28. *Putnam Republican Banner,* August 16, 1864.

29. D. W. Voorhees to Jno. G. Davis, May 15, 1864, microfilm, John Givan Davis Papers, William Henry Smith Memorial Library, IHS.

30. (Indianapolis) *Daily State Sentinel,* July 25, 1862.

31. Klement, *Copperheads in the Middle West,* 37–38; Emma Lou Thornbrough, *Indiana in the Civil War Era, 1850–1880* (Indianapolis: Indiana Historical Bureau, 1965), 122; (Indianapolis) *Daily State Sentinel,* February 18, 1863.

32. *Parke County Republican,* March 11, 1863; *Putnam Republican Banner,* March 5, 1863.

33. Dollie to [William], March 11, 1863, in *Love amid the Turmoil: The Civil War Letters of William and Mary Vermilion,* ed. Donald C. Elder III (Iowa City: University of Iowa Press, 2003), 68–69.

34. Scott Reynolds Nelson and Carol Sheriff, *A People at War: Civilians and Soldiers in America's Civil War, 1854–1877* (New York: Oxford University Press, 2007), 198.

35. C. Moore to O. P. Morton, July 30, 1862, John Hanna Manuscripts, Lilly Library, Indiana University, Bloomington; Robert Churchill, "Liberty, Conscription, and a Party Divided: The Sons of Liberty Conspiracy, 1863–1864," *Prologue* 30 (Winter 1998): 295–303.

36. Weber, *Copperheads,* 95–96; Thornbrough, *Indiana in the Civil War Era,* 202; Stephen E. Towne, "Killing the Serpent Speedily: Governor Morton, General Hascall, and the Suppression of the Democratic Press in Indiana, 1863," *Civil War History* 52 (March 2006): 41–65.

37. Report of Persons and Articles Hired, Provost Marshal Records, Record Group (RG) 110, National Archives–Great Lakes Region (hereafter cited as NA-GLR), Chicago. *Putnam Republican Banner,* June 18, 1863, lists fourteen enrolling officers, one for each township in the county. H. M. Rockwell to Capt. Thompson, June 9, 1863, Letters Received, Seventh District of Indiana, RG 110, NA-GLR.

38. Klement, *Copperheads in the Middle West,* 78–79; Weber, *Copperheads,* 104–105, 195; Thornbrough, *Indiana in the Civil War Era,* 200–201.

39. (Greencastle) *Indiana Press*, March 25, 1863, quoted in *Putnam Republican Banner*, August 24, 1865.

40. E. Cowgill to Col. R. W. Thompson, June 17, 1863, Letters Received, Seventh District of Indiana, RG 110, NA-GLR.

41. Matilda to Aden, June 18, 1863, copy of letter in the author's possession.

42. Report of Persons and Articles Hired; "A Tragedy on Deer Creek," Candace Sill Hopkins Papers, William Henry Smith Memorial Library, IHS; *Putnam Republican Banner*, June 18, November 26, 1863; *Parke County Republican*, June 17, 1863; Roll of Home Guards, Indiana Legion, Form of Articles of Association, Richard M. Hazelett, "'Little Black Book': Memoirs of Richard M. Hazelett," William Henry Smith Memorial Library, IHS; Record of Official Bonds, 1844–1911, Clerk's Office, Putnam County Courthouse, Greencastle, Ind., 5, 23, 36; *Greencastle Banner*, February 3, 1876; *Putnam Republican Banner*, November 26, 1863.

43. "Tragedy on Deer Creek"; *Putnam Republican Banner*, June 18, 1863; *Parke County Republican*, June 17, 1863; Roll of Home Guards, Memoirs of Richard M. Hazelett, IHS; Record of Official Bonds, 1844–1911, Clerk's Office, Putnam County Courthouse, Greencastle, Ind., 5, 23, 36; *Greencastle Banner*, February 3, 1876.

44. "Tragedy on Deer Creek"; *Putnam Republican Banner*, August 20, 1863.

45. *Putnam Republican Banner*, July 2, 1863.

46. *Lafayette Daily Journal*, June 19, 1863; *Sullivan Democrat*, June 25, 1863; *Greencastle Press*, quoted in ibid.

47. "Tragedy on Deer Creek"; *Putnam Republican Banner*, August 20, 1863.

48. *Putnam Republican Banner*, November 12, 1863.

49. Ibid., October 1, 1863, February 11, 1864, March 8, 1866; *Biographical and Historical Record of Putnam County, Indiana* (Chicago: Lewis Publishing, 1887; reprinted 1975), 467–468; *Atlas of Putnam Co., Indiana to Which Are Added Various General Maps, History, Statistics, Illustrations* (Chicago: J. H. Beers, 1879), 18.

50. Milton A. Crane to Col R. W. Thompson, July 2, 1863, Letters Received, Seventh District of Indiana, RG 110, NA-GLR; *Putnam Republican Banner*, June 18, 1863; W. F. Vermilion to [Dollie], June 26, 1863, in *Love amid the Turmoil: The Civil War Letters of William and Mary Vermilion*, ed. Donald C. Elder III (Iowa City: University of Iowa Press, 2003), 144–145.

51. *Putnam Republican Banner*, June 18, 1863; *Greencastle Banner*, February 3, 1876.

52. *Putnam Republican Banner*, June 18, 1863.

53. *Greencastle Banner*, February 3, 1876; H. J. Rockwell to Col. R. W. Thompson, June 19, 1864, Letters Received, Seventh District of Indiana, RG 110, NA-GLR.

54. *Putnam Republican Banner*, August 13, 1863; Putnam County Sesquicentennial Committee, *Journey through Putnam County History*, 41.

55. *Putnam Republican Banner*, November 5, 1863. Putnam men also participated in a military drill outside Brazil, in Clay County, that was dispersed by troops of the Indiana Legion. *Indianapolis Daily Journal*, May 4, 5, 10, 16, 1864.

56. *Parke County Republican*, November 4, 1863; *Putnam Republican Banner*, November 5, 19, 1863.

57. *Putnam Republican Banner*, June 18, July 2, 1863; Robert H. Churchill, *To Shake Their Guns in the Tyrant's Face: Libertarian Political Violence and the Origins of the Militia Movement* (Ann Arbor: University of Michigan Press, 2009), 125.

58. Entries for February 18, 26, March 1–5, 10, 1864, Thomas V. Lyon Diary, Archives and Special Collections, DePauw University, Greencastle, Ind.

59. *Putnam Republican Banner*, May 19, 1864.

60. Ibid., November 12, 1863, January 26, 1865; Thornbrough, *Indiana in the Civil War Era,* 136–137; Average Amount of Bounties Paid by Townships in the 7th District of Indiana under the Call of July 18th, 1864, Letters Received, Seventh District of Indiana, RG 110, NA-GLR.

61. 1862 Draft Records, Indiana State Archives, Commission on Public Records, Indianapolis.

62. Dollie to [William], March 9, 1863, in *Love amid the Turmoil: The Civil War Letters of William and Mary Vermilion,* ed. Donald C. Elder III (Iowa City: University of Iowa Press, 2003), 67–68.

63. *Putnam Republican Banner,* December 31, 1863; Nelson and Sheriff, *People at War,* 199; W. B. Williams to Josiah, October 1864, folder 1, box 3, Worthington B. Williams Family Papers, William Henry Smith Memorial Library, IHS; R. W. Thompson to Brig. Gen. H. B. Carrington, October 26, 1864, Statements of Substitutes, Seventh District of Indiana, RG 110, NA-GLR.

64. *Putnam Republican Banner,* April 27, 1865.

65. Ibid., January 5, 12, 19, February 9, July 27, December 16, 23, 1865; Gillum Ridpath, "Putnam County, Ind.," in *Atlas of Putnam Co., Indiana to Which Are Added Various General Maps, History, Statistics, Illustrations* (Chicago: J. H. Beers, 1879), 8; Thornbrough, *Indiana in the Civil War Era,* 136–137; Churchill, *To Shake Their Guns,* 139. See also Susan M. Sterett, *Public Pensions: Gender and Civic Service in the States, 1850–1937* (Ithaca, N.Y.: Cornell University Press, 2003), 36–37.

66. Klement, *Copperheads in the Middle West,* 179–180; Weber, *Copperheads,* 128–129; Dollie to [William], March 11, 1863.

67. Report of Persons and Articles Hired.

68. Churchill, "Liberty, Conscription, and a Party Divided," 295–313; Weber, *Copperheads,* 147–149, 243n36; Klement, *Copperheads in the Middle West,* 187–199.

69. Samuel Klaus, ed., *The Milligan Case* (New York: Da Capo Press, 1970), 258–261; Churchill, *To Shake Their Guns,* 134–138.

70. *Putnam Republican Banner,* October 27, 1864.

71. *Wabash Weekly Express,* April 20, 1864; *Indiana State Sentinel,* April 25, 1864; *Indianapolis Daily Journal,* April 30, 1864; D. Voorhees to Jno. G. Davis, April 22, 1864, microfilm, John Givan Davis Papers, William Henry Smith Memorial Library, IHS; D. W. Voorhees to Jno. G. Davis, May 15, 1864, ibid.

72. Klement, *Copperheads in the Middle West,* 195–199.

73. *Putnam Republican Banner,* September 17, October 15, 22, 1863; Mel McKee to John G. Davis, March 14, 1864, microfilm, John Givan Davis Papers, William Henry Smith Memorial Library, IHS; E. T. Keightley to John G. Davis, March 14, 1864, ibid.; 1850 U.S. Federal Census, AncestryLibrary.com; Mel McKee, Jas A Scott, W. D. Allen, Executive Committee to James Edwards, October 15, 1864, DC 287, folder 3, Andrew W. Crandall Papers, Archives and Special Collections, DePauw University, Greencastle, Ind.; Mel McKee to John G. Davis, May 19, 1864, folder 14, box 4, John Givan Davis Papers, William Henry Smith Memorial Library, IHS; Jno. Wilcox to [John G. Davis], June 7, 1864, ibid.

74. Henry B. Pickett to J. G. Davis, April 8, 1864, microfilm, John Givan Davis Papers, William Henry Smith Memorial Library, IHS.

75. Carl A. Zenor, "Putnam County in the Civil War: Local History of a Critical Period" (master's thesis, DePauw University, 1956), 142; Civil War Service Records, AncestryLibrary.com; American Civil War Soldiers, ibid.

76. *Indianapolis Daily Journal,* July 21, 23, 1864; Weik, *History of Putnam County,* 212–213; Affidavit of A. S. Morrison, April 19, 1866, Indiana Legion, Indiana State Archives, Indianapolis;

Notes of Interview with John W. Cooper, December 5, 1913, Group V, Herndon-Weik Collection, Library of Congress, Washington, D.C.

77. Zenor, "Putnam County in the Civil War," 142.

78. *Indianapolis Daily Journal,* July 23, 1864.

79. Hesseltine, *Lincoln and the War Governors,* 294–295; Melinda Lawson, *Patriot Fires: Forging a New American Nationalism in the Civil War North* (Lawrence: University Press of Kansas, 2002), 79–80; *Indianapolis Daily Journal,* September 12, 1864.

80. C. C. Matson to Gov. O. P. Morton, July 12, 1864, Correspondence of the 71st Indiana Volunteer Regiment, Indiana State Archives, Commission on Public Records, Indianapolis; Klement, *Copperheads in the Middle West,* 217–219; Thornbrough, *Indiana in the Civil War Era,* 219–222; Entries of October 5, 7, 1864, Thomas V. Lyon Diary, Archives and Special Collections, DePauw University, Greencastle, Ind.

81. Klement, *Copperheads in the Middle West,* 217–219; Thornbrough, *Indiana in the Civil War Era,* 219–222; *Putnam Republican Banner,* September 8, 22, October 20, 1864; Frank Smith Bogardus, "Daniel W. Voorhees," *Indiana Magazine of History* 27 (June 1931): 91–103.

82. *Putnam Republican Banner,* October 20, 27, 1864, February 14, 23, 1865; Thornbrough, *Indiana in the Civil War Era,* 227.

83. *Putnam Republican Banner,* October 25, 27, 1864, January 12, February 9, 16, 1865.

84. Ibid., November 10, 17, 1864; *Indianapolis Journal,* November 19, 1864.

85. *Daily State Sentinel,* October 18, 1864; *Indianapolis Daily Journal,* February 16, 1865.

86. Lucy to Brother, November 7, 1864, box 3, Ransom Hawley Papers, Manuscripts of the Indiana Division, Indiana State Library, Indianapolis.

87. *Indianapolis Daily Journal,* December 8, 1864; — to Cownover, May 4, 1865, Letters Received, Seventh District of Indiana, RG 110, NA-GLR. There was also a crime spree at Groveland. Some blamed escaped murderer Harpers Evans, but a note found in a burned store implicated the Copperheads. *Putnam Republican Banner,* April 27, May 4, 1865.

88. *Putnam Republican Banner,* May 11, 1865; *Indianapolis Daily Journal,* May 10, 1865; Elijah T. Keightley v. Solomon Akers et al., Order Book 6, May 1964 [*sic*]–Oct. 1867, Clerk's Office, Putnam County Courthouse, Greencastle, Ind., 46–47, 106.

89. Dollie to [William], July 15, 1863, in *Love amid the Turmoil: The Civil War Letters of William and Mary Vermilion,* ed. Donald C. Elder III (Iowa City: University of Iowa Press, 2003), 166–167; *Putnam Republican Banner,* July 2, 9, 1863.

Chapter Five. Their Own Corner

1. [Alice] to My Own Husband, January 29, 1862, folder 1, box 1, Lucius Chapin Papers, William Henry Smith Memorial Library, Indiana Historical Society (hereafter cited as IHS), Indianapolis.

2. Affidavit of Lucius P. Chapin, December 18, 1880, Lucius Chapin Pension File, National Archives, Washington, D.C.; Daniel W. Layman Account Books, vol. 1850–56, pp. 183, 268, vol. 1855–1862, p. 98, Manuscripts of the Indiana Division, Indiana State Library (hereafter cited as ISL), Indianapolis; Bro. G. L. Chapin to Dear Bro., April 23, 1861, folder 1, box 1, Lucius Chapin Papers, William Henry Smith Memorial Library, IHS.

3. [Alice] to My Own Husband, January 29, 1862.

4. Jesse W. Weik, *History of Putnam County, Indiana* (Indianapolis: Bowen, 1910), 490–494.

5. [Alice] to My Own Husband, January 29, 1862.

6. J. W. Osborn to L. P. Chapin, July 20, 1862, folder 1, box 1, Lucius Chapin Papers, William Henry Smith Memorial Library, IHS.

7. L. P. C. to Wife, August 26, 1862, ibid.

8. Ibid.; Wifey to My Own Love, October 7, 1862, folder 3, ibid.

9. L. P. C. to Wife, October 25, 1862, folder 3, ibid.

10. Historians have debated whether soldiers' motivations for fighting were mainly ideological or economic. James M. McPherson, *For Cause and Comrades: Why Men Fought in the Civil War* (New York: Oxford University Press, 1997), 23–24; Russell L. Johnson, "'Volunteer While You May': Manpower Mobilization in Dubuque, Iowa," in *Union Soldiers and the Northern Home Front: Wartime Experiences, Postwar Adjustments,* ed. Paul A. Cimbala and Randall M. Miller (New York: Fordham University Press, 2002), 30–68; Mark A. Snell, "'If They Would Know What I Know It Would Be Pretty Hard to Raise One Company in York': Recruiting, the Draft, and Society's Response in York County, Pennsylvania, 1861–1865," in *Union Soldiers and the Northern Home Front,* ed. Paul A. Cimbala and Randall M. Miller (New York: Fordham University Press, 2002), 69–115. Tyler Anbinder shows that draftees tended to be young, rural men rather than urban immigrants. See Anbinder, "Which Poor Man's Fight? Immigrants and the Federal Conscription of 1863," *Civil War History* 52 (December 2006): 344–373. Those with the least property—unskilled laborers, clerks, farmhands—were the most likely to enlist although no clear political connection to enlistment existed. Economics could be even more important than political ideology as a determinant for serving, with soldiers more likely to come from the Democratic town than the Republican one in one study of New Hampshire. Larry M. Logue, *To Appomattox and Beyond: The Civil War Soldier in War and Peace* (Chicago: Ivan R. Dee, 1996), 14–17. In Indiana, many volunteers were from southern and western counties, such as Putnam, that were Democratic bastions. Emma Lou Thornbrough, *Indiana in the Civil War Era: 1850–1880* (Indianapolis: Indiana Historical Bureau, 1965), 105. Thomas E. Rodgers disputes the conclusion that Democrats enlisted equally with Republicans. In a case study of Indiana's Seventh Congressional District, which included Putnam County, before the institution of the militia draft in 1862, Rodgers found no Democrats among the volunteers whose partisan affiliation could be identified. He attributes the heavy volunteering in Democratic counties to "nonpersisters," transient young men relatively new to those counties. Established local Democratic families did not have sons in the army. See Rodgers, "Republicans and Drifters: Political Affiliation and Union Army Volunteers in West-Central Indiana," *Indiana Magazine of History* 92 (December 1996): 321–334. Almost 95 percent of Union soldiers were volunteers. James W. Geary, *We Need Men: The Union Draft in the Civil War* (DeKalb: Northern Illinois University Press, 1991), 88.

11. Nancy Grey Osterud, *Bonds of Community: The Lives of Farm Women in Nineteenth-Century New York* (Ithaca, N.Y.: Cornell University Press, 1991), 57–67. An overview of Indiana women during the Civil War emphasizes the ways that Governor Oliver P. Morton's unorthodox procedures created avenues for women to become more independent even though woman's rights activists in the state turned from campaigning for rights to war work such as nursing and soldiers' aid. Anita Ashendel, "'Woman as Force' in Indiana History," in *The State of Indiana History 2000: Papers Presented at the Indiana Historical Society's Grand Opening,* ed. Robert M. Taylor, Jr. (Indianapolis: Indiana Historical Society, 2001), 1–36, esp. 14–15. Thomas E. Rodgers, however, in his study of the congressional districts in west-central Indiana, including Putnam County, does not see significant changes in "gender routines." What changes did occur in women's public roles proved temporary. See Rodgers, "Hoosier Women and the Civil War Home Front," *Indiana Magazine of History* 97 (June 2001): 105–128, esp. 128. Peggy Brase

Seigel says women's war work was linked to woman's rights, but many of her examples show nursing as an extension of women's traditional care for their menfolk. See Brase Siegel, "She Went to War: Indiana Women Nurses in the Civil War," *Indiana Magazine of History* 86 (March 1990): 1–27; also Nina Silber, *Daughters of the Union: Northern Women Fight the Civil War* (Cambridge, Mass.: Harvard University Press, 2005), 10–12. Southern women as well felt a profound sense of loss at the war's disruption of normal gender roles. "Warborn independence and autonomy were lamented rather than celebrated," writes Drew Gilpin Faust in *Mothers of Invention: Women of the Slaveholding South in the American Civil War* (Chapel Hill: University of North Carolina Press, 1996), 114–123.

12. Alice R. Chapin to Husband, September 17, 1862, folder 2, box 1, Lucius Chapin Papers, William Henry Smith Memorial Library, IHS; [Alice to ?], September 21, 1862, ibid.; Alice to Husband, September 27, 1863, folder 9, ibid.

13. [Alice to ?], September 21, 1862, folder 2, ibid.

14. S. Chapin to Dearest Son, April 21, 1863, folder 7, ibid.

15. Alice to Husband, May 14, 1863, ibid.

16. J. E. Chapin to Lew, April 19, 1863, ibid.; Anna Chapin to Brother, May 20, 1863, ibid.

17. Alice R. Chapin to Husband, February 1, 1863, folder 5, ibid.

18. Ibid.

19. Alice R. Chapin to Husband, March 28, 1863, folder 6, ibid.

20. Geary, *We Need Men*, 88; Weik, *History of Putnam County*, 204–205; Genealogy, Chapin Family Papers, William Henry Smith Memorial Library, IHS; George Chapin, "American Civil War Soldiers," AncestryLibrary.com.

21. *Putnam Republican Banner,* July 11, 1861; Weik, *History of Putnam County*, 207, 250–254; "List of Asbury Guards," Civil War and Thomas Lyon Papers, Archives and Special Collections, DePauw University, Greencastle, Ind.; Putnam County Sesquicentennial Committee, *A Journey through Putnam County History* (n.p., 1966), 14–15, 343; Muster Card for Courtland Matson, Civil War Records, Indiana State Archives, Commission on Public Records, Indianapolis, Ind.; William Blair, "We Are Coming, Father Abraham—Eventually: The Problem of Northern Nationalism in the Pennsylvania Recruiting Drives of 1862," in *The War Was You and Me: Civilians in the American Civil War,* ed. Joan E. Cashin (Princeton, N.J.: Princeton University Press, 2002), 183–208. The adjutant general credited Putnam with 3,257 total enlistments, but this number included reenlistments. Weik estimated the total number of men from Putnam County was 2,000; see Weik, *History of Putnam County*, 213–214. Julie A. Doyle, John David Smith, and Richard M. McMurry, eds., *The Wilderness of War: The Civil War Letters of George W. Squier, Hoosier Volunteer* (Knoxville: University of Tennessee Press, 1998), xv; Thornbrough, *Indiana in the Civil War Era*, 124; McPherson, *For Cause and Comrades*, viii; Edmund J. Raus, Jr., *Banners South: A Northern Community at War* (Kent, Ohio: Kent State University Press, 2005), 251; Ransom to Parents, Sisters &, All, [1863], folder 1, Ransom E. Hawley Letters, Special Collections, Vigo County Public Library (hereafter cited as VCPL), Terre Haute, Ind.

22. Ransom to Parents and Sister, April 22, 1861, box 3, Ransom Hawley Papers, Manuscripts of the Indiana Division, ISL; Ransom to Parents, February 24 [1862], ibid.; Ransom to Sister, April 7, 1862, ibid.; Ransom to Parents, June 4, 1862, ibid.; Ransom to Parents, Sisters & All, July 29 [1862], ibid.; American Civil War Soldiers, AncestryLibrary.com; [R. E. Hawley] to Miss Crawford, n.d., folder 3, Ransom E. Hawley Letters, Special Collections, VCPL.

23. Ransom to Father, Mother, and Sisters, June 23, [1863], box 3, Ransom Hawley Papers, Manuscripts of the Indiana Division, ISL.

24. Ransom to Lucy, September 21 [1863], ibid.; American Civil War Soldiers, AncestryLibrary.com; Ransom Hawley's Discharge Certificate issued by B. Pritchard, January 2, 1865, box 3, Ransom Hawley Papers, Manuscripts of the Indiana Division, ISL; Ransom to Parents, April 1865, ibid.; Ransom to Parents, May 27, 1864, folder 2, Ransom E. Hawley Letters, Special Collections, VCPL; Ransom to Ma, June 13, 1862, ibid.

25. Gerald Linderman has argued that soldiers became distanced from civilians by the experience of combat, which created an unbridgeable gulf between them. Chandra Manning has emphasized the importance of family to the experience of Confederate soldiers. Concern for protecting one's family caused Southerners first to join the war and then to falter in their support of a Confederacy that seemed to leave families vulnerable. See Linderman, *Embattled Courage: The Experience of Combat in the American Civil War* (New York: Free Press, 1987); Manning, *What This Cruel War Was Over: Soldiers, Slavery, and the Civil War* (New York: Vintage, 2007). McPherson, *For Cause and Comrades*, 22–24, emphasizes abstract concepts of duty and honor that motivated soldiers—and that frequently distanced them from family members, especially wives, who expected them to do their duty at home. Larry M. Logue, *To Appomattox and Beyond*, 14, concentrates on economic motives for enlistment. Reid Mitchell does study how family and community shaped the experience of the Northern soldier in *The Vacant Chair: The Northern Soldier Leaves Home* (New York: Oxford University Press, 1993). *Putnam Republican Banner*, April 18, August 22, 1861; Weik, *History of Putnam County*, 202–203; *Greencastle Banner*, November 2, 1876; *Weekly Indiana Press*, October 26, 1870; *Indianapolis Daily Journal*, July 31, 1862.

26. *Indianapolis Daily Journal*, October 4, 1861.

27. Josiah C. Williams to Grand Father, October 30, 1861, Worthington B. Williams Family Papers, William Henry Smith Memorial Library, IHS; A. R. C. to Husband, [June 8, 1863], folder 8, box 1, Lucius Chapin Papers, William Henry Smith Memorial Library, IHS.

28. *Putnam Republican Banner*, May 2, 1861.

29. Entry of August 20, 1862, William H. Anderson Diary, folder 4, Eleanore A. Cammack Papers, DePauw University, Greencastle, Ind.

30. *Putnam Republican Banner*, May 9, 1861.

31. [Alice] to Husband, December 19, 1862, folder 4, box 1, Lucius Chapin Papers, William Henry Smith Memorial Library, IHS.

32. Anna to Brother, December 20, 1862, ibid.

33. Mother LAL Williams to Josiah, May 1, 1864, folder 6, box 2, Worthington B. Williams Family Papers, William Henry Smith Memorial Library, IHS.

34. *Putnam Republican Banner*, September 15, 1864.

35. Ibid., July 7, 1864.

36. "In the Good Old Days," *Banner*, January 7, 1861, in folder "Clippings," Civil War and Thomas Lyon Papers, Archives and Special Collections, DePauw University, Greencastle, Ind.; Weik, *History of Putnam County*, 204–206; *Putnam Republican Banner*, May 9, 1861.

37. "In the Good Old Days"; Weik, *History of Putnam County*, 204–206; *Putnam Republican Banner*, September 17, October 8, 1863.

38. *Putnam Republican Banner*, September 17, October 8, 1863.

39. Bro. G. T. Chapin to Dear Bro., April 23, 1861, folder 1, box 1, Lucius Chapin Papers, William Henry Smith Memorial Library, IHS.

40. *Putnam Republican Banner*, October 8, 1863.

41. Ibid., August 22, 1861; Mother to Gertrude, note on the back of Josiah C. Williams to

Sister, May 12, 1861, folder 10, box 1, Worthington B. Williams Family Papers, William Henry Smith Memorial Library, IHS.

42. George Born Manhart, *The Presbyterian Church, 1825–1950* (Greencastle, Ind.: Graphic Press, 1950), 14; *Putnam Republican Banner,* December 12, 1861, June 4, 1863; Jos. M. Sadd to Bro. Hawley, February 24, 1862, folder 1, Ransom E. Hawley Letters, Special Collections, VCPL; Jeanie Attie, *Patriotic Toil: Northern Women and the American Civil War* (Ithaca, N.Y.: Cornell University Press, 1998), 30–31; Weik, *History of Putnam County*, 209–210.

43. *Putnam Republican Banner,* August 28, 1864.

44. Josiah C. Williams to Grand Father, October 30, 1861, folder 10, box 1, Worthington B. Williams Family Papers, William Henry Smith Memorial Library, IHS.

45. J. C. Williams to Grand Father, December 8, 1861, ibid.

46. Ransom to Ma, June 13, 1864, folder 2, Ransom E. Hawley Letters, Special Collections, VCPL; Father to Ransom, June 17, 1864, ibid.

47. George T. Chapin to brother [John E. Chapin], February 17, 1863, Chapin Family Papers, William Henry Smith Memorial Library, IHS.

48. Josiah C. Williams to Father, December 28, 1861, folder 10, box 1, Worthington B. Williams Family Papers, William Henry Smith Memorial Library, IHS.

49. Simps to Father, December 23, 1861, Simpson Hamrick Letters, William Henry Smith Memorial Library, IHS; Geo. T. Chapin to Bro., November 25, 1863, Chapin Family Papers, William Henry Smith Memorial Library, IHS.

50. Letters of January 26, March 3, October 9, 1863, *War Letters of Aden G. Cavins, Written to His Wife Matilda Livingston Cavins* (Evansville, Ind.: Rosenthal-Kuebler Printing, n.d.), 35–36, 40–41, 66; Alice Chapin to Husband, September 5, 1862, folder 2, box 1, Lucius Chapin Papers, William Henry Smith Memorial Library, IHS; [Alice] to Husband, December 19, 1862, folder 4, ibid.; L. P. Chapin to Wifey, December 21, 1862, ibid.

51. [Alice] to Husband, December 29, 1862, Lucius Chapin Papers, William Henry Smith Memorial Library, IHS.

52. L. P. Chapin to Wifey, July 13, [1863], folder 8, ibid.

53. John to Wife, January 28, 1863, John Applegate Manuscripts, Lilly Library, Indiana University, Bloomington.

54. Frances Clarke, "'Let All Nations See': Civil War Nationalism and the Memorialization of Wartime Voluntarism," *Civil War History* 52 (March 2006): 66–93, esp. 77–78.

55. Eliza to Dear Cousin, December 21, 1861, folder 3, box 5, Lucius C. Embree Papers, Manuscripts of the Indiana Division, ISL.

56. Dollie to [William], January 23, 1863, in *Love amid the Turmoil: The Civil War Letters of William and Mary Vermilion*, ed. Donald C. Elder III (Iowa City: University of Iowa Press, 2003), 45–46.

57. Simp S. Hamrick to Father, October 13, 1862, Simpson Hamrick Letters, William Henry Smith Memorial Library, IHS.

58. L. P. Chapin to Wifey, October 4 [1862], 4th Cavalry (77th Indiana Volunteers) Regimental Correspondence, Indiana State Archives (hereafter cited as ISA), Indianapolis.

59. L. P. Chapin to Wifey, December 21, 1862, folder 4, box 1, Lucius Chapin Papers, William Henry Smith Memorial Library, IHS.

60. Patricia L. Richard, "'Listen Ladies One and All': Union Soldiers Yearn for the Society of Their 'Fair Cousins of the North,'" in *Union Soldiers and the Northern Home Front: Wartime Experiences, Postwar Adjustments*, ed. Paul A. Cimbala and Randall M. Miller (New York: Fordham

University Press, 2002), 143–181, esp. 180–181; Wifey to Dearie, September 1, 1862, folder 2, box 1, Lucius Chapin Papers, William Henry Smith Memorial Library, IHS.

61. Entry of August 15, 1862, Anderson Diary, folder 4, Eleanore A. Cammack Papers, DePauw University, Greencastle, Ind.

62. See, for example, the letters from Aden and Matilda Cavins for descriptions of wives visiting from Putnam County. Letters dated January 8, March 23, April 5, 15, and 26, May 31, June 3, 1863, January 24, February 8, 1864, *War Letters of Aden G. Cavins*, 30, 42–48, 77–79; L. P. Chapin to Wife, September 30, 1862, folder 2, box 1, Lucius Chapin Papers, William Henry Smith Memorial Library, IHS.

63. E. S. Applegate to Husband, May 8, 1863, John Applegate Manuscripts, Lilly Library, Indiana University, Bloomington.

64. John to Wife, August 4, 1863, ibid.

65. John to Wife, April 28, 1863, ibid.

66. John to Wife, June 29, 1863, ibid.

67. John to Wife, April 14, 1864, ibid.

68. John to Wife, March 1, 1864, ibid.

69. John S. Applegate to Wife, November 23, [1863], ibid.; John to Wife, April 21, 1864, ibid.; John to Wife, September 8 [1865], ibid.; ES Applegate to Husband, September 12, 1865, ibid.

70. [Alice] to Husband, September 28, 1862, folder 2, box 1, Lucius Chapin Papers, William Henry Smith Memorial Library, IHS; A. R. C. to Husband, [June 8, 1863], folder 8, ibid.

71. Alice to My Love, June 16, 1863, 4th Cavalry (77th Indiana Volunteers) Regimental Correspondence, ISA.

72. Alice to My Beloved, January 24, 1864, folder 1, box 2, Lucius Chapin Papers, William Henry Smith Memorial Library, IHS.

73. [Alice] to Dearest, September 17, 1862, folder 2, box 1, ibid.

74. [L. P. Chapin] to Wifey, October 2, 1862, folder 3, ibid.; Alice to Father, December 19, 1862, folder 4, ibid.

75. George Chapin to Ella, October 14, 1862, Chapin Family Papers, William Henry Smith Memorial Library, IHS; Geo. T. Chapin to Brother, June 22, 1863, ibid.; Geo. T. Chapin to Bro., November 25, 1863, ibid.

76. 1850 U.S. Census, AncestryLibrary.com; 1860 U.S. Census, AncestryLibrary.com; Folder of Biographical Information, John Applegate Manuscripts, Lilly Library, Indiana University, Bloomington.

77. John to Wife, November 10, 1862, John Applegate Manuscripts, Lilly Library, Indiana University, Bloomington; John to Wife and Daughter, August 27, 1863, ibid.

78. John to Wife, February 24, 1864, ibid.; John to Wife, April 14, 1864, ibid.; J. H. Sands to Mrs. J. S. Applegate, November 27, 1864, ibid.

79. John to Wife, June 29, 1865, ibid.

80. E. S. Applegate to Husband, July 5, 1865, ibid.

81. John to Wife, July 9, 1865, ibid.

82. Thornbrough, *Indiana in the Civil War Era*, 177–179.

83. Gillum Ridpath, "Putnam County, Ind.," in *Atlas of Putnam Co., Indiana to Which Are Added Various General Maps, History, Statistics, Illustrations* (Chicago: J. H. Beers, 1879), 8; *Putnam Republican Banner*, September 19, December 12, 1861.

84. *Indianapolis Daily Journal*, July 31, 1862.

85. *Putnam Republican Banner,* November 19, 1863; Weik, *History of Putnam County,* 205–206, 209.

86. *Putnam Republican Banner,* November 19, 1863.

87. Ibid., November 26, December 10, 17, 30, 1863, January 14, 1864; Matilda to Aden, December 25, 1863, Aden G. Cavins, Alumni Files, DePauw University, Greencastle, Ind.

88. Alice Chapin to Husband, September 5, 1862, folder 2, box 1, Lucius Chapin Papers, William Henry Smith Memorial Library, IHS.

89. Alice R. Chapin to Husband, September 17, 1862, ibid.

90. Alice to Father, December 19, 1862, folder 4, ibid.

91. [Alice] to Husband, December 23, 1862, ibid.

92. *Putnam Republican Banner,* October 17, 1861.

93. Alice to Husband, April 3, 1863, folder 7, box 1, Lucius Chapin Papers, William Henry Smith Memorial Library, IHS.

94. Alice Chapin to Husband, September 5, 1862, folder 2, box 1, Lucius Chapin Papers, William Henry Smith Memorial Library, IHS; L. P. Chapin to Wife, July 21, [1863], folder 8, ibid.; A. R. Chapin to Husband, July 21, 1863, folder 8, ibid.

95. Alice R. Chapin to Husband, August 4, 1863, folder 9, ibid.

96. Lida to Brother, July 9, 1864, folder 2, box 2, ibid.; S. Chapin to Lew, July 10, 1864, ibid.; A. R. Chapin to Husband, March 23, 1865, folder 4, ibid.

97. Alice R. Chapin to Husband, March 28, 1863, folder 6, box 1, ibid.

98. L. P. Chapin to Wifey, March 1, 1863, ibid.; L. P. Chapin to Wife, February 12, 1865, folder 4, box 2, ibid.; L. P. Chapin to Wifey, February 2, 1865, ibid.; Alice R. Chapin to Husband, April 30, 1865, ibid.; J. W. Osborn to Lucius, September 14, 1865, folder 5, ibid.

99. L. P. Chapin to Dearest Wife, May 18, 1865, ibid.; Hannah Harriet Haret Elica Lide Lida Lidyer Chapin to Brother, November 25, 1865, ibid.; H. S. Cowgill to Gov. Morton, December 26, 1864, 4th Calvary (77th Indiana Volunteers) Regimental Correspondence, ISA.

100. [Alice] to Husband, September 28, 1862, folder 2, box 1, Lucius Chapin Papers, William Henry Smith Memorial Library, IHS.

101. Wifey to My Own Love, October 7, 1862, folder 3, ibid.

102. [Alice] to My Dear Love, December 21, 1863, folder 10, ibid.

103. [L. P. Chapin] to Wifey, October 2, 1862, folder 3, ibid.; J. E. Chapin to Lew, April 19, 1863, folder 7, ibid.

104. [Alice] to My Dear Husband, October 15, 1862, folder 3, ibid.

105. L. P. Chapin to Wifey, December 21, 1862, folder 4, ibid.

106. L. P. Chapin to Wifey, October 30, 1864, folder 3, ibid.

107. John to Wife, August 1, 1863, John Applegate Manuscripts, Lilly Library, Indiana University, Bloomington.

108. Pa, J. S. Applegate to Daughter, March 1, 1864, ibid.

109. John to Wife, October 11, 1863, ibid.

110. Ibid.

111. Pa, J. S. Applegate to Daughter, March 1, 1864, ibid.

112. John to Wife, May 22, 1863, ibid.

113. Pa to Miss Alma Apple[gate], n.d., ibid.

114. E. S Applegate to Husband, July 26, 1864, ibid.; E. S. Applegate to husband, August 10, 1864, ibid.

115. John to Wife, July 26, 1864, ibid.

116. James Marten, *The Children's Civil War* (Chapel Hill: University of North Carolina Press, 1998), 70, 89.

117. Pa to Miss Alma Apple[gate], n.d., John Applegate Manuscripts, Lilly Library, Indiana University, Bloomington.

118. Simp S. Hamrick to Father, October 13, 1862, Simpson Hamrick Letters, William Henry Smith Memorial Library, IHS.

119. *Putnam Republican Banner,* June 9, 1864.

120. Simps S Hamrick to Father, November 23, 1862, Simpson Hamrick Letters, William Henry Smith Memorial Library, IHS; Father to Ransom, October 3, 1864, box 3, Ransom Hawley Papers, Manuscripts of the Indiana Division, ISL; Simps S Hamrick to Father, November 23, 1862, Simpson Hamrick Letters, William Henry Smith Memorial Library, IHS; Father to Ransom, October 3, 1864, box 3, Hawley Papers, ISL.

121. E. S. Applegate to Husband, July 29, 1863, John Applegate Manuscripts, Lilly Library, Indiana University, Bloomington.

122. E. S. Applegate to Husband, August 3, 1864, ibid.

123. *Putnam Republican Banner,* July 21, 1864.

124. Ibid., August 4, 1864.

125. Ibid., August 11, 1864.

126. Ibid.

127. Josiah to Parents, August 9, 1862, folder 10, box 1, Worthington B. Williams Papers, William Henry Smith Memorial Library, IHS.

128. Entry of August 10, 1862, Captain Josiah C. Williams Civil War Diary, folder 10, box 2, ibid.

129. J. C. Williams to Parents, September 4, 1862, folder 10, box 1, ibid.

130. Josiah C. Williams to Parents, December 27, 1862, ibid.

131. Jos. C. Williams to Parents, January 2, 1863, folder 1, box 2, ibid.

132. W to Edistina, [1863], ibid.

133. J. A. Crose to Mr. Hamrick, May 4, 1863, Simpson Hamrick Letters, William Smith Memorial Library, IHS.

134. J. A. Crose to Mr. Hamrick, May 17, 1863, ibid.

135. J. T. Duffield to Dudley Hamrick, May 20, 1863, ibid.

136. J. A. Crose to Mr. Hamrick, May 4, 1863, ibid.

137. Isaac W. Montfort to [A. D. Hamrick], ibid.; A. C. Grooms to Bro. A. D. Hamrick, May 14, 1863, ibid.; Capt. J. W. Wilcoxson to A. D. Hamrick, June 2, 1863, ibid.; John W. Wilcoxson to Mr. Hamrick, May 21, 1863, ibid.; Capt. J. W. Wilcoxson to A. D. Hamrick, June 2, 1863, ibid.; John W. Wilcoxson to Mr. Hamrick, May 21, 1863, ibid. After the war, Simpson Hamrick's body was interred in the National Cemetery at Fredericksburg.

138. *Putnam Republican Banner,* April 16, 1863.

139. L. P. Chapin to Wife, April 14, 1863, folder 7, box 1, Lucius Chapin Papers, William Henry Smith Memorial Library, IHS.

140. J. E. Chapin to Lew, April 19, 1863, ibid.

141. S. Chapin to Son, June 5, 1864, folder 2, box 2, ibid.; S. Chapin to Lew, July 10, 1864, ibid.; J. E. Chapin to Lew, April 19, 1863, folder 7, box 1, ibid.; Alice R. Chapin to [Lucius], April 28, 1863, ibid.; Gary Laderman, *The Sacred Remains: American Attitudes toward Death, 1799–1883* (New Haven, Conn.: Yale University Press, 1996), 27–38, 104, 109–110; Franny Nudelman, *John Brown's Body: Slavery, Violence, & the Culture of War* (Chapel Hill: University of North Carolina Press, 2004), 113–115.

142. Weik, *History of Putnam County*, 205.

143. *Putnam Republican Banner*, September 15, 1864.

144. E. S. Applegate to Husband, July 26, 1864, John Applegate Manuscripts, Lilly Library, Indiana University, Bloomington.

145. E. S. Applegate to Husband, August 3, 1864, ibid.

146. E. S. Applegate to Husband, August 10, 1864, ibid.

147. J. S. Applegate to Wife, April 3, 1865, ibid.; E. S. Applegate to Husband, July 5, 1865, ibid.; John to Wife, July 9, 1865, ibid.

148. S. S. Hamrick to Father, October 1, 1862, ibid.; Miles J. Fletcher, n.d., Correspondence of the 27th Indiana Volunteer Regiment, ISA; S. S. Hamrick to Father, December 5, 1862, Simpson Hamrick Letters, William Henry Smith Memorial Library, IHS.

149. J. A. Matson to Gov. Morton, August 1, 1862, Correspondence of the 71st Indiana Volunteer Regiment, ISA; J. A. Matson to O. P. Morton, August 18, 1862, ibid.

150. Josiah to Parrents, November 29, 1863, Josiah C. Williams Letters, Manuscripts of the Indiana Division, ISL; A. D. Hamrick to W. B. Williams, November 16, 1863, folder 2, box 2, Worthington B. Williams Family Papers, William Henry Smith Memorial Library, IHS; J. A. Matson to Gov. Morton, November 27, 1863, ibid.

151. To His Excellency Hon O. P. Morton, November 18, 1863, ibid.; [W] to Josiah, December 6, 1863, ibid.; J. C. Williams to Grand Father, April 8, 1864, folder 5, ibid.; J. C. Williams to Parents, August 31, 1864, folder 6, ibid.; American Civil War Soldiers, AncestryLibrary.com; U.S. Civil War Soldiers, 1861–1865, AncestryLibrary.com; Your Mother L. A. L. Williams to [Josiah], [late 1864], folder 1, box 3, Worthington B. Williams Family Papers, William Henry Smith Memorial Library, IHS.

152. A. R. Chapin, September 23, 1863, folder 9, box 1, Lucius Chapin Papers, William Henry Smith Memorial Library, IHS.

153. S. Chapin to Son, June 5, 1864, folder 2, box 2, ibid.; S. Chapin to Lew, July 10, 1864, ibid.; S. Chapin to Son, June 5, 1864, ibid.

154. S. Chapin to Lew, July 10, 1864, ibid.

155. A. C. Grooms to Bro. A. D. Hamrick, May 14, 1863, Simpson Hamrick Papers, William Henry Smith Memorial Library, IHS; J. T. Duffield to Dudley Hamrick, May 20, 1863, ibid.

156. L. P. C. to Wife, June 7, 1864, folder 2, box 2, Lucius Chapin Papers, William Henry Smith Memorial Library, IHS.

157. E. S. Applegate to Husband, August 10, 1864, John Applegate Manuscripts, Lilly Library, Indiana University, Bloomington.

Chapter Six. Shoulder-Strapped Negroes

1. *Indiana State Sentinel*, March 2, 1863. See Joseph T. Glatthaar, *Forged in Battle: The Civil War Alliance of Black Soldiers and White Officers* (Baton Rouge: Louisiana State University Press, 2000).

2. U.S. Census Office, *Population Schedules of the Eighth Census of the United States, 1860* (Washington, D.C.: National Archives, 1967); Affidavit of Charity Townsend, October 1864, Robert Townsend Pension File, National Archives (hereafter cited as NA), Washington, D.C.; Declaration of Invalid Pension, September 12, 1864, ibid.; Affidavit of Daniel W. Layman, July 24, 1884, ibid.; Affidavit of John R. Miller, October 8, 1884, ibid.; 1860 U.S. Federal Census, AncestryLibrary.com; Affidavit of Charity Townsend, October 1884, Robert Townsend Pension File, NA.

3. Affidavit of John C. Albin, June 23, 1864, Robert Townsend Pension File, NA; Affidavit of John Summers, June 21, 1884, ibid.

4. American Civil War Soldiers, AncestryLibrary.com; William R. Forstchen's dissertation is still the authoritative account of the 28th. See Forstchen, "The 28th United States Colored Troops: Indiana's African-Americans Go to War, 1863–1865" (Ph.D. diss., Purdue University, 1994), 44–45, 52–53, 59, 61–64, 70, 77. Forstchen has also published a novel about the 28th: *We Look Like Men of War* (New York: Forge Books, 2001). William B. Hesseltine, *Lincoln and the War Governors* (New York: Knopf, 1948), 288–289; George P. Clark and Shirley E. Clark, "Heroes Carved in Ebony: Indiana's Black Civil War Regiment, the 28th USCT," *Traces of Indiana and Midwestern History* 7 (Summer 1995): 4–16.

5. Fortschen, "28th United States Colored Troops," 91; "Colored Men! To Arms," [December 1863], folder 2, Anna W. Wright Collection, Manuscripts of the Indiana Division, Indiana State Library (hereafter cited as ISL), Indianapolis.

6. Ibid.

7. James M. McPherson, *Battle Cry of Freedom: The Civil War Era* (New York: Oxford University Press, 1988), 563–564.

8. Richard Slotkin, *No Quarter: The Battle of the Crater, 1864* (New York: Random House, 2009), 232–253; Clark and Clark, "Heroes Carved in Ebony," 4–16; McPherson, *Battle Cry of Freedom*, 758–760.

9. On the battle of the Crater, see Slotkin, *No Quarter*; Noah Andre Trudeau, *Like Men of War: Black Troops in the Civil War, 1862–1865* (Boston: Little, Brown, 1998), 220–251; Edwin S. Redkey, ed., *A Grand Army of Black Men: Letters from African-American Soldiers in the Union Army, 1861–1865* (Cambridge: Cambridge University Press, 1992), 110–113.

10. Redkey, *Grand Army of Black Men*, 175–178, 200–202; Clark and Clark, "Heroes Carved in Ebony," 4–16.

11. There is a notation on Robert Townsend's service record that he deserted, but this was an error. U.S. Colored Troops Military Service Records, 1861–1865, AncestryLibrary.com; J. P. Martin, August 9, 1871, Robert Townsend Pension File, NA; Affidavit of Wyatt James, August 13, 1872, ibid.; Affidavit of William Jordan, August 16, 1872, ibid.; Affidavit of William H. Jordan and William Taylor, June 9, 1884, ibid.; Dependent Parents, 1885, ibid. For accounts of poisoned food being sold to soldiers, see *Putnam Republican Banner*, May 2, 1861; *Liberator*, May 17, June 28, 1861. Declaration of Invalid Pension, September 12, 1864, Robert Townsend Pension File, NA; Affidavit of Charity Townsend, October 1884, ibid.; Affidavit of John C. Albin, June 23, 1884, ibid. Although the examining surgeon reported that Robert was "totally incapacitated for obtaining his subsistence by manual labor" with a "Probably Permanent" disability from "incurable" heart disease, his application for an invalid pension was rejected. Examining Surgeon's Certificate, September 12, 1864, ibid.; Dependent Parents, 1885, ibid.

12. Affidavit of D. W. Layman, July 24, 1884, Robert Townsend Pension Files, NA. In others of the many affidavits Dr. Layman gave, he mentioned asthmatic and lung conditions as well as "Rhematic Disease" as among Robert's ailments. Affidavit of Daniel W. Layman, December 30, 1871, ibid.; Affidavit of Daniel W. Layman, June 12, 1884, ibid.; Declaration for Mother's Army Pension, June 27, 1884, ibid.

13. Fortschen, "28th United States Colored Troops," 99–102.

14. Jeremiah Bum to Calvin Fletcher, March 6, 1863, folder 5, box 10, Calvin Fletcher Papers, William Henry Smith Memorial Library, Indiana Historical Society (hereafter cited as IHS), Indianapolis.

15. Entry of [December] 1862, folder 4, William H. Anderson Diary, Eleanore A. Cammack Papers, DePauw University, Greencastle, Ind.

16. Dollie to My Dear Love, November 12, 1862, in *Love amid the Turmoil: The Civil War Letters of William and Mary Vermilion*, ed. Donald C. Elder III (Iowa City: University of Iowa Press, 2003), 15.

17. W. F. Vermilion to Dollie, December 7, 1862, ibid., 23.

18. *Putnam Republican Banner,* April 2, 1863.

19. L. P. Chapin to Wife, December 21, 1862, folder 4, box 1, Lucius Chapin Papers, William Henry Smith Memorial Library, IHS.

20. George Chapin to Ella, October 14, 1862, Chapin Family Papers, William Henry Smith Memorial Library, IHS.

21. Geo. T. Chapin to Bro., January 12, 1864, ibid.

22. Dollie to Dearest Love, December 23, 1862, in *Love amid the Turmoil: The Civil War Letters of William and Mary Vermilion*, ed. Donald C. Elder III (Iowa City: University of Iowa Press, 2003), 35–37.

23. "The Negro Slave," Civil War and Thomas Lyon Papers, Archives and Special Collections, DePauw University, Greencastle, Ind.

24. "The Song of the Fetter," folder 6, box 2, Lucius Chapin Papers, William Henry Smith Memorial Library, IHS.

25. John to Wife, January 23, 1863, John Applegate Manuscripts, Lilly Library, Indiana University, Bloomington.

26. Entry of September 1, 1862, folder 4, William H. Anderson Diary, Eleanore A. Cammack Papers, DePauw University, Greencastle, Ind.

27. Stephen Keyes Fletcher to Father, January 21, 1861 [1862], in *The Diary of Calvin Fletcher,* ed. Gayle Thornbrough, Dorothy L. Riker, and Paula Corpuz, 9 vols. (Indianapolis: Indiana Historical Society, 1972–1983), 7:308–309.

28. Loriman S. Brigham, ed., "The Civil War Journal of William B. Fletcher," *Indiana Magazine of History* 57 (March 1961): 43–76, esp. 68.

29. Stephen Keyes Fletcher to his father, December 25, 1863, in *Diary of Calvin Fletcher*, ed. Gayle Thornbrough, Dorothy L. Riker, and Paula Corpuz, 9 vols. (Indianapolis: Indiana Historical Society, 1972–1983), 8:289. For the practice of sending contrabands north, see Leslie A. Schwalm, "'Overrun with Free Negroes': Emancipation and Wartime Migration in the Upper Midwest," *Civil War History* 50 (June 2004): 145–174.

30. Thornbrough, Riker, and Corpuz, *Diary of Calvin Fletcher*, 8:61.

31. Entry of September 10, 1862, folder 4, William H. Anderson Diary, Eleanore A. Cammack Papers, DePauw University, Greencastle, Ind.

32. R. E. Hawley to Gertrude and Mattie, May 26, 1926, folder 4, box 3, Worthington B. Williams Family Papers, William Henry Smith Memorial Library, IHS.

33. Entry of May 2, 1862, Captain Josiah C. Williams Civil War Diary, folder 10, box 2, ibid.

34. — to J. B. Martin, August 25 [no year], folder 8, DC 287, Andrew W. Crandall Papers, Archives and Special Collections, DePauw University, Greencastle, Ind.

35. Perry McCandless, ed., "The Civil War Journal of Stephen Keyes Fletcher," *Indiana Magazine of History* 54 (June 1958): 141–190, esp. 185.

36. W. F. V. to [Mary], October 20, 1863, in *Love amid the Turmoil: The Civil War Letters of William and Mary Vermilion*, ed. Donald C. Elder III (Iowa City: University of Iowa Press, 2003), 251.

37. Christine Leigh Heyrman, *Southern Cross: The Beginning of the Bible Belt* (New York: Knopf, 1997), 218–219; Entries of September 4, 11, 18, October 16, 23, 1864, Thomas V. Lyon Diary, Archives and Special Collections, DePauw University, Greencastle, Ind.

38. Stephen Keyes Fletcher to His Brother Dax [Albert], February 29, 1863, in *Diary of Calvin Fletcher*, ed. Gayle Thornbrough, Dorothy L. Riker, and Paula Corpuz, 9 vols. (Indianapolis: Indiana Historical Society, 1972–1983), 8:55–57.

39. Simps Hamrick to Father, January 7, 1862, Simpson Hamrick Letters, William Henry Smith Memorial Library, IHS.

40. Josiah C. Williams to Father, April 21, 1862, folder 10, box 1, Worthington B. Williams Family Papers, William Henry Smith Memorial Library, IHS.

41. Will to [Mary], December 27, 1862, in *Love amid the Turmoil: The Civil War Letters of William and Mary Vermilion*, ed. Donald C. Elder III (Iowa City: University of Iowa Press, 2003), 38.

42. *War Letters of Aden G. Cavins, Written to His Wife Matilda Livingston Cavins* (Evansville, Ind.: Rosenthal-Kuebler Printing, n.d.); Aden G. Cavins, Alumni Files, Archives and Special Collections, DePauw University, Greencastle, Ind., 80.

43. J. E. Chapin to Sister [Anna Chapin], May 24, 1864, J. E. Chapin Letters, William Henry Smith Memorial Library, IHS.

44. T. H. Nance to Mr. Hamrick, July 27, 1862, Simpson Hamrick Letters, William Henry Smith Memorial Library, IHS; Simps to Father, July 28, 1862, ibid.

45. Entry of September 10, 1862, folder 4, William H. Anderson Diary, Eleanore A. Cammack Papers, DePauw University, Greencastle, Ind.

46. [S. S. Hamrick] to Lou, October 12, 1861, Simpson Hamrick Letters, William Henry Smith Memorial Library, IHS.

47. *War Letters of Aden G. Cavins*, 96–97.

48. Simps S Hamrick to Father, January 23, 1862, Simpson Hamrick Letters, William Henry Smith Memorial Library, IHS.

49. L. P. Chapin to Wife, April 11, 1865, folder 4, box 2, Lucius Chapin Papers, William Henry Smith Memorial Library, IHS.

50. Entry of October 11, 1862, folder 4, William H. Anderson Diary, Eleanore A. Cammack Papers, DePauw University, Greencastle, Ind.

51. J. C. Williams to Edwin, April 8, 1862, folder 10, box 1, Worthington B. Williams Family Papers, William Henry Smith Memorial Library, IHS.

52. Geo. T. Chapin to Bro., January 12, 1864, Chapin Family Papers, William Henry Smith Memorial Library, IHS.

53. L. P. Chapin to Wife, April 18, 1865, folder 4, box 2, Lucius Chapin Papers, William Henry Smith Memorial Library, IHS.

54. *Putnam Republican Banner*, June 9, 1864.

55. Simps Hamrick to Father, January 7, 1862, Simpson Hamrick Letters, William Henry Smith Memorial Library, IHS.

56. Stephen Keyes Fletcher to His Brother Dax [Albert], February 29, 1863, in *Diary of Calvin Fletcher*, ed. Gayle Thornbrough, Dorothy L. Riker, and Paula Corpuz, 9 vols. (Indianapolis: Indiana Historical Society, 1972–1983), 8:55–57.

57. Will to Dollie, February 14, 1863, in *Love amid the Turmoil: The Civil War Letters of William and Mary Vermilion*, ed. Donald C. Elder III (Iowa City: University of Iowa Press, 2003), 57.

58. *Putnam Republican Banner*, October 20, 1864.

59. Ibid.

60. Jonas Seely to Brother John, April 11, 1863, folder 7, box 1, Lucius Chapin Papers, William Henry Smith Memorial Library, IHS.

61. Josiah C. Williams to Father, February 24, 1863, folder 1, box 2, Worthington B. Williams Family Papers, William Henry Smith Memorial Library, IHS.

62. Entries of December 5, 7, 1864, Thomas V. Lyon Diary, Archives and Special Collections, DePauw University, Greencastle, Ind.

63. W. F. Vermilion to Dollie, December 7, 1862, in *Love amid the Turmoil: The Civil War Letters of William and Mary Vermilion,* ed. Donald C. Elder III (Iowa City: University of Iowa Press, 2003), 23.

64. *Putnam Republican Banner,* April 2, 1863.

65. James M. McPherson, *For Cause & Comrades: Why Men Fought in the Civil War* (New York: Oxford University Press, 1997), 117–130; Chandra Manning argues that in addition to pragmatic reasons, Union soldiers recognized that emancipation enabled the United States to fulfill its principles of liberty. See Manning, *What This Cruel War Was Over: Soldiers, Slavery, and the Civil War* (New York: Vintage, 2007).

66. Dudley Taylor Cornish, *The Sable Arm: Negro Troops in the Union Army, 1861–1865* (New York: Norton, 1966), 214–215; W. F. Vermilion to Dollie, May 21, 1863, in *Love amid the Turmoil: The Civil War Letters of William and Mary Vermilion,* ed. Donald C. Elder III (Iowa City: University of Iowa Press, 2003), 104–105.

67. Geo. T. Chapin to Bro., January 12, 1864, Chapin Family Papers, William Henry Smith Memorial Library, IHS.

68. *Indianapolis Daily Journal,* April 4, 1865; *Putnam Republican Banner,* July 20, 1865; Dollie to [William], December 18, 1862, in *Love amid the Turmoil: The Civil War Letters of William and Mary Vermilion,* ed. Donald C. Elder III (Iowa City: University of Iowa Press, 2003), 29–30.

69. *Putnam Republican Banner,* September 12, 1864.

70. Ibid., February 16, 1865.

71. Four of the other dissenting senators were from the border South states of Kentucky and Delaware and the fifth from California. Michael Vorenberg, *Final Freedom: The Civil War, the Abolition of Slavery, and the Thirteenth Amendment* (Cambridge: Cambridge University Press, 2001), 113, 220–221. The laws against black migration to Indiana and black suffrage were considered null after the Reconstruction amendments to the U.S. Constitution but were not formally repealed in Indiana until the state constitution was revised in 1881. Clifton J. Phillips, *Indiana in Transition: The Emergence of an Industrial Commonwealth, 1880–1920* (Indianapolis: Indiana Historical Bureau, 1968), 18. Joan E. Cashin has remarked on the "ambivalence" with which white Northerners reacted to emancipation and race change. See Cashin, "Editor's Introduction," in *The War Was You and Me: Civilians in the American Civil War,* ed. Joan E. Cashin (Princeton, N.J.: Princeton University Press, 2002), 1–5. Melinda Lawson argues that although Democrats maintained adherence to white supremacy as part of their definition of nationalism, Republicans increasingly found a place for African Americans. See Lawson, *Patriot Fires: Forging a New American Nationalism in the Civil War North* (Lawrence: University Press of Kansas, 2002), 96. Lex Renda argues that it is hard to tell whether the war eroded racism. See Lex Renda, "'A White Man's State in New England': Race, Party, and Suffrage in Civil War Connecticut," in *An Uncommon Time: The Civil War and the Northern Home Front,* ed. Paul A. Cimbala and Randall M. Miller (New York: Fordham University Press, 2002), 243–279.

72. *Putnam Republican Banner,* April 13, 1865.

73. Ibid., April 12, 13, 20, 1865.

74. Ibid., April 13, 20, 1865; Entry of May 2 [1865], p. 37, F. M. Harris Civil War Diary, Archives and Special Collections, DePauw University, Greencastle, Ind.

75. *Putnam Republican Banner,* April 20, 1865.

76. Matilda to Aden, April 21, 1865, Aden G. Cavins, Alumni Files, Archives and Special Collections, DePauw University, Greencastle, Ind.

77. Ibid.; *Putnam Republican Banner,* April 27, 1865.

78. Father to Ransom, April 28, 1865, box 3, Ransom Hawley Papers, Manuscripts of the Indiana Division, ISL. For the condition of Lincoln's corpse, see Michael Burlingame, *Abraham Lincoln: A Life,* 2 vols. (Baltimore, Md.: Johns Hopkins University Press, 2008), 2:823.

79. Ma to Son, April 15, 1865, Ransom Hawley Papers, Manuscripts of the Indiana Division, ISL.

80. Josiah to Parents, April 27, 1865, Josiah C. Williams Letters, Manuscripts of the Indiana Division, ISL.

81. Entry of May 2 [1865], p. 37, F. M. Harris Civil War Diary, Archives and Special Collections, DePauw University, Greencastle, Ind.

82. *Putnam Republican Banner,* April 20, 1865.

83. Ibid., April 20, 1865.

84. Ibid., March 16, 1865.

85. George B. Manhart, *DePauw through the Years,* 2 vols. (Greencastle, Ind.: DePauw University, 1962), 1:150–151.

86. *Putnam Republican Banner,* July 20, 1865.

87. (Greencastle) *Weekly Indiana Press,* August 9, 1865.

88. Emma Lou Thornbrough, *Indiana in the Civil War Era, 1850–1880* (Indianapolis: Indiana Historical Bureau, 1965), 541–543; Richard B. Pierce, "Negotiated Freedom: African Americans in Indiana," in *The State of Indiana History 2000: Papers Presented at the Indiana Historical Society's Grand Opening,* ed. Robert M. Taylor, Jr. (Indianapolis: Indiana Historical Society, 2001), 319–341, esp. 325–326; U.S. Census Office, *Population Schedules of the Eighth Census;* U.S. Census Office, *Population Schedules of the Ninth Census of the United States, 1870* (Washington, D.C.: National Archives, 1965).

89. *Putnam Republican Banner,* November 25, 1865.

90. Wyatt James Pension File, Native Archives, Washington, D.C.; *Putnam Republican Banner,* August 9, 1866.

91. Clark and Clark, "Heroes Carved in Ebony," 4–16.

92. Redkey, *Grand Army of Black Men,* 200–202.

93. Ibid., 223–225.

Chapter Seven. Radicals and Conservatives

1. *Putnam Republican Banner,* September 9, 1868. The classic history of postwar politics and finances is Irwin Unger, *The Greenback Era: A Social and Political History of American Finance, 1865–1879* (Princeton, N.J.: Princeton University Press, 1964). Although Unger acknowledges the Civil War origins of greenbacks, he is more interested in detailing the ideologies of soft and hard money, their reception by the major political parties, and the history of the third-party movements of the Grange and Greenbackers. Similarly, Gretchen Ritter emphasizes the

feasibility of the antimonopoly tradition and its attempt to ensure economic opportunity. See Ritter, *Goldbugs and Greenbacks: The Antimonopoly Tradition and the Politics of Finance in America* (Cambridge: Cambridge University Press, 1997), ix, 19. Industrial change and political corruption sparked a movement for reform that eroded northern commitment to Reconstruction, according to Eric Foner, *Reconstruction: America's Unfinished Revolution, 1863–1877* (New York: Harper & Row, 1988), 488–499. Michael O'Malley explicitly links racial and economic policy, arguing that the Civil War unsettled essentialist notions of the "intrinsic value" of currency and people by creating greenbacks and altering African Americans' status. Specie resumption and restoration of white supremacy reaffirmed the idea of "intrinsic value." See O'Malley, "Specie and Species: Race and the Money Question in Nineteenth-Century America," *American Historical Review* 99 (April 1994): 369–395.

2. (Indianapolis) *Daily State Sentinel*, April 8, 1865; *Weekly Indiana Press*, August 19, 1868.

3. R. M. Hazelett to Br James B. Kelly, March 16, 1862, Martha Goehring Materials, folder 10, DC 287, Andrew W. Crandall Papers, Archives and Special Collections, DePauw University, Greencastle, Ind.

4. *Greencastle Banner*, January 15, 1875.

5. *Putnam Republican Banner*, May 11, August 17, 24, 1865.

6. Michael W. Fitzgerald, *Splendid Failure: Postwar Reconstruction in the American South* (Chicago: Ivan R. Dee, 2007), 36–37; *Daily State Sentinel*, May 25, 1865; *Indianapolis Daily Journal*, August 25, 27, 1866; *Putnam Republican Banner*, September 30, 1865; *Indianapolis Daily Herald*, March 9, June 19, 1866.

7. *Weekly Indiana Press*, February 12, July 29, September 30, 1868.

8. Fitzgerald, *Splendid Failure*, 72–73, 89; *Putnam Republican Banner*, May 20, 1868; *Weekly Indiana Press*, May 20, 1868.

9. *Putnam Republican Banner*, July 15, 1868; *Weekly Indiana Press*, July 15, 1868.

10. *Putnam Republican Banner*, July 15, 1868; *Weekly Indiana Press*, July 22, August 19, 22, 1868; Emma Lou Thornbrough, *Indiana in the Civil War Era, 1850–1880* (Indianapolis: Indiana Historical Bureau, 1965), 240.

11. *Weekly Indiana Press*, August 5, 1868.

12. *Putnam Republican Banner*, August 12, 1868.

13. *Weekly Indiana Press*, August 5, 1868.

14. *Putnam Republican Banner*, July 4, 1867.

15. *Weekly Indiana Press*, August 5, 1868; *Indiana Press*, June 7, November 22, 1871; *Greencastle Press*, August 16, 1876; *Putnam Republican Banner*, September 2, 1868; *Greencastle Banner*, July 31, 1873. For threats in Bainbridge, see ibid., September 16, 1873.

16. *Putnam Republican Banner*, August 17, 1865, July 19, August 30, 1866; *Indianapolis Daily Journal*, August 27, 1866.

17. *Indianapolis Daily Journal*, August 27, 1866.

18. *Weekly Indiana Press*, September 16, 1868.

19. Fitzgerald, *Splendid Failure*, 44; William R. Forstchen, "The 28th United States Colored Troops: Indiana's African Americans Go to War, 1863–1865" (Ph.D. diss., Purdue University, 1994), 50–51; *Indianapolis Journal*, June 25, 1869.

20. *Indianapolis Journal*, June 25, 1869.

21. *Putnam Republican Banner*, September 30, 1865.

22. *Weekly Indiana Press*, January 8, 1868; *Putnam Republican Banner*, September 30, 1865, June 14, 1866.

23. *Weekly Indiana Press,* January 22, 1868; *Putnam Republican Banner,* March 18, 1869.

24. *Indiana Press,* July 5, 1871; *Greencastle Banner,* August 1, 15, 1878; *Greencastle Press,* August 7, 1878.

25. *Indianapolis Journal,* June 25, 1869; *Putnam Republican Banner,* March 18, 1869; Thornbrough, *Indiana in the Civil War Era,* 242–246; *Putnam Republican Banner,* December 9, 1869.

26. *Weekly Indiana Press,* February 16, 1870.

27. *Indianapolis Journal,* February 16, 1870.

28. *Indiana Press,* January 10, March 20, 1872.

29. *Weekly Indiana Press,* March 2, 1870.

30. *Indianapolis Journal,* June 6, 1870; *Indianapolis Daily Sentinel,* May 9, 1870; *Indiana Press,* September 4, 18, 1872; *Putnam Republican Banner,* July 18, 1867; *Weekly Indiana Press,* January 22, 1868; *Greencastle Press,* October 18, 1876.

31. Thornbrough, *Indiana in the Civil War Era,* 237–238; *Putnam Republican Banner,* June 14, August 9, October 18, 1866.

32. *Weekly Indiana Press,* June 8, 1870.

33. Ann L. Skene and Denise DeBoy, *Putnam County, Indiana Naturalization Records, 1854–1929* (Indianapolis: Indiana State Archives, 1999). In the 1860s, 203 people were naturalized in Putnam County, down from 228 in the 1850s. During the 1870s, it was only 84. The predominance of the Irish also lessened. In the 1850s, the Irish were 71 percent of the immigrants. They were only 52 percent and 40 percent in the 1860s and 1870s, whereas German immigrants rose to 33 percent of the total in the 1870s. Indiana still received comparatively little foreign migration—less than 10 percent of Indiana's population was foreign born according to the 1880 census, compared to 14 percent in Ohio and 23 percent in Illinois. James J. Divita, "Without Tenement: The State of Indiana Ethnic History," in *The State of Indiana History 2000: Papers Presented at the Indiana Historical Society's Grand Opening,* ed. Robert M. Taylor, Jr. (Indianapolis: Indiana Historical Society, 2001), 91–124.

34. *Greencastle Banner,* March 7, April 18, May 2, 23, 30, 1878.

35. Ibid., September 12, 1878.

36. Ibid., July 11, August 8, 1878; *Greencastle Press,* May 29, June 5, 1878.

37. *Greencastle Banner,* September 12, 1878.

38. Ibid., October 24, 1878, September 23, 1880; *Greencastle Press,* June 12, 1878.

39. *Putnam Republican Banner,* February 7, March 7, 1867, May 27, 1868, February 4, 1869.

40. Ibid., September 23, October 7, November 4, 1868, February 4, 1869; *Weekly Indiana Press,* January 5, March 30, 1870; *Greencastle Banner,* September 7, 1876.

41. *Indianapolis Daily Herald,* June 19, 1866; *Putnam Republican Banner,* July 4, 1867.

42. *Putnam Republican Banner,* July 18, 1867; *Indianapolis Journal,* June 6, 1870.

43. *Weekly Indiana Press,* January 15, 1868; *Greencastle Press,* April 5, 1876; *Indianapolis Daily Sentinel,* December 23, 1879.

44. *Greencastle Press,* February 20, 1878; *Greencastle Banner,* September 2, 1880.

45. *Greencastle Banner,* September 2, 1880.

46. *Indianapolis Journal,* June 9, 1868; *Weekly Indiana Press,* February 26, 1868.

47. *Putnam Republican Banner,* June 17, September 9, 16, 1868.

48. *Indianapolis Journal,* September 4, 1868; *Weekly Indiana Press,* September 9, 1868.

49. *Putnam Republican Banner,* September 9, 1868.

50. *Putnam Republican Banner,* September 9, 1868.

51. *Weekly Indiana Press,* September 9, 16, 1868; *Putnam Republican Banner,* December 9, 1869.

52. *Weekly Indiana Press,* October 14, 1868.

53. Record of Official Bonds, 1844–1911, Putnam County, Clerk's Office, Putnam County Courthouse, Greencastle, Ind., 70; *Indiana Press,* June 5, 1872; *Greencastle Press,* June 10, October 14, 1874.

54. *Greencastle Press,* January 16, 1878.

55. *Greencastle Banner,* January 6, 20, 27, 1876.

56. Ibid., September 26, 1878.

57. Ibid., January 20, 1876.

58. Ibid., February 3, 1876.

59. *Biographical and Historical Record of Putnam County, Indiana* (Chicago: Lewis Publishing, 1887; reprinted 1975), 467–468; *Greencastle Banner,* April 6, 1876, March 28, 1878.

60. Thornbrough, *Indiana in the Civil Era,* 398–399, 401.

61. *Greencastle Banner,* August 28, November 27, 1873.

62. Ibid., November 27, 1873, January 22, April 23, 1874.

63. William G. Carleton, "Why Was the Democratic Party in Indiana a Radical Party, 1865–1890?" *Indiana Magazine of History* 42 (September 1916): 207–228.

64. *Greencastle Banner,* January 22, 1874; Richard M. Hazelett, "'Little Black Book': Memoirs of Richard M. Hazelett," William Henry Smith Memorial Library, Indiana Historical Society (hereafter cited as IHS), Indianapolis, 14–17.

65. *Greencastle Banner,* January 29, 1874; *Greencastle Press,* June 17, 1874; Foner, *Reconstruction,* 523. Although Irwin Unger sees this convention as the origin of greenbackism with an agenda hostile to specie resumption, corruption drove Putnam Republicans into the third-party movement. See Unger, *Greenback Era,* 293–296.

66. *Greencastle Press,* June 24, 1874; *Greencastle Banner,* June 25, 1874.

67. Rebecca Edwards, *New Spirits: Americans in the Gilded Age, 1865–1905* (New York: Oxford University Press, 2006), 82–87; *Indianapolis Sentinel,* February 10, 1878; Mark Wahlgren Summers, *The Gilded Age or, The Hazard of New Functions* (Upper Saddle River, N.J.: Prentice Hall, 1997), 227–230.

68. *Greencastle Banner,* July 30, 1874.

69. Ibid., September 24, 1874.

70. Ibid.

71. Thornbrough, *Indiana in the Civil War Era,* 292–293; *Greencastle Banner,* December 30, 1875.

72. Thornbrough, *Indiana in the Civil War Era,* 285, 292–293, 398–399, 401; *Greencastle Banner,* August 13, 1874, September 5, 1878.

73. Thornbrough, *Indiana in the Civil War Era,* 286–287; *Greencastle Press,* February 27, 1878.

74. *Greencastle Press,* May 1, 1878.

75. *Greencastle Dollar Press,* February 11, 1880.

76. Ibid.; *Greencastle Banner,* September 14, 1876, March 28, April 4, 1878, January 15, 22, May 20, 1880; Circuit Court, Civil Order Book, 2, May 1855–December 1857, Clerk's Office, Putnam County Courthouse, Greencastle, Ind., 21.

77. *Greencastle Press,* April 3, May 8, July 17, October 9, 16, 1878; *Indianapolis Daily Sentinel,* August 19, 1878; *Greencastle Banner,* September 12, 1878, February 12, April 8, May 13, 1880.

78. *Greencastle Banner,* July 22, 1880.

79. Ibid., October 21, 1880; Edwards, *New Spirits,* 82–87.

80. *Greencastle Press,* August 21, 1878; *Greencastle Dollar Press,* January 22, 1879.

81. Charles S. Voorhees, comp., *Speeches of Daniel W. Voorhees* (Cincinnati, Ohio: Robert Clarke, 1875), 497.

82. *Indianapolis Journal*, November 3, 1873.

83. *Greencastle Press*, January 16, 1878.

84. *Indianapolis Daily Journal*, November 11, 1867; Putnam County Sesquicentennial Committee, *A Journey through Putnam County History* (n.p., 1966), 187; *Greencastle Banner*, August 5, 19, 1875; Edwards, *New Spirits*, 1–3; Jesse W. Weik, *History of Putnam County, Indiana* (Indianapolis, Ind.: Bowen, 1910), 243–45; *Indianapolis Journal*, March 17, September 1, 1873; *Greencastle Banner*, September 4, 1873, October 29, 1874, August 23, 1877.

85. *Indianapolis Journal*, November 3, 1873.

86. *Greencastle Press*, November 11, 1874; *Greencastle Banner*, October 1, 1874.

87. *Greencastle Banner*, November 5, 1874, November 5, 1875; Weik, *History of Putnam County*, 243–245; *Biographical and Historical Record of Putnam County*, 316–317; *Indianapolis Journal*, October 30, 1874; Father to Ransom, October 29, 1874, box 4, Ransom Hawley Papers, Manuscripts of the Indiana Division, Indiana State Library (hereafter cited as ISL), Indianapolis; *Greencastle Press*, November 4, 1874.

88. *Greencastle Press*, November 4, 1874; *Indianapolis Journal*, October 29, 30, 1874; Putnam County Sesquicentennial Committee, *Journey through Putnam County History*, 187–189.

89. Weik, *History of Putnam County*, 49–50, 243–245; *Biographical and Historical Record of Putnam County*, 316–317; *Indianapolis Journal*, October 30, 1874; *Greencastle Banner*, November 5, 1874.

90. Father to Ransom, December 1, 1874, box 4, Ransom Hawley Papers, Manuscripts of the Indiana Division, ISL.

91. *Greencastle Press*, November 4, 1874.

92. *Greencastle Banner*, November 5, 1874; *Indianapolis Sentinel*, November 9, 1874.

93. *Greencastle Press*, November 4, 1874.

94. *Greencastle Banner*, November 5, 1875. Timothy R. Mahoney argues that boosters "sought to subsume self-interest into cooperative public efforts." With this approach, they would not only promote development but also advance themselves as part of a town's elite. See Mahoney, *Provincial Lives: Middle-Class Experience in the Antebellum Middle West* (Cambridge: Cambridge University Press, 1999), 83–84.

95. *Greencastle Banner*, November 5, 1875.

96. *Indianapolis Journal*, October 25, 1875; *Greencastle Banner*, November 5, 1875.

97. *Greencastle Banner*, November 5, 1874.

98. Ibid., November 19, 1874; Weik, *History of Putnam County*, 243–245.

99. *Indianapolis Journal*, October 30, 1874; *Greencastle Banner*, November 5, 12, December 31, 1874; *Greencastle Press*, November 4, 1874.

100. *Greencastle Banner*, December 28, 1876.

101. Weik, *History of Putnam County*, 243–245; *Greencastle Banner*, March 11, 1875; Putnam County Sesquicentennial Committee, *Journey through Putnam County History*, 163; *Indianapolis Sentinel*, September 23, 1877; *Greencastle Banner*, October 24, 1878.

102. Weik, *History of Putnam County*, 243–245; *Indianapolis Journal*, October 25, 1875.

103. *Indianapolis Journal*, October 26, 27, 1875; *Indianapolis Sentinel*, October 26, 29, 1875.

104. *Biographical and Historical Record of Putnam County*, 343; *Greencastle Banner*, April 23, August 13, 1874, June 15, 1876; *Greencastle Press*, August 12, 1874, February 9, May 24, 1876.

105. *Greencastle Banner*, May 4, 1876.

106. *Greencastle Press*, June 21, July 12, 26, 1876; *Indianapolis Sentinel*, July 13, 1876;

Greencastle Banner, July 13, 1876, May 30, July 18, 1878; *Indianapolis Daily Sentinel,* July 27, November 18, 1880.

107. *Greencastle Banner,* July 20, 1876.

108. Ibid., November 29, 1877.

109. Ibid., July 20, 1876.

110. *Greencastle Press,* April 12, 1876.

111. For the Hamburg massacre, see Foner, *Reconstruction,* 570–571; *Greencastle Banner,* October 5, 1876.

112. *Indianapolis Journal,* September 7, 1876; *Greencastle Banner,* September 14, 1876. Republicans also hoped to benefit from the fact that Harrison was the grandson of former Indiana territorial governor and president William Henry Harrison. Greencastle organized the Tippecanoe Veteran Republican Club, composed of men who had voted for William Henry Harrison for president in 1836 and 1840. The club had over 200 members. *Greencastle Banner,* September 7, 14, 1876.

113. *Greencastle Banner,* June 15, October 12, 19, 1876; *Greencastle Press,* October 4, 1876; *Indianapolis Sentinel,* August 24, October 10, 1876; Linda C. Gugin and James E. St. Clair, *The Governors of Indiana* (Indianapolis: Indiana Historical Society Press, 2006), 167; *Greencastle Press,* October 18, 1876.

114. Thornbrough, *Indiana in the Civil War Era,* 302–304; *Greencastle Press,* July 5, November 8, December 13, 1876; *Greencastle Banner,* November 9, 1876; Foner, *Reconstruction,* 568, 575.

115. *Greencastle Banner,* November 16, 1876.

116. *Greencastle Press,* December 27, 1876.

117. *Greencastle Banner,* December 28, 1876.

118. *Indianapolis Sentinel,* January 4, 1877; *Greencastle Banner,* January 4, 1877.

119. *Greencastle Banner,* August 22, 1878.

120. Jas. F. Darnall to O. P. Morton, January 20, 1877, Oliver Perry Morton Papers, Manuscripts of the Indiana Division, ISL; *Indianapolis Journal,* April 23, 1879.

121. Foner, *Reconstruction,* 579–582; C. Vann Woodward, *Reunion and Reform: The Compromise of 1877 and the End of Reconstruction* (Boston: Little, Brown, 1951), 195–197; Father to Ransom, February 26, 1877, box 5, Ransom Hawley Papers, Manuscripts of the Indiana Division, ISL.

122. *Indianapolis Journal,* March 6, 1877; *Indianapolis Sentinel,* February 10, 1878.

123. During the same period, purists also felt that the Fourth of July was not being properly solemnized. The orations and traditional reading of the Declaration of Independence began to be overshadowed by picnics and dancing. *Greencastle Banner,* July 10, 1873; July 9, 1874, July 8, 1875; *Putnam Republican Banner,* May 4, 18, 25, June 1, 1871.

124. *Indianapolis Daily Sentinel,* July 30, 1880; *Greencastle Press,* June 1, 1881.

125. *Greencastle Dollar Press,* July 23, 1879.

126. *Greencastle Press,* October 20, 1875.

127. *Greencastle Banner,* June 4, 1874.

128. Kate McIlvain to Mr. & Mrs. Hawley, May 21, 1875, box 5, Ransom Hawley Papers, Manuscripts of the Indiana Division, ISL. Decoration Day in Greencastle is the most consistently recorded, but, of course, ceremonies were held throughout the county. Reverend Hawley frequently recorded laying flowers on the soldiers' graves at Putnamville. See boxes 4 and 5, Ransom Hawley Papers, Manuscripts of the Indiana Division, ISL; *Greencastle Banner,* June 3, 1875.

129. *Greencastle Banner,* June 10, 1875; *Greencastle Press,* June 2, 1875.

130. Father to Ransom, June 2, 1876, box 5, Ransom Hawley Papers, Manuscripts of the Indiana Division, ISL; *Greencastle Banner,* June 1, 8, 1876; *Indianapolis Journal,* November 12, 1875; *Greencastle Banner,* December 9, 1875, May 31, June 7, 1877; *Greencastle Press,* June 1, 1881.

131. *Greencastle Press,* June 5, 1879; *Indianapolis Journal,* May 31, 1879.

132. *Greencastle Banner,* June 26, 1879; *Greencastle Press,* December 15, 1875.

133. *Greencastle Banner,* June 1, 1876, June 3, 1880; *Indianapolis Journal,* June 1, 1880.

134. *Greencastle Press,* June 1, 1881.

135. Foner, *Reconstruction,* 460–499.

Chapter Eight. Pensioners

1. Lucius Chapin grave, 8-5-4, Forest Hill Cemetery, Greencastle, Ind. Alice Chapin died in 1907 and is buried with Lucius. Her gravestone has not survived. Her parents are also buried nearby. Cemetery Lots, Book 1, p. 86, Forest Hill Cemetery, Greencastle, Ind.

2. *Congressional Record Appendix,* 50th Cong., 1st sess. (Washington, D.C.: Government Printing Office, 1888), 378–382. Sadly, the National Archives has misplaced C. C. Matson's pension records. Letter from National Archives and Records Administration, June 2, 2009, in the author's possession.

3. E. W. Morgan to Catherine James, October 17, 1932, Wyatt James Pension File, National Archives, Washington, D.C.; *Congressional Record Appendix,* 48th Cong., 1st sess. (Washington, D.C.: Government Printing Office, 1884), 728; *Congressional Record,* 47th Cong., 1st sess. (Washington, D.C.: Government Printing Office, 1882), 4744.

4. David W. Blight has written the seminal work on the war's memory. Blight argues that a reconciliationist memory of the war triumphed over one that valued emancipation and black rights. Reconciliation emphasized the honor and sacrifice of soldiers on both sides. Because it downplayed the importance of African Americans, reconciliation accommodated the goals of white supremacists. See Blight, *Race and Reunion: The Civil War in American Memory* (Cambridge, Mass.: Belknap Press, 2001), 1–5. Mark Wahlgren Summers says that veterans' organizations such as the Grand Army of the Republic prized "increased devotion to the honored dead" at the expense of "the new birth of freedom." See Summers, *The Gilded Age or, The Hazard of New Functions* (Upper Saddle River, N.J.: Prentice Hall, 1997), 55. John R. Neff, however, suggests that the very act of remembering the dead subverted the goal of reconciliation. To remember the dead was to remember their cause, although he faults both sides as being willing to sacrifice the memory of African Americans. See Neff, *Honoring the Civil War Dead: Commemoration and the Problem of Reconciliation* (Lawrence: University Press of Kansas, 2005), 1–15.

5. Much of the literature on pensions has concentrated on how veterans got their pensions—the political lobbying of veterans' organizations and legislative maneuvering—rather than on what those pensions meant to them. Theda Skocpol is interested in how the Civil War pension system helped delay a general European-style system of old-age benefits. She calls the veterans' pensions "non-economic," but they were awarded on the basis of disabilities that prevented veterans from working at manual labor. See Skocpol, *Protecting Soldiers and Mothers: The Political Origins of Social Policy in the United States* (Cambridge, Mass.: Belknap Press, 1992), viii, 26, 102–151. Stuart McConnell does an excellent job of explaining the evolution of pension law. Although he argues that the 1890 Dependent Pension Act amounted to a service pension that any honorably discharged veteran could receive, it was still premised on the veteran's dependency, his disability. See McConnell, *Glorious Contentment: The Grand Army of the Republic,*

1865–1900 (Chapel Hill: University of North Carolina Press, 1992), 149–153. Susan M. Sterett emphasizes that pensions were seen as the reward for service, not as charity, and that men who became disabled were, like women, then considered dependent. See Sterett, *Public Pensions: Gender and Civic Service in the States, 1850–1937* (Ithaca, N.Y.: Cornell University Press, 2003), 2–4, 25.

6. L. P. Chapin to [Alice], May 18, 1865, folder 5, box 2, Lucius Chapin Papers, William Henry Smith Memorial Library, Indiana Historical Society (hereafter cited as IHS), Indianapolis; L. P. Chapin to Wife, July 3, 1865, ibid.; Your Sister to Brother [Lucius], November 25, 1865, ibid.; "Declaration for Original Invalid Pension," March 22, 1879, Lucius Chapin Pension File, National Archives (hereafter cited as NA), Washington, D.C.; L. P. Chapin to [Alice], May 18, 1865, folder 5, box 2, Lucius Chapin Papers, William Henry Smith Memorial Library, IHS; J. W. Osborn to Lucius, September 14, 1865, ibid.

7. Affidavit of Lucius P. Chapin, December 18, 1880, Lucius Chapin Pension File, NA; Declaration for Original Invalid Pension, March 22, 1879, ibid.; *Weekly Indiana Press*, February 12, 1868; John M. Knight, Physician's Affidavit, December 24, 1891, Lucius Chapin Pension File, NA; Dr. John M. Knight, December 29, 1880, ibid.

8. Affidavit of Lucius P. Chapin, December 18, 1880, Lucius Chapin Pension File, NA; Affidavit of John M. Knight, February 23, 1881, ibid.

9. Affidavit of Lucius P. Chapin, December 18, 1880, ibid.; Jesse W. Weik, *History of Putnam County, Indiana* (Indianapolis, Ind.: Bowen, 1910), 493–494; Declaration for Original Invalid Pension, March 22, 1879, Lucius Chapin Pension File, NA; Circuit Court, Order Book 7, December 1867–October 1871, Clerk's Office, Putnam County Courthouse, Greencastle, Ind., 229; *Greencastle Press*, May 28, 1873, January 16, 1878; Circuit Court, Order Book Cir-Ct, 11 Civil, September 1875–August 1876, Clerk's Office, Putnam County Courthouse, Greencastle, Ind., 11; Affidavit of Lucius P. Chapin, December 18, 1880, Lucius Chapin Pension File, NA.

10. *Putnam Republican Banner*, February 8, 15, 1866, May 16, June 13, 1867; *Greencastle Banner*, March 4, 1880.

11. *Greencastle Banner*, May 25, 4, 1876, May 2, 1878.

12. Weik, *History of Putnam County*, 253; C. C. Matson to W. H. H. Terrell, July 8, 1865, Correspondence of the 71st Indiana Volunteer Regiment (6th Cavalry), Indiana State Archives (hereafter cited as ISA), Commission on Public Records, Indianapolis; Wm. H. Schlater, July 14, 1865, ibid.; Courtland Matson Muster Card, Civil War Records, ibid. C. C. Matson's father, John A. Matson, had also been called "Colonel," but the designation seems to have been more reflective of social position than of military service.

13. C. C. Matson to Gov. O. P. Morton, August 26, 1863, Correspondence of the 71st Indiana Volunteer Regiment (6th Cavalry), ISA.

14. Weik, *History of Putnam County*, 252; *Indianapolis Daily Herald*, June 19, 1866; *Indianapolis Sentinel*, November 25, 27, 1880.

15. *Putnam Republican Banner*, July 12, 1866.

16. Ibid., October 11, 1866.

17. Ibid., July 15, 1868; *Weekly Indiana Press*, July 22, 1868.

18. *Greencastle Banner*, February 19, 1880.

19. *Indianapolis Journal*, June 4, 1880.

20. *Greencastle Banner*, January 15, 1880; J. C. Williams to Father, May 20, 1888, folder 4, box 3, Worthington B. Williams Family Papers, William Henry Smith Memorial Library, IHS; Weik, *History of Putnam County*, 252–253; *Indianapolis Daily Sentinel*, December 13, 1871.

21. Affidavit of Enos Townsend and Jay Townsend, August 14, 1882, Wyatt James Pension

File, NA; Affidavit of Albert Meuse, March 22, 1890, ibid.; Affidavit of Luke Ennos Townsend, February 19, 1891, ibid.

22. Department of the Interior, Bureau of Pensions, August 18, 1898, ibid.; Wyatt James to Department of Interior, August 8, 1898, ibid.; Widow's Pension, July 15, 1927, ibid.; Department of the Interior, Bureau of Pensions, August 18, 1898, ibid.

23. Declaration for the Increase of Invalid Pension, March 3, 1888, ibid.; Commissioner to J. B. Cralls and Co., November 4, 1911, ibid.

24. *Putnam Republican Banner*, May 21, 1863.

25. Ibid., May 11, 1865.

26. Ibid., May 25, June 1, 1865, September 13, 1866; Weik, *History of Putnam County*, 214–215.

27. *Putnam Republican Banner*, February 1, 1866.

28. Gillum Ridpath, "Putnam County, Ind.," in *Atlas of Putnam Co., Indiana to Which Are Added Various General Maps, History, Statistics, Illustrations* (Chicago: J. H. Beers, 1879), 8; *Indianapolis Daily Journal*, December 28, 1866.

29. Ridpath, "Putnam County, Ind.," 8; Weik, *History of Putnam County*, 214–215; *Weekly Indiana Press*, July 6, 1870.

30. *Indianapolis Daily Journal*, December 28, 1866; Kirk Savage, *Standing Soldiers, Kneeling Slaves: Race, War, and Monument in Nineteenth-Century America* (Princeton, N.J.: Princeton University Press, 1997), 4–5, 162–167, 174, 177, 186–192.

31. *Greencastle Banner*, June 5, 1873, June 3, 1875, June 1, 1876, May 8, 1879, May 27, 1880.

32. *Putnam Republican Banner*, May 27, June 3, 1868.

33. Ibid., May 24, 1866; James H. Madison, "Civil War Memories and 'Pardnership Forgittin,' 1865–1913," *Indiana Magazine of History* 99 (September 2003): 204; *Indianapolis Journal*, September 15, 29, 1879; Emma Lou Thornbrough, *Indiana in the Civil War Era, 1850–1880* (Indianapolis: Indiana Historical Bureau, 1965), 234; *Greencastle Banner*, December 4, 1879, December 16, 1880; Donald R. Shaffer, "'I Would Rather Shake Hands with the Blackest Nigger in the Land': Northern Black Civil War Veterans and the Grand Army of the Republic," in *Union Soldiers and the Northern Home Front: Wartime Experiences and Postwar Adjustments*, ed. Paul A. Cimbala and Randall M. Miller (New York: Fordham University Press, 2002), 442–462; Donald R. Shaffer, *After the Glory: The Struggles of Black Civil War Veterans* (Lawrence: University Press of Kansas, 2004), 153–154; Weik, *History of Putnam County*, 253.

34. *Greencastle Press*, October 12, 1881.

35. Ibid., November 20, 1879.

36. Ibid., January 15, 1880. Greencastle was not the only post. There were posts in Russell Township, Bainbridge, and even the Democratic stronghold of Cloverdale. Putnam County Sesquicentennial Committee, *A Journey through Putnam County History* (n.p., 1966), 343; Weik, *History of Putnam County*, 188, 539–540, 649–651.

37. Madison, "Civil War Memories and 'Pardnership Forgittin,'" 204; *Greencastle Banner*, October 7, 21, 1875.

38. Edistina Williams to [Josiah], [1886], folder 2, box 3, Worthington B. Williams Family Papers, William Henry Smith Memorial Library, IHS.

39. *Putnam Republican Banner*, February 12, 1868.

40. Ibid., April 8, 1869; Maris A. Vinovskis, "Have Social Historians Lost the Civil War? Some Preliminary Demographic Speculations," in *Toward a Social History of the American Civil War: Exploratory Essays*, ed. Vinovskis (New York: Cambridge University Press, 1990), 1–30, esp.

27; Declaration for the Increase of an Invalid Pension, April 15, 1904, Lucius Chapin Pension File, NA; Increase Declaration, April 4, 1905, Wyatt James Pension File, NA; Skocpol, *Protecting Soldiers and Mothers*, 138.

41. Diarrhea was a common soldiers' disease caused by bacteria passed in the unsanitary camp conditions of the war. Scott Reynolds Nelson and Carol Sheriff, *A People at War: Civilians and Soldiers in America's Civil War, 1854–1877* (New York: Oxford University Press, 2007), 216. Eric T. Dean, Jr., however, notes that physical ailments such as diarrhea could be induced or aggravated by stress. In particular, Lucius's claims of sunstroke are suggestive, as Dean argues that sunstroke became a way to explain a Civil War soldier's breakdown from what today would be called combat fatigue. See Dean, *Shook over Hell: Post-traumatic Stress, Vietnam, and the Civil War* (Cambridge, Mass.: Harvard University Press, 1997), 131–132.

42. Affidavit of D. W. Layman, March 3, 1879, Lucius Chapin Pension File, NA.

43. Affidavit of S. J. Dickerson, April 18, 1879, ibid.

44. Affidavit of Jonas Seely, February 28, 1879, ibid.

45. Affidavit of Lucius P. Chapin, December 18, 1880, ibid.

46. Dr. H[iram] R. Pitchlynn, March 1, 1881, ibid.; Samuel Fisher, Examining Surgeon's Certificate, January 25, 1881, ibid.

47. Original Invalid Pension, ibid.; Increase of Pension, August 5, 1885, ibid.; John M. Knight, Physician's Affidavit, December 24, 1891, ibid.; L. H. Dickerson to Commissioner of Pensions, May 2, 1892, ibid.; Surgeon's Certificate, February 4, 1891, ibid.; L. H. Dickerson to Commissioner of Pensions, May 2, 1892, ibid.

48. George W. Wood, Neighbor or Citizen's Affidavit, May 13, 1891, ibid.; Joseph B. Sellers, Neighbor or Citizen's Affidavit, May 29, 1891, ibid.

49. Certificate No. 192084, ibid.; Invalid Pension: Reissue to Allow Additional Disability, ibid.

50. Medical Division, Bureau of Pensions, September 15, 1904, ibid.; Invalid Pension: Increase & Reissue to Allow Additional Disability, July 27, 1904, ibid.

51. Affidavit of Lucius P. Chapin, September 29, 1904, ibid.

52. Surgeon's Certificate, July 6, 1904, ibid.; Certificate No. 192084, ibid.; Hannah Lee Chapin Pettyjohn to Commissioner of Pension, April 14, 1915, ibid.

53. Affidavit of Albert Meuse, March 22, 1890, ibid.

54. Declaration for an Increase of an Invalid Pension, March 12, 1892, ibid.

55. Surgeon's Certificate, August 9, 1911, ibid.; Surgeon's Certificate, June 7, 1905, ibid.; Affidavit of Enos Townsend and Jay Townsend, August 14, 1882, ibid.; W. M. McGaughey, Medical Affidavit, August 17, 1911, ibid.; Affidavit of W. M. McGaughey, April 24, 1912, ibid.; Medical Affidavit, April 18, 1912, ibid.; Affidavit of Wyatt James, July 19, 1926, ibid.; Certificate of Death, Indiana State Board of Health, March 22, 1927, ibid.; Act of May 1, 1920 Increase, July 2, 1926, ibid.

56. McConnell, *Glorious Contentment*, 143–153. The attention—and pensions—received by Union veterans spurred veterans of the Mexican War to demand their share. See *Greencastle Banner*, March 19, 1874; *Indianapolis Sentinel*, February 10, 1878; *Congressional Record Appendix*, 47th Cong., 1st sess. (Washington, D.C.: Government Printing Office, 1882), 463–464.

57. *Congressional Record Appendix*, 48th Cong., 1st sess. (Washington, D.C.: Government Printing Office, 1884), 125.

58. *Congressional Record*, 48th Cong., 2nd sess. (Washington, D.C.: Government Printing Office, 1885), 495, 739, 2224–2226; McConnell, *Glorious Contentment*, 149–153; Skocpol, *Protecting Soldiers and Mothers*, 65, 129, 148.

59. John to Wife, July 9, 1865, John Applegate Manuscripts, Lilly Library, Indiana University, Bloomington.

60. Ibid.; Affidavit of Courtland C. Matson, February 25, 1868, John Applegate Pension File, NA; *Greencastle Banner*, January 22, 1880; James M. McPherson, *Battle Cry of Freedom: The Civil War Era* (New York: Ballantine Books, 1988), 796; "Declaration for Invalid Pension," May 2, 1866, John Applegate Pension File, NA; *Putnam Republican Banner*, December 4, 1867; Nelson and Sheriff, *People at War*, 227–228.

61. "Declaration for Invalid Pension," May 2, 1866; *Putnam Republican Banner*, December 4, 1867; Affidavit of John Applegate, August 15, 1867, John Applegate Pension File, NA; "Claim for Widow's Pension," ibid.

62. Affidavit of John Applegate, August 15, 1867, John Applegate Pension File, NA; "Claim for Widow's Pension," ibid.; "Declaration for Invalid Pension," May 2, 1866, ibid.; Affidavit of Rufus R. Town, September 6, 1867, ibid.

63. Affidavit of John Applegate, August 15, 1867, ibid.; "Claim for Widow's Pension," ibid.; Record of Official Bonds, No. 1, Putnam County, Clerk's Office, Putnam County Courthouse, Greencastle, Ind., 398; *Putnam Republican Banner*, October 2, December 4, 1867; Affidavit of John Applegate, August 15, 1867.

64. Folder, 1865–1886, John Applegate Manuscripts, Lilly Library, Indiana University, Bloomington.

65. "Claim for an Invalid Pension," John Applegate Pension File, NA; Richard S. Skidmore, *Civil War Veterans Buried in Forest Hill Cemetery, Greencastle, Indiana* (n.p., 1987), William Henry Smith Memorial Library, IHS; "Declaration for Invalid Pension," May 2, 1866, John Applegate Pension File, NA; Affidavit of John Applegate, August 15, 1867, ibid.; Samuel Fisher, M.D., "Examining Surgeon Certificate," April 10, 1866, ibid.; Affidavit of Rufus R. Town, ibid.; "Surgeon's Certificate of Biennial, Annual, or Semi-annual Examination, on Which the Pensioner Draws His Pension," August 27, 1867, ibid.; John S. Jennings to D. W. Hannamar, October 15, 1869, Correspondence of the 71st Indiana Volunteer Regiment (6th Cavalry), ISA.

66. Sterett, *Public Pensions*, 8; Megan J. McClintock, "Civil War Pensions and the Reconstruction of Union Families," *Journal of American History* 83 (September 1996): 456–480. McClintock argues that the generous policy toward dependents cannot be explained by the political influence historians generally ascribe. Women and children did not vote. Rather, McClintock sees the pensions for family members as aimed at encouraging enlistment by reassuring recruits that their families would be cared for. For a discussion of Confederate widows, see Jennifer L. Gross, "The United Daughters of the Confederacy, Confederate Widows, and the Lost Cause: 'We Must Not Forget or Neglect the Widows,'" in *Women on Their Own: Interdisciplinary Perspectives on Being Single*, ed. Rudolph M. Bell and Virginia Yans (New Brunswick, N.J.: Rutgers University Press, 2008), 180–200; Nancy Grey Osterud, *Bonds of Community: The Lives of Farm Women in Nineteenth-Century New York* (Ithaca, N.Y.: Cornell University Press, 1991), 72, 134–135.

67. Amy E. Holmes has found that 12 to 17 percent of widows in Indiana in 1890 were Civil War widows. Most of these women were between thirty-five and fifty-five at that time, meaning that many were probably of marriageable age after their husbands' deaths. See Holmes, "'Such Is the Price We Pay': American Widows and the Civil War Pension System," in *Toward a Social History of the American Civil War: Exploratory Essays*, ed. Maris A. Vinovskis (New York: Cambridge University Press, 1990), 171–195.

68. Irving E. Showerman and Maranda Showerman to Mrs. Applegate, January 5, 1867 [1868], John Applegate Manuscripts, Lilly Library, Indiana University, Bloomington.

69. P. W. Applegate to Kind and Affectionate Grand Daughter, May 31, 1871, ibid.

70. *Greencastle Banner,* April 5, 1877.

71. 1870 U.S. Federal Census, AncestryLibrary.com; Susan Ingalls Lewis, "Business Widows in Nineteenth-Century Albany, New York, 1813–1885," in *Women on Their Own: Interdisciplinary Perspectives on Being Single,* ed. Rudolph M. Bell and Virginia Yans (New Brunswick, N.J.: Rutgers University Press, 2008), 115–139; ES Applegate to Allie, January 8, 1888, John Applegate Manuscripts, Lilly Library, Indiana University, Bloomington; 1880 U.S. Federal Census, AncestryLibrary.com; *Indiana Press,* April 3, 10, 1872; Folder for Finances, 1869–1890, John Applegate Manuscripts, Lilly Library, Indiana University, Bloomington; Receipt, October 17, 1889, ibid.; Receipt, April 5, 1890, ibid.; Thomas J. Bowser to Mrs. Applegate, October 26, 1887, ibid.; Thomas J. Bowser to Mrs. Applegate, January 5, 1888, ibid.; T. J. Bowser to Mrs. Applegate, January 12, 1888, ibid.; Thomas J. Bowser to Mrs. Applegate, January 9, 1890, ibid.; Thomas J. Bowser to Mrs. Applegate, February 3, 1890, ibid.; Thomas J. Bowser to Elizabeth Applegate, February 26, 1890, ibid.; E. S. Applegate to Allie, December 28, 1887, ibid.; Madie Spotswood Rhoads to Mrs. Applegate, October 23, 1889, ibid.; Tax Receipts, ibid.; *Greencastle Press,* August 30, 1876; Affidavit of Elizabeth S. Applegate, June 18, 1885, John Applegate Pension File, NA; E. S. A. to Allie, January 1, 1888, John Applegate Manuscripts, Lilly Library, Indiana University, Bloomington.

72. *Greencastle Banner,* July 4, 1878; Thornbrough, *Indiana in the Civil War Era,* 477; 1880 U.S. Federal Census, AncestryLibrary.com.

73. *Putnam Republican Banner,* April 4, 1867, April 29, 1868, September 30, 1869; *Greencastle Banner,* January 2, February 6, 1873, November 26, 1874; *Indianapolis Journal,* September 18, 1871.

74. *Greencastle Banner,* September 18, 1873, November 5, 1875. The state attendance rate was 70 percent in 1873. In 1879, the average school term was 136 days in Indiana; it had been 68 days in 1866. Thornbrough, *Indiana in the Civil War Era,* 461–485; *Greencastle Banner,* September 25, October 23, 1873, November 5, 1875, June 3, 1880; *Indianapolis Journal,* May 13, 1867, July 10, 1877. The small numbers were consistent with high schools across the state, where few who entered graduated. Thornbrough, *Indiana in the Civil War,* 491; *Putnam Republican Banner,* May 6, 1868.

75. Folder of Printed Material, John Applegate Manuscripts, Lilly Library, Indiana University, Bloomington. The Applegates belonged to the Disciples of Christ Church. Allie converted to Methodism when she married White.

76. E. S. A. to Allie, January 1, 1888, John Applegate Manuscripts, Lilly Library, Indiana University, Bloomington.

77. E. S. A. to Allie, January 23, 1888, ibid.

78. E. S. A to —, October 16, 1887, ibid.; E. S. A. to Allie, October 7, 1887, ibid.; Gramma to Allie, December 18, 1887, ibid.; E. S. Applegate to Allie, December 28, 1887, ibid.; E. S. Applegate to Allie, February 12, 1888, ibid.; E. S. Applegate to Allie, January 8, 1888, ibid.; Granma to Allie, November 11, 1888, ibid.; E. S. Applegate to Allie, September 9 [no year], ibid.; E. S. A. to Allie, October 7, 1887, ibid.; *Putnam Republican Banner,* December 4, 1867; [E. S. Applegate] to Allie, June 28, [1888], John Applegate Manuscripts, Lilly Library, Indiana University, Bloomington; S. A. Ross to Mrs. Applegate, June 15, 1890, ibid.; E. S. Applegate to Allie, February 8, 1888, ibid.; E. S. Applegate to Allie, [February 27, 1888], ibid.

79. Affidavit of Elizabeth S. Applegate, June 18, 1885, John Applegate Pension File, NA; S. T. Johnston to Elizabeth S. Applegate, February 15, 1888, Folder for January–May 1888, John Applegate Manuscripts, Lilly Library, Indiana University, Bloomington; E. S. Applegate to Allie,

[February 27, 1888], ibid.; Jesse W. Weik to E. S. Applegate, February 14, 1890, ibid.; Jesse W. Weik to Mr. White, May 9, 1890, ibid.; J. H. Franklin to Alma E. White, June 29, 1890, ibid.

80. Order from Hoffman & Long Dealers in Bronze, Granite, Marble and Stone Monuments, June 23, 1890, John Applegate Manuscripts, Lilly Library, Indiana University, Bloomington; John S. Applegate, 5-3-7, Forest Hill Cemetery, Greencastle, Ind.; Skidmore, *Civil War Veterans Buried in Forest Hill Cemetery.*

81. Declaration for Widow's Army Pension, January 31, 1868, John Applegate Pension File, NA; Affidavit of Charity Townsend, October 1884, Robert Townsend Pension File, NA.

82. Affidavit of Charity Townsend, October 1884, Townsend Pension File, NA; Affidavit of Daniel W. Layman, June 12, 1884, ibid.; Affidavit of D. W. Layman, July 24, 1884, ibid.; Declaration for Mother's Army Pension, June 27, 1884, ibid.; Affidavit of William D. Butler, November 1, 1884, ibid.

83. Affidavit of Charity Townsend, October 1884, ibid.; Affidavit of D. W. Layman, July 24, 1884, ibid.

84. Affidavit of Charity Townsend, October 1884, ibid.

85. Affidavit of Charity Townsend, December 6, 1871, ibid.; Certificate No. 212299, Affidavit of Charity Townsend, October 1884, ibid.; Affidavit of William Townsend, February 2, 1872, ibid.; Declaration for Mother's or Father's Application for Army Pension, July 1, 1878, ibid.; Dependent Parents, February 21, 1885, ibid.; Shaffer, *After the Glory,* 122; Murray L. Townsend, Jr., *Townsend-Pittman Family Reunion* (privately published, 2005), 24.

86. Charity died in 1892. Indiana Works Progress Administration, *Index to Death Records, Putnam County, Indiana 1880–1920* (Greencastle, Ind.: n.p., 1940). Charity's daughter, Catherine, Wyatt James's widow, also received a pension, from 1927 to her death in 1939. Widow's Pension, July 15, 1927, Wyatt James Pension File, NA; Reimbursement, ibid.

87. Thornbrough, *Indiana in the Civil War Era,* 522; George B. Manhart, *DePauw through the Years,* 2 vols. (Greencastle, Ind.: DePauw University, 1962), 1:79–85; *Indianapolis Sentinel,* December 14, 1872, November 18, 1873; *Indianapolis Journal,* June 12, 1875; *Indianapolis Daily Sentinel,* June 11, 1875. A surviving example of female students' work is Martha Jane Ridpath's address, "Ancient Classical Oration: The Influence of Greek Culture," June 19, 1879, folder 2, Martha Jane Ridpath Papers, Archives and Special Collections, DePauw University, Greencastle, Ind.

88. Putnam County Sesquicentennial Committee, *Journey through Putnam County History,* 212; Weik, *History of Putnam County,* 128; Elizabeth Ames and Eleanor Cammack, *The Woman's Club, Greencastle, Indiana* (Greencastle, Ind.: Woman's Club, 1974), 1–5; Anne Ruggles Gere, *Intimate Practices: Literacy and Cultural Work in U.S. Women's Clubs, 1880–1930* (Urbana: University of Illinois Press, 1997), 24, 252; *Indianapolis Journal,* July 10, 1877, September 11, 1878; *Greencastle Banner,* May 2, 1878. Gere has emphasized the diversity of many clubwomen, but the Greencastle club reflected the white, native-born, Protestant background of most residents. See Gere, *Intimate Practices,* 2–16, 252; Box 1, Martha Jane Ridpath Papers, Archives and Special Collections, DePauw University, Greencastle, Ind.

89. *Indianapolis Journal,* October 31, 1870; *Greencastle Banner,* January 2, 1863, February 27, 1873.

90. *Indianapolis Journal,* December 3, 1872; *Greencastle Banner,* January 23, 1873.

91. *Putnam Republican Banner,* April 22, 1869.

92. Ibid., August 19, 1869.

93. *Indiana Press,* December 18, 1872.

94. *Greencastle Press,* January 22, 1873.

95. *Indiana Press,* December 11, 1872; *Greencastle Banner,* January 23, 1873; *Indianapolis Journal,* July 9, 1869.

96. *Putnam Republican Banner,* March 4, 1868; *Weekly Indiana Press,* March 11, 1868.

97. *Greencastle Banner,* November 18, 1880.

98. *Putnam Republican Banner,* April 22, 29, 1869; Thornbrough, *Indiana in the Civil War Era,* 258–261.

99. *Greencastle Press,* February 5, 1873.

100. Thornbrough, *Indiana in the Civil War Era,* 258–261; Clifton J. Phillips, *Indiana in Transition: The Emergence of an Industrial Commonwealth, 1880–1920* (Indianapolis: Indiana Historical Bureau, 1968), 498–502.

101. *Greencastle Banner,* January 11, 1877.

102. *Putnam Republican Banner,* April 29, 1869.

103. *Greencastle Banner,* March 20, 1873.

104. Phillips, *Indiana in Transition,* 498–502.

105. *Putnam Republican Banner,* March 28, April 11, 1867; Summers, *Gilded Age,* 174–176; Mrs. Felix McWhirter to Mrs. Applegate, April 10, 1880, John Applegate Manuscripts, Lilly Library, Indiana University, Bloomington; *Indiana Press,* December 21, 1870; Linda Gordon, "U.S. Women's History," in *The New American History,* ed. Eric Foner (Philadelphia: Temple University Press, 1990), 185–210, esp. 186. Jack S. Blocker, Jr., believes women were motivated by the real evils of alcoholism and saw the saloons as a threat to their menfolk. Barbara Leslie Epstein believes that the middle-class women who made up the crusaders faced little real threat from alcohol and were reacting to a perceived threat to the "family" as an ideal rather than to their own families specifically. Contrary to Blocker, she argues per capita alcohol consumption was on the decline. For Barbara Leslie Epstein, the crusade was a "proto feminist" movement that pitted women against "the institutions of male culture" and whose failure convinced them of the necessity of woman suffrage to achieve reform. See Blocker, *"Give to the Winds Thy Fears": The Women's Temperance Crusade, 1873–1874* (Westport, Conn.: Greenwood Press, 1985); Epstein, *The Politics of Domesticity: Women, Evangelism, and Temperance in Nineteenth-Century America* (Middletown, Conn.: Wesleyan University Press, 1981), 1–4.

106. *Indiana Press,* December 21, 1870.

107. *Greencastle Banner,* March 9, 1871; *Indiana Press,* March 1, 8, 1871.

108. *Greencastle Banner,* March 9, 1871.

109. *Indiana Press,* April 12, 1871.

110. *Greencastle Banner,* March 16, 1871.

111. Ibid., April 20, 1871.

112. Ibid., March 16, 30, 1871.

113. Ibid.; *Indiana Press,* March 15, 22, 1871; *Indianapolis Journal,* March 15, 1871.

114. *Indiana Press,* June 14, July 26, 1871, February 14, 1872; John Cawley v. James D. Stevenson et al., Circuit Court, Order Book 7, December 1867—October 1871, Clerk's Office, Putnam County Courthouse, Greencastle, Ind., 630–635; *Indianapolis Journal,* December 18, 1871; Order Book 8, October 1871–October 1873, Clerk's Office, Putnam County Courthouse, Greencastle, Ind., 289, 349; State of Indiana v. John Cawley, Order Book, Civil 9, September 1873–October 1874, ibid., 52; James E. Downey v. John Cawley and the City of Greencastle, Order Book Cir-Ct 11, September 1875–August 1876, ibid., 13, 132, 235–236; ibid., 228–229.

115. Thornbrough, *Indiana in the Civil War Era,* 262–265.

116. Father to Ransom, March 20, 1873, box 4, Ransom Hawley Papers, Manuscripts of the Indiana Division, Indiana State Library, Indianapolis.

117. *Greencastle Banner*, March 20, 1873.

118. Ibid., April 3, 1873.

119. Ibid., April 10, 1873.

120. Ibid., April 17, 1873.

121. *Greencastle Press*, August 13, 1873.

122. Ibid., May 28, 1873; *Greencastle Banner*, September 4, 11, 1873; *Indianapolis Journal*, September 12, 1873.

123. *Greencastle Press*, March 26, December 9, 1874; *Indianapolis Journal*, September 12, 1873.

124. Blocker, *"Give to the Winds Thy Fears,"* 3–5, 10–12, 25, 37–38; Epstein, *Politics of Domesticity*, 98. Although students of the crusade have emphasized that it was a woman's movement against the male culture of the saloon, the woman's crusade in Greencastle remained—as the local temperance movement long had been—an alliance of men and women. Men did most of the speaking at meetings, but the officers were almost all women, including Desire A. Pitchlynn, the doctor's wife, and Jennie Fletcher Allen. *Greencastle Press*, March 18, March 26, December 9, 1874; *Greencastle Banner*, April 9, 1874.

125. *Greencastle Banner*, January 29, 1874.

126. Ibid., March 26, 1874.

127. Ibid.

128. *Greencastle Press*, March 18, March 26, December 9, 1874; *Greencastle Banner*, April 9, 1874.

129. *Greencastle Press*, April 8, 22, 1874; *Indianapolis Sentinel*, April 9, 1874; *Greencastle Banner*, April 16, 1874.

130. *Greencastle Banner*, July 30, August 13, September 3, 17, 1874.

131. Ibid., April 16, 1874.

132. Ibid.

133. *Greencastle Banner*, April 16, 1874.

134. Ibid., April 30, 1874; *Indianapolis Sentinel*, May 4, 1874; *Greencastle Press*, May 20, June 17, November 18, 1874.

135. *Greencastle Press*, June 17, July 29, 1874.

136. Ibid., February 3, June 9, November 10, 1875.

137. Summers, *Gilded Age*, 10–11.

138. *Greencastle Press*, July 24, 1878; *Putnam Republican Banner*, April 4, 1867.

139. *Greencastle Banner*, April 23, 1874.

140. Ibid., November 10, 1875.

141. Ibid., September 2, 1874.

142. *Indiana Press*, September 6, 1871.

143. *Putnam Republican Banner*, February 5, 1868.

144. *Indianapolis Journal*, July 23, 1875; *Greencastle Banner*, July 31, 1873; *Greencastle Press*, July 30, 1873.

145. *Greencastle Press*, August 26, 1874. Scott C. Martin argues there was a misogynistic strain in the temperance movement despite women's importance to it. See Martin, *Devil of the Domestic Sphere: Temperance, Gender, and Middle-Class Ideology, 1800–1860* (DeKalb: Northern Illinois University Press, 2008), 8.

146. Thornbrough, *Indiana in the Civil War Era*, 262–265; Blocker, *"Give to the Winds Thy Fears,"* 220; Summers, *Gilded Age*, 10–11; Epstein, *Politics of Domesticity*, 117.

147. *Greencastle Banner*, September 24, 1874.

148. Epstein, *Politics of Domesticity*, 115, 121.

149. Thornbrough, *Indiana in the Civil War Era*, 265; *Greencastle Banner*, January 3, June 20, 1878.

150. *Indianapolis Journal*, August 7, 1877, August 6, 1878, February 5, April 15, 1879.

Chapter Nine. Exodusters

1. *Putnam Republican Banner*, August 9, 1866.

2. The well-known Exodus to Kansas is detailed in Nell Irvin Painter, *Exodusters: Black Migration to Kansas after Reconstruction* (New York: Knopf, 1977), and Robert G. Athearn, *In Search of Canaan: Black Migration to Kansas, 1879–1880* (Lawrence: University Press of Kansas, 1978). Leslie A. Schwalm studies Iowa, Minnesota, and Wisconsin in *Emancipation's Diaspora: Race and Reconstruction in the Upper Midwest* (Chapel Hill: University of North Carolina Press, 2009), 1–7, 83, 105.

3. Darrel E. Bigham, *On Jordan's Banks: Emancipation and Its Aftermath in the Ohio River Valley* (Lexington: University Press of Kentucky, 2006), 152; 1870 U.S. Census, Heritage Quest; 1880 U.S. Census, Heritage Quest; U.S. Senate, *Report and Testimony of the Select Committee of the United States Senate to Investigate the Causes of the Removal of the Negroes from the Southern States to the Northern States,* 46th Cong., 2nd sess., 1880, Report 693, (hereafter cited as Voorhees Report) (Washington, D.C.: Government Printing Office, 1880), pt. 1, pp. 162–190.

4. Emma Lou Thornbrough, *Indiana in the Civil War Era, 1850–1880* (Indianapolis: Indiana Historical Bureau, 1965), 417, 419, 423; Mark Wahlgren Summers, *The Gilded Age or, The Hazard of New Functions* (Upper Saddle River, N.J.: Prentice Hall, 1997), 90–91; *Indianapolis Daily Sentinel*, March 14, 1870.

5. *Indianapolis Journal*, May 13, 1867; *Putnam Republican Banner*, February 26, 1868; Putnam County Sesquicentennial Committee, *A Journey through Putnam County History* (n.p., 1966), 168–169.

6. *Indianapolis Sentinel*, October 9, 1873.

7. *Putnam Republican Banner*, May 16, 1867, April 22, 1869; *Indianapolis Journal*, September 6, 1870.

8. *Indianapolis Journal*, March 10, 1870.

9. Ibid., September 3, 1873, August 1, 1879.

10. Ibid., April 17, 1873.

11. Jesse W. Weik, *History of Putnam County, Indiana* (Indianapolis, Ind.: Bowen, 1910), 148; *Indianapolis Daily Sentinel*, September 19, 1868, September 15, 1871; *Indianapolis Journal*, September 15, 1871, September 21, 1872, August 21, 1874.

12. *Indianapolis Journal*, July 10, 1877; *Greencastle Banner*, November 13, 20, 1879.

13. William G. Carleton, "Why Was the Democratic Party in Indiana a Radical Party, 1865–1890?" *Indiana Magazine of History* 42 (September 1916): 207–228; Paul Salstrom, *From Pioneering to Persevering: Family Farming in Indiana to 1880* (West Lafayette, Ind.: Purdue University Press, 2007), 118–119; *Weekly Indiana Press*, October 22, 1870; Weik, *History of Putnam County*, 462–464.

14. Heather Cox Richardson, *The Greatest Nation on Earth: Republican Economic Policies during the Civil War* (Cambridge, Mass.: Harvard University Press, 1997), 168; *Greencastle Banner*, June 25, 1874.

15. Elmer Thomas, "'Forty Years a Legislator': Memoir of a Hoosier Boyhood," *Indiana Magazine of History* 103 (December 2007): 384–410.

16. Ibid.

17. Folder 1, box 1, Vincent H. Day Family Collection, William Henry Smith Memorial Library, Indiana Historical Society (hereafter cited as IHS), Indianapolis; folder 4, ibid.; 1870 U.S. Census, AncestryLibrary.com. The average price for improved Indiana farmland in 1880 was $60 per acre, but this would include the less valuable land in the extreme northern and southern parts of the state. Robert P. Porter, *The West, from the Census of 1880: A History of the Industrial, Commercial, Social, and Political Development of the States and Territories of the West from 1800 to 1880* (Chicago: Rand, McNally, 1882), 145.

18. Thornbrough, *Indiana in the Civil War Era*, 369; R. Douglas Hurt, *American Agriculture: A Brief History* (Ames: Iowa State University Press, 1994), 165, 172, 215–216.

19. Lowell H. Harrison, ed., "A British View of Indiana's Agriculture, 1879," *Indiana Magazine of History* 68 (December 1972): 307–314; Jeremy Atack and Fred Bateman, *To Their Own Soil: Agriculture in the Antebellum North* (Ames: Iowa State University Press, 1987), 110–111; U.S. Census Office, *Report of the Productions of Agriculture as Returned at the Tenth Census* (Washington, D.C.: Government Printing Office, 1883), 28–29.

20. *Greencastle Banner,* October 2, 9, 23, November 3, 1873.

21. Ibid., November 27, 1873.

22. Thornbrough, *Indiana in the Civil War Era,* 512–514.

23. *Greencastle Banner,* October 12, 1876.

24. *Greencastle Press,* June 17, 1874.

25. *Indianapolis Journal,* December 16, 1876; *Indianapolis Sentinel,* December 18, 1877.

26. *Greencastle Press,* August 7, 1878.

27. Summers, *Gilded Age,* xiv–xv.

28. Heather Cox Richardson, *The Death of Reconstruction: Race, Labor, and Politics in the Post–Civil War North, 1865–1901* (Cambridge, Mass.: Harvard University Press, 2001), ix–xv.

29. *Putnam Republican Banner,* June 1, 1865; *Greencastle Press,* July 26, 1876.

30. *Greencastle Banner,* February 29, May 10, 1877; *Putnam Republican Banner,* January 14, 28, 1869.

31. *Greencastle Banner,* August 3, 1876.

32. 1880 Census, AncestryLibrary.com.

33. Thornbrough, *Indiana in the Civil War Era,* 481–483.

34. *Greencastle Banner,* January 1, 1880.

35. Ibid., April 3, 1879.

36. Ibid., January 1, 1880.

37. Ibid., February 26, 1880.

38. Ibid., January 1, 1880.

39. Putnam County Sesquicentennial Committee, *Journey through Putnam County History,* 199.

40. *Putnam Republican Banner,* March 18, 1869.

41. Putnam County Sesquicentennial Committee, *Journey through Putnam County History,* 290–291; Clifton Phillips, ed., *From Frontier Circuit to Urban Church: A History of Greencastle Methodism* (Greencastle, Ind.: Gobin Memorial United Methodist Church, 1989), 61–62; Weik, *History of Putnam County,* 117; Gillum Ridpath, "Putnam County, Ind.," in *Atlas of Putnam Co., Indiana to Which Are Added Various General Maps, History, Statistics, Illustrations* (Chicago: J. H. Beers, 1879), 8; *Greencastle Banner,* December 9, 1880.

42. Murray L. Townsend, Jr., *Townsend-Pittman Family Reunion* (privately published, 2005), 205–206; Ridpath, "Putnam County, Ind.," 8; Phillips, *From Frontier Circuit to Urban Church,* 61–62;

Putnam County Sesquicentennial Committee, *Journey through Putnam County History*, 190–191. See also *Greencastle Banner*, July 24, August 14, 1879; *Indianapolis Journal*, August 11, 18, 1879.

43. *Greencastle Press*, February 2, 1876.

44. Ibid., August 14, 1878.

45. *Greencastle Banner*, May 25, June 22, 1876.

46. Ibid., December 27, 1877.

47. Ibid., June 1, 1876, December 6, 1877; *Indianapolis Journal*, December 1, 1876.

48. *Greencastle Banner*, April 11, 1878; *Indianapolis Journal*, August 1, 12, 1878.

49. *Greencastle Banner*, October 3, 1878.

50. Ibid., December 9, 1875; Louis R. Harlan, *Booker T. Washington: The Making of a Black Leader, 1856–1901* (New York: Oxford University Press, 1972), vii–x.

51. *Greencastle Press*, June 26, 1878.

52. *Greencastle Banner*, July 4, 1878.

53. Ibid., December 12, 1878.

54. Ibid., March 20, 1879.

55. Ibid., April 24, 1879.

56. Emma Lou Thornbrough, *The Negro in Indiana before 1900: A Study of a Minority* (1957; reprint, Bloomington: Indiana University Press, 1993), 215–223; *Indianapolis Daily Sentinel*, December 22, 1879; Voorhees Report, pt. 2, pp. 243–247.

57. Thornbrough, *Negro in Indiana before 1900*, 215–223; *Indianapolis Daily Sentinel*, December 22, 1879; *Indianapolis Journal*, February 18, 1880.

58. Voorhees Report, pt. 1, pp. 280–303.

59. *Greencastle Banner*, April 10, 1879; *Indianapolis Journal*, April 12, 1879.

60. *Greencastle Banner*, December 25, 1879, January 1, 29, 1880; Voorhees Report, pt. 1, pp. 133–134, 280–303.

61. *Indianapolis Daily Sentinel*, December 3, 1879.

62. Ibid., December 22, 1879.

63. Most of the migrants were from Greene, Jones, Lenoir, and Wayne counties. Joseph H. Taylor, "The Great Migration from North Carolina in 1879," *North Carolina Historical Review* 31 (January 1954): 18–33. John G. Van Deusen estimates that less than half the migrants were adult male voters. See Van Deusen, "Did Republicans 'Colonize' Indiana in 1879?" *Indiana Magazine of History* 30 (September 1934): 334–346.

64. *Greencastle Banner*, January 8, 1880.

65. Voorhees Report, pt. 1, pp. 162–190.

66. Jeffrey J. Crow, Paul D. Escott, and Flora J. Hatley, *A History of African Americans in North Carolina* (Raleigh: North Carolina Office of Archives and History, 2002), 71, 91–92; *Greencastle Banner*, March 4, 1880; Voorhees Report, pt. 1, pp. 280–303, pt. 2, pp. 302–338; Claude A. Clegg III, *The Price of Liberty: African Americans and the Making of Liberia* (Chapel Hill: University of North Carolina Press, 2004), 256, 260.

67. *Greencastle Banner*, December 11, 1879.

68. Voorhees Report, pt. 2, pp. 302–338, 506–512.

69. *Indianapolis Journal*, December 19, 1879; *Greencastle Banner*, January 1, 1880.

70. *Greencastle Banner*, January 8, 1880; Thornbrough, *Negro in Indiana before 1900*, 215–223; *Indianapolis Journal*, December 19, 1879.

71. *Greencastle Banner*, January 29, 1880; Van Deusen, "Did Republicans 'Colonize' Indiana in 1879?" 338; *Indianapolis Sentinel*, September 18, 1880; *Indianapolis Journal*, November 25, 1879.

72. *Greencastle Banner,* December 4, 1879.

73. Ibid., January 1, 8, 1880.

74. *Biographical and Historical Record of Putnam County, Indiana* (Chicago: Lewis Publishing, 1887, reprinted 1975), 359; *Greencastle Dollar Press,* November 12, December 10, 1879, January 7, 1880; *Indianapolis Daily Sentinel,* November 15, 1879, January 28, 1880; Voorhees Report, pt. 1, pp. 162–190, pt. 2, pp. 302–338.

75. *Greencastle Banner,* January 15, 1880.

76. Ibid., December 4, 1879.

77. Ibid., January 29, 1880.

78. Ibid., November 20, December 18, 1879.

79. *Greencastle Dollar Press,* November 19, 1879.

80. Voorhees Report, pt. 1, pp. 162–190.

81. *Greencastle Dollar Press,* April 2, 1879.

82. Ibid., October 29, 1879.

83. Ibid., December 3, 1879.

84. *Greencastle Banner,* August 28, 1879. Republicans claimed that Democrats responded by colonizing their own voters, including recently pardoned Kentucky convicts. *Indianapolis Journal,* March 2, October 1, 1880; *Greencastle Banner,* March 4, April 8, 1880.

85. *Greencastle Banner,* January 15, 1880; *Greencastle Dollar Press,* January 14, 1880.

86. *Greencastle Banner,* December 4, 1879.

87. Ibid.

88. Voorhees Report, pt. 2, pp. 506–512; Van Deusen, "Did Republicans 'Colonize' Indiana in 1879?" 343.

89. *Greencastle Banner,* January 1, 1880.

90. Ibid., December 11, 1879.

91. Ibid., December 25, 1879.

92. Ibid., January 29, 1880.

93. Ibid., February 26, 1880.

94. *Indianapolis Journal,* August 13, 1880.

95. *Indianapolis Daily Sentinel,* December 3, 1879.

96. *Greencastle Banner,* September 23, 1880.

97. Ibid., April 8, 1880.

98. *Indianapolis Journal,* August 7, 1880; *Greencastle Banner,* October 21, 28, November 3, 1880.

99. *Indianapolis Daily Sentinel,* April 7, May 5, 1880; *Greencastle Banner,* July 22, 1880; *Greencastle Dollar Press,* December 3, 31, 1879.

100. *Greencastle Banner,* July 22, 1880.

101. *Greencastle Dollar Press,* February 4, 18, 1880.

102. *Greencastle Banner,* January 15, 1880; *Greencastle Dollar Press,* January 14, 1880.

103. *Greencastle Dollar Press,* October 29, 1879; Voorhees Report, pt. 1, pp. 162–190, pt. 2, pp. 506–512; *Indianapolis Daily Sentinel,* November 11, 1879.

104. *Greencastle Banner,* October 30, 1879.

105. Voorhees Report, pt. 2, pp. 485–512.

106. *Indianapolis Journal,* November 25, 1879.

107. *Greencastle Banner,* December 4, 1879, March 4, 1880.

108. Ibid., December 25, 1879, January 8, February 5, 1880. Although most of the

discussion was of farm labor, blacks found employment in the stone quarries, in limekilns, and on the railroads.

109. *Indianapolis Daily Sentinel,* December 9, 22, 1879; *Greencastle Banner,* January 1, 15, 1880.

110. *Greencastle Banner,* February 21, 1878, August 3, 1876; *Greencastle Dollar Press,* November 26, 1879.

111. *Greencastle Dollar Press,* December 17, 1879.

112. Voorhees Report, pt. 1, pp. 371–378.

113. Ibid., pp. 426–430.

114. *Greencastle Banner,* December 4, 1879.

115. Ibid., December 11, 1879; *Indianapolis Journal,* November 25, 1879; Voorhees Report, pt. 1, pp. 162–190.

116. *Greencastle Banner,* January 29, 1880.

117. Ibid., December 4, 1879, January 1, 1880.

118. Ibid., December 4, 1879.

119. Ibid., January 1, 1880.

120. Ibid., January 29, 1880.

121. Ibid., February 26, 1880.

122. Ibid., November 13, 1879, February 26, 1880.

123. Ibid., December 4, 1879.

124. Ibid., December 11, 1879.

125. Ibid., December 4, 1879.

126. Ibid.

127. Ibid., January 8, 1880; Voorhees Report, pt. 2, pp. 302–338.

128. George P. Rawick, ed., *The American Slave: A Composite Autobiography,* supplement, ser. 1, vol. 5, *Indiana and Ohio Narratives* (Westport, Conn.: Greenwood Press, 1977), 160–163.

129. *Chicago Daily Inter-Ocean,* February 10, 1880, quoted in Nell Irvin Painter, *Exodusters: Black Migration to Kansas after Reconstruction* (New York: Knopf, 1977), 251–252n50.

130. *Greencastle Banner,* November 20, December 18, 1879; Voorhees Report, pt. 1, pp. 162–190.

131. Voorhees Report, pt. 1, pp. 220–222.

132. Ibid., pp. 220–222, 225–226, 426–430; *Greencastle Dollar Press,* February 4, 1880.

133. *Greencastle Banner,* January 29, 1880; Voorhees Report, pt. 2, pp. 302–338.

134. *Indianapolis Journal,* February 17, 1880; Voorhees Report, pt. 1, pp. 371–378, pt. 2, pp. 302–338; *Greencastle Banner,* December 4, 1879, February 12, June 24, 1880; *Indianapolis Sentinel,* December 3, 1879, September 14, 18, 1880.

135. *Indianapolis Daily Sentinel,* December 9, 1879.

136. Ibid., December 3, 1879; *Greencastle Dollar Press,* March 24, 1880; *Indianapolis Sentinel,* September 18, 1880.

137. *Greencastle Dollar Press,* March 24, 1880.

138. *Greencastle Banner,* December 4, 1879.

139. Ibid., December 11, 18, 1879, February 26, 1880.

140. Voorhees Report, pt. 1, pp. 264–276; *Greencastle Banner,* January 1, 1880.

141. *Greencastle Banner,* January 29, 1880.

142. *Indianapolis Sentinel,* September 18, 1880; *Indianapolis Journal,* February 18, 1880; *Greencastle Banner,* December 18, 1879, January 1, 29, February 12, March 18, September 9, 1880.

143. *Greencastle Banner,* December 18, 1879.

144. *Indianapolis Journal,* February 18, 1880.

145. Voorhees Report, pt. 1, pp. 426–430; *Greencastle Banner,* December 25, 1879; *Greencastle Dollar Press,* December 31, 1879.

146. Voorhees Report, pt. 1, pp. 162–190.

147. *Greencastle Dollar Press,* June 9, 1880.

148. Voorhees Report, pt. 1, pp. 371–378.

149. *Indianapolis Journal,* January 29, February 11, 15, March 14, 1880. In addition to Voorhees, the committee included two Democrats, Zebulon B. Vance and George Pendleton, and two Republicans, William Windom and Henry W. Blair. U.S. Senate, *Miscellaneous Documents,* 46th Cong., 2nd sess., 1879, serial 1890, no. 15 (Washington, D.C.: Government Printing Office, 1880); Voorhees Report, pt. 1, p. xi.

150. Voorhees Report, pt. 1, pp. iii–viii.

151. Ibid., pp. ix–xxv; Thornbrough, *Negro in Indiana before 1900,* 215–223.

152. *Greencastle Banner,* November 25, 1880.

153. Ibid., December 16, 1880. In September 1880, Clay left Greencastle for a new post in Bloomington. He was succeeded by Reverend Burleigh, who came from Bloomington. Ibid., September 9, 1880.

154. Putnam County Sesquicentennial Committee, *Journey through Putnam County History,* 221; 1870 U.S. Census, AncestryLibrary.com; 1900 U.S. Census, AncestryLibrary.com; *Greencastle Banner,* December 18, 1879; 1890 U.S. Census, Census.gov, vol. 1, pt. 1, p. 409.

155. *Greencastle Dollar Press,* March 10, 1880.

156. Thornbrough, *Negro in Indiana before 1900,* 223.

157. 1900 U.S. Census, AncestryLibrary.com.

158. Affidavit of Stan Pittman, August 12, 1928, Wyatt James Pension File, National Archives, Washington, D.C.; Townsend, *Townsend-Pittman Family Reunion.*

Conclusion: The Monument Builder

1. *Biographical and Historical Record of Putnam County, Indiana* (Chicago: Lewis Publishing, 1887; reprinted 1975), 359; Jesse W. Weik, *History of Putnam County, Indiana* (Indianapolis, Ind.: Bowen, 1910), 129–130.

2. Kirk Savage, *Standing Soldiers, Kneeling Slaves: Race, War, and Monument in Nineteenth-Century America* (Princeton, N.J.: Princeton University Press, 1997), 4–8.

3. *Indianapolis Sentinel,* May 16, 1902.

4. Ibid., June 2, 1901; Ernestine Bradford Rose, *The Circle: "The Center of Our Universe"* (Indianapolis: Indiana Historical Society, 1957), 397–412; James Philip Fadely, "The Veteran and the Memorial: George J. Langsdale and the Soldiers and Sailors Monument," *Traces of Indiana and Midwestern History* 18 (Winter 2006): 27–35.

5. *Indianapolis Journal,* August 22, 23, 1889.

6. David J. Bodenhamer and Robert G. Barrows, *The Encyclopedia of Indianapolis* (Bloomington: Indiana University Press, 1994), 30, 1016.

7. Rose, *Circle,* 397–412; Fadely, "Veteran and the Memorial," 27–35; Anthony Eugene Grimaldi, "The Indiana Soldiers' and Sailors' Monument and Its Dedication: A Study of a Nineteenth Century American Monument and Its Allied Arts of Pageantry" (Ph.D. diss., Ohio

University, 1982), 27–28, 57–58; Bodenhamer and Barrows, *Encyclopedia of Indianapolis,* 908, 1242, 1279; *Indianapolis Journal,* May 16, 1902.

8. Rose, *Circle,* 397–412. John Bodnar comments that the statues of George Rogers Clark, William Henry Harrison, James Whitcomb (governor during the Mexican War), and Morton served to remind viewers of this monument to "ordinary soldiers" of the importance of elites. See Bodnar, "Commemorative Activity in Twentieth-Century Indianapolis: The Invention of Civic Traditions," *Indiana Magazine of History* 87 (March 1991): 1–23, esp. 5. *Indianapolis Sentinel,* May 16, 1902. Ransom E. Hawley opposed the monument, preferring to see the resources spent on the orphans' home. Before a veterans' reunion, he urged a friend, "We must fight the Indianapolis boys who want to build a stone monument." But his was an isolated complaint. R. E. Hawley to Comrade Agnew, n.d., box 3, Ransom Hawley Papers, Manuscripts of the Indiana Division, Indiana State Library, Indianapolis.

9. *Indiana Press,* December 4, 1872; *Indianapolis Sentinel,* February 20, 1874; Emma Lou Thornbrough, *Indiana in the Civil War Era, 1850–1880* (Indianapolis: Indiana Historical Bureau, 1965), 265–266.

10. U.S. Senate, *Report and Testimony of the Select Committee of the United States Senate to Investigate the Causes of the Removal of the Negroes from the Southern States to the Northern States,* 46th Cong., 2nd sess., 1880, Report 693 [Voorhees Report] (Washington, D.C.: Government Printing Office, 1880), pt. 2, p. 512.

11. *Greencastle Banner,* August 21, 28, September 11, 1873, December 3, 17, 1874, August 14, 1879; *Greencastle Press,* December 2, 1874.

12. Grimaldi, "Indiana Soldiers' and Sailors' Monument," 38–39, 40–45, 52, 58, 61; Rose, *Circle,* 397–412.

13. *Indianapolis Sentinel,* May 16, 1902.

14. As Kirk Savage documents, sculptors of post–Civil War monuments found it difficult to represent emancipation. Statues of Abraham Lincoln with a kneeling slave, either implied or present, receiving emancipation became a substitute. Not until the Robert Gould Shaw Memorial of the 1890s were blacks, in this case armed men, represented as agents in their own freedom. Savage, *Standing Soldiers, Kneeling Slaves,* 52–128, 195–208; Rose, *Circle,* 397–412; James H. Madison, "Civil War Memories and 'Pardnership Forgittin,' 1865–1913," *Indiana Magazine of History* 99 (September 2003): 198–230.

15. *Indianapolis Recorder,* May 17, 1902; *Indianapolis Journal,* May 16, 1902.

16. Fadely, "Veteran and the Memorial," 27–35; W. H. English to General, June 9, 1893, folder 1, box 3, General Mahlon D. Manson Family Papers, William Henry Smith Memorial Library, Indiana Historical Society (hereafter cited as IHS), Indianapolis; Rose, *Circle,* 397–412.

17. *Indianapolis Sentinel,* May 16, 1902.

18. Ibid.

19. Ibid., June 2, 1901.

20. Grimaldi, "Indiana Soldiers' and Sailors' Monument," 23, 69; Nathan Kimball to Wm. H. English, October 14, 1892, folder 5, box 5, William Hayden English Family Papers, William Henry Smith Memorial Library, IHS.

21. Geo. J. Langsdale to Col. Johnston, February 11, 1895, folder 10, box 1, George and William Johnston Collection, William Henry Smith Memorial Library, IHS. For more examples of disputes on the monument commission, see Geo. W. Johnston to Geo. J. Langsdale, July 11, 1891, folder 7, ibid.; Geo. J. Langsdale to Col. Johnston, March 25, 1895, folder 10, ibid.; W. H. English to Genl., February 18, 1893, folder 12, box 2, General Mahlon D. Manson

Family Papers, William Henry Smith Memorial Library, IHS; Wm. H. English to Genl. M. D. Manson, July 27, 1893, folder 1, box 3, ibid.; D. C. McCollum to W. H. English, December 7, 1894, folder 7, box 5, William Hayden English Family Papers, IHS; D. C. McCollum to Friend English, February 1, 1895, folder 8, ibid.

22. C. O. Waggoner to Wm. H. English and others, [1893], folder 7, William Hayden English Family Papers, IHS.

23. D. C. McCollum to W. H. English, February 14, 1895, folder 8, ibid.

24. *Indianapolis Sentinel*, May 15, 16, 1902.

25. *Indianapolis Journal*, May 16, 1902; *Indianapolis Sentinel*, May 16, 1902; Bodnar, "Commemorative Activity in Twentieth-Century Indianapolis," 1–23; Grimaldi, "Indiana Soldiers' and Sailors' Monument," 100–102.

26. *Indianapolis Sentinel*, May 16, 1902.

27. David W. Blight, *Race and Reunion: The Civil War in American Memory* (Cambridge, Mass.: Harvard University Press, 2001), 383–391.

28. W. E. B. DuBois, *Black Reconstruction in America* (New York: Atheneum, 1969), 30.

29. For a discussion of Indiana during the Prohibition era, see James H. Madison, *Indiana through Tradition and Change: A History of the Hoosier State and Its People, 1920–1945* (Indianapolis: Indiana Historical Society, 1982), 40–44, 97, 334, and Albert E. Monger to Bruce Lane, February 18, 1935, folder 10, box 3, Oscar Bruce Lane Papers, William Henry Smith Memorial Library, IHS. For Putnam County in the post–Civil War period, see Weik, *History of Putnam County*, 150, and John J. Baughman, *Our Past, Their Present: Historical Essays on Putnam County, Indiana* (Greencastle, Ind.: Putnam County Museum, 2008), 162–164, 317, 386–388, 439–441.

30. "Memorial Day," in *The Essential Holmes: Selections from the Letters, Speeches, Judicial Opinions, and Other Writings of Oliver Wendell Holmes, Jr.,* ed. Richard A. Posner (Chicago: University of Chicago Press, 1992), 186.

31. C. O. Waggoner to Wm. H. English and others, [1893], folder 7, box 5, William Hayden English Family Papers, IHS.

32. Grimaldi, "Indiana Soldiers' and Sailors' Monument," 124.

Bibliography

Newspapers

The African Repository
Indiana Press (also *Greencastle Press* or *Dollar Press*)
Indiana State Journal
Indiana State Sentinel
Parke County Republican
Putnam Banner (also *Putnam Republican Banner, Greencastle Banner*)
Putnam County Sentinel

Primary Sources

William H. Anderson Diary. Eleanore A. Cammack Papers. Archives and Special Collections. DePauw University, Greencastle, Ind.

John Applegate Manuscripts. Lilly Library. Indiana University, Bloomington.

Applications for Pardon, Parole, Remission of Fines, 1857–1858. Indiana State Archives. Commission on Public Records, Indianapolis.

Bainbridge Male and Female Academy Minutes, 1859–1860. Indiana History Manuscripts. Lilly Library. Indiana University, Bloomington.

Orion Bartholomew Papers. Manuscripts of the Indiana Division. Indiana State Library, Indianapolis.

Bence Family Papers. Manuscripts of the Indiana Division. Indiana State Library, Indianapolis.

Jeremiah S. Black Papers. Library of Congress, Washington, D.C.

Brown-Bolton Family Papers. William Henry Smith Memorial Library. Indiana Historical Society, Indianapolis.

James Buchanan Papers. Historical Society of Pennsylvania. On microfilm at Library of Congress, Washington, D.C.

Cauthorn-Stout Family Papers. William Henry Smith Memorial Library. Indiana Historical Society, Indianapolis.

Aden G. Cavins. Alumni Files. Archives and Special Collections. DePauw University, Greencastle, Ind.

Elijah H. C. Cavins Papers. William Henry Smith Memorial Library. Indiana Historical Society, Indianapolis.

Cemetery Records. Forest Hill Cemetery, Greencastle, Ind.

Chapin Family Papers. William Henry Smith Memorial Library. Indiana Historical Society, Indianapolis.

J. E. Chapin Letter. William Henry Smith Memorial Library. Indiana Historical Society, Indianapolis.

Lucius Chapin Papers. William Henry Smith Memorial Library. Indiana Historical Society, Indianapolis.

Lucius P. Chapin Papers. Archives and Special Collections. DePauw University, Greencastle, Ind.

Chapin Putnam County Genealogy. Cyril Johnson Room for Local History and Genealogy. Putnam County Public Library, Greencastle, Ind.

Church History—Baptist Records, 1798–1912. Manuscripts of the Indiana Division. Indiana State Library, Indianapolis.

Circuit Court. Putnam County. Clerk's Office. Putnam County Courthouse, Greencastle, Ind.

Civil War and Thomas Lyon Papers. Archives and Special Collections. DePauw University, Greencastle, Ind.

Civil War Claims by Veterans. Manuscripts of the Indiana Division. Indiana State Library, Indianapolis.

Civil War Records. Indiana State Archives. Commission on Public Records, Indianapolis.

John Coburn Papers. Manuscripts of the Indiana Division. Indiana State Library, Indianapolis.

Common Pleas Court. Clerk's Office. Putnam County Courthouse, Greencastle, Ind.

Correspondence of the 27th Indiana Volunteer Regiment. Indiana State Archives. Commission on Public Records, Indianapolis.

Correspondence of the 71st Indiana Volunteer Regiment (6th Cavalry). Indiana State Archives. Commission on Public Records, Indianapolis.

Correspondence of the 77th Indiana Volunteer Regiment (4th Cavalry). Indiana State Archives. Commission on Public Records, Indianapolis.

Cowgill Family. Boatwright Collection. Cyril Johnson Room for Local History and Genealogy. Putnam County Public Library, Greencastle, Ind.

Cowgill Putnam County Genealogy. Cyril Johnson. Room for Local History and Genealogy. Putnam County Public Library, Greencastle, Ind.

Andrew W. Crandall Papers. Archives and Special Collections. DePauw University, Greencastle, Ind.

Crane Family. Boatwright Collection. Cyril Johnson Room for Local History and Genealogy. Putnam County Public Library, Greencastle, Ind.

Abiathar Crane Papers. William Henry Smith Memorial Library. Indiana Historical Society, Indianapolis.

John Givan Davis Papers. William Henry Smith Memorial Library. Indiana Historical Society, Indianapolis.

Vincent H. Day Family Collection. William Henry Smith Memorial Library. Indiana Historical Society, Indianapolis.

Lucius C. Embree Papers. Manuscripts of the Indiana Division. Indiana State Library, Indianapolis.

Elijah Edward Evans Papers. Manuscripts of the Indiana Division. Indiana State Library, Indianapolis.

Exemptions and Other Papers. Seventh District of Indiana. RG 110, National Archives–Great Lakes Region, Chicago.

Calvin Fletcher Papers. William Henry Smith Memorial Library. Indiana Historical Society, Indianapolis.

Hillary Asbury Gobin Papers. Archives and Special Collections. DePauw University, Greencastle, Ind.

Simpson Hamrick Letters. William Henry Smith Memorial Library. Indiana Historical Society, Indianapolis.

John Hanna Manuscripts. Lilly Library. Indiana University, Bloomington.

Almira Maria Scott Harrah Papers. William Henry Smith Memorial Library. Indiana Historical Society, Indianapolis.

F. M. Harris Civil War Diary. Archives and Special Collections. DePauw University, Greencastle, Ind.

Ransom E. Hawley Letters. Special Collections. Vigo County Public Library, Terre Haute, Ind.

Ransom Hawley Papers. Manuscripts of the Indiana Division. Indiana State Library, Indianapolis.

Richard M. Hazelett. "'Little Black Book': Memoirs of Richard M. Hazelett." William Henry Smith Memorial Library. Indiana Historical Society, Indianapolis.

William P. Heath Letters. William Henry Smith Memorial Library. Indiana Historical Society, Indianapolis.

Herndon-Weik Collection. Library of Congress, Washington, D.C.

William Robeson Holloway Papers. William Henry Smith Memorial Library. Indiana Historical Society, Indianapolis.

Candace Sill Hopkins Papers. William Henry Smith Memorial Library. Indiana Historical Society, Indianapolis.

Indiana Conference Trials, 1859–1937. Archives and Special Collections. DePauw University, Greencastle, Ind.

Indiana Legion. Indiana State Archives. Commission on Public Records, Indianapolis.

John Ing Papers. Archives and Special Collections. DePauw University, Greencastle, Ind.

Internal Revenue Assessment Lists, Indiana, 1862–66. Microfilm, roll 28–31. Indiana State Library, Indianapolis.

H. S. Lane Manuscripts. Lilly Library. Indiana University, Bloomington.

Henry Smith Lane Papers. William Henry Smith Memorial Library. Indiana Historical Society, Indianapolis.

Oscar Bruce Lane Papers. William Henry Smith Memorial Library. Indiana Historical Society, Indianapolis.

Lane-Elston Family Papers. William Henry Smith Memorial Library. Indiana Historical Society, Indianapolis.

Daniel W. Layman Account Books. Manuscripts of the Indiana Division. Indiana State Library, Indianapolis.

Letters Received, Seventh District of Indiana. RG 110. National Archives–Great Lakes Region, Chicago.

Lists of Drafted Men. Warren Township, Putnam County. RG 110. Entry 5246, vol. 11. National Archives–Great Lakes Region, Chicago.

Lists of Drafted Men. Washington Township, Putnam County. RG 110. Entry 5246, vol. 11. National Archives—Great Lakes Region, Chicago.

Thomas J. McGan Record Books. Manuscripts of the Indiana Division. Indiana State Library, Indianapolis.

William Miller Papers. William Henry Smith Memorial Library. Indiana Historical Society, Indianapolis.

Oliver Perry Morton Papers. Manuscripts of the Indiana Division. Indiana State Library, Indianapolis.

Mullinix Family. Boatwright Collection. Cyril Johnson Room for Local History and Genealogy. Putnam County Public Library, Greencastle, Ind.

Pardons and Remissions, vol. 1. Indiana State Archives. Commission on Public Records, Indianapolis.

Pension Files. National Archives, Washington, D.C.

Petitions for Pardons and Paroles. Indiana State Archives. Commission on Public Records, Indianapolis.

Probate Records. Putnam County. Clerk's Office. Putnam County Courthouse, Greencastle, Ind.

Provost Marshal Papers. RG 110. Seventh District of Indiana. National Archives–Great Lakes Region, Chicago.

Putnam County Will Records. Microfilm. Indiana State Library, Indianapolis.

John W. Ray Papers. William Henry Smith Memorial Library. Indiana Historical Society, Indianapolis.

Record of Official Bonds. Putnam County. Clerk's Office. Putnam County Courthouse, Greencastle, Ind.

Records of the Office of the Pardon Attorney. RG 204. National Archives, Washington, D.C.

Returns for Quotas and Credits for Counties and Districts 1864. Entry 5068. RG 110. National Archives–Great Lakes Region, Chicago.

James Madison Reynolds Papers. William Henry Smith Memorial Library. Indiana Historical Society, Indianapolis.

Martha Jane Ridpath Papers. Archives and Special Collections. DePauw University, Greencastle, Ind.

Richard S. Skidmore. *Civil War Veterans Buried in Forest Hill Cemetery, Greencastle, Indiana.* N.p., 1987. William Henry Smith Memorial Library. Indiana Historical Society, Indianapolis.

Statements of Substitutes. Seventh District of Indiana. RG 110. National Archives–Great Lakes Region, Chicago.

Solon Turman Papers. Manuscripts of the Indiana Division. Indiana State Library, Indianapolis.

William L. Wharton Papers. Manuscripts of the Indiana Division. Indiana State Library, Indianapolis.

Asbury Wilkinson Papers. William Henry Smith Memorial Library. Indiana Historical Society, Indianapolis.

Josiah C. Williams Letters. Manuscripts of the Indiana Division. Indiana State Library, Indianapolis.

Worthington B. Williams Family Papers. William Henry Smith Memorial Library. Indiana Historical Society, Indianapolis.

Anna W. Wright Collection. Manuscripts of the Indiana Division. Indiana State Library, Indianapolis.

Published Primary Sources

Ames, Elizabeth, and Eleanore Cammack. *The Woman's Club, Greencastle, Indiana.* Greencastle, Ind.: Woman's Club, 1974.

Atlas of Putnam Co., Indiana to Which Are Added Various General Maps, History, Statistics, Illustrations. Chicago: J. H. Beers, 1879.

Baker, Ronald L. *Homeless, Friendless, and Penniless: The WPA Interviews with Former Slaves Living in Indiana.* Bloomington: Indiana University Press, 2000.

Basler, Roy P. *The Collected Works of Abraham Lincoln,* 8 vols. New Brunswick, N.J.: Rutgers University Press, 1953.

Baugh, Lauralee, Jinsie Bingham, Marilyn Clearwaters, and Rita W. Harlan, comps. *Putnam County, Indiana, Land Patents.* Evansville, Ind.: Evansville Bindery, 2003.

Baxter, Nancy Niblack, ed. *Hooiser Farm Boy in Lincoln's Army: The Civil War Letters of Pvt. John R. McClure.* N.p., 1971.

Beste, J. Richard. *The Wabash: Or Adventures of an English Gentleman's Family in the Interior of America,* 2 vols. London: Hurst and Blackett, 1855.

Blue, William E. *Pioneers of Putnam County, Indiana: Cooper, Clearwaters, Goss.* N.p., 1997.

Brakmo, Georgia. *William McGahey-McGaughey, Putnam County, Indiana Russell Twp.* Los Angeles: n.p., 1951.

Brigham, Loriman S., ed. "The Civil War Journal of William B. Fletcher." *Indiana Magazine of History* 57 (March 1961): 43–76.

Brown, Caroline. *Knights in Fustian: A War Time Story of Indiana.* Boston: Houghton Mifflin, 1900.

Congressional Directory, volumes from 1850–1885. Washington, D.C.

Congressional Globe. 35th Cong., 1st sess. Washington, D.C., 1858.

Congressional Record. Washington, D.C., 1882–1890.

[Davis, John G.] *Speech of Hon. Jno. G. Davis, of Indiana, against the Admission of Kansas into the Union under the Lecompton Constitution.* Pamphlet Collection. William Henry Smith Memorial Library. Indiana Historical Society, Indianapolis.

Doyle, Julie A., John David Smith, and Richard M. McMurry, eds. *The Wilderness of War: The Civil War Letters of George W. Squier, Hoosier Volunteer.* Knoxville: University of Tennessee Press, 1998.

Eggleston, George Cary. *A Rebel's Recollections.* Bloomington: Indiana University Press, 1959.

Elder, Donald C., III, ed. *Love amid the Turmoil: The Civil War Letters of William and Mary Vermilion.* Iowa City: University of Iowa Press, 2003.

Harrison, Lowell H., ed. "A British View of Indiana's Agriculture, 1879." *Indiana Magazine of History* 68 (December 1972): 307–314.

Hendershot, Steven, ed. *Putnam County Memories.* Greencastle, Ind.: BannerGraphic, 1990.

Henry Lane Stone. New York: James T. White, 1925. Pamphlet. Filson Historical Society, Louisville, Ky.

Hesseltine, William B., ed. *Three against Lincoln: Murat Halstead Reports the Caucuses of 1860.* Baton Rouge: Louisiana State University Press, 1960.

Jones, R. T., H. A. Mills, and T. J. Bassett, comps. *Souvenir of Greencastle, Indiana.* Greencastle, Ind.: M. J. Beckett, [1892].

Kellogg, Mary E., comp. *Army Life of an Illinois Soldier Including a Day-by-Day Record of Sherman's March to the Sea: Letters and Diary of Charles W. Wills.* Carbondale: Southern Illinois University Press, 1996.

Klaus, Samuel, ed. *The Milligan Case.* New York: Da Capo Press, 1970.

McCandless, Perry, ed. "The Civil War Journal of Stephen Keyes Fletcher." *Indiana Magazine of History* 54 (June 1958): 141–190.

Mandleco, Jessie Brothers, comp. *A History of the Bowers, Brothers, Fosher, Guilliams, Landis, Moss, Turner, and Webster Families of Putnam County, Indiana.* Terre Haute, Ind.: N.p., [1987].

Martis, Kenneth C. *The Historical Atlas of United States Congressional District, 1789–1983.* New York: Free Press, 1982.

Moore, John Bassett, ed. *The Works of James Buchanan.* New York: Antiquarian Press, 1960.

Moses, Wilson Jeremiah, ed. *Liberian Dreams: Back-to-Africa Narratives from the 1850s.* University Park: Pennsylvania State University Press, 1998.

Posner, Richard A., ed. *The Essential Holmes: Selections from the Letters, Speeches, Judicial Opinions, and Other Writings of Oliver Wendell Holmes, Jr.* Chicago: University of Chicago Press, 1992.

Rawick, George P., ed. *The American Slave: A Composite Autobiography.* Supp., ser. 1, vol. 5, *Indiana and Ohio Narratives.* Westport, Conn.: Greenwood Press, 1977.

Redkey, Edwin S., ed. *A Grand Army of Black Men: Letters from African-American Soldiers in the Union Army, 1861–1865.* Cambridge: Cambridge University Press, 1992.

Reports of the Debates and Proceedings of the Convention for the Revision of the Constitution of the State of Indiana. 2 vols. Indianapolis, Ind.: Brown, 1850.

Riker, Dorothy, and Gayle Thornbrough. *Indiana Election Returns, 1816–1851.* Indianapolis: Indiana Historical Bureau, 1960.

Sampson, Edward E., comp. *The History of the Kauffman/Kaufman/Coffman Family of Pennsylvania; Hampshire; Hardy County, Virginia; Bourbon Co., Kentucky; Monroe and Putnam County, Indiana.* N.p., 1982.

Scott, Harvey D. *Letter of Harvey D. Scott to His Constituents of the Seventh Congressional District of Indiana.* Washington, D.C.: Buell & Blanchard, 1856.

[Shoemaker, James]. "Reminiscences of James Shoemaker." *Indiana Magazine of History* 1 (December 1905): 173–176.

Skene, Ann L., and Denise DeBoy. *Putnam County, Indiana Naturalization Records, 1854–1929.* Indianapolis: Indiana State Archives, 1999.

Stone, Henry Lane. *"Morgan's Men": A Narrative of Personal Experiences.* Louisville, Ky.: Westerfield-Bonte, 1919.

Thomas, Elmer. "'Forty Years a Legislator': Memoir of a Hoosier Boyhood." *Indiana Magazine of History* 103 (December 2007): 384–410.

Thompson, Donald E., and Lorna Lutes Sylvester, eds. "The Autobiography of Isaac Reed, Frontier Missionary." *Indiana Magazine of History* 78 (September 1982); 193–214.

Thornbrough, Gayle, Dorothy L. Riker, and Paula Corpuz, eds. *The Diary of Calvin Fletcher.* 9 vols. Indianapolis: Indiana Historical Society, 1972–1983.

Townsend, Murray L., Jr. *Townsend-Pittman Family Reunion.* Privately published, 2005.

Turner, John Frank. "The Hoosier Huckster." *Indiana Magazine of History* 50 (March 1954): 51–60.

Upson, Theodore F. *With Sherman to the Sea: The Civil War Letters, Diaries & Reminiscences of Theodore F. Upson,* ed. Oscar Osburn Winther. Baton Rouge: Louisiana State University Press, 1943.

U.S. Bureau of the Census. *Historical Statistics of the United States: Colonial Times to 1957.* Washington, D.C.: Department of Commerce, 1965.

U.S. Census Office. *Population Schedules of the Eighth Census of the United States, 1860.* Washington, D.C.: National Archives, 1967.

———. *Population Schedules of the Ninth Census of the United States, 1870.* Washington, D.C.: National Archives, 1965.

———. *Population Schedules of the Seventh Census of the United States, 1850.* Washington, D.C.: National Archives, 1963.

———. *Population Schedules of the Sixth Census of the United States, 1840.* Washington, D.C.: National Archives, 1967.

———. *Sixth Census or Enumeration of the Inhabitants of the United States, 1840*. Washington, D.C.: Blair and Rives, 1841.

———. *The Statistics of Wealth and Industry in the United States*. Washington, D.C.: Government Printing Office, 1872.

U.S. Senate. *Miscellaneous Documents*. 46th Cong., 2nd sess., 1879, serial 1890, no. 15. Washington, D.C.: Government Printing Office, 1880.

———. *Report and Testimony of the Select Committee of the United States Senate to Investigate the Causes of the Removal of the Negroes from the Southern States to the Northern States*. 46th Cong., 2nd sess., 1880, Report 693 [Voorhees Report]. Washington, D.C.: Government Printing Office, 1880.

Vineyard, John, Mrs., comp. *Newton County, Missouri Marriage Records through 1869*. Independence, Mo.: n.p., 1965.

Voorhees, Charles S., comp. *Speeches of Daniel W. Voorhees*. Cincinnati, Ohio: Robert Clarke, 1875.

"Voting for America: United States Politics, 1840–2008." Available at http://americanpast .richmond.edu/voting.

Webb, Frank J. *The Garies and Their Friends*. New York: Arno, 1969.

Wiley, Bell I., ed. *Slaves No More: Letters from Liberia, 1833–1869*. Lexington: University Press of Kentucky, 1980.

Wilson, Harriet E. *Our Nig or, Sketches from the Life of a Free Black*, in *Three Classic African-American Novels*, ed. William L. Andrews. New York: Mentor, 1990.

Wright, Sarah Seller, and Minetta L. Wright. *The Seller Family in Putnam County, Indiana*. Greencastle, Ind.: Putnam County Historical Society, 1956.

Secondary Sources

Abbott, Carl. "The Plank Road Enthusiasm in the Antebellum Middle West." *Indiana Magazine of History* 67 (June 1971): 95–116.

Anbinder, Tyler. *Nativism and Slavery: The Northern Know Nothings and the Politics of the 1850s*. New York: Oxford University Press, 1992.

———. "Which Poor Man's Fight? Immigrants and the Federal Conscription of 1863." *Civil War History* 52 (December 2006): 344–372.

Andreasen, Bryon C. "Civil War Church Trials: Repressing Dissent on the Northern Home Front." In *An Uncommon Time: The Civil War and the Northern Home Front*, ed. Paul A. Cimbala and Randall M. Miller. New York: Fordham University Press, 2002, 214–242.

Anthrop, Mary E. "The Road Less Traveled: Hoosier African Americans and Liberia." *Traces of Indiana and Midwestern History* 19 (Winter 2007): 12–21.

Araya, Takeshiro. *A Short History of To-O Gijuku, 1872–1972*. Hirosaki, Japan: To-O Gijuku, 1972.

Ash, Stephen V. *Middle Tennessee Society Transformed, 1860–1870: War and Peace in the Upper South*. Baton Rouge: Louisiana State University Press, 1988.

Ashendel, Anita. "'Woman as Force' in Indiana History." In *The State of Indiana History 2000: Papers Presented at the Indiana Historical Society's Grand Opening*, ed. Robert M. Taylor, Jr. Indianapolis: Indiana Historical Society, 2001, 1–36.

Athearn, Robert G. *In Search of Canaan: Black Migration to Kansas, 1879–1880*. Lawrence: University Press of Kansas, 1978.

Attie, Jeanie. *Patriotic Toil: Northern Women and the American Civil War.* Ithaca, N.Y.: Cornell University Press, 1998.

Ayers, Edward L. *In the Presence of Mine Enemies: War in the Heart of America, 1859–1863.* New York: Norton, 2003.

Ball, Edward. *Slaves in the Family.* New York: Ballantine Books, 1999.

Banks, Jenifer. "'A New Home' for Whom? Caroline Kirkland Exposes Domestic Abuse on the Michigan Frontier." In *Over the Threshold: Intimate Violence in Early America,* ed. Christine Daniels and Michael V. Kennedy. New York: Routledge, 1999, 135–147.

Barnhart, John D., and Dorothy L. Riker. *Indiana to 1816: The Colonial Period.* Indianapolis: Indiana Historical Bureau and Indiana Historical Society, 1971.

Baughman, John J. *Our Past, Their Present: Historical Essays on Putnam County, Indiana.* Greencastle, Ind.: Putnam County Museum, 2008.

Bell, Rudolph M., and Virginia Yans. "Introduction." In *Women on Their Own: Interdisciplinary Perspectives on Being Single,* ed. Rudolph M. Bell and Virginia Yans. New Brunswick, N.J.: Rutgers University Press, 2008, 1–15.

Bigham, Darrel E. *On Jordan's Banks: Emancipation and Its Aftermath in the Ohio River Valley.* Lexington: University Press of Kentucky, 2006.

Bigler, David L. "The Aiken Party Executions and the Utah War, 1857–1858." *Western Historical Quarterly* 38 (Winter 2007): 457–476.

Biographical and Historical Record of Putnam County, Indiana. Chicago: Lewis Publishing, 1887; reprinted 1975.

Biographical Directory of the American Congress, 1774–1971. Washington, D.C.: Government Printing Office, 1971.

A Biographical History of Eminent and Self-Made Men of the State of Indiana. Vol. 1. Cincinnati, Ohio: Western Biographical Publishing, 1880.

Blair, William. *Virginia's Private War: Feeding Body and Soul in the Confederacy, 1861–1865.* New York: Oxford University Press, 1998.

———. "We Are Coming, Father Abraham—Eventually: The Problem of Northern Nationalism in the Pennsylvania Recruiting Drives of 1862." In *The War Was You and Me: Civilians in the American Civil War,* ed. Joan E. Cashin. Princeton, N.J.: Princeton University Press, 2002, 183–208.

Blee, Kathleen M. *Women of the Klan: Racism and Gender in the 1920s.* Berkeley: University of California Press, 2009.

Blight, David W. *Race and Reunion: The Civil War in American Memory.* Cambridge, Mass.: Belknap Press, 2001.

Blocker, Jack S., Jr. *"Give to the Winds Thy Fears": The Women's Temperance Crusade, 1873–1874.* Westport, Conn.: Greenwood Press, 1985.

Bodnar, John. "Commemorative Activity in Twentieth-Century Indianapolis: The Invention of Civic Traditions." *Indiana Magazine of History* 87 (March 1991): 1–23.

Bogardus, Frank Smith. "Daniel W. Voorhees." *Indiana Magazine of History* 27 (June 1931): 91–103.

Bourke, Paul, and Donald DeBats. *Washington County: Politics and Community in Antebellum America.* Baltimore, Md.: Johns Hopkins University Press, 1995.

Boylan, Anne M. *Sunday School: The Formation of an American Institution, 1790–1880.* New Haven, Conn.: Yale University Press, 1988.

Brakebill, Tina Stewart. *"Circumstances are destiny": An Antebellum Woman's Struggle to Define Sphere.* Kent, Ohio: Kent State University Press, 2006.

Bratt, James D. "Religious Anti-revivalism in Antebellum America." *Journal of the Early Republic* 24 (Spring 2004): 65–106.

Braukman, Stacy Lorraine, and Michael A. Ross. "Married Women's Property and Male Coercion: United States' Courts and the Privy Examination, 1864–1887." *Journal of Women's History* 12 (Summer 2000): 57–80.

Brown, Richard D. "Microhistory and the Post-modern Challenge." *Journal of the Early Republic* 23 (Spring 2003): 1–20.

Burin, Eric. *Slavery and the Peculiar Solution: A History of the American Colonization Society.* Gainesville: University Press of Florida, 2005.

Burlingame, Michael. *Abraham Lincoln: A Life.* 2 vols. Baltimore, Md.: Johns Hopkins University Press, 2008.

Carleton, William G. "Why Was the Democratic Party in Indiana a Radical Party, 1865–1890?" *Indiana Magazine of History* 42 (September 1916): 207–228.

Carmichael, Peter S. *The Last Generation: Young Virginians in Peace, War, and Reunion.* Chapel Hill: University of North Carolina Press, 2005.

Carmony, Donald F. *Indiana, 1816–1850: The Pioneer Era.* Indianapolis: Indiana Historical Bureau, 1998.

Carwardine, Richard. *Lincoln: A Life of Purpose and Power.* New York: Vintage, 2007.

———. *Transatlantic Revivalism: Popular Evangelicalism in Britain and America, 1790–1865.* Westport, Conn.: Greenwood Press, 1978.

Cashin, Joan E. "Deserters, Civilians, and Draft Resistance in the North." In *The War Was You and Me: Civilians in the American Civil War,* ed. Joan E. Cashin. Princeton, N.J.: Princeton University Press, 2002, 262–285.

———. "Editor's Introduction." In *The War Was You and Me: Civilians in the American Civil War,* ed. by Joan E. Cashin. Princeton, N.J.: Princeton University Press, 2002, 1–5.

———. *First Lady of the Confederacy: Varina Davis's Civil War.* Cambridge, Mass.: Belknap Press, 2006.

Churchill, Robert. "Liberty, Conscription, and a Party Divided: The Sons of Liberty Conspiracy, 1863–1864." *Prologue* 30 (Winter 1998): 295–313.

———. *To Shake Their Guns in the Tyrant's Face: Libertarian Political Violence and the Origins of the Militia Movement.* Ann Arbor: University of Michigan Press, 2009.

Cimbala, Paul A. "Soldiering on the Home Front: The Veteran Reserve Corps and the Northern People." In *Union Soldiers and the Northern Home Front: Wartime Experiences, Postwar Adjustments,* ed. Paul A. Cimbala and Randall M. Miller. New York: Fordham University Press, 2002, 182–218.

Clark, George P., and Shirley E. Clark. "Heroes Carved in Ebony: Indiana's Black Civil War Regiment, the 28th USCT." *Traces of Indiana and Midwestern History* 7 (Summer 1995): 4–16.

Clarke, Frances. "'Honorable Scars': Northern Amputees and the Meaning of Civil War Injuries." In *Union Soldiers and the Northern Home Front: Wartime Experiences, Postwar Adjustments,* ed. Paul A. Cimbala and Randall M. Miller. New York: Fordham University Press, 2002, 361–394.

———. "'Let All Nations See': Civil War Nationalism and the Memorialization of Wartime Voluntarism." *Civil War History* 52 (March 2006): 66–93.

Clegg, Claude A., III. *The Price of Liberty: African Americans and the Making of Liberia.* Chapel Hill: University of North Carolina Press, 2004.

Connelley, William Elsey, ed. "Official Roster of Kansas, 1854–1925." In *Collections of the Kansas State Historical Society, 1923–1925,* vol. 16. Topeka, Kans.: B. P. Walker, 1925, 658–745.

Conover, Paula. "The Civil War and Putnam County." Archives and Special Collections Manu-
    script prepared for Prof. John Schlotterbeck, DePauw University, Greencastle, Ind.
Cornish, Dudley Taylor. *The Sable Arm: Negro Troops in the Union Army, 1861–1865.* New York:
    Norton, 1966.
Cott, Nancy F. *The Bonds of Womanhood: "Woman's Sphere" in New England, 1780–1835.* New Ha-
    ven, Conn.: Yale University Press, 1977.
―――. *Public Vows: A History of Marriage and the Nation.* Cambridge, Mass.: Harvard University
    Press, 2000.
Crawford, Martin. *Ashe County's Civil War: Community and Society in the Appalachian South.* Char-
    lottesville: University Press of Virginia, 2001.
Crenshaw, Ollinger. *The Slave States in the Presidential Election of 1860.* Baltimore, Md.: Johns
    Hopkins University Press, 1945.
Crofts, Daniel W. *Old Southampton: Politics and Society in a Virginia County, 1834–1869.* Charlot-
    tesville: University Press of Virginia, 1992.
Crow, Jeffrey J., Paul D. Escott, and Flora J. Hatley. *A History of African Americans in North Caro-
    lina.* Raleigh: North Carolina Office of Archives and History, 2002.
Danhof, Clarence H. *Change in Agriculture: The Northern United States, 1820–1870.* Cambridge,
    Mass.: Harvard University Press, 1969.
Davis, William. *Lincoln's Men: How President Lincoln Became Father to an Army and a Nation.* New
    York: Free Press, 1999.
Dean, Eric T., Jr. *Shook over Hell: Post-traumatic Stress, Vietnam, and the Civil War.* Cambridge,
    Mass.: Harvard University Press, 1997.
Divita, James J. "Without Tenement: The State of Indiana Ethnic History." In *The State of Indi-
    ana History 2000: Papers Presented at the Indiana Historical Society's Grand Opening,* ed. Robert
    M. Taylor, Jr. Indianapolis: Indiana Historical Society, 2001, 91–124.
Dollar, Kent T. "Strangers in a Strange Land: Christian Soldiers in the Early Months of the
    Civil War." In *The View from the Ground: Experiences of Civil War Soldiers,* ed. Aaron Sheehan-
    Dean. Lexington: University of Kentucky Press, 2007, 145–169.
Donald, David Herbert. *Lincoln.* New York: Simon & Schuster, 1995.
Doyle, Don Harrison. *The Social Order of a Frontier Community: Jacksonville, Illinois, 1825–70.*
    Urbana: University of Illinois Press, 1978.
DuBois, W. E. B. *Black Reconstruction in America.* New York: Atheneum, 1969.
Dunn, D. Elwood, and Svend E. Holsoe. *Historical Dictionary of Liberia.* Metuchen, N.J.: Scare-
    crow Press, 1985.
Dykstra, Robert R. *Bright Radical Star: Black Freedom and White Supremacy on the Hawkeye Frontier.*
    Cambridge, Mass.: Harvard University Press, 1993.
Edmunds, R. David. *The Potawatomis: Keepers of the Fire.* Norman: University of Oklahoma Press,
    1978.
Edwards, Rebecca. *New Spirits: Americans in the Gilded Age, 1865–1905.* New York: Oxford Uni-
    versity Press, 2006.
Egnal, Marc. *Clash of Extremes: The Economic Origins of the Civil War.* New York: Hill and Wang, 2009.
Epstein, Barbara Leslie. *The Politics of Domesticity: Women, Evangelism, and Temperance in Nine-
    teenth-Century America.* Middletown, Conn.: Wesleyan University Press, 1981.
Etcheson, Nicole. *The Emerging Midwest: Upland Southerners and the Political Culture of the Old
    Northwest, 1787–1861.* Bloomington: Indiana University Press, 1996, 2–3.
Evans, Clement Anselm. *Confederate Military History: A Library of Confederate States History.* At-
    lanta, Ga.: Confederate Publishing, 1899.

[Evens, Thursa]. "Bainbridge Christian Church." N.p., 2009.

Fadely, James Philip. "The Veteran and the Memorial: George J. Langsdale and the Soldiers and Sailors Monument." *Traces of Indiana and Midwestern History* 18 (Winter 2006): 27–35.

Fahs, Alice. "A Thrilling Northern War: Gender, Race, and Sensational Popular War Literature." In *An Uncommon Time: The Civil War and the Northern Home Front,* ed. Paul A. Cimbala and Randall M. Miller. New York: Fordham University Press, 2002, 27–60.

Faragher, John Mack. "History from the Inside-Out: Writing the History of Women in Rural America." *American Quarterly* 33 (Winter 1981): 537–557.

———. *Sugar Creek: Life on the Illinois Prairie.* New Haven, Conn.: Yale University Press, 1986.

———. *Women and Men on the Overland Trail.* New Haven, Conn.: Yale University Press, 1979.

Faust, Drew Gilpin. *Mothers of Invention: Women of the Slaveholding South in the American Civil War.* Chapel Hill: University of North Carolina Press, 1996.

Ferrie, Joseph P. *Yankeys Now: Immigrants in the Antebellum United States, 1840–1860.* New York: Oxford University Press, 1999.

Fite, Emerson David. *The Presidential Campaign of 1860.* Port Washington, N.Y.: Kennikat Press, 1967, orig. 1911.

Fitzgerald, Michael W. *Splendid Failure: Postwar Reconstruction in the American South.* Chicago: Ivan R. Dee, 2007.

Foner, Eric. *Free Soil, Free Labor, Free Men: The Ideology the Republican Party before the Civil War.* New York: Oxford University Press, 1995.

———. "The Ideology of the Republican Party." In *The Birth of the Grand Old Party: The Republicans' First Generation,* ed. Robert F. Engs and Randall M. Miller. Philadelphia: University of Pennsylvania Press, 2002, 8–28.

———. *Politics and Ideology in the Age of the Civil War.* New York: Oxford University Press, 1980.

———. *Reconstruction: America's Unfinished Revolution, 1863–1877.* New York: Harper & Row, 1988.

Foote, Lorien. "Rich Man's War, Rich Man's Fight: Class, Ideology, and Discipline in the Union Army." *Civil War History* 51 (September 2005): 269–287.

Forstchen, William R. "The 28th United States Colored Troops: Indiana's African-Americans Go to War, 1863–1865." Ph.D. diss., Purdue University, 1994.

Foster, John Michael, Jr. "'For the Good of the Cause and the Protection of the Border': The Service of the Indiana Legion in the Civil War, 1861–1865." *Civil War History* 55 (March 2009): 31–55.

Fredrickson, George M. *The Inner Civil War: Northern Intellectuals and the Crisis of the Union.* New York: Harper & Row, 1965.

———. "Nineteenth-Century American History." In *Imagined Histories: American Historians Interpret the Past,* ed. Anthony Molho and Gordon S. Wood. Princeton, N.J.: Princeton University Press, 1998, 164–184.

Frisch, Michael H. *Town into City: Springfield, Massachusetts, and the Meaning of Community, 1840–1880.* Cambridge, Mass.: Harvard University Press, 1972.

Gallman, J. Matthew. "Afterward." In *An Uncommon Time: The Civil War and the Northern Home Front,* ed. Paul A. Cimbala and Randall M. Miller. New York: Fordham University Press, 2002, 345–351.

———. *Mastering Wartime: A Social History of Philadelphia during the Civil War.* Cambridge: Cambridge University Press, 1990.

———. *The North Fights the Civil War: The Home Front.* Chicago: Ivan R. Dee, 1994.

Geary, James W. *We Need Men: The Union Draft in the Civil War.* DeKalb: Northern Illinois University Press, 1991.

Gere, Anne Ruggles. *Intimate Practices: Literacy and Cultural Work in U.S. Women's Clubs, 1880–1920.* Urbana: University of Illinois Press, 1997.

Gienapp, William E. *The Origins of the Republican Party, 1852–56.* New York: Oxford University Press, 1987.

Gillispie, James M. *Andersonvilles of the North: The Myths and Realities of Northern Treatment of Civil War Confederate Prisoners.* Denton: University of North Texas Press, 2008.

Glatthaar, Joseph T. "Afterword." In *The View from the Ground: Experiences of Civil War Soldiers,* ed. Aaron Sheehan-Dean. Lexington: University of Kentucky Press, 2007, 249–253.

———. "Duty, Country, Race, and Party: The Evans Family of Ohio." In *The War Was You and Me: Civilians in the American Civil War,* ed. Joan E. Cashin. Princeton, N.J.: Princeton University Press, 2002, 333–357.

———. *Forged in Battle: The Civil War Alliance of Black Soldiers and White Officers.* Baton Rouge: Louisiana State University Press, 2000.

Glover, Lorri. *Southern Sons: Becoming Men in the New Nation.* Baltimore, Md.: Johns Hopkins University Press, 2007.

Goodwin, Doris Kearns. *Team of Rivals: The Political Genius of Abraham Lincoln.* New York: Simon & Schuster, 2005.

Gordon, Linda. "U.S. Women's History." In *The New American History,* ed. Eric Foner. Philadelphia: Temple University Press, 1990, 185–210.

Grant, Susan-Mary. "'The Charter of Its Birthright': The Civil War and American Nationalism." In *Legacy of Disunion: The Enduring Significance of the American Civil War,* ed. Susan-Mary Grant and Peter J. Parish. Baton Rouge: Louisiana State University Press, 2003, 188–206.

Grant, Susan Mary, and Peter J. Parish. "Introduction." In *Legacy of Disunion: The Enduring Significance of the American Civil War,* ed. Susan-Mary Grant and Peter J. Parish. Baton Rouge: Louisiana State University Press, 2003, 1–13.

Grimaldi, Anthony Eugene. "The Indiana Soldiers' and Sailors' Monument and Its Dedication: A Study of a Nineteenth Century American Monument and Its Allied Arts of Pageantry." Ph.D. diss., Ohio University, 1982.

Grimsley, Mark. "In Not So Dubious Battle: The Motivations of American Civil War Soldiers." *Journal of Military History* 62 (January 1998): 175–188.

Gross, Jennifer L. "The United Daughters of the Confederacy, Confederate Widows, and the Lost Cause: 'We Must Not Forget or Neglect the Widows.'" In *Women on Their Own: Interdisciplinary Perspectives on Being Single,* ed. Rudolph M. Bell and Virginia Yans. New Brunswick, N.J.: Rutgers University Press, 2008, 180–200.

Gross, Robert A. *The Minutemen and Their World.* New York: Hill and Wang, 1976.

Gugin, Linda C., and James E. St. Clair. *The Governors of Indiana.* Indianapolis: Indiana Historical Society Press, 2006.

Guyatt, Nicholas. "'The Outskirts of Our Happiness': Race and the Lure of Colonization in the Early Republic." *Journal of American History* 95 (March 2009): 986–1011.

Hahn, Steven, and Jonathan Prude, eds. *The Countryside in the Age of Capitalist Transformation.* Chapel Hill: University of North Carolina Press, 1985.

Hall, James R. "The Hoosier Rebels." *Civil War Times* 39 (October 2000): 39–40.

Hammond, John Craig. *Slavery, Freedom, and Expansion in the Early American West.* Charlottesville: University of Virginia Press, 2007.

Harlan, Louis R. *Booker T. Washington: The Making of a Black Leader, 1856–1901.* New York: Oxford University Press, 1972.

Hartman, Grover L. *A School for God's People: A History of the Sunday School Movement in Indiana.* Indianapolis: Central Publishing, 1980.

Hatch, Nathan O. *The Democratization of American Christianity.* New Haven, Conn.: Yale University Press, 1989.

Hatton, Ed. "'He Murdered Her Because He Loved Her': Passion, Masculinity, and Intimate Homicide in Antebellum America." In *Over the Threshold: Intimate Violence in Early America,* ed. Christine Daniels and Michael V. Kennedy. New York: Routledge, 1999, 111–134.

Hempton, David. *Methodism: Empire of the Spirit.* New Haven, Conn.: Yale University Press, 2005.

Hess, Earl J. *Liberty, Virtue, and Progress: Northerners and Their War for the Union.* New York: Fordham University Press, 1977.

———. "'Tell Me What the Sensations Are': The Northern Home Front Learns about Combat." In *Union Soldiers and the Northern Home Front: Wartime Experiences, Postwar Adjustments,* ed. Paul A. Cimbala and Randall M. Miller. New York: Fordham University Press, 2002, 119–142.

———. "A Terrible Fascination: The Portrayal of Combat in the Civil War Media." In *An Uncommon Time: The Civil War and the Northern Home Front,* ed. Paul A. Cimbala and Randall M. Miller. New York: Fordham University Press, 2002, 1–26.

Hesseltine, William B. *Lincoln and the War Governors.* New York: Knopf, 1948.

Heyrman, Christine Leigh. *Southern Cross: The Beginnings of the Bible Belt.* Chapel Hill: University of North Carolina Press, 1997.

History of Newton, Lawrence, Barry and McDonald Counties, Missouri. Chicago: Goodspeed Publishing, 1888.

Hodes, Martha. *The Sea Captain's Wife: A True Story of Love, Race, and War in the Nineteenth Century.* New York: Norton, 2006.

Holt, Michael F. "Making and Mobilizing the Republican Party, 1854–1860." In *The Birth of the Grand Old Party: The Republicans' First Generation,* ed. Robert F. Engs and Randall M. Miller. Philadelphia: University of Pennsylvania Press, 2002, 29–59.

———. *The Rise and Fall of the American Whig Party: Jacksonian Politics and the Onset of the Civil War.* New York: Oxford University Press, 1999.

Holzer, Harold. *Lincoln President-Elect: Abraham Lincoln and the Great Secession Winter, 1860–1861.* New York: Simon & Schuster, 2008.

Howe, Daniel Walker. *Making the American Self: Jonathan Edwards to Abraham Lincoln.* Cambridge, Mass.: Harvard University Press, 1997.

———. *What Hath God Wrought: The Transformation of America, 1815–1848.* New York: Oxford University Press, 2007.

Hunter, Jane. *The Gospel of Gentility: American Women Missionaries in Turn-of-the-Century China.* New Haven, Conn.: Yale University Press, 1984.

Hurt, R. Douglas. *American Agriculture: A Brief History.* Ames: Iowa State University Press, 1994.

Huston, James L. *Stephen A. Douglas and the Dilemmas of Democratic Equality.* Lanham, Md.: Rowman & Littlefield, 2007.

Jensen, Joan M. *Calling This Place Home: Women on the Wisconsin Frontier, 1850–1925.* St. Paul: Minnesota Historical Society Press, 2006.

———. *Loosening the Bonds: Mid-Atlantic Farm Women, 1750–1850.* New Haven, Conn.: Yale University Press, 1986.

Jimerson, Randall C. *The Private Civil War: Popular Thought during the Sectional Conflict*. Baton Rouge: Louisiana State University Press, 1988.

Johnson, E. Polk. *A History of Kentucky and Kentuckians: The Leaders and Representative Men in Commerce, Industry and Modern Activities*. Chicago: Lewis Publishing, 1912.

Johnson, Paul E. *A Shopkeeper's Millennium: Society and Revivals in Rochester, New York, 1815–1837*. New York: Hill and Wang, 1978.

Johnson, Russell L. "The Civil War Generation: Military Service and Mobility in Dubuque, Iowa, 1860–1870." *Journal of Social History* 32 (Summer 1999): 791–820.

———. "'Volunteer While You May': Manpower Mobilization in Dubuque, Iowa." In *Union Soldiers and the Northern Home Front: Wartime Experiences, Postwar Adjustments*, ed. Paul A. Cimbala and Randall M. Miller. New York: Fordham University Press, 2002, 30–68.

Johnston, J. Stoddard. *Memorial History of Louisville from Its First Settlement to the Year 1896*. Chicago: American Biographical Publishing, 1896.

Jones, Abeodu B. *Grand Cape Mount County: An Historical and Cultural Study of a Developing Society in Liberia*. Monrovia: Tubman Centre for African Culture, 1964.

Karamanski, Theodore J. *Rally 'Round the Flag: Chicago and the Civil War*. Chicago: Nelson-Hall, 1993.

Kelley, Mary. *Learning to Stand & Speak: Women, Education, and Public Life in America's Republic*. Chapel Hill: University of North Carolina, 2006.

Kentucky State Bar Association. *Proceedings of the Annual Meeting of the Kentucky State Bar Association*. Louisville, Ky.: n.p., 1922.

Kete, Mary Louise. "Slavery's Shadows: Narrative Chiaroscuro and *Our Nig*." In *Harriet Wilson's New England: Race, Writing, and Region*, ed. JerriAnne Boggis, Eve Allegra Raimon, and Barbara A. White. Durham: University of New Hampshire Press, 2007, 109–122.

Kett, Joseph F. *Rites of Passage: Adolescence in America, 1790 to the Present*. New York: Basic Books, 1977.

Kettleborough, Charles. *Constitution Making in Indiana*. Vol. 1, *1780–1851*. Indianapolis: Indiana Historical Bureau, 1971.

Kinsel, Amy J. "American Identity, National Reconciliation, and the Memory of the Civil War." *Proteus: A Journal of Ideas* 17 (Fall 2000): 5–14.

Klement, Frank L. *The Copperheads in the Middle West*. Gloucester, Mass., 1972, orig. 1960.

Laderman, Gary. *The Sacred Remains: American Attitudes toward Death, 1799–1883*. New Haven, Conn.: Yale University Press, 1996.

Laurie, Bruce. *Beyond Garrison: Antislavery and Social Reform*. Cambridge: Cambridge University Press, 2005.

Lawson, Melinda. *Patriot Fires: Forging a New American Nationalism in the Civil War North*. Lawrence: University Press of Kansas, 2002.

Lepore, Jill. "Historians Who Love Too Much: Reflections on Microhistory and Biography." *Journal of American History* 88 (June 2001): 129–144.

Levin, H., ed. *The Lawyers and Lawmakers of Kentucky*. Chicago: Lewis Publishing, 1897.

Lewis, Susan Ingalls. "Business Widows in Nineteenth-Century Albany, New York, 1813–1885." In *Women on Their Own: Interdisciplinary Perspectives on Being Single*, ed. Rudolph M. Bell and Virginia Yans. New Brunswick, N.J.: Rutgers University Press, 2008, 115–139.

Linderman, Gerald F. *Embattled Courage: The Experience of Combat in the American Civil War*. New York: Free Press, 1987.

Litwack, Leon F. *North of Slavery: The Negro in the Free States, 1790–1860*. Chicago: University of Chicago Press, 1961.

Logue, Larry M. *To Appomattox and Beyond: The Civil War Soldier in War and Peace.* Chicago: Ivan R. Dee, 1996.

Lucas, Marion B. *A History of Blacks in Kentucky.* Vol. 1, *From Slavery to Segregation, 1760–1891.* Frankfort: Kentucky Historical Society, 1992.

Lystra, Karen. *Searching the Heart: Women, Men, and Romantic Love in Nineteenth-Century America.* New York: Oxford University Press, 1989.

McClintock, Megan J. "Civil War Pensions and the Reconstruction of Union Families." *Journal of American History* 83 (September 1996): 456–480.

McConnell, Stuart. *Glorious Contentment: The Grand Army of the Republic, 1865–1900.* Chapel Hill: University of North Carolina, 1992.

McCurry, Stephanie. *Confederate Reckoning: Power and Politics in the Civil War South.* Cambridge, Mass.: Harvard University Press, 2010.

McGerr, Michael E. *The Decline of Popular Politics: The American North, 1865–1928.* New York: Oxford University Press, 1986.

McKay, Ernest A. *The Civil War and New York City.* Syracuse, N.Y.: Syracuse University Press, 1990.

McKenzie, Robert Tracy. *Lincolnites and Rebels: A Divided Town in the American Civil War.* New York: Oxford University Press, 2006.

McMillen, Sally G. *Motherhood in the Old South: Pregnancy, Childbirth, and Infant Rearing.* Baton Rouge: Louisiana State University Press, 1990.

McPherson, James M. *Battle Cry of Freedom: The Civil War Era.* New York: Oxford University Press, 1988.

———. *Crossroads of Freedom: Antietam.* New York: Oxford University Press, 2002.

———. *For Cause & Comrades: Why Men Fought in the Civil War.* New York: Oxford University Press, 1997.

Mackey, Robert R. *The Uncivil War: Irregular Warfare in the Upper South, 1861–1865.* Norman: University of Oklahoma Press, 2004.

MacKinnon, William P. "Albert Gallatin Browne Jr.: Brief Life of an Early War Correspondent: 1832–1891." *Harvard Magazine* (November–December 2008): 48.

———. "'Unquestionably Authentic and Correct in Every Detail': Probing John I. Ginn and His Remarkable Utah War Story." *Utah Historical Quarterly* 72 (Fall 2004): 322–342.

Madison, James H. "Civil War Memories and 'Pardnership Forgittin,' 1865–1913." *Indiana Magazine of History* 99 (September 2003): 198–230.

———. *Indiana through Tradition and Change: A History of the Hoosier State and Its People, 1920–1945.* Indianapolis: Indiana Historical Society, 1982.

———. *The Indiana Way: A State History.* Bloomington: Indiana University Press, 1986.

———. "Race, Law, and the Burdens of Indiana History." In *The History of Indiana Law,* ed. David J. Bodenhamer and Randall T. Shepard. Athens: Ohio University Press, 2006, 37–59.

Mahoney, Timothy R. *Provincial Lives: Middle-Class Experience in the Antebellum American West.* Cambridge: Cambridge University Press, 1999.

Manhart, George B. *DePauw through the Years.* 2 vols. Greencastle, Ind.: DePauw University, 1962.

———. *The Presbyterian Church, 1825–1950.* Greencastle, Ind.: Graphic Press, 1950.

Manning, Chandra. *What This Cruel War Was Over: Soldiers, Slavery, and the Civil War.* New York: Vintage, 2007.

Marten, James. *The Children's Civil War.* Chapel Hill: University of North Carolina Press, 1998.

Martin, Charles H. "The Color Line in Midwestern College Sports, 1890–1960." *Indiana Magazine of History* 98 (June 2002): 85–112.

Martin, Scott C. *Devil of the Domestic Sphere: Temperance, Gender, and Middle-Class Ideology, 1800–1860*. DeKalb: Northern Illinois University Press, 2008.

Masur, Louis P. *Rites of Execution: Capital Punishment and the Transformation of American Culture, 1776–1865*. New York: Oxford University Press, 1989.

Melish, Joanne Pope. *Disowning Slavery: Gradual Emancipation and "Race" in New England, 1780–1860*. Ithaca, N.Y.: Cornell University Press, 1998.

Metcalf, Brandon J. "The Nauvoo Legion and the Prevention of the Utah War." *Utah Historical Quarterly* 72 (Fall 2004): 300–321.

Mihm, Stephen. *A Nation of Counterfeiters: Capitalists, Con Men, and the Making of the United States*. Cambridge, Mass.: Harvard University Press, 2007.

Miller, Randall M. "Introduction." In *Union Soldiers and the Northern Home Front: Wartime Experiences, Postwar Adjustments*, ed. Paul A. Cimbala and Randall M. Miller. New York: Fordham University Press, 2002, xi–xvi.

Miller, Tamara G. "'Those with Whom I Feel Most Nearly Connected': Kinship and Gender in Early Ohio." In *Midwestern Women: Work, Community, and Leadership at the Crossroads*, ed. Lucy Eldersveld Murphy and Wendy Hamand Venet. Bloomington: Indiana University Press, 1997, 121–140.

Mintz, Steven. *Huck's Raft: A History of American Childhood*. Cambridge, Mass.: Harvard University Press, 2004.

Mitchell, Reid. *Civil War Soldiers*. New York: Viking, 1988.

———. *The Vacant Chair: The Northern Soldier Leaves Home*. New York: Oxford University Press, 1993.

Modell, John. "Family and Fertility on the Indiana Frontier, 1820." *American Quarterly* 23 (December 1971): 615–634.

Moore, Leonard J. *Citizen Klansmen: The Ku Klux Klan in Indiana, 1921–1928*. Chapel Hill: University of North Carolina Press, 1991.

Morrison, Elting. "Election of 1860." In *History of American Presidential Elections, 1789–1968*, ed. Arthur M. Schlesinger, Jr., and Fred L. Israel. New York: McGraw-Hill, 1971, 1097–1122.

Morrison, Michael A. *Slavery and the American West: The Eclipse of Manifest Destiny and the Coming of the Civil War*. Chapel Hill: University of North Carolina Press, 1997.

Motz, Marilyn Ferris. *True Sisterhood: Michigan Women and Their Kin, 1820–1920*. Albany: State University of New York Press, 1983.

Murrell, Amy E. "Union Father, Rebel Son: Families and the Question of Civil War Loyalty." In *The War Was You and Me: Civilians in the American Civil War*, ed. Joan E. Cashin. Princeton, N.J.: Princeton University Press, 2002, 358–391.

Neff, John R. *Honoring the Civil War Dead: Commemoration and the Problem of Reconciliation*. Lawrence: University Press of Kansas, 2005.

Nelson, Scott Reynolds, and Carol Sheriff. *A People at War: Civilians and Soldiers in America's Civil War, 1854–1877*. New York: Oxford University Press, 2007.

Noll, Mark A. *The Civil War as a Theological Crisis*. Chapel Hill: University of North Carolina Press, 2006.

Nudelman, Franny. *John Brown's Body: Slavery, Violence, & the Culture of War*. Chapel Hill: University of North Carolina Press, 2004.

Nye, Robert A. "Western Masculinities in War and Peace." *American Historical Review* 112 (April 2007): 417–438.

O'Connor, Thomas H. *Civil War Boston: Home Front and Battlefield*. Boston: Northeastern University Press, 1997.

Olsen, Christopher J. *Political Culture and Secession in Mississippi: Masculinity, Honor, and the Antiparty Tradition, 1830–1860*. New York: Oxford University Press, 2000.

O'Malley, Michael. "Specie and Species: Race and the Money Question in Nineteenth-Century America." *American Historical Review* 99 (April 1994): 369–395.

Opal, J. M. *Beyond the Farm: National Ambitions in Rural New England*. Philadelphia: University of Pennsylvania Press, 2008.

O'Rear, Edward C. *History of the Montgomery County (Ky.) Bar*. Frankfort, Ky.: E. C. O'Rear, 1945.

Orr, Timothy J. "A Viler Enemy in Our Rear: Pennsylvania Soldiers Confront the North's Antiwar Movement." In *The View from the Ground: Experiences of Civil War Soldiers*, ed. Aaron Sheehan-Dean. Lexington: University of Kentucky Press, 2007, 171–198.

Osterud, Nancy Grey. *Bonds of Community: The Lives of Farm Women in Nineteenth-Century New York*. Ithaca, N.Y.: Cornell University Press, 1991.

Painter, Nell Irvin. *Exodusters: Black Migration to Kansas after Reconstruction*. New York: Knopf, 1977.

Palladino, Grace. *Another Civil War: Labor, Capital, and the State in the Anthracite Regions of Pennsylvania, 1840–68*. Urbana: University of Illinois Press, 1990.

Paludan, Phillip Shaw. *"A People's Contest": The Union and Civil War, 1861–1865*. Lawrence: University Press of Kansas, 1996.

Parish, Peter J. "Conflict by Consent." In Peter J. Parish, *The North and the Nation in the Era of the Civil War*, ed. Adam I. P. Smith and Susan-Mary Grant. New York: Fordham University Press, 2003, 149–170.

———. "From Necessary Evil to National Blessing: The Northern Protestant Clergy Interpret the Civil War." In *An Uncommon Time: The Civil War and the Northern Home Front*, ed. Paul A. Cimbala and Randall M. Miller. New York: Fordham University Press, 2002, 61–89.

Pease, Jane H., and William H. Pease. *They Who Would Be Free: Blacks' Search for Freedom, 1830–1861*. New York: Atheneum, 1974.

Peck, Graham Alexander. "Abraham Lincoln and the Triumph of an Antislavery Nationalism." *Journal of the Abraham Lincoln Association* 28 (Summer 2007): 1–27.

Pence, George, and Nellie C. Armstrong. *Indiana Boundaries: Territory, State, and County*. Indianapolis: Indiana Historical Bureau, 1967.

Phillips, Clifton, ed. *From Frontier Circuit to Urban Church: A History of Greencastle Methodism*. Greencastle, Ind.: Gobin Memorial United Methodist Church, 1989.

Phillips, Clifton J. *Indiana in Transition: The Emergence of an Industrial Commonwealth, 1880–1920*. Indianapolis: Indiana Historical Bureau, 1968.

Pierce, Richard B. "Negotiated Freedom: African Americans in Indiana." In *The State of Indiana History 2000: Papers Presented at the Indiana Historical Society's Grand Opening*, ed. Robert M. Taylor, Jr. Indianapolis: Indiana Historical Society, 2001, 319–341.

Porter, Jack W. *The Catholic Church in Greencastle, Putnam County, Indiana, 1848–1978*. Greencastle: Ind.: Saint Paul the Apostle Church, 1979.

Porter, Robert P. *The West, from the Census of 1880: A History of the Industrial, Commercial, Social, and Political Development of the States and Territories of the West from 1800 to 1880*. Chicago: Rand, McNally, 1882.

Potter, David M. *The Impending Crisis, 1848–1861*. New York: Harper & Row, 1976.

Powers, Doug. "Courtland Cushing Matson: A Political Life." Manuscript, Wabash College, 1992.

Pruitt, Lisa Joy. *"A Looking-Glass for Ladies": American Protestant Women and the Orient in the Nineteenth Century*. Macon, Ga.: Mercer University Press, 2005.

Putnam County Sesquicentennial Committee. *A Journey through Putnam County History*. N.p., 1966.

Rable, George C. "Hearth, Home, and Family in the Fredericksburg Campaign." In *The War Was You and Me: Civilians in the American Civil War*, ed. Joan E. Cashin. Princeton, N.J.: Princeton University Press, 2002, 85–111.

Rainville, Lynn. "Hanover Deathscapes: Mortuary Variability in New Hampshire, 1770–1920." *Ethnohistory* 46 (Summer 1999): 541–597.

Raus, Edmund J., Jr. *Banners South: A Northern Community at War*. Kent, Ohio: Kent State University Press, 2005.

Renda, Lex. "'A White Man's State in New England': Race, Party, and Suffrage in Civil War Connecticut." In *An Uncommon Time: The Civil War and the Northern Home Front*, ed. Paul A. Cimbala and Randall M. Miller. New York: Fordham University Press, 2002, 243–279.

Richard, Patricia L. "'Listen Ladies One and All': Union Soldiers Yearn for the Society of Their 'Fair Cousins of the North.'" In *Union Soldiers and the Northern Home Front: Wartime Experiences, Postwar Adjustments*, ed. Paul A. Cimbala and Randall M. Miller. New York: Fordham University Press, 2002, 143–181.

Richardson, Heather Cox. *The Death of Reconstruction: Race, Labor, and Politics in the Post–Civil War North, 1865–1901*. Cambridge, Mass.: Harvard University Press, 2001.

Richey, Russell E. *Early American Methodism*. Bloomington: Indiana University Press, 1991.

Ridgley, Ronald H. "Henry Smith Lane: Republican Progenitor." In *Their Infinite Variety: Essays on Indiana Politicians*, ed. Robert G. Barrows. Indianapolis: Indiana Historical Bureau, 1981, 49–75.

Robertson, James I., Jr. *Soldiers Blue and Gray*. Columbia: University of South Carolina Press, 1988.

Robertson, John. "Re-enlistment Patterns of Civil War Soldiers." *Journal of Interdisciplinary History* 32 (Summer 2001): 15–35.

Rodgers, Thomas E. "Hoosier Women and the Civil War Home Front." *Indiana Magazine of History* 97 (June 2001): 105–128.

———. "Republicans and Drifters: Political Affiliation and Union Army Volunteers in West-Central Indiana." *Indiana Magazine of History* 92 (December 1996): 321–334.

Rorabaugh, W. J. *The Alcoholic Republic: An American Tradition*. New York: Oxford University Press, 1979.

Rose, Ernestine Bradford. *The Circle: "The Center of Our Universe."* Indianapolis: Indiana Historical Society, 1957.

Rose, Gregory S. "The Distribution of Indiana's Ethnic and Racial Minorities in 1850." *Indiana Magazine of History* 87 (September 1991): 224–260.

———. "Hoosier Origins: The Nativity of Indiana's United States-Born Population in 1850." *Indiana Magazine of History* 81 (September 1985): 201–232.

Roth, Randolph A. "Spousal Murder in Northern New England, 1776–1865." In *Over the Threshold: Intimate Violence in Early America*, ed. Christine Daniels and Michael V. Kennedy. New York: Routledge, 1999, 65–93.

Rothman, Ellen K. *Hands and Hearts: A History of Courtship in America*. New York: Basic Books, 1984.

Rotundo, E. Anthony. *American Manhood: Transformations in Masculinity from the Revolution to the Modern Era*. New York: Basic Books, 1993.

Ryan, Mary P. *Cradle of the Middle Class: The Family in Oneida County, New York, 1790–1865*. Cambridge: Cambridge University Press, 1981.

Salstrom, Paul. *From Pioneering to Persevering: Family Farming in Indiana to 1880.* West Lafayette, Ind.: Purdue University Press, 2007.

———. "Sifting Indiana's Farm Past for Seeds to Plant a Future." In *The State of Indiana History 2000: Papers Presented at the Indiana Historical Society's Grand Opening,* ed. Robert M. Taylor, Jr. Indianapolis: Indiana Historical Society, 2001, 343–365.

Salvatore, Nick. *We All Got History: The Memory Books of Amos Webber.* New York: Random House, 1996.

Sarris, Jonathan Dean. *A Separate Civil War: Communities in Conflict in the Mountain South.* Charlottesville: University of Virginia Press, 2006.

Savage, Kirk. *Standing Soldiers, Kneeling Slaves: Race, War, and Monument in Nineteenth-Century America.* Princeton, N.J.: Princeton University Press, 1997.

Schneider, A. Gregory. *The Way of the Cross Leads Home: The Domestication of American Methodism.* Bloomington: Indiana University Press, 1993.

Schultz, Jane E. *Women at the Front: Hospital Workers in Civil War America.* Chapel Hill: University of North Carolina Press, 2004.

Schulze, Willi. *Liberia: Länderkundliche Dominanten und Regionale Strukturen.* Darmstadt, Germany: Wissenschafliche Buchgesellschaft, 1973.

Schwalm, Leslie A. *Emancipation's Diaspora: Race and Reconstruction in the Upper Midwest,* Chapel Hill: University of North Carolina Press, 2009.

———. "'Overrun with Free Negroes': Emancipation and Wartime Migration in the Upper Midwest." *Civil War History* 50 (June 2004): 145–174.

Seidman, Rachel Filene. "A Monstrous Doctrine? Northern Women on Dependency during the Civil War." In *An Uncommon Time: The Civil War and the Northern Home Front,* ed. Paul A. Cimbala and Randall M. Miller. New York: Fordham University Press, 2002, 170–188.

Seigel, Peggy Brase. "She Went to War: Indiana Women Nurses in the Civil War." *Indiana Magazine of History* 86 (March 1990): 1–27.

Sellers, Charles. *The Market Revolution: Jacksonian America, 1815–1846.* New York: Oxford University Press, 1991.

Shaffer, Donald R. *After the Glory: The Struggles of Black Civil War Veterans.* Lawrence: University Press of Kansas, 2004.

———. "'I Would Rather Shake Hands with the Blackest Nigger in the Land': Northern Black Civil War Veterans and the Grand Army of the Republic." In *Union Soldiers and the Northern Home Front: Wartime Experiences, Postwar Adjustments,* ed. Paul A. Cimbala and Randall M. Miller. New York: Fordham University Press, 2002, 442–462.

Shammas, Carole. *A History of Household Government in America.* Charlottesville: University of Virginia Press, 2002.

Shick, Tom W. *Behold the Promised Land: A History of Afro-American Settler Society in Nineteenth-Century Liberia.* Baltimore, Md.: Johns Hopkins University Press, 1980.

Shively, Jeffrey D. "The Asbury Guards: A History of a Company in the 14th Indiana Volunteer Regiment, 1861–1864." Manuscript. Archives and Special Collections, DePauw University, 1994.

Shoaf, Dana B. "'For Every Man Who Wore the Blue': The Military Order of the Loyal Legion of the United States and the Charges of Elitism after the Civil War." In *Union Soldiers and the Northern Home Front: Wartime Experiences, Postwar Adjustments,* ed. Paul A. Cimbala and Randall M. Miller. New York: Fordham University Press, 2002, 463–481.

Shortridge, Ray M. "The Voter Realignment in the Midwest during the 1850s." *American Politics Quarterly* 4 (April 1976): 193–222.

————. "Voting for Minor Parties in the Antebellum Midwest." *Indiana Magazine of History* 74 (June 1978): 117–134.

Shumaker, Arthur W. *A History of Indiana Literature.* Indianapolis: Indiana Historical Society, 1962.

Silber, Nina. *Daughters of the Union: Northern Women Fight the Civil War.* Cambridge, Mass.: Harvard University Press, 2005.

Simpson, Brooks D. "The Reforging of a Republican Majority." In *The Birth of the Grand Old Party: The Republicans' First Generation.* Philadelphia: University of Pennsylvania Press, 2002, 148–166.

Skocpol, Theda. *Protecting Soldiers and Mothers: The Political Origins of Social Policy in the United States.* Cambridge, Mass.: Belknap Press, 1992.

Slotkin, Richard. *No Quarter: The Battle of the Crater, 1864.* New York: Random House, 2009.

Smith, Adam I. P. *The American Civil War.* New York: Palgrave Macmillan, 2007.

————. "Beyond Politics: Patriotism and Partisanship on the Northern Home Front." In *An Uncommon Time: The Civil War and the Northern Home Front,* ed. Paul A. Cimbala and Randall M. Miller. New York: Fordham University Press, 2002, 145–169.

Smith, Daniel Scott. "Family Limitation, Sexual Control, and Domestic Feminism in Victorian America." In *Clio's Consciousness Raised: New Perspectives on the History of Women,* ed. Mary S. Hartman and Lois Banner. New York: Harper & Row, 1974, 119–136.

Smith, Mark M. "Of Bells, Booms, Sounds, and Silences: Listening to the Civil War South." In *The War Was You and Me: Civilians in the American Civil War,* ed. Joan E. Cashin. Princeton, N.J.: Princeton University Press, 2002, 9–34.

Smith-Rosenberg, Carroll. "The Hysterical Woman: Sex Roles and Role Conflict in 19th-Century America." *Social Research* 39 (Winter 1972): 652–678.

Snell, Mark A. "'If They Would Know What I Know It Would Be Pretty Hard to Raise One Company in York': Recruiting, the Draft, and Society's Response in York County, Pennsylvania, 1861–1865." In *Union Soldiers and the Northern Home Front: Wartime Experiences, Postwar Adjustments,* ed. Paul A. Cimbala and Randall M. Miller. New York: Fordham University Press, 2002, 69–115.

Stampp, Kenneth M. *America in 1857: A Nation on the Brink.* New York: Oxford University Press, 1990.

————. *Indiana Politics during the Civil War.* Bloomington: Indiana University Press, 1978, orig. 1949.

Stefanco, Carolyn J. "Poor Loving Prisoners of War: Nelly Kinzie Gordon and the Dilemma of Northern-Born Women in the Confederate South." In *Enemies of the Country: New Perspectives on Unionists in the Civil War South,* ed. John C. Inscoe and Robert C. Kenzer. Athens: University of Georgia Press, 2001, 148–171.

Steinson, Barbara J. "Rural Life in Indiana, 1800–1950." *Indiana Magazine of History* 90 (September 1984): 203–250.

Sterett, Susan M. *Public Pensions: Gender and Civic Service in the States, 1850–1937.* Ithaca, N.Y.: Cornell University Press, 2003.

Stevenson, Margaretta, comp. *Stevenson Family History from the Eastern Shore of Maryland to Woodford County, Kentucky to Putnam County, Indiana with Allied Families.* New York: privately published, 1966.

Strouse, Isaac R. *Parke County Indiana Centennial Memorial (1816–1916).* Rockville, Ind.: Rockville Chautauqua Association, 1916.

Summers, Mark Wahlgren. *The Gilded Age or, The Hazard of New Functions.* Upper Saddle River, N.J.: Prentice Hall, 1997.

———. *The Plundering Generation: Corruption and the Crisis of the Union, 1849–1861.* New York: Oxford University Press, 1987.

Sutherland, Daniel E. *Seasons of War: The Ordeal of a Confederate Community, 1861–1865.* New York: Free Press, 1995.

Tadmor, Naomi. *Family and Friends in Eighteenth-Century England.* Cambridge: Cambridge University Press, 2001.

Taylor, Amy Murrell. *The Divided Family in Civil War America.* Chapel Hill: University of North Carolina Press, 2005.

Terrell, W. H. H. *Indiana in the War of the Rebellion: Report of the Adjutant General.* 8 vols. Indianapolis: Indiana Historical Society, 1960, orig. 1869.

Thomas, William G., III, and Edward L. Ayers. "The Differences Slavery Made: A Close Analysis of Two American Communities." Available at http://www.vcdh.virginia.edu/AHR.

Thornbrough, Emma Lou. *Indiana in the Civil War Era, 1850–1880.* Indianapolis: Indiana Historical Bureau, 1965.

———. *The Negro in Indiana before 1900: A Study of a Minority.* Bloomington: Indiana University Press, 1993, orig. 1957.

Towne, Stephen E. "Killing the Serpent Speedily: Governor Morton, General Hascall, and the Suppression of the Democratic Press in Indiana, 1863." *Civil War History* 52 (March 2006): 41–65.

———. "Scorched Earth or Fertile Ground? Indiana in the Civil War Era, 1861–1865." In *The State of Indiana History 2000: Papers Presented at the Indiana Historical Society's Grand Opening,* ed. Robert M. Taylor, Jr. Indianapolis: Indiana Historical Society, 2001, 397–415.

Trask, Kerry A. *Fire Within: A Civil War Narrative from Wisconsin.* Kent, Ohio: Kent State University Press, 1995.

Tyrrell, Ian R. *Sobering Up: From Temperance to Prohibition in Antebellum America, 1800–1860.* Westport, Conn.: Greenwood Press, 1979.

Unger, Irwin. *The Greenback Era: A Social and Political History of American Finance, 1865–1879.* Princeton, N.J.: Princeton University Press, 1964.

Van Deusen, John G. "Did Republicans 'Colonize' Indiana in 1879?" *Indiana Magazine of History* 30 (September 1934): 335–346.

Varon, Elizabeth. *We Mean to Be Counted: White Women and Politics in Antebellum Virginia.* Chapel Hill: University of North Carolina Press, 1998.

Vedder, Richard K., and Lowell E. Gallaway. "Migration and the Old Northwest." In *Essays in Nineteenth Century Economic History: The Old Northwest,* ed. David C. Klingaman and Richard K. Vedder. Athens: Ohio University Press, 1975, 159–176.

Vincent, Steven A. *Southern Seed, Northern Soil: African-American Farm Communities in the Midwest, 1765–1900.* Bloomington: Indiana University Press, 1999.

Vinovskis, Maris A., ed. *Toward a Social History of the American Civil War: Exploratory Essays.* New York: Cambridge University Press, 1990.

Vorenberg, Michael. *Final Freedom: The Civil War, the Abolition of Slavery, and the Thirteenth Amendment.* Cambridge: Cambridge University Press, 2001.

Walsh, Justin E. *The Centennial History of the Indiana General Assembly, 1816–1978.* Indianapolis: Indiana Historical Bureau, 1987.

Watters, David H. "'As Soon as I Saw My Sable Brother, I Felt More at Home': Sampson Battis,

Harriet Wilson, and New Hampshire Town Memory." In *Harriet Wilson's New England: Race, Writing, and Region,* ed. JerriAnne Boggis, Eve Allegra Raimon, and Barbara A. White. Durham: University of New Hampshire Press, 2007, 67–96.

Webb, Stephen H. "Introducing Black Harry Hoosier: The History behind Indiana's Namesake." *Indiana Magazine of History* 98 (March 2002): 31–41.

Weber, Jennifer L. *Copperheads: The Rise and Fall of Lincoln's Opponents in the North.* New York: Oxford University Press, 2006.

Weigley, Russell F. *A Great Civil War: A Military and Political History, 1861–1865.* Bloomington: Indiana University Press, 2000.

Weik, Jesse W. *History of Putnam County, Indiana.* Indianapolis: Bowen, 1910.

Weisenburger, Steven. *Modern Medea: A Family Story of Slavery and Child-Murder from the Old South.* New York: Hill and Wang, 1998.

Whites, Lee Ann. *The Civil War as a Crisis in Gender: Augusta, Georgia, 1860–1890.* Athens: University of Georgia Press, 1995.

Wigger, John H. *Taking Heaven by Storm: Methodism and the Rise of Popular Christianity in America.* New York: Oxford University Press, 1998.

Wilentz, Sean. *The Rise of American Democracy: Jefferson to Lincoln.* New York: Norton, 2005.

Williams, David, Teresa Crisp Williams, and David Carlson. *Plain Folk in a Rich Man's War: Class and Dissent in Georgia.* Gainesville: University Press of Florida, 2002.

Wills, Brian Steel. *The War Hits Homes: The Civil War in Southeastern Virginia.* Charlottesville: University Press of Virginia, 2001.

Wilson, Lisa. *Ye Heart of a Man: The Domestic Life of Men in Colonial New England.* New Haven, Conn.: Yale University Press, 1999.

Winslow, Verl W. "Thomas V. Lyon, Union Soldier: His Experiences with the Army of the Cumberland as Taken from His Diary for 1864." Master's thesis, DePauw University, 1957.

Wood, Ann Douglas. "'The Fashionable Diseases': Women's Complaints and Their Treatment in Nineteenth-Century America." In *Clio's Consciousness Raised: New Perspectives on the History of Women,* ed. Mary S. Hartman and Lois Banner. New York: Harper & Row, 1974, 1–22.

Woodward, C. Vann. *Reunion and Reform: The Compromise of 1877 and the End of Reconstruction.* Boston: Little, Brown, 1951.

Wulf, Karin. *Not All Wives: Women of Colonial Philadelphia.* Philadelphia: University of Pennsylvania Press, 2005.

Wyatt-Brown, Bertram. *The Shaping of Southern Culture: Honor, Grace, and War, 1760s–1890s.* Chapel Hill: University of North Carolina Press, 2001.

Zagarri, Rosemarie. "Politics and Civil Society: A Discussion of Mary Kelley's Learning to Stand and Speak." *Journal of the Early Republic* 28 (Spring 2008): 61–73.

Zenor, Carl A. "Putnam County in the Civil War: Local History of a Critical Period." Master's thesis, DePauw University, 1956.

Index

CPSIA information can be obtained
at www.ICGtesting.com
Printed in the USA
JSHW021518020423
39776JS00001B/4